HISTORY

OF

EARLY CHRISTIAN LITERATURE

IN THE FIRST THREE CENTURIES

BY

DR. GUSTAV KRUGER

TRANSLATED BY

REV. CHARLES R. GILLETT

WITH CORRECTIONS AND ADDITIONS BY THE AUTHOR

WIPF & STOCK · Eugene, Oregon

Wipf and Stock Publishers
199 W 8th Ave, Suite 3
Eugene, OR 97401

History of Early Christian Literature in the First Three Centuries
With Corrections and Additions by the Author
By Krüger, Gustav and Gillett, Charles R.
Copyright © 1875 by Krüger, Gustav All rights reserved.
Softcover ISBN-13: 979-8-3852-4121-7
Hardcover ISBN-13: 979-8-3852-4122-4
eBook ISBN-13: 979-8-3852-4123-1
Publication date 12/10/2024
Previously published by Macmillan, 1875

This edition is a scanned facsimile of the original edition published in 1875.

PREFACE

THE account of the history of early Christian literature, contained in the following pages, does not lay claim to novelty It simply professes to be a compilation of facts already known, based upon a reexamination of them. It seemed to me important and profitable that the mass of material for the history of this literature, which has been accumulated by the unstinted diligence of almost countless workers during the last decades, should be made accessible in somewhat sifted form to those whose labors lie in a different field, but who have long sought for such help in finding their bearings The primary purpose of the book, however, is to furnish a manual to serve as a basis for lectures and as a student's handbook. In the directions given to secure a uniform mode of presentation in the "Outline" series (*Grundriss der theologischen Wissenschaften*) to which this book belongs, it was required that the accounts should be as condensed and brief as possible, while being at the same time smooth and readable; that they should be adapted to the practical needs of the learner (but not for memorizing), and that they should be clearly arranged and free from polemic. Such a book also requires that the author's personality should be held in abeyance Consequently it was necessary to suppress many observations and characterizations, in order that the work of the lecture room might not be forestalled. As a result, the reader will find many a paragraph which might serve as the subject of a whole lecture.

This book differs from the more recent handbooks on Patrology, both Catholic and Protestant, not only in many details of its conception of the subject, but in its arrangement and limitation of the treatment. It has been my special purpose to emphasize the literary point of view, since a history of literature has no occasion to explain the theological or ecclesiastical importance of a writer. I have also endeavored to substitute an organic method of treatment in place of a mechanical sequence based on chronology and biography, though I dare not hope that I have realized the ideal that has hovered before me. In my manner of conceiving of the subject I have adhered to the views expounded by Friedrich Nitzsch, now professor of Systematic Theology at Kiel, and by Franz Overbeck, professor of Church History at Basel (cf. § 1)

I am not aware of the existence, in English, of a book like the present. The work of C. T. Cruttwell is excellent in many respects, but it was intended for a different class of readers, being a book for continuous perusal rather than a text-book It does not take sufficient note of the results and hypotheses of the most recent investigations, and indeed, it was not the author's intention to do so. The references here made to the latest researches will give my book, perhaps, a special value for English-speaking people. The names of those who have rendered eminent services in this field are already well known. and on every page this volume indicates what I have learned from Harnack, Hilgenfeld, and Zahn, from Lightfoot and Westcott.

On one point I beg the reader's indulgence for a moment; namely, the inclusion of the New Testament Scriptures in the following account In various reviews of the book, especially in English, this feature has been condemned, or at least declared undesirable. But two questions must be considered in this connection : first, whether the New Testament Scriptures may properly be treated at all in a history of early Christian literature, that is, in connection with writings which are not included in our canon ; and second, whether the author's peculiar views concerning the circumstances which gave rise to the New Testament writings, are capable of justification The answer to the first is closely connected with the views which we entertain in general upon religious questions If, after the fashion of our forefathers, we hold to an inspiration of the Holy Scriptures in such a sense as to make the Holy Ghost wield the pens of their authors, we shall be inclined to regard it as sacrilege to subject them in any way to the methods of historical investigation. The author, on the contrary, is of the opinion that the value and sublimity of these writings lose nothing by being submitted to these processes; that for many, possibly, a distinct gain is involved. The second question can only be answered after one has obtained a view of the whole subject of primitive Christianity, its writings and teachings, based upon the sources. The author does not claim to be infallible. He is quite conscious of the immense difficulties involved in the investigation of the New Testament by our lack of material He believes himself to be free from traditional prejudices, critical or ecclesiastical If he is mistaken in this respect, he at least always holds himself ready to receive better instruction. The positive tone and the lack of detailed explanation which characterize the remarks on the New Testament writings may be displeasing to some, but they are merely the result of the fact that it was necessary to be brief because of the many excellent treatises which we already possess.

In the citation of literature, the reader will find enumerated all that is necessary for a thorough study of the subject. The latest works are also mentioned even when their permanent value may appear somewhat doubtful. Treatises on the history of dogma are mentioned, in accordance with the plan of the book, only when they contain original material bearing upon the history of the literature. The chronological conspectus is intended to portray the gradual progress of literary productivity in the several provinces of the Empire.

Finally, I wish to thank the translator for the pains which he has taken, and in the same connection I would express the hope that the volume may not be devoid of profit to the English-speaking reader.

GUSTAV KRUGER.

GIESSEN.

TRANSLATOR'S NOTE

THE translator's purpose in the following pages has been to render the thoughts of the original work into idiomatic English, while adhering as closely as possible to the author's own language. This task has involved some difficulty at various points on account of the brevity of style and the condensation of material which the projectors of the series required of the contributors. It has been a matter of surprise that the author was able to crowd so much information upon a single page or into a single paragraph, and the extraordinary potency of his system of abbreviations has received frequent illustration These qualities, while increasing the task of the translator, are of great advantage to the reader, and are beyond praise Sometimes it has been found necessary to break up the long sentences of the original, but this scarcely calls for apology.

The footnotes of the present volume originally appeared as part of the text, being enclosed in brackets. In transferring them to the foot of the page the translator has not been a mere copyist, but has taken the liberty of adding an occasional reference in order to greater clearness. It has also been thought advisable to make some additions to the citations of literature, especially in the case of English books.

The thanks of the reader are due to Dr. Kruger for the readiness with which he has acceded to the translator's request for corrections and additions to the text Some important alterations have been made, and many references to later works have found a place in this volume which entitle it to be regarded as the second edition of the *Geschichte*.

It is scarcely necessary for the translator to say anything in regard to the author's views His responsibility does not extend to these, but ceases when he has reproduced them faithfully in English But there can be no doubt that Dr. Kruger has rendered an important service in calling attention to the organic connection of the various remnants of the early Christian literature of which he treats.

CHARLES R GILLETT

Library, Union Theological Seminary, New York

TABLE OF CONTENTS

	PAGE
PREFACE	V
TRANSLATOR'S NOTE	IX
LIST OF ABBREVIATIONS	XXI
INTRODUCTION	1
§ 1. THE SUBJECT	1
§ 2. TRANSMISSION, COMPILATIONS, AIDS TO STUDY	1

1 Transmission Eusebius, Photius, Χρήσεις 'Ιερά Sacra Parallela, Catenae 2 Jerome and Others 3 Catholic and Protestant Compilations of the Seventeenth and Eighteenth Centuries. 4 More Recent Works 5 History of Greek and Roman Literature 6. Collections 7. Helps 8. Collections of the Works of Ecclesiastical Writers. 9. Translations.

DIVISION I

PRIMITIVE CHRISTIAN LITERATURE

§ 3. GENERAL	11

1. Transmission, The New Testament. 2. Its Forms. 3. Primitive Christian and Jewish Literature.

CHAPTER I.—EPISTLES

§ 4. THE PAULINE AND PSEUDO-PAULINE EPISTLES	15

1. The Epistles included in the New Testament. 2. Epistle to the Alexandrians and the Laodiceans. Correspondence between Paul and the Corinthians. Correspondence between Paul and Seneca.

§ 5. THE CATHOLIC EPISTLES	18

	PAGE
§ 6. THE EPISTLE OF BARNABAS	18
1. Transmission. 2. Attestation. 3. Author. Time and Place of Composition. 4 Contents, Character, Unity.	
§ 7. THE FIRST EPISTLE OF CLEMENT	21
1. Transmission. 2. Attestation. 3. Circumstances of Composition 4. Contents and Character.	
§ 8. THE EPISTLE OF POLYCARP	25
1. Transmission. 2. Attestation, Unity. 3. Contents 4. Fragments ascribed to Polycarp.	
§ 9. THE EPISTLES OF IGNATIUS	28
1. Transmission 2 Attestation. 3 Contents Personality of the Author. 4 Doubts as to Genuineness 5. Refutation of Doubts.	

CHAPTER II.—APOCALYPSES

§ 10. THE APOCALYPSE OF JOHN	35
§ 11. THE APOCALYPSE OF PETER	36
1. Attestations 2 The Akhmîn Manuscript. 3. Circumstances of Composition.	
§ 12. THE SHEPHERD OF HERMAS	38
1. Transmission. 2 Attestation. 3. Purpose, Form, Character of the Work. 4. Contents 5. Time of Composition; Unity.	

CHAPTER III.—HISTORICAL BOOKS

I. THE GOSPELS

§ 13. THE BEGINNINGS: PAPIAS	46
1. The *Logia*. 2. Papias. 3. The Rainer Papyrus.	
§ 14. THE SYNOPTIC GOSPELS	48
§ 15. THE GOSPEL OF JOHN	49
§ 16. APOCRYPHAL GOSPELS	50
1. The Gospel of the Hebrews. 2 The Gospel of Peter 3 The Gospel of the Egyptians. 4 The Gospels of Andrew, Barnabas, Bartholomew, Matthias, and Philip The *Traditiones Matthiae*. 5 The Gospel of Thomas. 6. The Protevangel of James 7. The *Acta Pilati*.	

II. THE ACTS OF THE APOSTLES

§ 17. THE ACTS OF THE APOSTLES 57

CHAPTER IV — DOCTRINAL WRITINGS

§ 18. THE SO-CALLED ROMAN SYMBOL 59
§ 19. THE "PREACHING" OF PETER 60
    1. The *Kerygma Petri* and the *Didascalia Petri*. 2. The Character of the "Preaching." 3. Circumstances of Composition. *Paulli Praedicatio.*
§ 20. THE SO-CALLED SECOND EPISTLE OF CLEMENT . . . 62
    1. Transmission and Attestation. 2 Contents and Circumstances of Composition.
§ 21. THE TEACHING OF THE APOSTLES 63
    1. Transmission Contents 2 Attestation. 3 Components. Authorship.

DIVISION II

GNOSTIC LITERATURE

§ 22. GENERAL 68

CHAPTER I. — THEOLOGICAL LITERATURE

§ 23. BASILIDES AND ISIDORE 70
    1 Basilides. 2. Isidore. 3. *Incantationes.*
§ 24. VALENTINUS AND HIS SCHOOL 71
    1 Valentinus. 2. Ptolemæus, Heracleon. 3. The *Excerpta Theodoti.*
§ 25. BARDESANES 75
    1 Life and Personality. 2. Writings.
§ 26. THE CARPOCRATIANS 77
§ 27. MARCION AND APELLES 77
    1. Marcion's Life 2 The Gospel and the Apostle 3 The *Antitheses.* 4 Apelles 5. Psalms. *Liber Propositi Finis.*
§ 28. OPHITIC ("GNOSTIC") WRITINGS 82
    1 Ophitic Writings. 2. Writings of the Severians, Sethites, *Archontici* (a) *Pistis-Sophia* (b) *Papyrus Brucianus.*
§ 29 JULIUS CASSIANUS 86

CHAPTER II.—ROMANCES

§ 30 ACTS 88
    1 General. 2 Acts of Peter. 3. Acts of John. 4. Acts of Thomas. 5 Acts of Andrew

SUPPLEMENTARY

§ 31. SYMMACHUS 96

DIVISION III

LITERATURE OF THE CHURCH

First Section. Patristic Literature in the Age of the Apologists and during the Conflict with Gnosticism

§ 32. GENERAL 97
    1. Apologetic Literature 2 Anti-Jewish Literature.
    3. Anti-Heretical Literature. 4. The Pastoral Epistles

CHAPTER I.—APOLOGETIC LITERATURE

§ 33 QUADRATUS 100
§ 34 ARISTIDES 101
    1 Transmission of the Apology 2 Contents and Character 3 The Epistle and the Homily.
§ 35 ARISTO OF PELLA 104
§ 36 JUSTIN 105
    1 Life and Literary Character. 2. Transmission. 3. Genuine Writings (a) The *Syntagma*, (b) The Apologies, (c) Dialogue with Trypho. Writings which may be genuine (a) *de Resurrectione*, (b) *Cohortatio*, (c) *Oratio*, (d) Fragments, (e) The Apology of Photius. 4 Spurious Writings (a) *de Monarchia*, (b) *Confutatio Dogmatum Aristotelis*, (c) and (d) *Quaestiones Christianorum ad Gentiles*, and *Quaestiones et Responsiones ad Orthodoxos*, (e) Epistle to Zenas and Serenus, (f) *Expositio Rectae Fidei* 5 Λόγος περὶ προνοίας Περὶ τοῦ παντός. Exposition of the Apocalypse. 6. Reference to the Epistle to Diognetus.

CONTENTS

		PAGE
§ 37.	TATIAN	117
	1. Life. 2. *Oratio ad Graecos* Literary Character. 3. Lost Writings. 4. The *Diatessaron*	
§ 38	MILTIADES	121
§ 39.	APOLLINARIS	122
§ 40.	MELITO	123
	1. Life and Personality. 2. Literary Character Transmission. 3 Writings mentioned by Eusebius. 4. Εἰς τὸ πάθος. 5 Fragments in *Catenae*. 6. Syriac Fragments. 7 The Syriac Apology. 8. Later Writings	
§ 41.	ATHENAGORAS	130
	1 Life 2. (a) *Supplicatio*, and (b) *de Resurrectione*. Characteristics.	
§ 42.	THEOPHILUS	132
	1. Circumstances of Composition of the Books *ad Autolycum* Theophilus of Antioch 2. Contents of the *ad Autolycum* 3 Lost Writings. The Gospel Commentary.	

SUPPLEMENTARY

§ 43	THE EPISTLE TO DIOGNETUS	135
§ 44.	HERMIAS	137
§ 45.	MINUCIUS FELIX	138
	1. Transmission and Contents of the *Octavius*. 2. Relation to Other Writings 3. Time of Composition. 4. *De Fato*.	

CHAPTER II.—ANTI-HERETICAL LITERATURE

§ 46.	AGRIPPA CASTOR	143
§ 47	RHODO	143
§ 48	MUSANUS	144
§ 49	PHILIP OF GORTYNA	144
§ 50.	MODESTUS	144
§ 51	HEGESIPPUS	145
	1. Life. 2 The *Hypomnemata*.	
§ 52.	IRENÆUS	146
	1. Life 2 Characteristics *Adversus Haereses* 3. Lost Writings Fragments 4 Pfaff's Fragments	
§ 53	MONTANISTS AND ANTI-MONTANISTS	152
	1, Montanistic Writings 2. Anti-Montanistic Writings	

CHAPTER III. — EPISCOPAL AND SYNODAL WRITINGS

	PAGE
§ 54. THE ROMAN BISHOPS	155
Soter. Eleutherus. Victor.	
§ 55 DIONYSIUS OF CORINTH	156
§ 56 SERAPION OF ANTIOCH	157
§ 57. WRITINGS IN THE PASCHAL CONTROVERSY	158

Second Section. Patristic Literature in the Age of the Rise of Theological Science

§ 58. GENERAL 159
 1. Christian Science. 2 Catechetical School of Alexandria.
 3. Scientific Tendencies Elsewhere in the East 4. The West.

CHAPTER I. — THE ORIENTALS

I. THE ALEXANDRIANS

§ 59. PANTÆNUS 162
§ 60. CLEMENT 162
 1. Life. 2. Characteristics. 3. Principal Works: (a) The *Protrepticos*, (b) The *Paedagogus*, (c) *Stromata*. 4 *Quis Dives?* 5. Fragments. 6. Title. 7. Disputed Writings.
§ 61. ORIGEN 173
 1. Sources. 2. Life. 3. Characteristics. 4. Transmission.
 5. Labors in Textual Criticism. 6. Exegetical Writings (a) The Scholia, (b) The Homilies; (c) Commentaries
 7. Apologetic, 8. Dogmatic, and 9. Devotional Writings.
 10. Epistles. 11. Disputed Writings.
§ 62. TRYPHO 205
§ 63 DIONYSIUS 205
 1. Life. 2. Characteristics. Transmission. 3. Treatises
 4. Epistles and Deliverances. 5. Uncertain and Forged Writings.
§ 64 ANATOLIUS 216
§ 65. THEOGNOSTUS 217
§ 66. PIERIUS 217

	PAGE
§ 67. Phileas, Hesychius, Pachomius, Theodorus	219
§ 68. Petrus (Peter)	219
§ 69. Alexander	221
§ 70. Hierax	223

Supplementary

§ 71. Judas 223
§ 72. Heraclitus, Maximus, Candidus, Apion, Sextus, Arabianus 224
§ 73. Ammonius 224
§ 74. Theonas 225

II. Writers of Asia Minor

§ 75. Gregorius Thaumaturgus 226
  1. Sources. 2. Life. 3. Genuine Writings (a) The Panegyric; (b) Ἔκθεσις πίστεως; (c) Ἐπιστολὴ κανονική, (d) Μετάφρασις, (e) To Theopompus, (f) To Ælianus 4 Writings apparently or certainly Spurious (a) Κατὰ μέρος πίστις, (b) To Philagrius, (c) Περὶ ψυχῆς (d) Ἀναθεματισμοί; (e) Homilies. 5. Fragments 6 Disputed Writings.

§ 76. Methodius 235
  1. Life. 2 Transmission. Characteristics. 3. Genuine Writings (a) Συμπόσιον; (b) Περὶ αὐτεξουσίου; (c) De Vita, (d) Περὶ ἀναστάσεως; (e) De Cibis, (f) De Lepra, (g) De Sanguisuga. 4. Fragments. 5 Lost, and 6 Spurious Writings.

§ 77. Firmilianus 242

III Writers of Syria and Palestine

§ 78. Paul of Samosata 243
§ 79. Lucian 244
§ 80. *Anonymous Dialogus de Recta Fide* . . . 245
§ 81. Alexander of Jerusalem 247
§ 82. Julius Africanus 248
  1. Life. 2 Characteristics. 3. Writings (a) Chronicle, (b) Κεστοί, (c) Letter on the History of Susanna, (d) Epistle to Aristides. 4. Disputed Writings.

		PAGE
§ 83	PAMPHILUS	253
§ 84	BERYLLUS OF BOSTRA IN ARABIA	255

CHAPTER II.—THE OCCIDENTALS
I AFRICAN WRITERS

§ 85 TERTULLIAN 256
    1 Life 2 Characteristics 3 Transmission 4 *De Pallio* 5 Apologetic Writings 6 *Adversus Judaeos* 7 Anti-Heretical Writings 8 *De Anima* 9 Writings on Questions of Morals and Church Discipline 10 Lost, and 11 Spurious Writings

§ 86 CYPRIAN . 280
    1 Life 2 Characteristics Transmission 3 Treatises 4 Letters 5 Writings of Doubtful Genuineness (a) *De Spectaculis*, (b) *De bono Pudicitiae*, (c) *De Laude Martyrii* 6 Spurious Writings.

§ 87. ARNOBIUS 304
    1 Transmission and Contents of the Book *Adversus Nationes*. 2 His Character as an Author. Sources Attestation

§ 88 LACTANTIUS 307
    1 Life 2 Characteristics Transmission 3 Writings during his Heathen Period 4 Writings during his Christian Period. 5 Lost Writings 6. *De Mortibus Persecutorum*. 7 Poems

SUPPLEMENTARY

§ 89 COMMODIANUS 317
    1. Life. 2 Characteristics. 3 (a) *Instructiones*, (b) *Carmen Apologeticum*.

II ROMAN WRITERS

§ 90 CAIUS 320
§ 91 HIPPOLYTUS 321
    1 Life 2 Transmission Characteristics 3 Exegetical Writings 4 Sermons 5. Polemical, 6 Dogmatic, 7 Chronographical, and 8 Ecclesiastical Writings 9 Poems (?) 10 Spurious Writings

	PAGE
§ 92. NOVATIANUS	344

1. Life   2 Characteristics   3 (a) *De Trinitate*, (b) *De Cibis Judaicis*   4 Lost Writings   5 Writings probably by Novatian (a) Letters, (b) *De Spectaculis*, and *De Bono Pudicitiae*.

III THE REMAINING OCCIDENTAL WRITERS

§ 93. VICTORINUS OF PETTAU	347

1 Writings   2 *Adversus Omnes Haereses*.

§ 94. RETICIUS OF AUTUN	349

CHAPTER III.— EPISCOPAL AND SYNODAL WRITINGS

§ 95. THE ROMAN BISHOPS	350

Zephyrinus. Callixtus   Pontianus. Cornelius. Stephanus Sixtus II. Dionysius. Felix

§ 96. ACTS OF SYNODS	352

1. Lost   2. Extant Acts of Synods.

Third Section. Ecclesiastical Literature

§ 97. SYMBOLS AND CREEDS	355
§ 98. CHURCH-ORDERS	356

1. The *Didascalia*   2 Ecclesiastical Canons.   3. *Duae Viae, vel Judicium sec. Petrum*.   4 The Egyptian Canons.

SUPPLEMENTARY

§ 99. THE PSEUDO-CLEMENTINE EPISTLES *De Virginitate* . .	361

Fourth Section. Legends

§ 100. GENERAL	363
§ 101 THE LEGEND OF ABGARUS	364
§ 102. THE ACTS OF PETER AND THE ACTS OF PAUL . . .	365

1. Acts of Paul.   2 Acts of Peter.   3 Acts of Paul and Thecla.

§ 103 THE PSEUDO-CLEMENTINE RECOGNITIONS AND HOMILIES .	371

1. Transmission   2 Contents.   3 Circumstances of Composition.   4 Attestation.

Fifth Section. Martyrologies

	PAGE
§ 104. GENERAL	378
§ 105. FROM ANTONINUS PIUS TO SEPTIMIUS SEVERUS	380

1. Polycarp. 2. Carpus 3. Justin. 4. Lyons and Vienne
5. The Scillitan Martyrs 6. Apollonius 7. Perpetua and Felicitas.

§ 106. FROM DECIUS TO LICINIUS 385

INDEX 393

CHRONOLOGICAL CONSPECTUS . . . . after 409

LIST OF ABBREVIATIONS

AA. *Acta Apost. Apocry*, edd. Lipsius et Bonnet (cf § 30).
AG. R. A. Lipsius, *Apokryph. Apostelgeschichten* (cf § 30, Literature).
ALG. *Archiv fur lateinische Lexikographie und Grammatik*, edited by E. Wolfflin
ANF. *Ante-Nicene Fathers*. Translations of the writings of the Fathers Edited by A C. Cox, D.D (§ 2. 9 *b*).
AS. Pitra, *Analecta Sacra* (cf § 2. 8 *b*).
ASGW *Abhandlungen der konigl. sachsischen Gesellschaft der Wissenschaften.*
BG. Fabricius-Harles, *Bibliotheca Graeca* (§ 2. 3 *b*). When the volume is not named, Vol VII is understood
BKV. *Bibliothek der Kirchenvater* (cf. § 2. 9 *a*)
BPL Schoenemann, *Bibliotheca*, Vol I (cf. § 2. 3 *b*).
BS Richardson, *Bibliographical Synopsis* (cf. § 2. 7 *c*).
CSE. *Corpus Scriptorum Ecclesiasticorum Latinorum* (§ 2. 8 *a*).
DCB *Dictionary of Christian Biography* (cf § 2 6 *a*), Vol. I, 1877; II, 1880, III, 1882, IV, 1887.
DLZ *Deutsche Litteraturzeitung*. Founded by M. Roediger, edited by P Hinneberg
Egh Lipsius, *Erganzungshefte* (cf § 30, Literature).
FGK. Zahn, *Forschungen zur Geschichte des Kanons*, etc. (§ 2 6 *b*), Vol I, 1881, II, 1883, III, 1884, IV, 1891, V, 1893.
GGA *Gottingische Gelehrte Anzeigen.*
GNK Zahn, *Geschichte des neutestamentlichen Kanons* (§ 2 6 *b*), Vol I, 1, 1888, I, 2, 1889, II, 1, 1890, II, 2, 1892.
HJG. *Historisches Jahrbuch der Gorresgesellschaft* Edited by H. Grauert, L Pastor, and G. Schnurer.
HZ. *Historische Zeitschrift*. Edited by H. von Sybel and Fr. Meinecke
JclPh. *Jahrbucher fur classische Philologie (Neue Jahrbucher fur Philologie und Padagogik)*. Edited by A Fleckeisen and R. Richter.
JdTh. *Jahrbucher fur deutsche Theologie*. Edited by K. Th. A. Liebner, J A. Dorner, *et al.*

LIST OF ABBREVIATIONS

JprTh. *Jahrbucher fur protestantische Theologie* Edited by Hase, Lipsius, Pfleiderer, Schrader
Kath *Der Katholik, Zeitschrift fur katholische Wissenschaft und kirchliches Leben* Edited by J M. Raich
KLex Wetzler and Welte, *Kirchenlexikon* (cf § 2 6 a), Vol. I, 1882, II, 1883, III, 1884, IV, 1886, V, 1888, VI, 1889, VII, 1891, VIII, 1893
LCB. *Litterarisches Centralblatt.* Founded by Fr. Zarncke; edited by E. Zarncke
LFC Library of the Fathers of the Holy Catholic Church (cf § 2. 9 b)
LG Harnack, *Litteraturgeschichte* (cf. § 2 4 b).
Lo. Lommatzsch's edition of Origen (§ 61).
NC. Maius, *Nova Collectio* (cf § 2 8 b).
NJdTh. *Neue Jahrbucher fur deutsche Theologie* Edited by L Lemme.
NKZ *Neue Kirchliche Zeitschrift* Edited by G Holzhauser
NPB Maius, *Nova Patrum Bibliotheca* (cf. § 2 8 b)
PG. Migne, *Patrologia Graeca* (cf. § 2. 8 a), Vol I, 1886, Vol II–V, 1857, VI, 1884, VII, 1882, VIII–XI, 1857, XII–XIV, 1862, XV, XVI, 1, 1862, XVI, 2, 3, 1863, XVII–XVIII, 1857.
PKZ. *Protestantische Kirchenzeitung* Edited by (H. Krause, F W. Schmidt, and) J. Websky.
PL. Migne, *Patrologia Latina* (cf § 2. 8 a), Vol I, II, 1866, III, IV, 1865, V–VII, 1844.
RE. *Realenzyklopadie fur Theologie und Kirche* (§ 2 6 a). Second edition, Vol. I, 1877, II, III, 1878, IV, V, 1879, VI, VII, 1880; VIII, IX, 1881, X, 1882, XI, XII, 1883, XIII, XIV, 1884, XV, XVI, 1885, XVII, 1886; XVIII, 1888.
RhM. *Rheinisches Museum* Edited by O. Ribbeck and F. Buecheler.
RQuH. *Revue des Questions historiques.*
RS. Routh, *Reliquiae Sacrae* (cf § 2. 8 b)
SAW. *Sitzungsberichte der kaiserl Akademie der Wissenschaften zu Wien.*
SBBA. *Sitzungsberichte der konigl. preussischen Akademie der Wissenschaften zu Berlin.*
SQu. *Sammlung kirchen- und dogmengeschichtlicher Quellenschriften* Edited by G Kruger, Freiburg, 1891 ff.
SpR. Maius, *Spicilegium Romanum* (cf. § 2 8 b).
SpS. Pitra, *Spicilegium Solesmense* (cf § 2 8 b).
StKr *Theologische Studien und Kritiken.* Edited by (E. Riehm and) J Kostlin, and E Kautzsch.
TSt *Texts and Studies* (cf. § 2. 6 b).

LIST OF ABBREVIATIONS xxiii

TU	*Texte und Untersuchungen* (§ 2 6 *b*)
ThJ.	*Theologische Jahrbucher.* Edited by F Chr. Baur and E. Zeller.
ThLB.	*Theologische Litteraturblatt.* Edited by Chr. E. Luthardt
ThLZ.	*Theologische Litteraturzeitung* Edited by A. Harnack and E Schurer
ThQu.	*Theologische Quartalschrift* Edited by von Kober, von Funk, *et al*
ThSt.	*Theologische Studien* Edited by F. E. Daubanton *et al*
ThT	*Theologische Tydschrift.* Edited by F. W. B. van Bell *et al.*
VJ	Jerome, *De Viris Illustribus* (cf § 2. 2)
WclPh	*Wochenschrift fur classische Philologie.* Edited by G. Andresen, H Draheim, and F Harder
ZhTh	*Zeitschrift fur die historische Theologie* Edited by (Chr F Illgen, Chr W Niedner, and) K F. A Kahnis
ZKG.	*Zeitschrift fur Kirchengeschichte* Edited by Th Brieger and B. Bess
ZkTh	*Zeitschrift fur katholische Theologie* Innsbruck
ZkWL.	*Zeitschrift fur kirchliche Wissenschaft und kirchliches Leben.* Edited by Chr E Luthardt.
ZwTh.	*Zeitschrift fur wissenschaftliche Theologie.* Edited by A. Hilgenfeld

Where the names of Epiphanius, Eusebius, and Irenæus occur without the mention of any particular work, the references are uniformly to the *Panarion*, the Church History, and the work *Adversus Haereses* respectively The citations of Irenæus follow the chapters in the edition of Stier, and those of Clement in that of Dindorf.

INTRODUCTION

§ 1. *The Subject*

Literature: H. J. Pestalozzi, *Grundlinien der Geschichte der kirchlichen Litteratur der ersten sechs Jahrhunderte*, Gottingen, 1811   G. C. F Lücke, in GGA, 1841, nos 186, 187, 1849–62 (Review of Moehler's *Patrologie*). F. Nitzsch, *Geschichtliches und Methodologisches zur Patristik*, in JdTh, X, 1865, 37–63   F. Overbeck, *Ueber die Anfange der patristischen Litteratur*, in HZ, XLVIII (XII), 1882, 417–472   A. Ehrhard, *Die altchristliche Litteratur*, etc. (cf. § 2. 8. *c*), 220–230. J. A. Deissmann, *Prolegomena zu den biblischen Briefen*, in *Biblische Studien*, Marburg, 1895, 187–252.

The history of early Christian literature is a guide to a correct understanding and appreciation of the literary productions to which the spirit of Christianity gave rise. It treats these works, both singly and in their mutual formal relations, from a purely literary point of view, without reference to their ecclesiastical or theological importance. Such a history is, therefore, to be distinguished from Patrology, which proceeds upon a purely dogmatic conception of the "Church Fathers," and which ranks as a special discipline belonging to Catholic theology by reason of its choice and treatment of its materials.

§ 2. *Transmission, Compilations, Helps*

1. The Christian literature of the first three centuries has been directly handed down to us only in a very fragmentary form, owing to the fact that a later age

soon outgrew the conceptions of an earlier time. Posterity has treated with pious reverence only the works of certain Fathers who were held in permanent high esteem. Our obligations are, therefore, the greater toward those who, by their copious quotations, have preserved to us fragments of the older literature. The importance of the Ἐκκλησιαστικὴ Ἱστορία of Eusebius, Bishop of Cæsarea (d. 340) for the history of early Christian literature, consists particularly in this feature, as well as in the biographical details which it gives Photius (Patriarch of Constantinople, circa 981) in his Ἀπογραφὴ καὶ συναρίθμησις τῶν ἀνεγνωσμένων ἡμῖν βιβλίων κ.τ.λ. (*Bibliotheca*), wrote with the same purpose, to make known to his readers the literature to which he had access. Others without this aim had recourse to ancient writers for quotations unacknowledged or explicit; and the great opponents of heresy — Irenæus, Clement, Tertullian, Hippolytus, and, later, Epiphanius and others — have involuntarily preserved a great deal of heretical matter from oblivion (§ 22) After the fourth and fifth centuries, *dicta probantia* (χρήσεις), taken from the early Fathers, were put to polemical use in the controversies within the church Quotations from the Fathers, some of them extensive, were combined with Biblical texts for hortatory and didactic purposes in the Ἱερά of Leontius and John, a work which originated in the sixth, or, at latest, in the seventh, century, and which is extant in the so-called *Sacra Parallela* (ascribed to John of Damascus, d. 754), and in similar manuscript recensions (Rupefucaldinus). Finally, from the sixth century onward (Procopius of Gaza), expositions taken from the writings of the older Fathers were compiled (*Catenae*) as aids to exegetical study.

INTRODUCTION 3

Harnack, LG, XXI–LXI, 835–842   Eusebius A C McGiffert, *The Church History of Eusebius*, translated with prolegomena and notes, in *A Select Library*, etc (see below, 9 *b*), 2d series,' Vol I, New York, 1890. C. F G Heinrici, *Das Urchristenthum in der Kirchengeschichte des Eusebius*, Lpz 1894, in *Beitrage zur Geschichte und Eklarung des neuen Testaments*, I, 1–70.—Photius · ed J Bekker, 1824–25   Fabricius, BG, VIII, 466–492 — **Heretical Books** see literature cited in § 22   — **Parallela** · K Holl, *Die Sacra Parallela des Johannes Damascenus*, in TU, XVI, 1, Lpz 1896. F Loofs, *Studien uber die dem Johannes Damascenus zugeschriebenen Parallelen*, Halle, 1892 — Compare also P. Wendland, *Neuentdeckte Fragmente Philos* Berl 1891   L Cohn, *Zur indirekten Ueberlieferung Philos und der alteren Kirchenvater*, in JprTh, XVIII, 1892, 475–492. **Catenae** · Th Ittigius (§ 2. 8 *b*), Fabricius, VIII, 637–700; E. Bratke, in StKr, LXVIII, 1895, 361–372.

2. Compilations begin with Jerome's (d. 421) *de Viris Illustribus Liber*, written in 392, which the author himself also styled *de Scriptoribus Ecclesiasticis*[1] It contains brief sections, 135 in number, which begin with Peter and close with a comparatively full account of the writer himself The information is superficially compiled and loosely connected; it embraces certain selected ecclesiastical and some heretical writers. Eusebius was the principal source, and the parts added by the author himself require in every instance the most searching verification The Greek version, said to have been made by Sophronius,[2] but of uncertain date, was apparently accessible to Photius Continuations of the work of Jerome were made by the Presbyter Gennadius of Massilia (*circa* 480), by Isidore, Bishop of Seville (d. 636), and by Ildefonsus, Bishop of Toledo (d. 667) Jerome's work was also the model followed by John Tritemius, Abbot of Sponheim,[3] who gave accounts of

[1] Cf. Ep 112, 3.   [2] Cf Jerome, 134
[3] *Liber de Scriptoribus Ecclesiasticis*, 1492

963 writers, many of whom belonged to the Middle Ages.

Editions: J. A Fabricius, *Bibliotheca Ecclesiastica*, Hamb. 1718.
— Separate editions of Jerome and Gennadius Guil. Herdingius, Lips 1879 C A Bernoulli, in SQu, 11, Freib 1895 — Literature. St v. Sychowski, *Hieronymus als Literarhistoriker*, in *Kirchengeschichtliche Studien*, by A Knopfler, H Schrors, and M Sdralek, 2 vols, Munster, 1894 J Huemer, in *Wiener Studien*, XVI, 1894, 121-158 C A Bernoulli, *Der Schriftstellercatalog des Hieronymus* Freib 1895 E C Richardson, *Hieronymus, Liber de Viris Illustribus*; *Gennadius, Liber de Viris Illustribus*, and O v Gebhardt, *Hieronymus de Viris Illustribus in griechischer Uebersetzung (der sogenannte Sophronius)* in TU, XIV, 1, 1896

3. Among Catholic and Protestant compilations of the seventeenth and eighteenth centuries, the following are worthy of mention: —

a) A Possevinus, *Apparatus Sacer ad Scriptores V. et N. T*, etc.
2 vols Venet 1603-1606 Colon Agripp (Cologne), 1608.
R Bellarminus, *De Scriptoribus Ecclesiasticis Liber*. Rome, 1613, and frequently.
L. E Dupin, *Nouvelle bibliothèque des auteurs ecclésiastiques*, etc.
47 vols Paris, 1686-1711 Also Latin. Compare the account given by Richardson, pp 120-121
S Le Nain de Tillemont, *Mémoires pour servir à l'histoire ecclésiastique des six premiers siècles* 16 vols Paris, 1693-1712, and frequently
D N Le Nourry, *Apparatus ad Bibliothecam Maximam Patrum Veterum et Scriptorum Ecclesiasticorum Lugduni editam*, etc.
2 vols Paris, 1694-97, and Tom I, 1703-15.
R. Ceillier, *Histoire générale des auteurs sacrés et ecclésiastiques* 23 vols Paris, 1729-63 New edition, 14 vols and 2 vols. Index. Paris, 1858-65 (69)
G Lumper, *Historia Theologica Critica de Vita, Scriptis atque Doctrina ss Patrum*, etc. 13 vols. August Vindel 1783-99 Incomplete

b) J. Gerhardius, *Patrologia*, etc. Jena, 1653, 2d edit, *sine loco*, 1668, 3d edit Gerae, 1673

INTRODUCTION 5

W Cave, *Historia Litteraria Scriptorum Ecclesiasticorum*
2 vols London, 1688-98 Best edition, Oxford, 1740-43
German edition, with index, Bremen, 1701

J. A Fabricius, *Bibliotheca sine Notitia Scriptorum Veterum Graecorum*, etc 12 vols Index Hamburg, 1705 ff 3d edit. 1716 (18) till 1728 14 vols 4th edit by Th Chi Harles, Hamburg, 1790-1809. 12 vols Index Incomplete

C Oudin, *Commentarius de Scriptoribus Ecclesiae Antiquis*. 3 vols Lips 1722

. J G. Walch, *Bibliotheca Patristica* Jena, 1770 Enlarged and improved edition by J T L Danz Jena, 1834 Also 1839

C. T G Schoenemann, *Bibliotheca Historico-Litteraria Patrum Latinorum*, etc 2 vols Lips 1792-94
On works of the Fathers of the primitive age, see Th Ittigius, *Schediasma de autoribus qui de scriptoribus ecclesiasticis egerunt*. Lips. 1711.

4. Among more recent works are the following: —

a) J. A. Moehler, *Patrologie oder Christliche Litteraturgeschichte*, edited by F. X Reithmayr 1 vol Regensburg, 1840

J. Fessler, *Institutiones Patrologiae* 2 vols Oenip. 1850-51 Newly edited by B Jungmann. Vols I and II, 1 Oenip 1890-92

J. Alzog, *Grundriss der Patrologie oder der alteren christlichen Literargeschichte*. Freib 1866 4th edit 1888

J Nirschl, *Lehrbuch der Patrologie und Patristik*. 3 vols. Mainz, 1881-85.

b) J. Donaldson, A critical history of Christian literature and doctrine from the death of the Apostles to the Nicene Council 3 vols. London, 1864-66 1 vol in 2d edit 1874 (Continued only as far as the apologists)

O. Zöckler, *Geschichte der theologischen Litteratur*. (*Handbuch der theologischen Wissenschaften* I Supplem) Gotha, 1890

Ch. Th Cruttwell, A literary history of early Christianity 2 vols London, 1893

A. Harnack, *Geschichte der altchristlichen Litteratur bis Eusebius* Part I, *Die Ueberlieferung und der Bestand*, bearbeitt unter Mitwirkung von Lic E Preuschen, Lpz, 189˙

The articles upon the following subjects are by Preuschen: Apocryphal Acts, Pseudo-Clementine writings, Irenæus, Clement of Alexandria, Origen, Gregory Thaumaturgus, Alexander of Alexandria, Methodius, Adamantius, Julius Africanus, Pamphilus, Eusebius, Novatian, Tertullian, Victorinus, Lactantius, Speeches of Sixtus, the Councils, Martyrdoms, Heathen matter (in reference to Christianity), the account of the *Catenae* and the indexes of initial words and manuscripts. Also A Harnack, in TU, XII, 1. 1894 (additions to the foregoing)

A. Harnack, *Die Chronologie der altchristlichen Litteratur bis Eusebius* (I . . *bis Irenaus*) Lpz 1897. (This volume arrived after the translation was completed)

5. Early Christian literature is also treated in the following works: —

J. F C. Bahr, *Geschichte der romischen Litteratur.* Vol. 4. *Die christlich-romische Litteratur.* I *Die christlichen Dichter und Geschichtschreiber* 2d edit Karlsruhe, 1873

A Ebert, *Allgemeine Geschichte der Litteratur des Mittelalters im Abendlande* 1 vol Lpz 1874 2d edit 1889

W S Teuffel, *Geschichte der romischen Litteratur.* 2 vols. Lpz 1870. 5th edit by L Schwabe, 1890

W Christ, *Geschichte der griechischen Litteratur bis auf die Zeit Justinians* (*Handb der klassischen Altertumswissenschaften* VII). Nordlingen, 1889 2d edit 1890

M. Manitus, *Geschichte der christlich-lateinischen Poesie.* Stuttgart, 1891

6. The following collections contain valuable contributions to the history of early Christian literature.

a) *Realencyklopadie fur protestantische Theologie und Kirche* von J. J Herzog † and G L Plitt †, continued by A. Hauck 2d edit. 18 vols Lpz. 1877–88

A Dictionary of Christian Biography, Literature, Sects, and Doctrines during the first eight centuries, edited by William Smith and Henry Wace 4 vols. London, 1877–87.

Kirchenlexikon oder Encyklopadie der katholischen Theologie und ihrer Hilfswissenschaften, edited by H J Wetzer and B Welte 2d edit by J Hergenroether † and Franz Kaulen. Freib 1882 ff

b) Th Zahn, *Forschungen zur Geschichte des neutestamentlichen Kanons und der altchristlichen Litteratur* Erlangen and Lpz 1881 ff (Thus far 5 volumes)

O v Gebhardt and Ad Harnack, *Texte und Untersuchungen zur Geschichte der altchristlichen Litteratur* Lpz 1882 Ser I, Vols I-XV.

J A Robinson, Texts and Studies Contributions to Biblical and Patristic Literature Cambridge, 1891 ff (4 volumes thus far.)

7 As aids to study the following may be mentioned:—

a) W Wattenbach. *Anleitung zur lateinischen Palaographie.* Lpz. 1865. 4th edit 1886.
—— *Anleitung zur griechischen Palaographie.* Lpz 1867 2d edit 1877
V Gardthausen, *Griechische Palaographie.* Lpz. 1879. 2d edit in preparation
Th Birt, *Das antike Buchwesen in seinem Verhaltnis zur Litteratur* Berl 1882

b) Th Ittigius, *De Bibliothecis et Catenis Patrum* Lips 1704
J G Dowling, *Notitia Scriptorum ss Patrum Aliorumque Vet eccl Monumentorum, quae in Collectionibus Anecdotor post a MDCC in lucem editis continentur.* Oxon 1839

c) H Hurter, *Nomenclator litterarius recentioris theologiae catholicae* I–III Innsbruck, 1871–86
W Englemann, *Bibliotheca scriptorum classicorum* 8th edit by E Preuss. 2 vols Lips 1880–82
E C Richardson, Bibliographical Synopsis in " The Ante-Nicene Fatheis," Vol X (cf § 2 9 *b*)
P Wendland, *Litteraturbericht* in the *Archiv fur Geschichte der Philosophie*, edited by L Stein in connection with H Diels, W Dilthey, B Erdmann, and E Zeller. Berl since 1887
C Sittl, *Litteraturbericht* in the *Jahresbericht uber die Fortschritte der Klassischen Altertumswissenschaften*, founded by C Bursian, edited by L v Muller Berl since 1888.

P Savi, *Delle scoperte e dei progressi realizzati nell' antica letteratura cristiana durante l' ultimo decennio.* Siena, 1893

A Ehrhard, *Die altchristliche Litteratur und ihre Erforschung seit 1880,* I (1880-84) in the *Strassb Theolog Studien* I, 4, 5 Strassb (Freib), 1894 (To be continued)

d) E A Sophocles, A Greek Lexicon of the Roman and Byzantine periods from BC 146 to AD 1100 New York (Lpz.), 1888

B G Winer, *Grammatik des neutestamentlichen Sprachidioms* 8th edit by P W Schmiedel Part I *Einleitung und Formenlehre* Gottingen, 1894

F W A Mullach, *Grammatik der griechischen Vulgarsprache in historischer Entwicklung* Berl 1856

G. Koffmane, *Geschichte des Kirchenlateins* Vol I *Entstehung und Entwicklung des Kirchenlateins bis Augustinus-Hieronymus* Berl 1879

e) A. Harnack, *Lehrbuch der Dogmengeschichte* 3 vols. Freib. 1886-90 Vol I, 3d edit Freib and Lpz 1894 *History of Dogma,* translated from the third German edition. Vols I, II London and Boston, 1895-97.

K J Neumann, *Der romische Staat und die allgemeine Kirche.* I, Lpz 1889

8 The following are the principal collections of the works of ecclesiastical writers: —

a) *Sacra Bibliotheca ss Patrum,* etc , edited by M de la Bigne 8 vols. Paris, 1575 Much augmented in the edition of A. Schott and others, in which it is called *Magna Bibliotheca Veterum Patrum* 15 vols Colonia, 1618-22

Maxima Bibliotheca Veterum Patrum et Antiquorum Scriptorum Eccl 27 vols Lugd 1677 Usually marked as edited by Ph Despont (Dupont), but actually the work of John and James Arvison

Bibliotheca Veterum Patrum Antiquorumque Scriptorum Eccl , edited by A Gallandius 14 vols and Appendix Venice, 1765-81 2d edit 1788

Cursus Patrologiae Completus, edited by J P Migne I *Patrologia Latina* 221 vols Paris, 1844-64 1844-49 (79 vols), 1850-55 (80-217), 1862-64 (218-221) Continued later than

1216 A D by Horoy II *Patrologia Graeca.* 161 vols in 166 Paris, 1857–66 1857–60 (104 vols), 1862–66 (105–161 [162]) Single volumes also in new editions
Corpus Scriptorum Ecclesiasticorum Latinorum, edit cons et imp. acad litt. caes. *Vindobonensis* (Up to 1896, 35 vols) Vindob (Prague and Lpz), 1867 ff.
Sanctorum Patrum Opuscula Selecta, ad Usum praesertim Studiosorum Theologiae. Edidit et commentariis auxit H. Hurter, S J. Oenip 1868 ff. [Innsbruck]. 1 Ser. 48 vols., 2 Ser now 6 vols

J L Dacherius, *Spicilegium sive Collectio Veter aliquot Scriptorum*, etc 13 vols Paris, 1645–77 New edition by L F J de la Barre 3 vols Paris, 1723.

J. B Cotelerius, *Ecclesiae Graecae Monumenta*, etc 3 vols. Paris, 1677–86 The fourth volume, Paris, 1692, is a titlepage edition of the *Analecta Graeca*, Paris, 1688

J E Grabe, *Spicilegium ss Patrum, ut et Haereticorum, saec.* I, II, III 2 vols Oxon 1698–99 2d edit 1700

L Zacagnius, *Collectanea Monumentorum Veter. Eccl. Graecae ac Latinae* 1 vol Rome, 1698

J. S Assemani, *Bibliotheca Orientalis Clementino-Vaticana* 3 vols Rome, 1719–28

A Maius, *Scriptorum Veterum Nova Collectio* 10 vols Rome, 1825–38

———, *Spicilegium Romanum* 10 vols Rome, 1839–44.

———, *Nova Patrum Bibliotheca.* 9 vols Rome, 1852–88 The 8th vol was edited by J Cozza-Luzi, 1871, the 9th, 1888

J Routh, *Reliquiae Sacrae.* 4 vols Oxon 1814–18 2d edit. 5 vols. 1846–48.

J. B Pitra, *Spicilegium Solesmense.* 4 vols Paris, 1852–58

———, *Analecta Sacra Spic Sol. parata* 4 vols ˗Paris. 1876–84 Volume 4 was edited by P Martinus There are two additional volumes of *Analecta Sacra et Classica* Paris, 1888–91. The last volume edited by A Battandier

Anecdota Maredsolana (thus far 3 vols). Mareds. 1893–94 III, 1, 1895

J. Bollandus, G. Henschenius, and others, *Acta Sanctorum quotquot toto orbe coluntur*, etc 56 (57) vols. Antwerp, Brussels, and Tongerloae, 1643–1794 (Reprint in 42 vols [to 14th

Sept inclus.ve] Venice, 1734–35) After an interruption in 1796, the work was resumed in 1837, and in 1894 had advanced as far as the 63d (Nov, II 1) volume   New edition by G J Camadet, 61 vols and Suppl   Paris and Rome, 1863–83   In addition, *Analecta Bollandiana*, edited by C de Smedt, J de Backer, and others   (Already 13 vols)   Brussels, 1882   An index to the old edition is in A Potthast's *Bibliotheca Historica Medii Aevi*   Berl 1862, pp. 575–942, 2d edit Berl 1895–96, pp 1129–1647   Th Ruinart, *Acta primorum Martyrum sincera et selecta*   Paris, 1689   New edition, Ratisbon, 1859

9. The following collections contain the best translations : —

a) *Bibliothek der Kirchenvater*   Auswahl der vorzuglichsten patristischen Werke in deutscher Uebersetzung   By F X Reithmayr and Thalhofer   420 parts in 80 volumes   Also a *Bericht uber die Bibliothek der Kirchenvater*   Kempton, 1869–88.

b) *Ante-Nicene Fathers*   Translations of the writings of the Fathers down to A D 325   The Rev Alexander Roberts, D D , and James Donaldson, LL D , editors   (Edinburgh edition, 1864–72   24 vols)   American reprint revised and chronologically arranged with brief prefaces and occasional notes by A Cleveland Coxe, D D   New York, new edition, 1896   10 vols   Vols IX and X are original additions to this edition ; IX, A Menzies, *Recently discovered Additions to Early Christian Literature*, and Origen's *Commentaries on John and Matthew* ; X, E C Richardson, *Bibliographical Synopsis*, and B Pick, *Comprehensive General Index* (to Vols I–VIII). (References in the following pages are to this edition)

A Library of the Fathers of the Holy Catholic Church, anterior to the division of the East and West   Translated by members of the English Church   Edited by E B. Pusey, John Keble, and J H Newman   Oxf 1838–85

A Select Library of the Nicene and Post-Nicene Fathers of the Christian Church   Second Series   Translated into English, with prolegomena and explanatory notes, under the editorial supervision of Philip Schaff, D D , LL.D , and Henry Wace, D D   New York, 1890 ff   (Thus far 12 vols)

DIVISION I

PRIMITIVE CHRISTIAN LITERATURE

Editions: The New Testament, S. P. Tregelles, C. Tischendorf, B F. Westcott and F J. A. Hort, O v. Gebhardt. — Extra-Canonical Writings · A Hilgenfeld, *Novum Testamentum extra canonem receptum.* Fasc IV². Lips. 1884. — The so-called Apostolic Fathers *SS. Patrum qui temp. apost. flor etc. opera etc.*, edited by J. B. Cotelerius. 2 vols. Paris, 1672. Autv. (Amst.) 1698. A. Hilgenfeld in *Novum Testamentum extra canonem receptum.* Fasc I–III. Lips. (1866), 1876–81 (Clement, Barnabas, Hermas). *Patrum Apostolicorum Opera*, edited by O de Gebhardt, A. Harnack, and Th. Zahn. 3 fasc. (Fasc. I²). Lips. 1876–78, smaller edition, Lips. 1877, reprinted 1894. *Opera Patrum Apostolicorum*, edited by F. X. Funk. 2 vols. Tubingen, 1881 The first volume was reprinted in 1887, augmented by the *Doctrina Apostolorum.* J. B. Lightfoot, *The Apostolic Fathers.* 2 Parts (Clement of Rome, Ignatius, Polycarp), Lond. 1885–90; 2d edit., Part I, 2 vols, 1890, Part II, 3 vols, 1889; smaller edition (all the Fathers), Lond. 1890. — **Translations:** *Das Neue Testament*, by C. Weizsacker, 6th and 7th edit, Freib. and Lpz. 1894. *Die apostolischen Vater*, by J Chr Mayer in BKV, 1869–80.

Literature · Introductions to the New Testament, particularly those of H. J. Holtzmann, 3d edit., Freib 1892, and A. Julicher, Freib. and Lpz. 1894 E. Reuss, *Die Geschichte der heiligen Schriften N. T.*, 6th edit., Braunschweig, 1887. A. Hilgenfeld, *Die apostolischen Vater*, Halle, 1853, J. Donaldson (§ 2. 4. *b*) ; C. Skworzow, *Patrologische Untersuchungen.* Lpz. 1875.

§ 3. *General*

1. As Christendom became consolidated in a Catholic Church, it collected into a New Testament a number of

writings which it regarded with reverence and holy awe, believing them to be permeated by the spirit of the Lord and his Apostles This new collection was a complement of the older Bible in which God had revealed himself to his covenant people, and which they had received from their fathers as Holy Scripture. This new collection was to be a memorial of the revelation made by God to his new people. It was meant to bequeath, as a sacred treasure, to all future generations of Christians, the choicest relics of an age of the highest religious fervor. This canonization has proved a great hindrance to the treatment of these writings from a purely literary and historical point of view, inasmuch as it has isolated the New Testament Scriptures, and tended to obscure their relation to other literary productions of early Christianity. At the same time it has been of decisive importance for the transmission of the early literature. For, while the New Testament has been copied over and over again, manuscript evidence for the uncanonical portion of the early literature is very slight; much of it has been preserved only in fragments, while more has been sacrificed to the disfavor of later times.

2. Jesus Christ left no writings behind him, and his Apostles and preachers were not writers in the strict sense of the word. They little knew that the **Letters**, in which they preached Christ to believers, in which they exhorted them to a sober and moral life, and in which they proved their love and care for them, would live on upon the lips and in the hearts of countless millions. Still less did they dream that these occasional writings would become the objects of ever-renewed labors, both pious and critical, on the part of learned and

unlearned alike. Nevertheless the new religious spirit produced monuments of real literary worth. The long and firmly held hope of a speedy coming of the Lord brought forth on Christian soil, also, the same kind of literature (viz. **Apocalypses**) which, under like circumstances, had arisen among the Jews.

The **Gospels** owe their origin to the desire to rescue the recollection of the words and deeds of the life, death, and resurrection of the Lord from the uncertainty of oral tradition, thus preserving it to the brethren; also to the desire to set forth the glad tidings of Christ as the very centre of the Christian faith. A like interest in the first generation of those who proclaimed the Gospel and a desire to record their labors, gave rise to the **Acts of the Apostles.** Finally, the practical needs of the churches occasioned the preparation of didactic and homiletic writings, and of works dealing with church government. What persons were engaged in this literary activity is, in many cases, only matter of conjecture; the personality of the writer withdrew into the background before that which he had to say. Nevertheless, it was the spirit of God and of Christ which spoke through him.

3. While Græco-Roman literature and its forms lay beyond the horizon of the early Christian writers, the *Devotional Literature of Judaism* had a widespread influence on the substance and the form of the early Christian literature, both on account of its affinity to early Christian ideas and because the representatives of those ideas sprang from the ranks of Judaism. The language, too, often bears a Hebraic stamp, although it was nearly always originally Greek in the specimens that have been preserved to us. Jewish writings were

worked over by Christians, and in the earliest Christian literature, specimens, such as the Apocalypse of John and the *Didache*, are found in which a Jewish substratum probably or demonstrably existed.

CHAPTER I

THE EPISTLES

§ 4 *The Pauline and the Pseudo-Pauline Epistles*

1. The New Testament includes fourteen writings supposed to be the work of **Paul**. They have not all, indeed, equal claim to be considered as genuine portions of the legacy bequeathed by him, but only that criticism which takes pleasure in completely obstructing with its baseless fancies the little light that, at best, is granted to us in the investigation of early Christian problems, can reject all, or nearly all, of these epistles as forgeries. In so doing, it banishes from history the figure of the great Apostle whose personality is incomprehensible to little minds. Neither convincing reasons, nor even probable doubts, have ever been maintained touching the genuineness of the first Epistle to the Thessalonians (written 54–55 A D), of the Epistle to the Galatians (55–57), of the two Epistles to the Corinthians (56–58 and 58–60), of the Epistle to the Romans (59–60, 61), or of the Epistles to the Philippians (62–64) and to Philemon (about the same date) Doubts as to the Epistle to the Colossians (63–64) are susceptible of solution, and the spurious character of the second Epistle to the Thessalonians (written not long after the first, if its genuineness is assumed), as also of the Epistle to the Ephesians (63–64), though maintained on weighty grounds, has not

been rigorously demonstrated. On the other hand, even tradition is not favorable to the Epistle to the Hebrews. In the West, in the middle of the fourth century, it was not universally regarded as Pauline or as a portion of the New Testament canon. Its contents point to the author as a Pauline Christian of Alexandrian culture,[1] who wrote later than the year 70 A.D., and earlier than Clement of Rome, probably under Domitian (81–96). The so-called **Pastoral Epistles** (two epistles to Timothy and Titus) were unknown to Marcion when he formed his canon of Pauline epistles. The situation presupposed in them cannot be explained by the Apostle's life as known to us; the language and the whole sphere of thought render their Pauline authorship highly improbable, and their relation to Gnosticism apparently excludes them from the first century. It is possible that genuine epistles, or fragments of epistles addressed to the same two persons, were at the disposal of their author.

2. Several epistles of the Apostle have been lost,[2] and an attempt was made to replace them by forgeries. The author of the Muratorian Fragment[3] knew of Epistles to the Laodiceans and to the Alexandrians, both of which he designated as Marcionite works. Concerning an *Epistle to the Alexandrians* nothing else is known certainly (but compare Zahn); on the other hand, a supposed *Epistle to the Laodiceans* is found in the *Codex Fuldensis* of Victor of Capua of the sixth century,[4] and in many other Latin manuscripts of the

---

[1] Jülicher, *Einleitung*, 107.
[2] Cf 1 Cor v 9, 2 Cor 11 3 f, Col iv 16, Phil. iii 1. Cf. also Polycarp, *ad Phil* 3.   [3] V. 63–65.
[4] Cf. also the *Speculum Augustini*, edited by Weihrich, in CSE, XII, 516.

Bible, as well as in Arabic in a Paris Codex[1] But it is uncertain whether the author of the Muratorian Fragment, and other ancient witnesses,[2] refer to this particular epistle. An apocryphal Correspondence between Paul and the Corinthians still existed at the time of Ephraem (about 350 A.D.) in the Syriac Bible,[3] and, though eliminated there, it passed over into the Armenian Bible, in which it appears to have been found as late as the fourteenth century. This correspondence has been preserved in Armenian, (1) in many Bibles, and (2) in the translation of Ephraem's Commentary on the Pauline Epistles; and in Latin, (1) in the manuscript Bible in the *Ambrosiana*,[4] apparently of the tenth century (Berger), and (2) in a different translation in the Laon manuscript of the Bible[5] (Bratke). The forgery was apparently aimed against the Bardesanites, its original language, whether Syriac or Greek, cannot now be determined. The Correspondence between Seneca and Paul[6] could scarcely have arisen before the fourth century.

E. Bratke, *Notiz zu einer arabischen Version des Laodicenerbriefes*, in ZwTh, XXXVII (II), 1894, 137 f. W F Rinck, *Das Sendschreiben der Korinther an Paulus*, etc Heidelb. 1823. P. Vetter, in ThQu, LXXII, 1890, 610-639. Th Zahn, GNK, II, 2, 565-621 S Berger, *La correspondance apocryphe de S. Paul et des Corinthiens* Paris, 1891. Also in connection therewith, A. Harnack, in ThLZ, XVII, 1892, 2-9, and in LG, 33-39, 763-765 E Bratke in ThLZ, XVII, 1892, 585-588 C Callewaert, *Une lettre perdue de S Paul et le "De aleatoribus"* Louvain, 1893 P Vetter, *Der apokryphische dritte Korintherbrief*. Wien, 1894 Cf Th Zahn, in ThLB, XV, 1894, 123-126.

[1] *Codex Paris. Arab* 80.   [2] Harnack, LG, 34 f.
[3] Cf. also the citations in Aphraates' *Homily VI*, edited by Bert, 105, and XXIII, 389 f
[4] E. 53, infr.   [5] Codex 45   [6] Jerome, *de Viris*, 12

§ 5. *The Catholic Epistles*

It is improbable that the seven **Catholic** (*i e.* General) **Epistles** of the New Testament were all the work of the authors to whom they are ascribed in their headings. In the case of the second and third Epistles of John, and the Epistle of Jude, but more especially in that of the second Epistle of Peter and the Epistle of James, this assumption is strengthened by the fact that all these writings became recognized as parts of sacred literature only gradually, after the third century. There exist no positive grounds for regarding their authors as men of the Apostolic age, and possibly the latest of the writings, the second Epistle of Peter, first came into existence about the middle of the second century. The tradition as to the first Epistle of Peter and the first Epistle of John is more favorable; but apart from its opening words there is nothing to justify the assumption that the former writing was the work of Peter, who, on this supposition, must have become Paul's pupil in his old age Nevertheless it remains quite possible that it was composed in the first century; but the Epistle of John stands or falls with the Gospel.

§ 6. *The Epistle of Barnabas*

Editions On the edition by J. Usserius, printed at Oxford in 1642, and destroyed by fire in 1644, see J H. Backhouse, The *editio princeps* of the epistle of Barnabas, etc Oxf 1883 H Menardus, Paris, 1645. J G Muller, Lpz 1869 A Hilgenfeld (§ 3), II², 1877 (The first edition of the whole epistle according to the collation by Bryennios) W Cunningham, Lond 1877. O de Gebhardt and A Harnack (§ 3), I, 2², 1878 F X Funk (§ 3), I², 1887 — **Translation** J Chr Mayer (§ 3) Roberts and Donaldson, ANF, I, 133-149 (§ 2 9 *b*)

Literature. The prolegomena and commentaries in the various editions. J. Hefele, *Das Sendschreiben des Apostels Barnabas.* Tubingen, 1840 K H Weizsacker, *Zur Kritik des Barnabas aus dem Kodex Sinaiticus* Tubingen, 1863. R A Lipsius in Schenkel's *Bibellexikon*, I, 1869, 363–373 W. Milligan in DCB, I, 260–265 F X Funk, *Der Codex Vaticanus graec.* 859. *und seine Descendenten*, in ThQu, LXII, 1880, 629–637 D Volter, in JprTh, XIV, 1888, 106–144 J Weiss, Berl 1888 — Fabricius, BG, IV, 827, 828. Richardson, BS, 16–19 Harnack, LG, 58–62.

1. The epistle entitled Βαρνάβα ἐπιστολή has been transmitted in Greek and Latin in the following manuscripts: (1) Greek, (*a*) in the *Codex Sinaiticus* (א), possibly of the fourth century, as a supplement to the New Testament, following the revelation of John, and preceding the *Shepherd* of Hermas; (*b*) in the *Codex Constantinopolitanus* (1056 A D), discovered by Bryennios in 1875, and now in the Patriarchal Library at Jerusalem. It stands between Chrysostom's Synopsis of the Old and New Testament and the Epistle of Clement. (*c*) Together with the Epistle of Polycarp, it is found in eight (nine) manuscripts (derived from the same archetype), in all of which the first chapters down to 5 7 (... τὸν λαὸν τὸν καινὸν ἑτοιμάζων) are wanting; (2) Latin: in a translation made before the year 700 (*Cod Biblioth. Imper. Petropol. Qu.* v I, 39, *saec.* x), which comprises only the first seventeen chapters.

2. Clement of Alexandria commented upon the Epistle[1] in his *Hypotyposes*,[2] and mentioned it in his *Stromata*[3] as a work of the Apostle Barnabas, and as a sacred writing, though not of equal standing with the Old Testament and the Gospels.[4] Origen called it an Ἐπιστολὴ καθολική, and he appears to have treated it

[1] Eusebius, *Eccl. Hist.* VI, 14, 1.
[2] Cf. § 60 5. *c.*
[3] II, 6, 31, cf II, 20, 116.
[4] Cf *Stromata*, II, 15, 67

as *Scriptura Divina*.[1] Later, the epistle was little read, even Eusebius[2] seeming to have doubts as to its apostolic origin. Apart from the manuscripts, it is only mentioned besides in the "List of Sixty Canonical Books,"[3] in the Stichometry of Nicephorus, and, possibly, in the Catalogus Claromontanus[4]—in the West it is not mentioned at all except in the translation and by Jerome.[5]

3. The assumption—which became fixed by tradition—that the epistle was the work of **Barnabas**, the companion of Paul, is chiefly contradicted by the writer's ignorance of Jewish ceremonial, which appears incomprehensible in a Palestinian Jew and Levite; and also by his avowed anti-Judaism. Definite conjectures as to the author can hardly be ventured, since the date of composition can only be placed somewhere between the destruction of Jerusalem,[6] on the one hand, and the time of Clement,[7] on the other. Furthermore, the reference to the "ten kings"[8] cannot be determined with certainty, nor can the "building of the temple"[9] be supposed to mean anything else than the building of the spiritual temple in the hearts of believers (in spite of the views of Weizsacker and others). Still, the epistle contains nothing that compels us to assign it to a date outside of the first century, and there is no convincing reason against the assumption that it was written under Nerva (or Vespasian). There are adequate grounds for regarding Alexandria as the place of its composition.

[1] *Contra Celsum*, I, 63, *Princ.* III, 2, 4, 7.
[2] Cf. *Hist. eccl* III, 25, 4, VI, 13, 6.
[3] Cf Zahn, GNK, II, 1, 292
[4] Cf. Zahn, GNK, II, 1, 169–171.
[5] *De Viris illust.* 6, etc.
[6] Cf. 4, 14; and 16.
[7] Cf however, § 21 3.
[8] 4, 4–6.
[9] 16, 3–4

4 The **writing** was not addressed to any single congregation, but to all Christendom, with the general purpose of establishing the faith of his readers by imparting to them complete Gnosis (1, 5). To this end the author showed that Judaism was an error with which Christianity could have nothing to do, but which it must reject; and also that the covenant made by God in the Old Testament applied to Christians, but that it never applied to the Jews. This Gnosis rested upon an unusually grotesque and bald typology to which the institutions of the Old Testament were sacrificed, and which gives as plain evidence of the author's narrowness and lack of culture as do his awkward language and the senseless way in which, from chapter 18 onward, he sets forth the precepts of the Book of the Two Ways.[1] Besides the Pauline Epistles, the author must have read the Evangelical records, possibly even the Gospel of Matthew.[2] There is no reason to doubt the unity of the epistle. The dismemberment attempted by Volter has no appearance of justification, and Weiss' hypothesis of a single complete redaction breaks down, owing to the absence of any such variety in its tendencies as he maintains.

§ 7. *The First Epistle of Clement*

Editions (1) Of the Greek text P Junius, Oxf 1633 Φ Βρυέννιος, Κωνσταντ 1875 (First edition of the complete epistle) O de Gebhardt and A Harnack (§ 3), I, 1, 2d edit, 1876 A Hilgenfeld (§ 3), I, 2d edit 1876 F. X Funk (§ 3), I, 2d edit 1887. J. B Lightfoot (§ 3), Part I, 2 vols, Lond 1890 (contains an autotype of the *Codex Constantinop.*). (2) Of the Latin translation G. Morin in *Anecdota Maredsolana*, Vol II, Maredsous, 1894 Cf. thereon, A. Harnack in ThLZ, XIX, 1894, 159-162, and SBBA,

---

[1] Cf. § 21 3   [2] See, however, Weiss, 94-119.

1894, 261–273, 601–621. J. Haussleiter in ThLB, XV, 1894, 169–174   Th Zahn in ThLB, XV, 1894, 195–200   E Woelfflein in ALG, IX, 1894, 81–100. G. Courtois, *L'Épitre de Clément de Rome*, Montauban, 1894 — Translations. J. Chr Mayer (§ 3), Roberts and Donaldson, ANF, I, pp 5–21 (§ 2 9 *b*). J Keith, ANF, IX, 229–248   (Revised from a more recently discovered manuscript) Literature   The prolegomena and commentaries in the various editions, especially that of Lightfoot. R. A. Lipsius, *De Clem Rom Epistola ad Corinthios priore Disquisitio*, Lips 1854   G Salmon in DCB, I, 554–559   Hasenclever, *Christliche Proselyten der hoheren Stande im ersten Jahrhundert*, in JprTh, VIII, 1882, 66–78, 230–271   W Wrede, *Untersuchungen zum ersten Clemensbriefe*, Gottingen, 1891. — Fabricius, BG, IV, 828–830   Richardson, BS, 1–5   Harnack, LG, 39–47

1. The so-called first Epistle of Clement to the Corinthians, Κλήμεντος πρὸς Κορινθίους ā, has been handed down in a threefold transmission: (1) Greek: (*a*) in the *Codex Alexandrinus* of the fifth century, as an appendix to the New Testament. A portion (from Chap 57, 6 πλήσθησον . . . to 64, 1 . . ιπον ὁ παντεόπτης) is wanting. (*b*) In the *Codex Constantinop*. (1056 A D), discovered by Bryennios in 1875, and now in the Patriarchal Library at Jerusalem   (2) Latin: in a translation which Harnack considers to be Roman, and Haussleiter African, in its origin. Probably it was made as early as the second century (Zahn : fifth century). It is found in the *Codex Florinens* of the eleventh century, and was discovered by Morin. (3) Syriac :· in an unpublished translation, being a part of the New Testament,[1] placed after the Catholic and before the Pauline Epistles.[2]

2. The **Epistle** was used by Polycarp[3] without any

---

[1] Codex Cantabr Add. MSS 1700 (A.D. 1170).
[2] Cf. Lightfoot, 2d edit I, 129–146.
[3] Cf. Harnack's edition, XXIV–XXVII.

explicit reference. It is first mentioned by Hegesippus,[1] who, however, does not name Clement as the author any more than does Irenæus.[2] Clement is named as the author by Dionysius of Corinth[3] and by Clement of Alexandria,[4] the latter of whom frequently made use of the Epistle,[5] both tacitly and expressly. He also reckoned it among the sacred writings. The same is the case also with Origen.[6] Eusebius held the epistle in high esteem, though he did not place it in any comparison with the New Testament scriptures.[7] For attestation of the epistle see Lightfoot[8] and Harnack.[9]

3. In the dedication the Roman church avows itself to be the sender of the epistle. Clement's name does not occur in it, but no valid proof can be adduced against the view that the **Clement**, who appears in the tradition of the Roman Catholic church as the third or fourth bishop of Rome, wrote it by order of the congregation. The identification of this Clement with the consul Flavius Clement, against whom his cousin, the Emperor Domitian, instituted proceedings on account of his shameful inactivity, suggests itself at once; but it is more or less contradicted by the fact that the epistle displays a finished and exact knowledge and a keen appreciation of the Old Testament. This leads one to conclude that the author was not a pagan by birth, still less a man of high rank, but more probably a Hellenis-

---

[1] Eusebius, *Eccl. Hist.* III, 16, IV, 22, 1.
[2] *Adversus Haer.* III, 3, 3, cf. Eusebius, V, 6, 2 ff.
[3] Eusebius, IV, 23, 9 ff.   [4] *Stromat.* IV, 17, 105.
[5] Cf. Harnack, LG, 41 f.
[6] *De Principiis*, II, 3, 6, *Select. in Ezech.* VIII, 3, *in Joann.* VI, 36.
[7] III, 16, 37, 4, 38, cf. III, 3, 25, cf. also Jerome, *De Viris.* 15, etc., Photius, *Codex*, 113 and 126.
[8] I, 2d edit. 148-200.   [9] LG, 40-47.

tic Jew, perhaps a freedman of the consul (thus Lightfoot, otherwise, Lipsius, Harnack, Hilgenfeld, and many others) Besides, if at this early date a high Roman official had held a distinguished position in the church, tradition would hardly have allowed the fact to escape unmentioned. In order to determine the date of composition, it is important to note that besides the persecution that took place under Nero,[1] a second is presupposed as having occurred in the immediate past:[2] a fact that points to the last years of the first century.[3]

4 The **authenticity and integrity** of the epistle have only been impugned occasionally and on weak grounds.[4] The writing is an exhortation occasioned by the controversies within the Corinthian church. The Roman church, throwing her authority into the balance, not without some consciousness of its weight, explains to her sister congregation that the unchristian behavior of certain younger members toward their elders and superiors cannot but injure the good repute of the Corinthian Christians[5] Variations on this theme, exhortations to discipline and good order, warnings against envy and jealousy, with the citation of numerous examples from ancient and later times, form the substance of a composition which, in spite of the smoothness and correctness of its diction,[6] is wearisome on account of its length. With rather abrupt transition the prayer used in the Roman congregation is recorded.[7] Quota-

---

[1] Chap. V, 6. [2] Chap. VII, 1; cf. I, 1.
[3] Cf Hegesippus in Eusebius, III, 16.
[4] Cf. Harnack's edition, XLIX f.
[5] Cf. I–III, 37, XLIV, 6, XLV, 3, XLVI, 5, 9; XLVII, 6; LIV, 1; LVII, 1.
[6] Cf Photius, 126. [7] Chaps. LIX, 3–LXI, 3.

tions from the Old Testament occupy nearly a quarter of the whole epistle, and use was also made of Pauline Epistles, the Epistles to the Hebrews, and apparently of the first Epistle of Peter and the Epistle of James, as well as of other writings that cannot now be determined.[1]

5. The following writings have been falsely ascribed to, or wittingly forged under the name of Clement: (1) The so-called second Epistle of Clement;[2] (2) the two Epistles to James;[3] (3) the two Epistles *de Virginitate*;[4] (4) canonical compositions (διαταγαὶ διὰ Κλήμεντος,[5] Apostolic Constitutions).

§ 8 *The Epistle of Polycarp*

Editions: J Faber, Paris, 1498 (Latin only) P Halloix, *Ill. Eccl. Orient. Scriptorum* . . *Vitae et Documenta*, I, Duaci, 1633, 525-532. J Usserius, Oxon 1644, cf J H Backhouse (§ 6) Theo. Zahn (§ 3), II, 1876 F. X Funk (§ 3), II, 1881. J. B. Lightfoot (§ 3), Part II, Lond, 1885 (2d edit., 1889). A Hilgenfeld in ZwTh, XXIX, 1886, 180-206 — **Translations:** J. Chr. Mayer (§ 3). Roberts and Donaldson, ANF, I, pp 33-36.

Literature: The prolegomena and notes of the various editions, particularly Lightfoot, I, 417-459, 530-704, II, 987-998. Also, Ritschl, A, *Die Entstehung der altkatholischen Kirche* (2d edit.), Bonn, 1857, 584-600. G Volkmar, *Epistulam Polycarpi Smyrnaei genuinam* . . . Zurich, 1885, cf A Harnack in ThLZ, XI, 1886, 53-55. G Salmon in DCB, IV, 423-431 Theo Zahn, *Zur Biographie des Polykarpus und Irenaus* in FGK, IV, 249-279 J M Cotterill, *The Epistle of Polycarp to the Philippians and the Homilies of Antiochus Palaestinensis* in the *Journ of Philol*, XIX, 1891, 241-285. Compare also the literature cited at § 9 — Fabricius, BG, 47-52. Richardson, BS, 7-10 Harnack, LG, 69-74.

---

[1] Cf XVII, 6; XXIII, 3 ff.; XXVI, 2; XXVII, 5; XLVI, 2; L, 4.
[2] Cf. § 20. [3] § 103. [4] § 99. [5] § 98.

1. An **Epistle to the Philippians** has been preserved under the name of **Polycarp**, Bishop of Smyrna, who, having been a disciple of John (the Presbyter) and a contemporary of Papias,[1] died on Feb 23, 155,[2] at the age of eighty-six[3] or even older[4] The Epistle is extant (1) in Greek, in a fragmentary form, together with the Epistle of Barnabas, in eight (nine) manuscripts (all descended from one archetype) In all these, the last chapters following Chap 9 2 ($\delta\iota'$ $\dot{\eta}\mu\hat{a}s$ $\dot{v}\pi\dot{o}$) are wanting (2) in Greek, in two fragments preserved by Eusebius,[5] which contain the whole of Chapter 9 and Chapter 13 except the last sentence (3) in Latin, in a somewhat free and not entirely correct translation, collected together with the spurious or interpolated Epistles of Ignatius Attempts at re-translations of the missing chapters into Greek will be found in Zahn and Lightfoot

2. Irenæus bears **witness** in his letter to Florinus[6] that Polycarp[7] wrote several Epistles both to congregations and to individuals, and he mentions one addressed to the Philippians, in a manner that seems to compel us to understand his words as referring to the Epistle now extant Nevertheless, the decision as to the genuine or spurious character of this Epistle as well as the determination of its date of composition, depends upon the solution of like problems touching the Epistles of Ignatius, with which it is closely connected by unmistakable references[8] Any explanation of these relations

---

[1] Irenæus, *Adv Haer* V, 33 4 Cf Papias in Eusebius, *Hist Eccl* III, 39 4

[2] Lightfoot, I, 629-702, II, 987-998, 2d edit, I, 646-722, III, 404-415 Cf, however, Réville, *Origines* (cf § 9, below), 454, note

[3] Martyr Polycarp 9 [6] Cf Eusebius, *Hist Eccl* V, 20 8

[4] Zahn [7] *Adv Haer* III, 3 4

[5] *Hist Eccl* III, 36, 13-15 [8] Cf Chaps 9 and 13 and the introduction.

by distinguishing between a genuine nucleus and a redaction[1] is inadmissible for internal reasons (e g use of the Epistle of Clement throughout and uniformity of style) in spite of the difficulties which remain on the assumption of its unity.[2] Identification of the author with the author of the Epistles of Ignatius is quite impossible According to Jerome[3] (a doubtful authority) the Epistle was still employed in divine service in his own time. It is possible that even Antiochus of St. Saba (seventh century) quoted sections from it in his *Pandectes*.

3. The **Epistle** was occasioned by a communication made by the church at Philippi to Polycarp. The request of the Philippians that he should strengthen them in their faith and conduct is met by the bishop by a reference to the foundations of their faith and to the duties binding upon every Christian, but particularly upon those who bear office. At the same time he recommends a strict though gentle treatment in a case of apostasy that had been mentioned by the Philippians. The composition abounds in quotations and reminiscences of Gospel literature, the Epistles of Paul, including the Pastoral Epistles, the first Epistle of John and, more especially, the first Epistle of Peter; apparently, also, the Acts of the Apostles The first Epistle of Clement is also freely used

4 Five fragments, in the form of answers to Biblical questions, which are ascribed to Polycarp, were discovered by Feuardentius and published in the notes to his edition of Irenæus.[4] With the exception of a single

---

[1] Ritschl, Volkmar, Hilgenfeld.
[2] Cf particularly Hilgenfeld.
[3] *De Viris Illust* 17.
[4] 1639, *Adv. Haer.* III, 3. 4

sentence they are regarded as genuine by Zahn,[1] while Lightfoot[2] and Harnack[3] reject them. Harnack considers that they may have been written at the beginning of the third century On the martyrdom of Polycarp (*Martyrium Polycarpi*) see § 98.

§ 9. *The Epistles of Ignatius*

Editions: J Faber, Paris, 1498 (12 epistles of the longer Latin recension [= L²], without the letter of Maria to Polycarp). S Champerius, Colon 1536 (13 epistles L²) V Paceus, Dillingen, 1557 (13 epistles of the longer Greek recension [= G²]) C Gesnerus, Tigur 1559 (13 epistles, G², L²) J Usserius, Oxon 1644 (first edition [of the shorter Latin recension =] L¹) J. Vossius, Amstelod. 1646 (first edition [of the shorter Greek recension =] G¹, without the Epistle to the Romans) Th Ruinart, Paris, 1689 (first edition of the Epistle to the Romans) Constantinople, 1783 (first edition of the Armenian translation, reprinted by G Petermann, Lips 1849) W Cureton, The ancient Syriac version of the Epistles of St Ignatius, etc Lond 1845, and *Corpus Ignatianum*, Lond 1849 (first edition of the three Syriac epistles) Migne, PG, V, 643–960 Theo Zahn (§ 3), II, 1876 F. X Funk (§ 3), II, 1881 P de Lagarde (extract from the *Abhandlungen der Gotting Gesellsch d Wissensch* XXIX), Gottingen, 1882 (the shorter Latin recension, L¹) J B Lightfoot (§ 3), Part II, Lond 1885, 2d edit 1889 G A Simcox, St Ignatius and the new Syriac Gospels, Academy, 1894, Nov 24, 424 —**Translations:** J Chr Mayer (§ 3) Roberts and Donaldson, ANF, I, 49–131 (Eph, Magnes, Trall, Rom, Philad, Smyrn, Polycarp, Syriac Ep, Spurious Ep, Mart)

Literature: J Ussher, *Dissertatio de Ignatio et Polycarpo*, 1644 (Works, edited by Elrington, VII, 87–295.) J. Dallæus, *De scriptis, quae sub Dionys Areop et Ignat Antioch nominibus circumferuntur, libri* II, Genev 1666 J. Pearson, *Vindiciae Ignatianae* Cantab 1672 Oxon 1852 (PG, 37–472) R Rothe, *Die Anfange der Christlichen Kirche*, etc I, Wittenb 1837, 713–784. W. Cure-

---

[1] GNK, I, 2, 782.   [3] LG, 73.
[2] II, 1003. (Second edition, 1889, III, 421.)

ton, *Vindiciae Ignatianae*, Lond 1846. C. C J. v. Bunsen, *Ignatius von Antiochien und seine Zeit*, Hamb 1847. F Chr Baur, *Die ignat. Briefe und ihr neuester Kritiker*, Tubingen, 1848 H Denzinger, *Ueber die Aechtheit des Textes des Ignat* Wurzb. 1849. (Latin in PG, 601-624) A Ritschl (§ 8), 1st edit, Bonn, 1850, 577-589 G. Uhlhorn, in ZhTh, XXI, 1851, 3-65, 247-341 (cf also RE, VI, 688-694). R. A. Lipsius, in ZhTh, XXVI, 1856, 3-160, and in *Abhandlungen für die Kunde des Morgenlandes*, I, 5, 1859 A Merx, *Meletemata Ignatiana*, Halle, 1861. Theo Zahn, *Ignatius von Antiochien*, Gotha, 1873 E Renan, *Les évangiles*, Paris, 1877, XV-XXXV (cf also *Journal des Savants*, 1874, 38) A Harnack, *Die Zeit des Ignatius von Antiochien*, etc. Lpz 1878 (cf Hart in Lightfoot, 461-466, and the whole section of Lightfoot) R. T. Smith in DCB, III, 209-222. F X Funk, *Die Echtheit der ignat. Briefe*, etc., Tubingen, 1883, and in KLex, VI, 581-590. W D. Killen, The Ignatian Epistles entirely spurious. Edin. 1886. D. Volter, *Die ignat Briefe*. etc Tubingen, 1892 See besides the prolegomena and notes in the various editions, particularly Lightfoot The literature on the origin of Episcopacy and of the Catholic church should also be compared, particularly J. Réville, in *Rev. de l'Hist. des Relig* XXII, 1890, 1-26, 123-160, 267-288. Also separately, Paris, 1891 Idem, *Les Origines de l'Épiscopat*, Paris, 1894, 442-481. See also the literature on the Apostolical Constitutions and their sources, particularly F. X. Funk, in ThQu, LXII, 1880, 355-384, and *Die apostolischen Konstitutionen*, Rottenb. 1891, 281-355. A. Harnack, in TU, II, 1, 2, 1884 (Edition of the *Didache*), 241-268, and in StKr, LXVI, 1893, 460-484 — Fabricus, BG, 32-44. Richardson, BS, 10-15. Harnack, LG, 75-86

1. A number of epistles have been preserved bearing the name of **Ignatius** Theophorus,[1] who, according to tradition, is known as the second (third) **bishop of Antioch**[2] and is reputed to have met a martyr's death at Rome under Trajan.[3] These **Epistles** exist (1) in a

---

[1] Cf. Lightfoot, I, 22-28.

[2] Origen, *Hom in Lucam*, VI, 1; Eusebius, *Hist Eccl* III, 22, *Chronicorum, anno Abrahami* 2085 [Migne, PG, 19 545 f.].

[3] Eusebius, *Chronicor Lib* II *anno Abrahami* 2123 [Migne, PG, 19: 553 c.], cf. Irenæus, *Adv. Haer.* V, 28. 4.

short form which embraces seven Epistles addressed to the Ephesians, Magnesians, Trallians, Romans, Philadelphians, Smyrnæans, and to Polycarp (*a*) in Greek (G^1), six being contained in a manuscript[1] at Florence (probably of the eleventh century), the missing Epistle to the Romans being found as part of the text of the *Martyrion* (Colbert) in the National Library at Paris[2] (belonging probably to the tenth century): (*b*) in Latin (L^1) in a translation made by Robert Grosseteste, about 1250 A D [3]: (*c*) in Armenian, in a translation made from the Syriac in the fifth century at the earliest[4] (2) In Syriac [S], in a still shorter form, as compared with G^1 and L^1, containing the Epistles to the Ephesians, Romans, and Polycarp. (3) In an interpolated and enlarged form, containing a number of additional epistles. (*a*) In Greek (G^2) 13 epistles, of Mary of Cassobola and of Ignatius to Mary, to the Trallians, Magnesians, Tarsians, Philippians, Philadelphians, Smyrnæans, to Polycarp, the Antiochians, Hero, the Ephesians, and to the Romans These are preserved in 10 (11) manuscripts. (*b*) in Latin (L^2), containing those named above (with the exception of the letter of Mary of Cassabola), and also the *Laus Heronis*, two epistles to the Apostle John, one to Mary, and one from Mary to Ignatius· all preserved in 13 manuscripts The epistle of Mary of Cassobola is preserved only in the *Codex Caiensis* (see above) It may be regarded as generally admitted that only the contents of the shorter recensions G^1 (and L^1)

---

[1] *Cod Medic. Laur. Plut.* LVII, 7.
[2] *Codex Paris.* 1451 [cf Lightfoot, I, 75. 2]
[3] *Codex Montacutian.* [now lost] and *Codex Caiensis* 395, 1440 A.D., at Cambridge.
[4] Thus Petermann, Lightfoot regards it as later.

EPISTLES OF IGNATIUS 31

are available for an investigation and estimate of the literary remains of Ignatius Even in his day, Ussher showed that a relationship existed between the longer recension G^2 (and L^2) and the Apostolic Constitutions, which was explicable only on the assumption of a common redactor, and opinions only vary as to whether the redactor (who labored either in the first part of the fifth century or in the second half of the fourth) was a semi-Arian (Zahn, Harnack), an Apollinarian (Funk), or a reconciler of the two (Lightfoot). The view that the shortest form in Syriac (S) was the original one, as is maintained by Bunsen, Ritschl, and Lipsius, was denied by Denzinger and Uhlhorn, and finally refuted by Zahn and Lightfoot. The fact that the Epistle to the Romans has been handed down separately is possibly accounted for by the fact that it was not contained in the first collection of Epistles made in Asia Minor.[1]

2. The fact that Ignatius wrote several epistles was attested by Polycarp, who, at the same time, sent such as were in his possession to the Philippians[2] Irenæus quoted a sentence from the Epistle to the Romans[3] without mentioning the author[4] Acquaintance with Ignatius is to be assumed in the case of Clement of Alexandria,[5] and Origen quoted Rom. iii. 3,[6] vii. 2,[7] and Eph xix 1[8] In the last two instances he named the martyr-bishop, Ignatius, as the author. Eusebius quoted Eph xix 1,[9] Rom v ; Smyrn iii. 1, 2, and

---

[1] *Epist. Polycarpi ad Philipp.* 13. 2.   [3] 4. 1.
[2] Cf. his Epistle, Chap. 13 2   [4] *Adv. Haer.* V, 28 4.
[5] Cf. *Paedagogus*, II, 8 63 [Eph. xvii 1], *Excerpta Theodoti*, 74 [Eph xix. 2], *Paedagogus*, I, 6 38 [*Trall* viii 1]
[6] *Orat.* 20.   [8] *Hom* VI, *in Lucam*
[7] *In Canticum Cant. prolegom*   [9] *Quaestiones ad Stephanum*, I.

Rom. iv. 1:¹ and Athanasius quoted and commented on Eph vii. 2.² Jerome³ had not read the Epistles. At the time of the Monophysite controversies, quotations from Ignatius were frequently used with effect Attestations (in part of doubtful character) are given by Zahn⁴ and Lightfoot.⁵

3 The seven epistles of the **shorter recension** purport to have been written by Ignatius from Smyrna or from Troas and Naples during his journey to Rome under the escort and guard of soldiers. Their object was to return thanks for the loving welcome that he had received in these cities, but their chief aim was to give exhortations against schismatical movements and against Docetism and Judaism. The Epistle to the Romans was meant to announce the arrival of the bishop, and it gave utterance to his ardent desire for martyrdom. It is presupposed in these epistles that a bishop was at the head of each separate congregation (see, however, the Epistle to the Romans), and the greatest stress is laid upon the maintenance of this order The epistles are written with an extravagant, almost histrionic, pathos, and in an original but artificial style They lead one to imagine the writer as a man possessing deep religious feeling, much theological naiveté, and subject to passionate emotion and excitement There is much which recalls various passages of Scripture, but actual quotations are few. E. v. d. Goltz⁶

¹ *Eccl. Hist* III, 36. 7-12 Cf V, 8 9, and III, 38 1, 5
² *Epistola de synodis Arimini et Seleuciae*, 47.
³ Cf *De Viris Illust* 16, etc.
⁴ II, pp. 326-373.
⁵ I, 127-221 [2d edit 1889, I, 135-232]
⁶ In his work on *Ignatius von Antiochien als Christen und Theologen*, in TU, XII, 3, 1894.

has carefully investigated the literary relations between
the Ignatian epistles and other portions of early Christian literature, with the result that we must assume that
Ignatius was acquainted with the principal epistles of
Paul, and, most probably, with the Pauline (?) Epistle
to the Ephesians, but not with the Epistle to the
Hebrews, the Pastoral Epistles, the Epistles of Peter,
the Epistle of James, or with the fourth Gospel, in
spite of his spiritual affinity with it

4. The doubts that have been raised as to the **genuineness** of the Epistles may be grouped under three
heads: (1) The situation presupposed in the Epistles,
the systematic method of their composition, and their
whole literary character make them appear like the
work of a forger, (2) The church polity presupposed in
the Epistles; and (3) The heresies which they combat
are inconceivable in the time of Trajan, to which tradition has assigned the martyrdom of Ignatius. The
motive of the forgery is alleged to have been a desire
to glorify the dignity of monarchical episcopacy to the
congregations of Asia Minor; and the time of Ignatius
is assigned as the *terminus ad quem* of the epistles;
i.e. the epoch in which the Catholic idea of the episcopate may be considered as everywhere realized. Under
these circumstances the Epistle of Polycarp to the
Philippians would appear to have been written as a
companion piece to facilitate the circulation of the
forgery.

5. The first argument may be met by reference to
the fact that the situation presents no other improbabilities than are often met with in authenticated history;
that the alleged systematic character of the composition
is fully explained by the situation; that the literary form

would be no more intelligible in the case of a forger than in the case of the author assigned by tradition, and that, on the other hand, there are countless concrete traits that make any theory of forgery well-nigh untenable. The force of the second and third arguments cannot be denied off-hand. Nevertheless, it should be considered (1) that our knowledge of the development both of church polity and of doctrine is far too uncertain for us to draw absolute conclusions from it, and that, therefore, any judgment as to that development may be drawn more correctly from the original documents than *vice versa;* (2) that the Epistles contain undeniable archaisms which are hardly conceivable even as late as 150 A D ; and (3) that these doubts presuppose that the traditional date of Ignatius, more especially the date of his martyrdom, is correct, whereas serious objections can be raised at this point. The *Martyria Ignatii* can lay no claim to historical worth, and the statements of Eusebius are of doubtful value, seeing that the list of Antiochian bishops, which he used, itself shows evident traces of an artificial chronology. It thus appears to be at least not impossible that a later date may be given for the martyrdom of Ignatius (Harnack; see, however, Hort). The natural result of this assumption would be to assign the Epistle of Polycarp also to a later date.

CHAPTER II

APOCALYPSES

§ 10. *The Apocalypse of John*

MORE than any other book in the New Testament, the Apocalypse of John shows a Jewish cast. The domain of Jewish apocalyptic thought was real to its author, and the evidences of a Christian spirit and a Christian temper, which are scattered like pearls throughout the whole Apocalypse, contrast strangely with the visions of an extravagant fancy, breathing hate and vengeance, which form the substratum of the book. The riddles which this Apocalypse offers to historico-literary criticism seem to be almost as difficult to solve as the problems which its contents presented as long as pious belief saw future history prophesied in it. The book is by no means uniform in its contents, written down at the prompting of the Spirit; but the author has incorporated foreign material clumsily and not without manifest self-contradiction. It also appears undeniable that Jewish material may be found among the rest. Nothing in the book points to the Apostle as the author, and the tradition (in itself not contemptible) may rest upon a confusion of the Apostle with the Presbyter. We must apparently be content with this statement: a Christian, named John, wrote the Apocalypse in Asia Minor toward the end of the first century, during the reign of Domitian.

§ 11. *The Apocalypse of Peter*

Editions: A Hilgenfeld (§ 3) IV, 2d edit 1884, 71-74 U Bouriant, in *Mémoires publiés par les membres de la mission archéologique française au Caire*, IX, 1, Paris, 1892. Cf. the photographic facsimile of the manuscript in Tom IX, 3, 1893. A Harnack, in SBBA, 1892, XLV, XLVI, 949-955; in TU, IX, 2, 1893, second edition J A. Robinson and M. R James, Lond 1892. A Lods, Paris (1892), 93. F. X. Funk, in ThQu, LXXV, 1893, 278-288 (263-265). O. v Gebhardt, Lpz 1893 (contains photographic facsimile). Rutherford, A , ANF, IX, 141 f

Literature: Besides the introductions and annotations in the editions mentioned above, see Theo. Zahn, in GNK, II, 2, 810-820 (written before the discovery of the manuscript). E Bratke, in ThLB, XIV, 1893, 99-102, 113-115, and his *Handschriftliche Ueberlieferung und Bruchstücke der arabisch-äthiopischen Petrusapokalypse*, in ZwTh, XXXVI, 1, 1893, 454-493 A. Dieterich, *Nekyia*, Lpz 1893. A Harnack, *Die Petrusapokalypse in der alten abendländischen Kirche*, in TU, XIII, 1, 1895, 71-73. — Harnack, LG, 29-33.

1 An Ἀποκάλυψις Πέτρου passed current for a time as holy scripture [1] in certain ecclesiastical circles. Clement of Alexandria commented upon it in his *Hypotyposes*,[2] and in the Eclogues [3] he quoted four (or, according to Zahn, three) passages from it. A quotation made by Methodius [4] may also be claimed as belonging to this Apocalypse. The philosopher, against whom Macarius Magnes (about 400 A D.) contended, made use of the book, and Macarius himself spoke of it not without respect.[5] While Eusebius [6] unmistakably rejected it, it

[1] Cf. Fragm. Murator. 71-73.
[2] Cf Eusebius, *Hist. Eccl.* VI, 14 1.
[3] 41, 48, 49.
[4] *Symposium*, II, 6, p. 16 of Jahn's edition.
[5] *Apokriticos*, IV, 6, 7, 16, pp 164, 185, Blondel's edition, Paris, 1876.
[6] *Hist. Eccl.* III, 25. 4.

was still read in Palestine in the fifth century.¹ In the *Catalogus Claromontanus* (Oriental, of the third or fourth century) it stands at the end of the list of writings which were classed with the New Testament, and in the Stichometry of Nicephorus ² (perhaps Palestinian, about 500 A.D.), it is placed with the Johannian Apocalypse among the Antilegomena. These lists respectively reckon its length at from 270 to 300 stichoi.

2. A parchment codex of the eighth or ninth century, found in a tomb at Akhmîm (Panopolis) in Upper Egypt and first published by Bouriant (1892), contains on seven leaves a large fragment ³ of an apocalypse, in which the old Apocalypse of Peter can be distinctly recognized. Conclusive proof that the fragment belonged to the Gospel of Peter cannot be presented (in spite of the opinion of Dieterich); probably the two writings have nothing to do with one another. The fragment opens in the middle of a discourse of the Lord, who, complying with the desire of his disciples, shows to them their righteous brethren who had departed this world before them, and afterward (apparently to Peter alone, who is brought forward as the narrator), heaven and hell, the abodes of the just and of the damned, whose punishments, conceived with a refinement of cruelty, are graphically described. The fragment does not include a description of the end of all things.

3. The Apocalypse of Peter has nothing in common with that of John. The fantastic conceptions which possess the author are of Græco-Orphic origin (Dieterich), and have their prototypes and parallels in the Jewish (Christian) Sibylline books. Numerous points

¹ Sozomen, *Hist. Eccl* VII, 19.   ³ 131 *stichoi*, according to Harnack.
² Migne, PG. C. 1055 f.

of resemblance to the second Epistle of Peter are very striking. Like this, the Apocalypse probably originated in Egypt and was written about the same time (*circa* 150 A D.), even if both writings did not have the same author. It is quite possible that Origen was acquainted with the Apocalypse.[1] It was much used in subsequent apocalyptic literature, and such use can be positively proved in the case of the Apocalypse of Paul and the Acts of Thomas[2] The Arabo-Ethiopic Apocalypse of Peter, revised in the eighth century, apparently does not stand in any direct relation to the Greek.

§ 12. *The Shepherd of Hermas*

Editions: (1) OF THE GREEK TEXT R. Anger (and Guil Dindorf), Lpz 1856 A F. C. Tischendorf, Lpz 1856 A. R M Dressel, Lpz. 1857, 1863 A Hilgenfeld (§ 3), III, 2d edit 1881. O de Gebhardt and A Harnack (§ 3), III, 1877, cf. Theo Zahn, in GGA, 1878, 33–64 F X Funk (§ 3), I, 1887, 2d edit. A Hilgenfeld, Lpz 1887 (2) OF THE VULGATE J Faber, in *Liber trium Virorum*, etc. Paris, 1513 A Hilgenfeld, Lips. 1873 O. de Gebhardt, as above (3) OF THE PALATINA, in the editions of Dressel (4) OF THE ETHIOPIC TRANSLATION A d'Abbadie, Lips 1860. (*Abhandlungen der deutschen morgenlandischen Gesellschaft*, II, 1) — **Translations:** J Chr Mayer, in BKV, 1869. F Crombie, ANF, II, 3–58 Chas. H Hoole, Lond 1870

Literature: The prolegomena and notes in the various editions Theo Zahn, *Der Hirt des Hermas* Gotha, 1868, cf R A Lipsius, in ZwTh, XII, 1869, 249–311, and also for the contrary view, Zahn, in JdTh, XV, 1870, 192–206 G Heyne, *Quo Tempore Hermae Pastor scriptus sit* Regiom. 1872 H M. T. Behm, *Ueber den Verfasser der Schrift, welche den Titel "Hirt" fuhrt*. Rostok, 1876 J Nirschl, *Der Hirt des Hermas* Passau, 1879 G Salmon, in DCB, II, 912–921 M (du) C(olombier), *Le pasteur d'Hermas* Paris, 1880. F X Funk, in KLex, V, 1839–44. A Link, *Die Einheit des Pastor Hermae*. Marburg, 1888 P Baumgartner,

---

[1] Bratke, 114   [2] Cf. pp 39–41, in the edition of Bonnet.

Die Einheit des Hermas-Buches Frieb 1/B 1889 Fabricius, BG, VII, 18–21 Richardson, BS, 30–33 Harnack, LG, 49–58.

1 An extensive work under the title Ποιμήν has been **preserved** in the following forms: (1) Greek: (*a*) two fragments (*Similitudes*, II, 7–10 and IV, 2–5) in a Fayûm papyrus now in Berlin,[1] written, perhaps, *circa* 400 A.D. (*b*) The section from the *Visions*, I, 1. 1, to the *Mandates*, IV, 3. 6 (... ἐγώ σοι λέγω) in the *Codex Sinaiticus* (א), perhaps of the fourth century, appended to the New Testament after the Apocalypse of John and the Epistle of Barnabas. (*c*) The entire book, with the exception of the closing portion (from *Similitudes* IX, 30. 3 [εἰ δὲ ...] onward) is continued in the *Codex Athous-Lipsiensis*, saec. *XIV vel XV*. Three leaves of this manuscript (Mandates, XII, 4 4–*Similitudes*, VIII, 4 3; and *Similitudes*, IX, 15. 1–30. 3) were sold by Simonides in Leipzig, and six leaves (*Visions*, I, 1 1– *Mandates*, XII, 4. 6, and *Similitudes*, VIII, 4. 3–IX, 14. 5) are still preserved in the monastery of Athos. Two copies of these six leaves, made by Simonides, are found in Leipzig, one of which is unreliable and the other forged. The final portion, which was published by Simonides and Draeseke,[2] must also be regarded as a forgery, at least until it is proved that Simonides really found the final leaf of the codex when he visited Athos (*d*) In numerous quotations, particularly by Clement of Alexandria, Pseudo-Athanasius (*Praecepta ad Antiochum*), and in the *Pandectes* of Antiochus of Saba (2) Latin: in two translations which are not entirely independent of one another, and which belong as far back as the time of the ancient church. (*a*) The socalled *Vulgata*, perhaps of the second century, which

[1] *Mus. Berol.* P 5513   [2] Cf Hilgenfeld's edition of 1887.

is preserved in a large number of manuscripts. L. Duchesne has described a new manuscript of the *Versio Vulgata* in the *Bulletin crit.* (1894, 14–16). (*b*) The so-called *Palatina*,[1] which, according to Harnack, was not made before the end of the fourth century, but which Haussleiter considers older than the Vulgate. (3) Ethiopic: in an ancient translation "possibly prepared as early as the time of the oldest Ethiopic version of the Bible" (Harnack).

U. Wilcken, *Tafeln zur älteren griechischen Paläographie.* Lpz. and Berl 1891. No. 3. H Diels and A Harnack, *Ueber einen Berliner Papyrus des Pastor Hermae*, in SBBA, 1894, 427–431. A. Ehrhard, *Hermasfragmente auf Papyrus*, in the *Centralblatt fur Bibliothekswesen*, 1892, 223–226 (ThQu, LXXIV, 1892, 294–303). A. Lykurgos, *Enthüllungen uber den Simonides-Dindorfschen Uranios* Lpz. 1856. C. Tischendorf, *De Herma graeco Lipsiensi*, in Dressel's edition. K. Simonides, Ὀρθοδόξων Ἑλλήνων θεολογικαὶ γραφαὶ τέσσαρες. Lond 1859, 203–210. J Draeseke, in ZwTh, XXX, 1887, 172–184. (Cf A Hilgenfeld, in ZwTh, XXX, 1887, 185–186, 256, 334–342, 384, 497–501; XXXVI, 11, 1893, 338–440 A. Hainack, in ThLZ, XII, 1887, 147–151; and F. X Funk, in ThQu, LXX, 1888, 51–71) Sp. P. Lambros, A Collation of the Athos Codex of the Shepherd of Hermas, translated and edited by J A Robinson, Lond 1888. (Cf. Harnack, in ThLZ, XIII, 1888, 303–305, and A. Hilgenfeld, in ZwTh, XXXII, 1889, 94–107 Cf. also Sp. P. Lambros, in *Byzant. Zeitschrift*, II, 1893, 610–611, and the accompanying reproductions of folio 1 v. and 3 r. of the Athos Codex) Guil. Dindorf, *Athanasii Alex. Praecepta ad Antiochum*, recog G. D Lips. 1857. J. Haussleiter, *Textkritische Bermerkungen zur palatinischen Uebersetzung des Hirten*, in ZwTh, XXVI, 1883, 345–356 The same, *De versionibus Pastoris Hermae latinis* (Acta Semin. philol III). Erlangen, 1884. (Different view, R. A. Lipsius, in ThLZ, X, 1885, 281–284.) A. Dillmann, *Bemerkungen zu dem athiopischen Hermas*, in *Zeitschrift der deutschen morgenländischen Gesellschaft*, XV, 1861, 111–125 (cf. Harnack's edition, XXVII–XXIX).

---

[1] *Codex Palatin.* 150, saec. XIV.

2. The **Shepherd** was held in high esteem in the churches of the West and of Alexandria, and was much read. Irenæus,[1] Tertullian, in his pre-montanistic period,[2] Pseudo-Cyprian (*adversus Aleatoribus*), Clement, and Origen, in whose writings there are numerous quotations from and allusions to it,[3] regarded the book as a sacred writing;[4] and the close resemblances to it found in the *Passion of Perpetua and Felicitas* appear to presuppose an equally high estimate. To be sure, Eusebius classed it with the Antilegomena and the writings which he thought should be rejected,[5] but he did not dispute its usefulness for the instruction of catechumens.[6] Athanasius[7] defended such employment of it by classing the book with the Old Testament Apocrypha. This use of the *Shepherd* recommended it permanently to the Latins,[8] and insured it a place in the Bible along with the Old Testament Scriptures, in spite of its condemnation by Gelasius. It was used and quoted by mediæval writers in martyrologies and in collections of canon law. It continued to be read in the Oriental church also, and its translation is evidence of the respect paid to it, particularly in the Ethiopic church.

3. The **purpose** of the book, which took its name from the author's guardian angel,[9] was to make an

[1] *Adv. Haer.* IV, 20. 2. Cf. Eusebius, *Hist. Eccl.* V, 8. 7.
[2] *Orat.* 16. Cf. the different judgment in his montanistic *de Pudicitia*, c. 20.
[3] Harnack, LG, 53–55.
[5] *Hist. Eccl.* III, 25.
[4] Cf. Codex ℵ.
[6] *Id.* III, 3. 6.
[7] Cf particularly, *Epist. Fest.* 39, anno 365.
[8] Cf. the *Muratorian Fragment*, v. 73–80; Jerome, *De Viris Illus.* 10, etc.; Rufinus, Cassian (*Collat.* VIII, 7; XIII, 12).
[9] Cf. *Visiones*, V, and *passim*.

energetic appeal to all Christendom[1] for a speedy abandonment of the lax and sinful mode of life into which it had sunk. As regards its form, it is to be classed with the Apocalypses. The author wrote by reason of a divine revelation, and in consequence of a special commission, like a prophet inspired by the divine spirit. But the aim and character of the work plainly distinguish it from the Apocalypses of John and Peter, and indeed from any of the apocalyptic writings whose authors seized upon some name famous in earlier times in order to accredit their own communications. In this sense the book is not a literary fiction, no matter how fanciful the garb in which it is presented. **Hermas** (Herma, or Hermes[2]) was, possibly, born in Arcadia,[3] and in his youth was sold as a slave and taken to Rome, where he was freed, and settled with his family.[4] He was a brother of Pius, the bishop.[5] He wrote without special culture,[6] in a naive and childlike style, diffuse and circumstantial, but popular and graphic. His language, if it does not imply Jewish extraction, at least indicates a Jewish education, or familiar intercourse with the Jewish elements of the church. We cannot determine with certainty what Christian (or Jewish) writings he had read; his knowledge of synoptic tradition, apocalyptic literature, and certain epistles,[7] as well as of the original *Didache*,[8] and the *Kerygma Petri*,[9]

---

[1] *Vis.* II, 4. 3.
[2] Cf. *Id.* I, 1. 4, etc.
[3] Cf. *Similitudes*, IX, 1, and Robinson (following Harris), 30–36.
[4] Cf. the Introduction
[5] Cf. *Catalog. Liberian Anno* 354, and the *Muratorian Fragment*, v. 76 ff.
[6] Cf. *Visions*, II, 4. 1.
[7] Eph., 1 Pet., James(?).
[8] Cf. § 21. 3.
[9] § 19.

may have been gathered from the readings and teachings which formed part of the service of the church.

4. This extensive book is divided into **three parts**: five Visions (ὁράσεις, *Visiones*), twelve Mandates or Commandments (ἐντολαί, *Mandata*), and ten Similitudes (παραβολαί, *Similitudines*). After a charming introduction, giving an account of some personal matters and experiences, the author relates certain **visions** in which the church appears to him as a woman, aged, but visibly renewing her youth. She shows to him in an image the necessity for speedy repentance, seeing that the building of the church will soon be completed, and that the distress of the last days is nigh at hand. The fifth vision marks the transition to the second part of the book, by the appearance of the "Shepherd," who henceforth remains beside his charge, imparting to him the Mandates, and presenting and explaining the Similitudes. The **Mandates** treat of those sins of deed and thought from which the true Christian should refrain. The following things are inculcated: belief in one God (Mandate 1), simplicity (2), truthfulness (3), chastity (4), forbearance and patience (5), the discerning of spirits (6), the fear of God (7), continence (8), confidence in prayer (9), and cheerful trust in God (10), discerning between true and false prophecy (11), and flight from evil desires (12) In their form, the **Similitudes** of the third part frequently recall the Visions. They have for their subject the following themes, among others: (1) the Christian as a stranger in this world; (2) the relation between rich and poor (the vine and the elm); (3 and 4) the present and the future ages of the world (trees in winter and summer); (5) the value of good works (the servant of God and his

deserts), (6) the value of a second repentance (the wandering sheep), (7) the value of punishment (the avenging angel); (8) Christendom and its moral condition (the willow tree and its branches); (9) the building of the church (the tower); (10) closing exhortation. The book is rich in concrete examples, and is a mine of information as to the life and customs of the Roman church toward the end of the first century and the beginning of the second.

5. The **date of composition** of the *Shepherd* cannot be fixed with certainty. A statement, which may be traced to Hippolytus, is made in the *Catalogus Liberianus*,[1] 354 A D , to the effect that Hermas wrote the book during the episcopate of his brother Pius (139/141-154/156 A D.). This statement is opposed by the fact that in the *Shepherd* the episcopal polity in the Roman church is not yet presupposed; and that there is no reference to developed forms of Gnosticism. The many references to the oppression and persecution of the church[2] apply to the time of Domitian just as well as to that of Trajan. Clement[3] is mentioned in such a way as to make it at least not impossible that the author of the Epistles to the Corinthians is meant. On the other hand, the statements as to the generation that had already passed away,[4] and the general corruption of things, as described by Hermas, forbid our assigning the writing to the time before Domitian, and identifying the author with the Hermes mentioned in Rom. xvi. 14.[5] While the book may thus have origi-

---
[1] Cf. also *Fragm. Murator.* v. 73-77.
[2] Cf the passage in Harnack's edition, LXXVI, n. 9   [3] *Vision* II, 4. 3.
[4] Cf. *Similitudes*, IX, 15. 4, 16. 5.   *Vision.* III, 5 1.
[5] Cf. Origen, *Com. in Rom.* X, 31.

nated about 100 A D, it should not be overlooked that it can scarcely have been written in a single draft Although the hypothesis of two[1] or three[2] authors is untenable, owing to uniformity of language, yet certain allusions make it probable that the single portions of the book were issued successively, perhaps as fugitive pieces, and afterwards revised. Certain contradictions, indeed, can only be explained upon this assumption. Separate copies of the Mandates have existed.[3]

[1] Champagny, *Les Antonins*, I. Paris, 1873, 3d edit. 144
[2] Hilgenfeld, edition of 1881, XX–XXIX
[3] Cf. Athanasius, *Epist fest.* 11, edition of Larsow, p. 117.

CHAPTER III

HISTORICAL BOOKS

I. THE GOSPELS

§ 13   *The Beginnings: Papias*

1. Concerning the beginnings of the Gospel literature, which are now lost to us, it can only be asserted with probability that as early as the primitive church, and before the destruction of Jerusalem, there existed an Aramaic Gospel whose author was said by tradition to be the Apostle **Matthew**.[1] Tradition, in giving this writing the title of Λόγια τοῦ κυρίου (λόγια κυριακά), described its essential contents correctly without, however, entirely excluding the possibility of a historical setting.

2. The writing by Matthew, in a Greek version, and, apparently, our Gospel of Mark, must have been in the hands of **Papias**, Bishop of Hierapolis, in Phrygia, when he undertook (presumably in the first decade of the second century), on the basis of the statements of men of the first and second (?) post-apostolic generation,[2] to supplement as far as possible, and to correct where it appeared necessary, the tradition that had already become fixed in writing This he did in a work entitled

---
[1] Cf. Papias, in Eusebius, *Hist. Eccl* III, 39. 16   See also V, 10. 3.
[2] Cf. Eusebius, *Hist. Eccl.* III, 39.

Λογίων κυριακῶν ἐξηγήσεως συγγράμματα (βιβλία) πέντε, which was dedicated to an unknown person. It is no longer possible to form a clear idea of his attempt, since the few extant fragments, together with Eusebius' remarks upon some of them, tend rather to obscure the facts than to clear them up. In particular, it cannot be certainly known in what relation the bare reproduction of traditional matter stood to the explanations which Papias appears to have added himself. What materials were furnished to him as excerpts from the genuine tradition is best seen in the fragment preserved by Irenæus.[1]

The Fragments (Irenæus, Eusebius, Apollinarius [of Laodicea?], Philippus Sidetes, and later writers), and Witnesses, collected by P. Halloix (§ 8) Routh, RS, I, 3-44 A. Hilgenfeld, in ZwTh, XVIII, 1875, 231-270 O. v. Gebhardt (§ 3), I, 2, 2d edit 1878, 87-104. F. X Funk (§ 3), II, 1881, 276-300, cf Pitra, AS, II, 157-159. C de Boor, in TU, V, 2, 1886, 170, cf 176 ff — Translation: Roberts and Donaldson, in ANF, I, 153-155.

Literature: Theo Zahn, in StKr, XXXIX, 1886, 649-696; GNK, I, 2, 849-903; II, 2, 790-797. W. Weiffenbach, *Das Papiasfragment bei Eusebius*, III, 39. 3-4. Giessen, 1874. C. L. Leimbach, *Das Papiasfragment*, etc Gotha, 1875 (also RE, XI, 194-206) H Holtzmann, in ZwTh, XXIII, 1880, 64-77. R A Lipsius, in JprTh, XI, 1885, 174-176. A Hilgenfeld, in ZwTh, XXIX, 1886, 257-291 (with references to earlier works). G Salmon, in DCB, IV, 185-190 — Richardson, BS, 19-21. Harnack, LG, 65-69.

3. It is possible that a stage prior to our group of Synoptic Gospels may be marked by a fragment on a papyrus dating from the third century and now in the collection of the Archduke Rainer in Vienna. It contains the pericope Mk. xiv. 26-30 and Matt. xxvi. 30-34 in abbreviated form. It is quite possible, however, that

---

[1] *Adv Haer*. V, 33. 3, 4.

the piece is only an extract from one of our Gospels, or that it belonged to a Gospel harmony, or even to a homily. To draw extensive conclusions from it is obviously unwarrantable.

G Bickell, in ZkTh, IX, 1885, 498–504. A. Harnack, in ThLZ, X, 1885, 277–281, in TU, V, 4, 1889, 481–497. K. Wessely, in ZkTh, XI, 1887, 507–515. Theo. Zahn, in GNK, II, 2, 780–790.

§ 14. *The Synoptic Gospels*

From among the numerous gospels current during the second century, the church designated the four which are attributed to Matthew, Mark, Luke, and John, as those which appeared to her to preserve most faithfully the tradition of the life and teaching of Jesus. The first three (which for about a hundred years past have been known as the synoptic Gospels) stand in a close relationship to each other. Scholars have been uninterruptedly engaged in investigating this relationship and in tracing it back to its source. According to the most probable view, the Gospel of Mark was the oldest of all. According to tradition,[1] it was compiled by Mark, the disciple of the Apostle, on the basis of the discourses of Peter. The Gospel of Matthew represents in its chief parts a combination of the original gospel[2] with the Gospel of Mark. According to his own statement, the author of the Gospel of Luke had already at command numerous compilations of gospel material. Legendary elements already show themselves unmistakably in the narrative (in the stories of Jesus' childhood and life after his resurrection) at those points where Matthew and Luke relate more than is contained

---

[1] Cf Papias, in Eusebius, *Hist Eccl* III, 39. 15. [2] § 13 1

in Mark (its spurious final paragraph excepted). All three Gospels were written after the destruction of Jerusalem, and their text can hardly have received its present shape before the second half of the second century.

§ 15. *The Gospel of John*

The Gospel of John occupies an entirely unique position as compared with the three synoptic Gospels. The controversy as to this gem of Biblical literature is as animated to-day as it was decades ago, and apparently there is no prospect of a speedy settlement of it. Whereas for a time the genuineness of the Gospel was apparently given up almost universally in the scientific camp, its defenders are now on the increase, and their arguments are not without their due weight But this magnificent poem of a highly endowed soul, who, like Paul, created a Christ of his own, cannot pass as the work of that simple man before whose eyes and in whose heart the actual history of Jesus of Nazareth was enacted. The author handles freely the material furnished by tradition, and transforms it with the purpose of depicting the earthly life of the Logos, who, being from all eternity with the Father, became flesh, and revealed in perfect fashion the divine light and truth and life to those who received him. He betrays knowledge of the Synoptic (and, in fact, of Luke's) type of narrative, and his representation presupposes the rise of Gnosticism. Still he may have been acquainted with sources which antedate ours, and it is not in itself inconceivable that he may have been connected in some way with the Apostle John (or the Johannine circle), although the tradition of the Apostle's residence in Asia Minor (Ephesus) is not unassailable. The author was a Jew, trained in the ideas of Alexandrian religious philosophy. The place of composition may possibly have been in Asia Minor (Ephesus) or even Syria (Antioch?). Care should be exercised in drawing conclusions as to the date of composition from the comparatively late use of the Gospel in ecclesiastical literature, since the elevation of its conceptions would prevent them from easily becoming common property. Nevertheless, its composition within the first century may be considered improbable.

§ 16. *Apocryphal Gospels*

It may be doubted whether the following gospels should be classed with early Christian literature; but their mention in this connection may be justified by their likeness of form to the Synoptic Gospels and their conscious dependence upon the early Christian tradition. The really legendary accounts of the antecedent history, and of the history of the Infancy and of the Passion of Jesus, for the most part belong to a far later period. At the same time, their sources go back into the time of the primitive literature.

1. The **Gospel according to the Hebrews**, Εὐαγγέλιον καθ' (κατὰ) Ἑβραίους, is cited at first hand by Hegesippus,[1] Clement of Alexandria,[2] Origen,[3] Eusebius,[4] and

---

[1] Eusebius, *Hist. Eccl.* IV, 22. 8.

[2] *Stromata*, II, 9. 45.

[3] *Hom. in Jerem.* XV, 4; *Comm. Joann.* II, 6; *Comm. ad Matth.* XIX, 16 ff.

[4] *Hist. Eccl.* III, 25. 5; 27. 4; Θεοφάνεια, p. 234, in Lee's edition; Mai, NPB, IV, 155.

frequently by Jerome[1] On the other hand, Irenæus,[2] Epiphanius,[3] and Theodoret[4] knew of it only by hearsay. Fragments, which have been preserved principally by Jerome, show that this Gospel was an Aramaic redaction of the original Gospel,[5] made to suit the Jewish congregations of Palestine and enriched from oral tradition. Only by a misconception (as old as Irenæus) has it been possible to discover the original of the Greek Matthew in this Gospel, which, apparently in imitation of its prototype, was designated as κατὰ Ματθαῖον. A comparison, however, proves the literary independence of the extant fragments of the Gospel according to the Hebrews, so far as the synoptic accounts are concerned In the fragments there appear to have been preserved not only minor details, but also portions of the original which were sacrificed in the redaction of the Synoptic Gospels — From the Gospel according to the Hebrews another Gospel is to be distinguished, which, according to Epiphanius,[6] was in use among the **Ebionites**, and which he designated as καθ' Ἑβραίους (κατὰ Ματθαῖον). The fragments quoted by Epiphanius allow the supposition that the Gospel was originally written in Greek, and they indicate that in form and contents it was a product of Gnostic Ebionism, which presupposes the canonical Matthew and Luke — A Gospel of the Twelve Apostles, *Evangelium duodecim Apostolorum*, mentioned by Origen,[7] Ambrose,[8] Jerome,[9] and Theophylact,[10] is identified by Jerome[11] with

[1] Handmann, TU, V, 3, 45–65.
[2] *Adv Haer* I, 26 2 Cf III, 11 7
[3] *Panarion*, XXIX, 9, cf. XXX, 3, 4
[4] *Haer Fab* I, 1.
[5] § 13 1
[6] *Panarion*, XXX.
[7] *Hom I. in Lucam*.
[8] *Prooem Comm in Luc*
[9] *Prooem Comm in Matth*.
[10] *Prooem Comm in Luc*
[11] *Adv Pelagianos*, II, init.

the Gospel according to the Hebrews — Epiphanius[1] asserts that the Jewish-Christian Cerinthus put forth his own redaction of the Gospel, but there is no ground for connecting it with the Gospel according to the Hebrews.

> E. B. Nicholson, *The Gospel according to the Hebrews*, Lond. 1879. A. Hilgenfeld (§ 3), IV, 2d edit 1884. R Handmann, in TU, V, 3, 1888. Cf A Hilgenfeld, in ZwTh, XXXII, 1889, 280-302. A Resch, *Agrapha*, in TU, V, 4, 1889, 322-342 Theo Zahn, GNK, II, 2, 642-742 E. Nestle, *Zur Philologia Sacra*, in *Evang. Kirchenblatt für Württemberg*, 1895, No. 26.

2. The parchment codex found at Akhmim[2] contains on nine leaves a large portion of a Gospel in which there may be recognized distinctly (in spite of the objections of Volter) the **Gospel of Peter**, Εὐαγγέλιον κατὰ Πέτρον, which Serapion, Bishop of Antioch,[3] found at Rhosus (Rhossos [in Syria]) on his visitation journey, and which, after careful examination, he forbade to be read,[4] on account of its Docetic errors. The fragment relates the story of the Passion, beginning with the Condemnation; also the history of the Resurrection down to the flight of the disciples to Galilee, and to Jesus' appearance to Peter (who is introduced as the narrator), Andrew, and Levi (*sic*) by the lake of Gennesaret. The story of the Passion is simply and plainly told, with an evident attempt at graphic effect; the story of the Resurrection is pervaded with echoes of Docetic theories, has a strong legendary coloring, and far exceeds in detail the accounts given by canonical tradition. A consensus of opinion has not been reached as to the character and value of the Gospel, and, more

---

[1] *Haer.* LI, 7.
[2] § 11.
[3] Cf § 9.
[4] Eusebius, *Hist. Eccl* VI, 12.

especially, as to its relation to the canonical Gospels Harnack, while recognizing the fact that this Gospel presupposes the canonical writings, inclusive of the Gospel of John,[1] ranks it along with the last on account of its peculiar character and its construction Others,[2] however, are unwilling to regard it as a work at all analogous to the canonical Gospels, but classify it among the popular Gnostic apocryphal writings Its close connection with the Pilate-Literature[3] gives special weight to the latter assumption The Gospel may have originated at Antioch, about 140 or 150 A D, among a circle which was "either identical with, or at least intimately allied to, the Oriental school of Valentinus" (Zahn, 75). The hypothesis of an apologetic (anti-Jewish or Roman) tendency in the Gospel and its kindred literature (v Schubert), is very tempting That Justin made use of this Gospel (as Harnack contends) is quite improbable.

Editions and Literature: See § 11 Besides, Theo Zahn, *Das Petrusevangelium*, Erlangen and Lpz 1893 J Kunze, *Das Petrusevangelium*, Lpz 1893 H. v Soden, in *Zeitschrift fur Theologie und Kirche*, III, 1893, 52–92 H v Schubert, Berl 1893 (with synoptic tables) Cf. A Harnack, ThLZ, XIX, 1894, 9–18 A. Hilgenfeld, in ZwTh. XXXVI, ii, 1893, 220-267 D Volter, *Petrusevangelium oder Aegypterevangelium ?* Tubingen, 1893 A Sabatier, *L'évangile de St. Pierre*, Paris, 1893 H B Swete, *The Akhmîn Fragment of the Apocryphal Gospel of St Peter*, Lond 1893 J A Robinson and M R James, *The Gospel according to Peter and the Revelation of Peter*, Lond 1892, 2d edit J A Armitage, *The Gospel of Peter* (translation) in ANF, IX, 1–31 A C. McGiffert (*The Gospel of Peter*) in *Papers*, American Soc of Church Hist VI, 1893, 101-130), N Y. 1894 (Contains an extensive bibliography)

[1] ThLZ, XIX, 1.
[2] Robinson, Harris, Zahn, von Schubert
[3] v. Schubert, 170–195.

Translation: J A. Robinson, ANF, IX, 7, 8-31.

3. **The Gospel according to the Egyptians**, Εὐαγγελιον κατ' Αἰγυπτίους, has been preserved in fragments found in Clement,[1] Hippolytus,[2] and Epiphanius,[3] and it is mentioned by Origen,[4] Jerome,[5] and Theophylact[6] It appears to have been employed in the interest of encratitic and ascetic tendencies (vegetarianism), and of philosophical speculation (transmigration of souls; the trinity). It originated in Egypt. Clement seems to assume that Julius Cassianus[7] made use of it: though Zahn holds another view. The Naassenes (Hippolytus) and Sabellians (Epiphanius) made use of it. Whether it was used in the so-called second Epistle of Clement is doubtful[8]

M. Schneckenburger, *Ueber das Evangelium der Aegypter*. Bern, 1834. A Hilgenfeld (§ 3), IV, 2d edit. 1884, 42-48. A. Resch in ZkWL, IX, 1888, 232-241; *Agrapha* in TU, V, 4, 1889, 316-319 (202, 203). Theo. Zahn, GNK, II, 2. 628-642. Harnack, LG, 12-14

4. It is impossible to determine what is meant by the **Gospels** of Andrew,[9] Barnabas,[10] Bartholomew,[11] Matthias,[12] and Philip.[13] The mention by Innocent and Augustine of a Gospel of Andrew is probably due

[1] *Stromata*, III, 6. 45; 9. 63, 64, 66; 13. 92 [15. 97]; *Excerpta Theodoti*, 67.
[2] *Philosophumena*, V, 7. [5] *Comm. Matth. praef.;* cf. *Luc.* I, 1.
[3] *Haer.* LXII, 2. [6] *Comm. Luc. prooem.*
[4] *Hom.* I *in Lucam.* [7] § 29.
[8] See II Clem. 12, however.
[9] Innocent I, *Epist.* 6. 13; Augustine, *Contra adversarium legis et prophetarum*, I, 20; *Decret Gelas.* [10] *Decret. Gelas.*
[11] Jerome, *Comm. Matth. Prooem ; Decret. Gelas.;* Beda, *Comm. Luc. init*
[12] Origen, *Hom.* II *in Luc.;* Eusebius, *Hist. Eccl.* III, 25. 6; Jerome, *Comm. Matth. prooem.; Decret Gelas.;* Beda, *Comm. Luc. init*
[13] Epiphanius, *Panarion*, XXVI, 13.

to some confusion of it with the Acts of Andrew[1] The Gospel of Matthias may be identical with the Παραδόσεις Ματθίου, which, according to Clement,[2] were held in high esteem by the Basilidians, since Basilides and Isidore were supposed to have received them as esoteric doctrine from Matthew himself.

For the *Traditiones Matthiae*, cf. A. Hilgenfeld (§ 3), IV, 2d edit 1884, 49 ff. Theo. Zahn, GNK, II, 2. 751–761. On the Gospel of Philip, see Zahn, 761–768. Harnack, LG, 4 f, 14 f, 17 f.

5 The **Gospel of Thomas**, Εὐαγγέλιον κατὰ Θωμᾶν (τὰ παιδικὰ τοῦ κυρίου, infancy of our Lord Jesus), has been preserved in several recensions, two Greek, one Latin, and one Syriac. The present text must represent a shortened form of the original narrative.[3] It is mentioned by Origen[4] and Eusebius,[5] and according to Hippolytus[6] it was read by the Naassenes. According to Irenæus,[7] the stories related by the Marcosians concerning the child Jesus may have been derived from this source. In the *Pistis-Sophia*[8] also, this gospel seems to have been used.[9] In it Jesus appears as a miracle-worker and magician when a child of five to eight (twelve) years. The author professes to be an Israelite, but both his language and his matter make this impossible. It cannot be proved certainly that the work originated in Gnostic circles, but this is strongly suggested by the circles in which it was read. It is not impossible that Justin[10] had read the book.

[1] § 30. 5.
[2] *Stromata*, VII, 17. 108 (cf. Hippolytus, *Philosophumena*, VII, 20); II, 9. 45, III, 4. 26, IV, 6. 35; VII, 13 82.
[3] *Stichometry* of Nicephorus.   [7] *Adv. Haer* I, 20. 1.
[4] *Hom.* I *in Luc.*   [8] § 28.
[5] *Hist Eccl.* III, 25. 6.   [9] p 69 ff. (Schwarze-Petermann).
[6] *Philos.* V, 7.   [10] *Dial. cum Trypho*, 88.

Editions: J. C Thilo, *Cod Apocr Nov. Test* I, Lips 1832, LXXIII–XCI, 275–315 C Tischendorf, *Evangelia Apocrypha,* 2d edit, Lips. 1876, XXXVI–XLVIII, 140–180 W. Wright, Contributions to the Apocryphal Literature of the N. T Lond. 1865.
Translations: K F. Borberg, *Die apokryphischen Evangelien und Apostelgeschichten,* Stuttgart, 1841, 57–84 Cf. also Theo. Zahn, GNK, II, 2. 768–773 Alex. Walker in ANF, VIII, 395 ff. Richardson, BS, 98. Harnack, LG, 15–17.

6. The so-called **Protevangel of James,** Ἡ ἱστορία Ἰακώβου περὶ τῆς γεννήσεως Μαρίας, has been preserved complete in the original in numerous manuscripts,[1] and the concluding portion is contained in a Syriac translation. The present text represents a later redaction, and it is possible that the references to it made by Justin[2] and Clement,[3] together with the quotation from the Βίβλος Ἰακώβου, made by Origen,[4] presuppose an older text. The book was very frequently used by the later Fathers[5] The narrative is couched in simple language, and extends from the birth of Mary to the slaughter of the Innocents at Bethlehem. In so far as the story is confined within the limits of the canonical narrative, it appears to be a diffuse paraphrase of the matter contained in Matthew and Luke; but written sources can hardly have been used for the tale of Anna and Mary. The author was probably of Jewish birth, and may have written, in Egypt or in Asia Minor, in the first decade of the second century.[6]

[1] Harnack, LG, 19.
[2] *Apol.* I, 33, *Dial.* 78, 100.
[3] *Stromata,* VII, 16 93
[4] *Comm Matt* X, 17, in the edition of Lommatzsch, III, 45.
[5] Cf. citations from the literature of the fourth to the eleventh century, made by Thilo and Tischendorf.
[6] So Zahn.

Editions: Th. Bibliander, Basil 1552 (Latin). M. Neander, Basil. 1564. J. C. Thilo, see above, XLV–LXXIII, 159–273 W. Wright, see above. C. Tischendorf, see above, XI–XXIV, 1–50 **Translations:** Alex Walker, ANF, VIII, 361 ff K. F. Borberg, see above, 1–56. F. C Conybeare (translation from an Armenian manuscript in the Library of the Mechitarists in Venice) Amer Jnl of Theol. I, 1897, pp 424–442. Cf. A. Hilgenfeld in ZwTh, XII, 1865, 339 f.; XIV, 1867, 87 note; L. Conrady, *Das Protevang. Jacobi in neuer Beleuchtung* in StKr, LXII, 1889, 728–784. Zahn, 774–780. A. Behrendts, *Studien uber Zacharias-Apokryphen und Zacharias-Legenden.* Lpz. 1895. Richardson, BS, 96 f. Harnack, LG, 19–21.

7. As early as the time of Justin,[1] appeal was made to certain alleged official Acts concerned with the trial of Jesus (τὰ ἐπὶ Ποντίου Πιλάτου γενόμενα ἄκτα). It is quite possible that Justin had before him something similar to the Ὑπομνήματα τοῦ κυρίου ἡμῶν Ἰησοῦ Χριστοῦ πραχθέντα ἐπὶ Ποντίου Πιλάτου, an account of the Passion, decked out with legendary details and interspersed with speeches by the principal actors. This work, however, can scarcely have originated before the fourth century. Compare with it the Gospel of Peter.

II. THE ACTS OF THE APOSTLES

§ 17. The Acts of the Apostles, incorporated in the New Testament Canon, were a direct continuation of the Gospel according to Luke, and were written by the same author and from the same point of view. The story of the life and work of the Lord was followed by an account of the deeds of his Apostles in whom his holy spirit continued to live. The actual occurrences of the Apostolic Age, and especially the controversies

[1] *Apol.* I, 35; 48.

which dominated it, were no longer known to the author. He made a faithful use, as he had done in his first book, of the sources which he could obtain, but for the earlier history tradition furnished him principally with legends, and it requires some pains to sift out from the rest whatever is of authentic value in the first half of the book. On the other hand, the second half is founded upon a source of the first order, the so-called "we-source," containing an account of Paul's journeys told by a companion of the Apostle, presumably Luke. The general character of the book (which, furthermore, cannot be traced in ecclesiastical literature with any certainty before the time of Irenæus) renders it improbable that it was written during the first century. Where it was written cannot be determined

CHAPTER IV

DOCTRINAL WRITINGS

§ 18. *The So-called Roman Symbol*

Literature · C. P Caspari, *Ungedruckte . . . Quellen zur Geschichte des Taufsymbols und der Glaubensregel*, III. Christiania, 1875. A. Hahn (G L. Hahn), *Bibliothek der Symbole und Glaubensregeln der alten Kirche* Breslau, 1877 2d edit. (texts). A. Harnack (§ 3), I, 2, 2d edit 1878, 115-142 (Testimony from the second century), *Das apostolische Glaubensbekenntnis*, Berl. (1892), 1894, 25th edit. W Bornemann, *Das Taufsymbol Justins der Martyrer*, in ZKG, III, 1879, 1-27. Theo. Zahn, *Das apostolische Symbolum* Erlangen and Lpz. 1893; cf. A Julicher, in *Christ. Welt*, VII, 1893, 246-252. 268-274, and A. Harnack, in *Zeitschrift fur Theologie und Kirche*, IV, 1894, 130-166. S Baeumer, *Das apostolische Glaubensbekenntniss*. Mainz, 1893. Cl. Blume, *Das apostolische Glaubensbekenntniss* Freib. 1893 L Lemme, in NJdTh, II, 1893, 1-53. J. Haussleiter, *Zur Vorgeschichte des apostolischen Glaubensbekenntnisses*. Marburg, 1893. F. Kattenbusch, *Das apostolische Symbol*, I, Lpz. 1894; cf. F. Loofs, in GGA, 1894, 665-680. C. Clemen, in NKZ, VI, 1895, 323-336. Harnack, LG, 115 f.

In the time of Justin Martyr, *i.e* about 150 A.D. at the latest, the Roman church possessed a formal **baptismal creed**, written in Greek; the earliest form of the so-called Apostles' Creed When and where it originated cannot be determined with certainty. All attempts to reconstruct its previous history on the basis of the earliest Christian documents have hitherto proved futile; though the possibility remains that it may have originated about 100 A.D. Possibly Rome was the place where it took shape, but the formula may equally well have been imported from the East. Its wording can be **restored** with almost absolute certainty, (1) in Greek, from the formulæ (*a*) in the letter of Marcellus of Ancyra and Julius of Rome (337–338? 341? A D.) preserved by Epiphanius,[1] and (*b*) in the so-called *Psalterium Aethelstani*[2] of the eighth or ninth century; and (2) in Latin, from the formulæ (*a*) in an Oxford manuscript[3] of the seventh century; (*b*) in a manuscript in the British Museum[4] of the eighth century, and (*c*) in the *Expositio Symb. Apost.* of Rufinus of Aquileia (died 410). The legend that this symbol was composed by the Apostles in common soon after the first Pentecost was possibly well known at Rome as early as the third century, though it is first mentioned by Rufinus in connection with an erroneous exposition of the symbol. The baptismal confessions of the other Western churches can be traced back to the Roman symbol.

§ 19 *The "Preaching" of Peter*

Literature: A Hilgenfeld (§ 3), IV, 2d edit 1884, 51–65; same, in ZwTh, XXXVI, 11, 1893, 518–541 J. R Harris, in TSt I, 1. (The Apology of Aristides), 1891, 86–99 Theo Zahn, GNK, II, 820–832. E. v Dobschutz, in TU, XI, 1, 1893. Harnack, LG, 25–28, 29

1. Clement[5] of Alexandria has preserved a number

---

[1] *Panarion*, LXXII, 2
[2] *Cod. Biblioth Cotton Mus Britt* [Galba A, XVIII].
[3] *Cod. Laud.* 35, *Biblioth. Bodlei*
[4] *Codex Mus. Brit.* 2 A, XX.
[5] Cf *Stromata*, I, 29 182, II, 15 68, VI, 5. 39–43; VI, 6. 48, VI, 7. 58; VI, 15. 128; *Eclogae*, 58.

PREACHING OF PETER

of longer or shorter fragments of the Πέτρου Κήρυγμα, which had previously been employed by Heracleon,[1] the Valentinian, and apparently by Apollonius,[2] the Anti-Montanist. While Clement spoke of this writing with high respect, Origen[1] expressed doubts as to its genuineness, though without giving a definite opinion, and Eusebius[3] rejected it as apocryphal. The *Petri Doctrina*, Πέτρου Διδασκαλία, is very probably identical with this *Preaching*. Some passages from it have been preserved by Origen,[4] by Gregory Nazianzen,[5] and in the *Sacra Parallela*.[6] Compare also Origen[7] and possibly Œcumenius.[8]

2. From these **fragments** it appears that the writing was a missionary sermon, placed in the mouth of Peter and addressed to the heathen If the fragments may be read in the light of the *Apology* of Aristides,[9] it is possible that an exposition of the true idea of God formed the introductory portion. Then followed discussions and refutations of Greek and Jewish belief, while a laudatory account of Christian ethics may have formed the conclusion. Such a plan would denote that the work was a forerunner of the apologetic literature. There is no basis for the conjecture that it formed a continuation of (Hilgenfeld), or an analogue (v. Dobschutz) to, the Acts of the Apostles.

3. As the *Preaching* was very probably used in the *Apology* of Aristides, it probably was composed as early

---

[1] Cf. Origen, *in Joann*. XIII, 17.   [3] *Hist Eccl*. III, 3. 2.
[2] Cf. Eusebius, *Hist. Eccl*. V, 18. 14.   [4] *De principiis, praef* 8.
[5] *Orat*. 14 (old, 16), *Epist*. 16 (old, 20).
[6] John of Damascus, *Opera*, edition of Le Quien, II, 336 A and 475
[7] *Hom. in Lev*. 10.
[8] *Comm. ad Jacob*. 5, 16; *Opera* II, 478.
[9] § 34. 2.

as the first quarter of the second century. If the relationship of the *Preaching* to the *Shepherd* of Hermas could be traced back with certainty to a use of it in the *Shepherd*, then it must have originated during the first century, and nothing conclusive can be adduced against this view. The place of composition may have been either Egypt or Greece (Hilgenfeld). The supposed relations of the *Preaching* to the κηρύγματα Πέτρου of the pseudo-Clementine literature, allow of no certain explanation. From the statements of Clement of Alexandria,[1] Pseudo-Cyprian[2] (*Paulli praedicatio*), and Lactantius,[3] Hilgenfeld considers it allowable to assert that the *Preaching* was originally known as Πέτρου καὶ Παύλου κηρύγμα.

§ 20. *The So-called Second Epistle of Clement*

Editions, Translation, and Literature, see § 7. Also, Hagemann, in ThQu, XLIII, 1861, 509–531. A Harnack, in ZKG, I, 1877, 264–283, 329–364, *Idem*, *Ueber den Ursprung des Lectoramts*, etc, in TU, II, 5, 1886, 82–84; transl by L. A. Wheatley, in Harnack's Sources of the Apost Canons, Lond 1895 — Harnack, LG, 47–49. J Keith, in ANF, IX, 251–256 (revised translation)

1 The manuscript transmission of the so-called **Second Epistle of Clement** is the same as that of the First Epistle,[4] though the *Codex Alexandrinus* contains only the Chapters 1–12, 5 (τοῦτο ...) The writing is first mentioned by Eusebius, who described it as an epistle,[5] though presumably he had not read it. Jerome[6] simply copied Eusebius. Excepting the index of the *Codex Alexandrinus*, it is first mentioned as the

---

[1] *Stromata*, VI, 5 42 ff.
[2] *De 1 epaptismo*, 17
[3] *Divinae Institutiones*, IV, 21. 2.
[4] § 7, 1.
[5] *Hist. Eccl.* III, 38. 4.
[6] *De Viris Illust.* 15

Second Epistle of Clement to the Corinthians in the *Responsiones ad Orthodoxos*, 74, of Pseudo-Justin.[1]

2. Since the discovery of the complete text, there is no longer any doubt that we have to do, not with an epistle, but with a **homily**,[2] which may have been read[3] to the congregation by the lector (Harnack). The preacher exhorts to the fulfilment of Christ's commands by showing "that therein consists the true confession of Jesus which corresponds to the greatness of redemption; that therein is expressed opposition to the world, and that therefor the reward of resurrection and of a future life is assured."[4] No conjectures can be formed as to the personality of the **author.** Even Photius[5] knew that he could not have been Clement of Rome. Corinth (Lightfoot) and Rome (Harnack) have been indicated as the place of its composition. The author's theology and the possibility of his having used the Gospel to the Egyptians[6] appear to make it impossible that the date of composition could have been later than the middle of the second century.

§ 21. *The Teaching of the Apostles*

Editions: Φ. Βρυέννιος, Κωνσταντ. 1883. A. Hilgenfeld (§ 3), IV, 2d edit 1884. A Harnack, in TU, II, 1, 2, 1884 (Greek and German), reprinted 1893 A Wunsche, Lpz 18?4 (Greek and German) P. Sabatier, Paris, 1885 H. D M Spence, Lond 1885 Hitchcock and Brown, 2d edit, N. Y 1885 Ph Schaff, N Y. (1885) 1889, 3d edit F. X Funk (§ 3), Tubingen, 1887 (G ͚ ͡ ͩ and Latin). J R. Harris, Baltimore, 1887 (with fac-simile of the entire manuscript). — **Translation:** I H. Hall and J T Napier,

[1] Cf Justin, *Opera*, III, p. 108, 3d edit Otto, 1880 Lightfoot, I, 1, p 178 f
[2] Cf. 15. 2; 17. 3; 19. 1.
[5] *Codex*, 113.
[3] Cf. 19. 1.
[6] § 16. 3.
[4] Ritschl, *Altkatholische Kirche*, 2d edit. p. 286 f.

ANF, VIII, 377-382. (Several of the editions mentioned above contain translations) **Literature**: The prolegomena and notes in the above editions. Most careful collection of the literature by Schaff, cf. also S. Baumer, in *Litterar Handw.* XXVII, 1888, 393-398, 425-430 Theo Zahn, FGK, III, 278-319, *Idem, Justinus und die Lehre der zwölf Apostel*, in ZKG, VIII, 1885, 66-84. A. Krawutzcky, in ThQu, LXVI, 1884, 547-606, *Idem*, in KLex, III, 1869-1872. L. Massebieau, *L'enseignement des douze apôtres*, Paris, 1884 A. Hilgenfeld, in ZwTh, XXVIII, 1885, 73-102. H. Holtzmann, *Die Didache und ihre Nebenformen*, in JprTh, XI, 1885, 154-166. C Fr. Arnold, in *Zeitschrift fur Kirchenrecht*, 1885, 407-454. J R Harris, The Teaching of the Apostles and the Sibylline Books, Camb 1885 E Bratke, *Die Einheitlichkeit der Didache*, in JprTh, XII, 1886, 302-312 Ch. Taylor, The Teaching, etc, with Illustrations from the Talmud, Camb 1886. B B. Warfield, Texts, Sources, and Contents of *The Two Ways*, in *Bibliotheca Sacra*, 1886, 100-160. A C McGiffert, The *Didache* viewed in its relations to other writings, in *Andover Review*, V, 1886, 430-442. A Harnack, *Die Apostellehre und die judischen beiden Wege*, Lpz 1886 (with texts; cf. RE, XVII, 656-675); *Idem*, in ThLZ, XI, 1886, 271-273, 344-347, XII, 1887, 32-34 F X Funk, *Zur alten lateinischen Uebersetzung der Doctrina apostolorum*, in ThQu, LXVIII, 1886, 650-655; *Idem, Zur Apostellehre und apostolischen Kirchenordnung*, in ThQu, LXIX, 1887, 276-306, 355-374 G Wohlenberg, *Die Lehre der zwolf Apostel in ihrem Verhaltnis zum neutestamentlichen Schrifttum*, Erlangen, 1888. P Batiffol, *Le Syntagma Doctrinae, dit de Saint Athanase*, in *Studia Patristica*, II, Paris, 1890, 117-160. H Amoneit, *Die Apostellehre und ihr Verhaltnis zu verwandten Schriften*, in *Untersuchungen zur alten Kirchengeschichte, Program*, Wehlau, 1892 P Savi, *La "dottrina degli Apostoli"* Roma, 1893 (from *Studi e documenti di storia e diritto*, XIII, 1892), cf. F X. Funk, in ThQu, LXXVI, 1894, p 703 ff L E Iselin and A. Heusler, *Eine bisheru nbekannte Version des ersten Teiles der "Apostellehre*," in TU, XIII, 1, 1895 Richardson, BS, 83-86. Harnack, LG, 86-92.

1. **The Teaching of the Twelve Apostles**, Διδαχὴ τῶν δώδεκα ἀποστόλων (Διδαχή κυρίου διὰ τῶν δώδεκα ἀπο-

στόλων τοῖς ἔθνεσιν), is preserved in the *Codex Hierosol.*[1] (Constantinople) of the year 1056 A.D. It was first made known in print in 1883, and since then has become the subject of an almost unlimited literature. It was a sort of guide to Christian practice and church life, and was intended to be used in the instruction preliminary to baptism. The first part (1–6) presents, under the image of the two paths of life and of death, the moral precepts with which the catechumen was to be made acquainted before baptism; while the second part (or the last two parts) was addressed to those who had received baptism, and treated of acts of worship (7–10, baptism, fasts, the eucharist) and of the " offices " in the church, *i e.* of prophets, apostles, teachers, bishops, and deacons (11–15). It closed with an exhortation in which reference was made to the second coming of the Lord (16).

2. Eusebius[2] enumerates the so-called διδαχαὶ τῶν ἀποστόλων in the last group of the Scriptures [the "rejected writings"], and in the list of Athanasius,[3] the so-called διδαχὴ τῶν ἀποστόλων follows Judith and Tobit, and precedes the *Shepherd* of Hermas In the List of the Sixty Canonical Books,[4] the περίοδοι καὶ διδαχαὶ τῶν ἀποστόλων are mentioned between the Apocalypse of Peter and the Epistle of Barnabas; and the *Stichometry* of Nicephorus mentions the διδαχὴ τῶν ἀποστόλων (200 stichoi) after the Gospel of Thomas, and before the Epistle of Clement. Funk[5] has shown the existence of traces of the *Didache* in the writings of Optatus of Milevis (Mileum). From the West, only one

---

[1] § 6. 1.
[2] *Hist. Eccl* III, 25
[3] *Epist. fest* 39.
[4] Zahn, GNK, II, 292.
[5] ThQu, LXXVI, 1894, 601–604.

unequivocal attestation is known: viz. in the writing *de Aleatoribus*[1] of Pseudo-Cyprian (*doctrinae Apostolorum*), Rufinus, in his transcript of the canonical list[2] of Athanasius, put a writing called *Duae viae vel judicium secundum Petrum*[3] in place of the διδαχή. Since the discovery of the text, it appears that the sentence quoted by Clement[4] as Holy Scripture is found in the *Didache*,[5] that besides Clement,[6] Origen,[7] Dionysius,[8] and perhaps Gregory of Nyssa[9] were also acquainted with the *Didache*, and that it was much used in the Pseudo-Athanasian writing περὶ παρθενίας.[10]

3. The question as to the time and place of **composition** of the Teaching of the Apostles, as also its relation to other writings, can only be answered when the preliminary problem as to its component parts has been solved. The form of the document as it is contained in the manuscript may be regarded as a redaction of earlier copies. Probably it is to be traced back to a Jewish catechism for proselytes, which contained the first five chapters and a part of the sixth (in the form of *The Two Ways*), and, presumably, also considerable portions of the succeeding chapters: commands as to food, instruction, and the general practices of worship (6, 8), teachers (11–13), celebration of

---

[1] Chap 4.
[2] *Exposit. in Symb. Apost.* 36–38.
[3] § 98. 3.
[4] *Stromata*, I, 20 100.
[5] 3. 5.
[6] Cf. also *Protrepticos*, 10, 109; *Paedagogus*, II, 10. 89, III, 12. 89, *Quis divis*, 29.
[7] *Hom.* VI *in Jud.;* edition of Lommatzsch, XI, 258. Cf. also *Princ.* III, 2. 7.
[8] *Sacra Parallela*, edition of Le Quien, 674.
[9] Ep. 2, Migne, PG, XLVI, 1012
[10] Migne, PG, XXVIII, 251–282

the Sabbath (14-15), other gatherings for divine worship (16), and the crown of the same, readiness for the Messianic kingdom. These instructions underwent Christian revision, probably in Egypt (= the original *Didache*), and out of this revision there grew up, probably in Syria,[1] earlier even than 150 A D., the form preserved in our manuscript (= *Didache*) The older form (various recensions?) probably underlay the fragment of a Latin translation in the *Codex Mellicensis*[2] of the twelfth century,[3] the citation in the treatise *de Aleatoribus*, the recension contained in the Ecclesiastical Canons,[4] and also that in the Pseudo-Athanasian Σύνταγμα διδασκαλίας[5] and the closely allied Pseudo-Athanasian *Fides Nicaena*[6] This same form may have been used in the concluding chapters[7] of the Epistle of Barnabas, in case these chapters do not go back to the original source. Hermas,[8] like Aristides,[9] also probably had read the writing in this or in a similar form. On the other hand, the recension of it in the seventh book of the Apostolic Constitutions[10] was based upon a text almost exactly identical with that of the manuscript.

[1] Cf. chap. 9. 10   [2] *Codex Mellicensis*, Qu 52, Saec. XII.
[3] v Gebhardt, in Harnack's TU, II, 2, pp. 275-286   Cf also Funk.
[4] § 98. 2.   [6] Migne, PG, XXVIII, 1. 637-1644.
[5] Migne, PG, XXVIII, 835-846   [7] 17-20.
[8] § 12.   [9] § 34.   [10] § 98. 3

DIVISION II

GNOSTIC LITERATURE

Literature: R. A. Lipsius, *Zur Quellenkritik des Epiphanios* Wien, 1865; *Idem, Die Quellen der ältesten Ketzergeschichte*, Lpz. 1875. A. Harnack, *Zur Quellenkritik des Gnosticismus*, Lpz 1873; *Idem* in ZhTh, XLIV, 1874, 143–226. A. Hilgenfeld, *Die Ketzergeschichte des Urchristentums*, Lpz. 1884, *Idem, Judentum und Judenchristentum*, Lpz. 1886. J. Kunze, *De historiae gnosticismi fontibus novae quaestiones criticae*, Lips. 1894, cf. Harnack, in ThLZ, XIX, 1894, 340 f.

§ 22. *General*

With few exceptions, our knowledge of Gnostic literature is derived solely from those **fragments** which Catholic theologians and ecclesiastics included in their works that they might combat and refute them. Although these remains allow us only very scanty insight into the nature and contents of Gnostic literature, they nevertheless suffice to produce the impression that it must have been most important and varied. To be sure, the leaders of Gnostic sects were not all authors. We are not told on good authority that either Cleobius and Dositheus, or Simon, Menander, Satornilus, Cerinthus, and others, left literary works behind them.[1] We have no tangible evidence that others, such as

---

[1] See, however, Origen, *in Johan.* XIII, 27; *Constitutiones apost.* VI, 16. Fabricius, BG, 176 f. Harnack, LG, 152–157.

Hermogenes,[1] were authors   But the principal Gnostic leaders, notably Basilides, Valentinus, and their disciples, anticipated, both in form and matter, much that played a part in Patristic literature; and the singular class of edifying tales [which later attained great vogue] seems to have been fostered first in Gnostic circles.

[1] Harnack, LG, 200.

CHAPTER I

THEOLOGICAL LITERATURE

§ 23. *Basilides and Isidore*

Fragments: J E Grabe, *Spicilegium* (§ 2 8. *b*), II, 1699, 35–43. A Hilgenfeld, *Die Ketzergeschichte des Urchristentums*, Lpz. 1884, 207–218, cf F A Hort, in DCB, II, 268–281. — Fabricius, BG, 177 f Harnack, LG, 157–161.

1 **Basilides**, a pupil of Glaucias, who is alleged to have been the interpreter of Peter,[1] was a teacher in Alexandria[2] in the time of Hadrian.[3] That he had been in Antioch with Satornilus, a pupil of Menander, is an assertion of Epiphanius[4] which cannot now be verified. We gather from the *Acta Archelai* of the fourth century, that he preached among the Persians[5] Origen[6] says of him, possibly incorrectly, that he wrote a gospel of his own, Εὐαγγέλιον κατὰ Βασιλίδην It is certain that he wrote twenty-four βιβλία on the Gospel,[7] which, according to Clement of Alexandria,[8] were en-

---

[1] Clement, *Stromata*, VII, 17. 107.
[2] Irenæus, *Adv Haer* I, 24. 1, and, following him, Eusebius, *Hist Eccl* IV, 7 3
[3] Clement, *loc. cit.* Eusebius, *Chronic. ad ann* 133.
[4] *Panarion*, XXIII, 1
[5] Chap 55.
[6] *Hom* I *in Luc* V, edit. of Lommatzsch, V, 86; cf. 87.
[7] Agrippa Castor, in Eusebius, *Hist. Eccl* IV, 7 7.
[8] *Stromata*, IV, 12 83

titled 'Εξηγητικά. Fragments from Books XIII and XXIII have been preserved by Clement and in the *Acta Archelai*, and these serve materially to brighten the picture of Basilides which his opponents drew of him. Compare also the sentence in Origen's *Comm in epist. ad Rom.* V.[1]

2. **Isidore**, the son of Basilides, wrote the following three works, fragments of which have been preserved by Clement of Alexandria: (a) Περὶ προσφυοῦς ψυχῆς.[2] By this is meant the lower soul in man, with all belonging to it,[3] which is to be ruled by the rational soul. (b) 'Εξηγητικὰ τοῦ προφήτου Παρχώρ[4] (in at least two books), which attempts, among other things, to prove the Oriental origin of Greek learning. (c) 'Ηθικά[5] This extensive fragment is connected with an explanation of a saying of the Lord analogous to Matt. xix. 10 f., and it proves that the author's ethics were of a strict type According to Epiphanius,[6] Isidore wrote certain Παραινετικά, which, supposing the statement to be correct, may be identical with the 'Ηθικά.

3 Irenæus[7] mentions the **Incantationes** of the followers of Basilides Concerning the Παραδόσεις Ματθίου, which they held in high esteem, see § 16, 4.

§ 24. *Valentinus and his School*

Literature: G. Heinrici. *Die valentinianische Gnosis und die heilige Schrift*, Berl. 1871. — Fabricius, BG, 178 f Harnack, LG, 174-184.

1. **Valentinus**, according to a statement of Clement,[8] was a pupil of Theodas, who was a disciple (γνώριμος)

---

[1] Edition of Lommatzsch, VI, 336.
[2] *Stromata*, II, 20 113
[3] Cf. § 60 7. d. 2.
[4] *Stromata*, VI, 6. 53

[5] *Stromata*, III, 1. 1-3.
[6] *Panarion*, XXXII, 3
[7] *Adv. Haer.* I, 24. 3.
[8] *Stromata*, VII, 17. 106.

of Paul. He was born somewhere on the north coast of Egypt, was educated as a Greek in Alexandria,[1] and possibly came under the influence of Basilides. According to Irenæus,[2] he went to Rome in the time of Hyginus (about 136–140 A.D.), flourished there under Pius (about 140–155 A.D.), and remained till the time of Anicetus (154/5–166/7 A.D.). Tertullian,[3] who praises his genius and eloquence, asserts that his break with the church was occasioned by his being overlooked in the appointment to an (the Roman) episcopal see. The place and time of his death are unknown. The statement that he went from Rome to Cyprus, that he might there withdraw from the church,[4] is to be received with caution. Clement[5] has preserved fragments with anthropological, psychological, and Christological contents, taken from the **Letters** of Valentinus (ἐπιστολή τις περὶ τῶν προσαρτημάτων [sc. τῆς ψυχῆς] πρὸς Ἀγαθοπόδα); also fragments of **Homilies**,[6] which give some conception of the author's rhetorical power, together with their evident relationship to Pauline and Johannine thought. The Valentinian fragment preserved by Hippolytus[7] possibly came also from a homily. Tertullian[8] bears witness to **Psalms** composed by Valentinus, and a fragment is given by Hippolytus.[9] No writing entitled Σοφία[10] ever existed. Irenæus[11] knew of an *Evangelium Veri-*

---

[1] Epiphanius, *Panarion*, XXXI, 2.
[2] *Adv. Haer.* III, 4. 3; cf. Eusebius, *Chronic. ad ann.* 138 and 144.
[3] *Adv. Valent.* 4.
[4] Epiphanius, *Panarion*, XXXI, 7.
[5] *Stromata*, II, 8 36; 20 114; III, 7. 59.
[6] *Stromata*, IV, 13 91; VI, 6. 52.   [8] *Carne Christi*, 17. 20.
[7] *Philosophumena*, VI, 42.   [9] *Philos.* VI, 37.
[10] Grabe, *Spicilegium*, II, 49, following Tertullian, *Adv. Valent.* 1.
[11] *Adv. Haer.* III, 11. 9; cf Pseudo-Tertullian, 12.

SCHOOL OF VALENTINUS 73

'atis of the Valentinians, though he did not ascribe it to Valentinus.

Fragments are collected in A. Hilgenfeld's *Die Ketzergeschichte*, 1884, 292-307. Cf. A Hilgenfeld, in ZwTh, XXIII, 1880, 280-300 Cf. XXVI, 1883, 356 f R. A. Lipsius, in DCB, IV, 1076-1099 (in German, in JprTh, XIII, 1887, 585-658).

2. According to Hippolytus,[1] the numerous **disciples of Valentinus** were divided into an Italian and an Oriental branch (ἰταλιωτικὴ and ἀνατολικὴ διδασκαλία). Ptolemæus and Heracleon were authors of the Italian school. **Ptolemæus**, as to the circumstances of whose life we know nothing, wrote a Letter to a highly cultured woman, named Flora, to allay her doubts concerning the Mosaic law, on the strength of a distinction between its eternal and its temporal parts. Irenæus[2] appears to have known of other writings (ὑπομνήματα) of Ptolemæus (Explanation of the Prologue to John's Gospel).[3] **Heracleon**, whom Clement[4] ranks as the most illustrious of the Valentinians, may have been a direct pupil of Valentinus,[5] although Tertullian makes him out to have been a follower of Ptolemæus.[6] The statement of Prædestinatus[7] that Heracleon was a Sicilian probably arose from confusing him with Heraclius. Heracleon left behind Ὑπομνήματα,[8] which contained comments on passages of the Gospels of Matthew (?) and Luke,[9] but more especially on the Gospel of John.

[1] *Philosophumena*, VI, 35.
[2] *Adv. Haer.* I, 1-8. 4   Cf. particularly, I. 8. 5.
[3] Zahn.
[4] *Stromata*, IV, 9. 71.
[5] Origen, *in Joann.* II, 8, edition of Lommatzsch, I, 117.
[6] *Adv. Valent.* 4.
[7] Chap 16 [Migne, PL, LIII, 592].
[8] Origen, *in Joann.* VI, 8; edition of Lommatzsch, IV, 117.
[9] Two fragments in Clement's *Eclogae proph* § 25, edition of Potter, 995, and *Stromata*, IV, 9. 73.

Origen, in his commentary on John, included extensive excerpts from Heracleon's expositions, which betray, indeed, a purely dogmatic method of exegesis, but one which is deep and also often in accord with the spirit of the Gospel. **Florinus** also belonged to the Italian school, and he wrote "a detestable book."[1]

Ptolemaei Epist ad Floram, in Stieren's edition of Irenæus, I, 922–936, and in A Hilgenfeld's article, in ZwTh, XXIV, 1881, 214–230, cf Theo Zahn, GNK, II, 2 956-961. — *Heracleon*: Fragments, in Hilgenfeld, *Die Ketzergeschichte*, 1884, 472–505, and A. E Brooke in TSt, I, 4, 1891 (with introduction and extensive notes). Cf R A Lipsius, *Die Zeit des Markion und des Herakleon*, in ZwTh, X, 1867, 75–183

3. The **Excerpts of Theodotus**, Ἐκ τῶν Θεοδότου καὶ τῆς ἀνατολικῆς καλουμένης διδασκαλίας κατὰ τοὺς Οὐαλεντίνου χρόνους ἐπιτομαί, had their origin in the Oriental school, and Clement of Alexandria used them with the aim of refuting their heresies, perhaps in preparation for the eighth book of his *Stromata*[2] Theodotus is nowhere mentioned as a pupil of Valentinus. It is possible that the writing contained doctrines that were attributed by the Valentinians to Theodas.[3] The Excerpts present an older (perhaps merely a more conservative?) form of the doctrine. Von Arnim sees in the Ἐκ τῶν προφητῶν ἐκλογαί[4] likewise a collection of excerpts from Gnostic writings.

The *Excerpts* are given in Potter's edition of Clement, 966–989 (Dindorf, III, 424–455) Some emendations are given by A E. Brook, TSt, I, 4. 105 f. The *Eclogues* are given by Potter, 989–1004 (Dindorf, III, 456–478) Cf Theo. Zahn, FGK, III, 117 f, 122–130 P Ruben, *Clemen. Alex. Excerpta ex Theodoto.* Lips.

[1] Cf. *Fragm. Syr.* XXVIII, in Harvey's edition of Irenæus, II, 457.
[2] Cf § 60, 3. c. [3] Cf. No. 1, above. [4] § 60, 3. c.

1892   J ab Arnim, *De octavo Clementis Stromateorum libro*   Ind
Schol   Rostock, 1894 — Translated by Wm Wilson, in ANF, VIII,
39 ff.

§ 25   Bardesanes

A Hahn Lips 1819 W Cureton, *Spicilegium Syriacum*
Lond 1855 (Book of Laws and Countries) A Merx Halle, 1863
A Hilgenfeld Lpz 1864 Cf R A Lipsius, in PKZ, XIV, 1865,
689–696 F J A Hort, in DCB, III, 250–260 F Boll, *Studien
uber Claudius Ptolemaus*, in JclPh, Suppl XXI, 181–188 — Fabricius, BG, 172–175 Richardson, BS, 108 Harnack, LG, 184–191

1 According to Hippolytus,[1] **Bardesanes** (Bar-Daisan) belonged to the Oriental school   He was born on July 11, 154, at Edessa [now Orfa], on the Daisan,[2] and received a secular education at court.[3]   He was at first a priest of the Syrian goddess, and afterward a Christian[4] Abgarus of Edessa (probably Bar Manu, 202–217 A D) embraced Christianity at the instigation of Bardasanes   When Caracalla captured Edessa, in 217, Bardasanes fled to Armenia, and preached there without success[5]   He probably returned to Edessa (218 ?), and died at the age of sixty-eight.[6]   The numerous contradictory accounts as to the nature of his Christianity make it probable that he was influenced by Valentinianism, but they show him to have been an independent theologian who followed paths of his own.[7]

[1] *Philosophumena*, VI, 35.
[2] *Chron Edess*, edited by J S Assemani, *Bibliotheca Orientalis*, I, 389. Barhebræus, *Chron eccl*, edited by J B Abbeloos and Lamy, 1872, 49
[3] Cf Julius Africanus, *Cesti*, 29, edited by Thevenot, in *Veterum Mathematicorum opera*, 275 f.
[4] Barhebræus
[5] Moses of Chorene, *Hist. Armen* II, 63; Whiston's edition, 1736, 185 ff.
[6] Barhebræus
[7] Cf. also Jerome, *De Viris Illust.* 33.

2. The writings of Bardesanes have been preserved only in meagre fragments. Eusebius[1] and Theodoret[2] mention writings in the form of dialogues directed against Marcion, which were translated into Greek;[3] Eusebius[4] and Epiphanius[5] mention an *Apology* addressed to Antoninus (Heliogabalus?) occasioned by the persecution. A *History of Armenian Kings* (Valarses and Kosru, till 216 A D.), which he composed, was used by Moses of Chorene (fifth, seventh, or eighth century?) as a source for his own work. Ephraem, the Syrian, was acquainted with a book containing 150 *Psalms* (*Hymns*) through which Bardesanes sought to win the popular heart. In his own anti-heretical hymns, Ephraem[3] made use of the material supplied by Bardesanes by substituting orthodox for heretical matter. Through these Hymns, Bardesanes (and his son **Harmonius**[7]) became the creator of Syrian church hymnody. The Book of the Laws of Countries was the work not of Bardesanes, but of his school (third century). It is preserved in Syriac[8] (the original language?); was used in the Pseudo-Clementine Recognitions,[9] and is identical with the dialogue Περὶ εἱμαρμένης (*de Fato*) mentioned by Eusebius,[10] Epiphanius,[11] and Theodoret.[12] In it Bardesanes is introduced in the third person. Persian and

[1] *Hist Eccl* IV, 30 [2] *Haer fab* I, 22.
[3] Cf. also Jerome, *Epist.* 70, 4, edited by Vallarsius, I, 428.
[4] *Hist Eccl.* IV, 30 [5] *Haer* LVI, 1.
[6] Ephraem Syr, *Opera*, edition of Benedetti, II, 437-560, cf. particularly, Nos 51-60.
[7] See Hort, DCB, II, 252. [H. Burgess, Hymns and Homilies of Ephraem Syrus, Lond 1853, pp xxviii-xl]
[8] *Codex Brit. Mus Add* 14658 [9] IX, 19.
[10] *Hist. Eccl* IV, 30. Cf. the fragment in his *Praepar evang.* VI, 10. 1-48
[11] *Haer.* LVI, 1. [12] *Haer. fab.* I, 22.

Manichæan influences are apparently presupposed in the writings ascribed by the Fihrist[1] to 'Ibn Deisân ([Bardaisan] Bardesanes): *Light and Darkness, The Spiritual Nature of Truth, The Movable and the Fixed;* consequently these works may belong to a later period[2]

§ 26 The Carpocratians

Irenæus[3] was acquainted with writings of the Carpocratians Epiphanes, a son of Carpocrates, who lived about or before 150 A D, and who died at the age of seventeen, was the author of a book, Περὶ δικαιοσύνης, from which Clement[4] made extensive quotations In this writing Epiphanes contended for community of goods and of wives. On the question whether characteristics of the moon-god (θεὸς ἐπιφανής) worshipped at Same may not have been transferred to him, see G Volkmar's view,[5] and the contrary view of A Hilgenfeld.[6]

§ 27. Marcion and Apelles

Literature: R A Lipsius, *Die Zeit des Markion und des Herakleon*, in ZwTh, X, 1867, 75–183 ; cf his *Quellen zur alt Ketzergesch*, Beilage II, 225–258   A Hilgenfeld, *Cerdon und Marcion*, in ZwTh, XXIV, 1881, 1–37 ; cf *Ketzergeschichte*, etc , 316–341   G Salmon, in DCB, III, 816–824   Meyboom, *Marcion en de Marcionieten*, 1888 , cf Theo Zahn, GNK, II, 2 418   H Usener, *Religionsgeschichtliche Untersuchungen*, I, Bonn, 1889, 103–108. G Kruger, in JprTh, XVI, 1890, 592 f — Fabricius, BG, 179 f Harnack, LG, 191–200.

1. **Marcion**, the founder of the religious society of

---

[1] Flugel, *Mani*, Lpz. 1862, p. 85.   [3] *Adv Haer.* I, 25. 5.
[2] Cf also, § 30, 4   [4] *Stromata*, III, 2 5–9
[5] *Monatschrift des wissensch Vereins in Zurich*, 1858, 276 f.
[6] ZwTh, V, 1862, 426.

the Marcionites, was a native of Pontus¹ and a wealthy shipowner.² He was regarded as a most dangerous heretic by Justin when he wrote his *Apology* (138 A D? *circa* 150 A.D?) and even earlier³ According to Irenæus⁴ he went to Rome about 140 A.D, became a pupil (?) of the Syrian Cerdo, and separated from the Roman congregation in consequence of his connection with him⁵ According to Irenæus he developed his full activity for the first time under Anicetus, that is, after 154 A D.; a statement which disagrees with the assertion of Clement of Alexandria⁶ that he stood in the relation of πρεσβύτης to Basilides and Valentinus. Hippolytus and the writers who followed his statements maintained that Marcion was the son of a bishop, that he passed a frivolous youth, was excommunicated by his father, etc, but these statements are to be received with caution. The story of his disputation with Roman presbyters on certain passages in the Bible may be founded on fact.

2. Marcion successfully undertook a dogmatic perversion of tradition by altering the Gospel of Luke and the ten Epistles of Paul, which he regarded as genuine, to correspond with his anti-Jewish conception of Christianity.⁷ The Εὐαγγέλιον (with no author's name: τοῦ κυρίου? τοῦ χριστοῦ?) can be reconstructed from Ter-

---

¹ Justin, *Apol.* I, 26. 58. Irenæus, *Adv. Haer.* I, 27. 2. Sinope is mentioned as his birthplace by Philastrius, *de Haer.* XLV, and Epiphanius, *Haer.* XLII, 1, following Hippolytus, *Syntagma*

² Rhodo, quoted by Eusebius, *Hist. Eccl.* V, 13. 3. Tertullian, *Adv Marcion.* I, 18, III, 6.

³ *Syntagma.*

⁴ *Adv. Haer.* I, 27, 2, III, 4. 3.

⁵ Tertullian, *Adv. Marcion.* I, 2, 18, 22, III, 6, IV, 17.

⁶ *Stromata*, VII, 17 107

⁷ Irenæus, *Adv. Haer.* I, 27. 2, III, 12. 12.

tullian's[1] and Epiphanius'[2] extensive refutations, also from the dialogue *De recta fide*[3] and some other accounts[4] Omitting all particulars of the childhood of Jesus, Marcion began by combining Luke iii 1 and iv. 31, and in the course of his narrative rejecting or altering (on the ground that it had been falsified by tradition) everything that was opposed to his own ideas, but more particularly, whatever pointed to a connection between Judaism and Christianity In the face of the plainest indications to the contrary, the statement made by the Tubingen school (following Semler and Eichhorn) and for a time by Ritschl also, to the effect that the Gospel of Luke was a canonical redaction of Marcion's Gospel, cannot be maintained, although possibly Marcion, as compared with the present text of Luke, frequently presents the original setting[5] This Gospel possessed canonical authority in Marcionite congregations It is also possible to reconstruct the 'Ἀποστολικὸν (sc βιβλίον), the second half of the Marcionite New Testament, at any rate in all its essential parts. It contained ten Pauline epistles in the following order: Galatians, 1 and 2 Corinthians, Romans, 1 and 2 Thessalonians, Laodiceans (Ephesians), Colossians, Philippians, and Philemon (Epiphanius: Philemon, Philippians) Hebrews and the Pastoral Epistles were omitted as non-Pauline

Attempted Reconstruction A Hahn, *Das Evangelium Marcions*, Konigsb 1823, and in J C Thilo, *Cod apocr nov Test* I, Lips 1832, 401-486 A Hilgenfeld, *Kritische Untersuchungen uber die Evangelien Justins*, etc Halle, 1850, 391-475, and in ZhTh, XXV, 1855, 426-484 (*Apostolicum*) Cf also ThJ, XII, 1853, 192-244

[1] *Adv. Marcion libri* V, especially Lib IV
[2] *Haer* XLII
[3] § 80 2
[4] Zahn, GNK, I, 608 ff
[5] See Reuss, Usener

G Volkmar, *Das Evangelium Marcions*. Zurich, 1852 W C van Manen, in ThT, 1887, 382-404 (Galatians) Theo Zahn, GNK, II, 2, 409-529 (Gospel and *Apostolicum*). Cf also A Schwegler, in ThJ, II, 1843, 575-590, and *Das nachapostolische Zeitalter*, I, Lpz 1846, 260-284 A Ritschl, *Das Evangelium Marcions und das kanonische Evangelium des Lukas*, 1846 (another view, ThJ, X. 1851, 528-533) E Reuss, *Die Geschichte der heiligen Schriften N T* 6th edit. Braunschweig, 1887, 281. Theo. Zahn, *Die Dialoge des "Adamantius" mit den Gnostikern*, in ZKG, IX, 1888, 193-239, and in GNK, I, 2, 585-718 H. Usener, *Religionsgeschichtliche Untersuchungen*, I, Bonn, 1889, 80-91.

3 In justification of his undertaking, Marcion wrote his Ἀντιθέσεις (**Antitheses**),[1] a sort of dogmatic system (*dos fidei*),[2] which derived its name from the comparison of contradictory passages from the Old and New Testaments which it contained. (*Opus ex contrarietatum oppositionibus Antitheses cognominatum et ad separationem legis et evangelii coactum*) The work occupied a position independent of the Marcionite canon and possessed unity of character (Hahn holds the opposite view) It was intended to prove a *diversitas deorum* from a *diversitas instrumentorum*, and thence the arrangement of the *diversitas ingeniorum, legum et virtutum*[3] was perhaps taken These antithetical sentences[4] may have been used as the chief arguments, being illustrated and strengthened by the quotations of proof passages. The proof of the *diversitas deorum* was apparently followed by an exposition of the true revelation of God and of its falsification through tradition under Jewish

[1] Tertullian, *Adv. Marc* IV, 1; the title given as ἀντιπαραθέσεις by Hippolytus, *Philosoph* VII, 30, is inexact
[2] Tertullian, *loc. cit*
[3] Tertullian, *Adv Marc*. I, 19, II, 29, IV, 1; 6.
[4] Cf, for instance, *Idem*, IV, 28

influence, and finally by proof of the genuineness of the Marcionite Gospel. For our knowledge of the work we are dependent upon Tertullian (whose controversial treatise against Marcion, more especially in the fourth and fifth books, is full of references to the *Antitheses*) and the *Dialogus de recte Fide*. These writings, however, do not make a reconstruction possible (against Hahn). It cannot be proved that other writers were acquainted with the *Antitheses*. In Tertullian's time Marcion's work passed as a symbolic book,[1] but it must have lost this canonical importance speedily. The existence of a separate Commentary on the Gospels, written by Marcion, cannot be proved[2] from the statements of Ephraem Syrus (*Evangelii concordantis expositio*). Tertullian[3] had knowledge of a letter (*quaedam epistula*) of Marcion, a sort of manifesto, with an elaborate justification of his secession from the church.

A Hahn, *Antitheses Marcionis Gnost.*, Regiomont 1823. Theo. Zahn, in ZKG, IX, 1888, 193–239.

4. **Apelles**, a distinguished pupil of Marcion, was called upon when an old man, by Rhodo, the apologist, to give an account of his heretical views[4]. He wrote Συλλογισμοί, the 38th *Tomus* of which is cited by Ambrose[5]. From the fragments preserved by Origen[6] and Ambrose[7] it appears that the statement of Pseudo-Tertullian[8] to the effect that in this work Apelles pur-

[1] Tertullian, *Adv Marc* I, 19, IV, 4
[2] Contrary view, Harnack, in ZKG, IV, 1881, 500.
[3] *De Carne Christi*, 2
[4] Eusebius, *Hist Eccl* V, 13. Cf also § 47 below.
[5] *De Paradis* V, 28
[6] *Homil. in Genes* II, 2, Lommatzsch's edition, VIII, 134 ff.
[7] *De Paradis* V, 28, VI, 30–32, VII, 35, VIII, 38, 40, 41.
[8] *Haer.* 19

posed to show the falsehood of the Mosaic conception of divine things, is correct [1] In his work called Φανερώσεις [2] (no fragment of which has been preserved), Apelles recorded the revelations of Philumene, a prophetess of the sect It cannot be determined whether Apelles' Gospel [3] was identical with that of Marcion, or whether it represented a further elaboration of it

A Harnack, *De Apellis gnosi monarchica*, Lips. 1874; and *Sieben neue Bruchstucke der Syllogismen des Apelles*, in TU, VI, 3, 1890, 109-120

5 The writer of the Muratorian Fragment [4] and *Anonymus Arabicus* [5] knew of certain Psalms of Marcion (Marcionites), the latter was acquainted also with a *Liber propositi Finis* Esnic, the Armenian, borrowed some interesting notices from a dogmatic work of the Marcionites (fourth century)

Harnack, in ZwTh, XIX, 1876, 80-120, *passim*

§ 28. *Ophitic ("Gnostic") Writings*

1. In the large group of **Ophites** and "Gnostics," in the narrower sense, numerous writings were in circulation, of which almost nothing has survived except the titles. Irenæus,[6] Hippolytus, and Epiphanius (vv. ll) in their accounts of the "**Gnostics**," Ophites, Cainites, Sethites, Severians, Naassenes, Peratæ, Docetæ, and of the Gnostic Justin and Monoimus, used a number of

[1] Cf also Rhodo, in Eusebius, *Hist. Eccl* V, 13. See also § 47, below
[2] Tertullian, *Praescrip Haer* 30
[3] Jerome, *Comm in Matth Prooem* following Origen
[4] V, 82-84
[5] *Praef ad Conc Nic* Mansi, II, 1057
[6] *Adv. Haer* I, 29-31.

sources of which they have given us no further description Irenæus[1] mentions the use by the Cainites of a Gospel of Judas, in their opinion the only one of the disciples who understood Jesus; and a Gospel of Eve was used by the "Gnostics" and perhaps by the Peratæ[2] Gospels of Thomas, Philip, and other Apostles[3] were used by other "Gnostics."[4] Epiphanius[5] also mentions "many books" written and used by the "Gnostics," among them being the following: Ἐρωτήσεις Μαρίας μεγάλαι and μικραί, the former containing matter that was obscene and altogether foreign to genuine tradition; the Γέννα Μαρίας (progeny? of Mary containing a cynical account of the death of Zacharias) the Ἀποκαλύψεις τοῦ Ἀδὰμ εἰς τὸν Ἰαλδαβαώθ, which was also in use among others besides, εἰς ὄνομα τοῦ Σήθ (see below). A work, Ἀναβατικὸν Παύλου, was in circulation among the Cainites and "Gnostics"[6] According to Epiphanius[7] the Sethites had seven books bearing the name of Seth, other books entitled Ἀλλογενεῖς, an Apocalypse of Abraham, some books bearing the name of Moses, and, according to Hippolytus,[8] a Παράφρασις Σήθ. The Archontici[9] used a large and a small book of "Συμφωνία," the book Ἀλλογενεῖς (see above), an Ἀναβατικὸν Ἡσαίου, etc. Hippolytus[10] has preserved a fragment of the *Hymns* of the Naassenes, also a Psalm.[11] This sect made use of the Ἀπόφασις μεγάλη.[12]

[1] *Adv. Haer.* I, 31. 1.
[2] Epiphanius, *Haer* XXVI, 2, 3, 5, in the third section there is a fragment of an apocalyptic character Cf also Hippolytus, *Philosoph.* V, 16
[3] Cf § 16 4-5.
[4] Epiphanius, *loc cit* and Hippolytus
[5] *Haer* XXVI, 8 12
[6] Epiphanius, *Haer* XXXVIII, 2
[7] *Haer* XXXIX, 5.
[8] *Philosoph* V, 22.
[9] Epiphanius, *Haer.* XL.
[10] *Philosoph.* V, 6.
[11] *Idem*, V, 10.
[12] *Idem*, V, 9.

In connection with the above list, which does not profess to be complete, see Harnack, LG, 162–171, 662 f A Behrendts (§ 16 6), 32–37

2. The only **Gnostic writings** that have been preserved complete have been handed down in Coptic translations. They consist of the literary productions of the Severians, Sethites, and Archontici, who, in contrast with the lascivious Nicolaitans, Cainites, etc., sought to found their life and doctrine upon a strict moral basis

(a) The so-called Πίστις-Σοφία,[1] in four books, is not a literary unit, the fourth book is evidently different from the others and appears to be older than they; the first three books are apparently identical with the Ἐρωτήσεις Μαρίας μικραί (see above), or at least, a recension of the same[2] All the books are in the form of dialogues (question and answer) between the risen Jesus and his disciples, more especially Mary Magdalene. The main emphasis is laid upon the answering of practical questions "as to the conditions and hindrances, the degrees and stages of blessedness" (Koestlin) Interest in questions of systematic theology is kept in the background The central idea is that of the fall from and the return to the Infinite Books I and II contain the history of Σοφία, the type of that which is to be accomplished in humanity, (Books III and IV.) The work in its existing form very probably originated in the second half of the third century. Among its sources, besides extensive use of the literature of the Old and New Testaments, two large Books of Jeû are mentioned. Scattered throughout are Psalms, partly

[1] *Codex Askew Brit Mus. Saec* V–VI. Title not original.
[2] Renan, Harnack.

composed by the author himself, partly selected; for instance, the Odes of Solomon¹

Editions M G Schwartze and J H Petermann, *Pistis-Sophia*. Gotha, 1851, 53 (Coptic and Latin)
Literature F Munter, *Odae gnosticae Salomoni tributae*, 1812 K R Kostlin, *Das gnostische System der Pistis-Sophia* in ThJ, XIII, 1854, 1–104, 137–196 E Renan, *Marc-Aurèle* Paris, 1882, p 120, note 3 R. A Lipsius in DCB, IV, 405–415 A. Harnack in TU, VII, 2, 1891.

(*b*) Certain writings, without titles, contained in the *Papyrus Brucianus* (Oxford; of the fifth or sixth century) may have been taken from the tomb of a "Gnostic" According to Schmidt there are two works which are jumbled together in the manuscript, but which are to be distinguished from each other Originally they were written in Greek and translated into Coptic The *first*, whose conclusion is wanting, has been identified by Schmidt with the two Books of Jeû (see above) as the book of the great Λόγος κατὰ μυστήριον Schmidt, therefore, thinks that it was written about the middle of the third century at the latest The *second* (which lacks both beginning and conclusion) is referred by Schmidt to the second century, between 170 and 200 A D. The two Books of Jeû (and the *Pistis-Sophia*), according to Schmidt, would represent productions of the Severians. The second, the title of which is unknown, belonged to the Sethites and Archontici Between the system developed in this work and that which was opposed by Plotinus,² there existed a remarkable simi-

¹ Munter, cf Harnack, TU, VII, 2 35–49, revised Latin translation
² *Ennead*, II, 9; cf. Porphyry, *Vita Plotini*, 16, οἱ περὶ 'Ἀδέλφιον καὶ 'Ἀκυλῖνον.

larity. In the opinion of Preuschen there is no adequate proof either of the unity of the first book or of its identity with the source cited in the *Pistis-Sophia* He thinks rather, that "Jeû I" is considerably later than the *Pistis-Sophia*, that the close relation between "Jeû II" and the *Pistis-Sophia* IV (the doctrine of the Mysteries) still awaits explanation, and that the date of composition of the second work must for the present remain doubtful   It is certain, however, that the second work, which is of systematic contents throughout, gives an impression of greater antiquity than the first or than the *Pistis-Sophia*. The first work, in the form of communications made by Jesus to his disciples, both male and female (see above), contains, besides speculative and systematic expositions, practical directions, explanations as to initiations and the mysteries, and also hymns.

C Schmidt, *Gnostische Schriften in koptischer Sprache aus dem Codex Brucian* in TU, VIII, 1, 2, 1892 , cf E Preuschen in ThLZ, XIX, 1894, 183–187, and Schmidt's reply in *idem*, 284, and in ZwTh, XXXVII, 1894, 555–585 (an elaborate refutation of Preuschen's contentions)   Harnack, LG, 171–174, 661–663.

§ 29 *Julius Cassianus*

G Salmon in DCB, I, 412 f   Theo Zahn, GNK, II, 2, 632–636. Fabricius, BG, 182   Harnack, LG, 201–204.

Julius Cassianus, after his secession from the Oriental school of Valentinus, became the founder of a distinct Docetic (and Encratic) sect,[1] perhaps about 170 A.D.[2] or earlier[3]   He wrote a work Περὶ ἐγκρατείας ἢ περὶ εὐνου-

---
[1] Clement, *Stromata*, III, 13 91, 92   [3] Harnack.
[2] Zahn.

χίας, which was attacked by Clement,[1] and of which the latter preserved three fragments of an Encratic character. Besides this work, Clement[2] knew of another book called 'Εξηγητικά in which the age of Moses was calculated.

[1] Loc. cit
[2] Stromata, I, 21. 101, cf Eusebius, Praeparat. evang X, 12. 1.

CHAPTER II

ROMANCES

§ 30. Acts

Editions: J. A. Fabricius, *Codex apocryphus*, N.T. II (*Acta apostolorum apocrypha*). Hamb. 1703 C. Tischendorf, *Acta apost apocry*. Lips. 1851. M. Bonnet, *Supplementum Cod. apocry*. I (*Acta Thomae*). Lips. 1883. *Acta apost. apocrypha*, edd. R. A. Lipsius et M. Bonnet, I, Lips. 1891 (in the following sections marked AA). — Literature: J C. Thilo, *Acta S. Thomae apostoli*, Lips. 1823, I–CXXVI. A. v. Gutschmid, *Die Königsnamen in den apokryphen Apostelgeschichten*, in RhM, XIX, 1864, 161–183, 382–401 (and in his *Kleine Schriften*, II, 1890, 332–394). R. A. Lipsius, *Die apokryphen Apostelgeschichten und Apostellegenden*, I, II, 1, 2, and *Erganzungsheft*. Braunschw. 1883–1890 (marked AG and Egh, in following). H. Lietz, in ZwTh, XXXVII, 1894, 34–57 Richardson, BS, 100, 103 Preuschen, in Harnack's LG, 116–128, 131–134.

1. According to Eusebius [1] there were in circulation among the heretics **Acts** of Andrew, John, and other apostles, which were not thought worthy of mention by other ecclesiastical writers. Such acts were in use among the Bardesanites,[2] the Ebionites,[3] the Encratites,[4] the Apostolici,[5] and the Origenists [6] Later they appear among the Manichæans,[7] and even Faustus seems to

[1] *Hist. Eccl.* III, 25. 6
[2] Ephraem Syrus, cf. Zahn, GNK, II, 2, 598 f.
[3] Epiphanius, *Haer.* XXX, 16
[4] *Idem*, XLVII, 1.
[5] *Idem*, LXI, 1.
[6] *Idem*, LXIII, 2.
[7] Philastrius, *De Haer.* 88 [Migne, LP, XII], Augustine, *De Actis cum Felice Manichaeo*, II, 6 [Migne, PL, XLII, 539]; *Idem, Contra Adversarium Legis et Prophetarum*, I, 20. 39 [Migne, PL, XLII, 626]; *Idem*,

have cited from Acts of Peter, Andrew, Thomas, and John.[1] Even Photius[2] possessed a collection of such Acts (Peter, John, Andrew, Thomas, and Paul), which he assumed to be the work of Leucius Charinus, who may have been the disciple of the Apostles[3] mentioned by Epiphanius[4] and Pacianus.[5] Innocent I[6] and Leo I[7] rejected them on account of their heretical character,[8] and the decretal of Gelasius[9] gave official force to this judgment as regards the Acts of (Andrew), Thomas, Peter, and Philip, and the writings of Leucius generally. The *Stichometry* of Nicephorus enumerates the Acts of Peter, John, and Thomas, among the New Testament apocrypha. With the exception of some fragments, these Gnostic Acts in their original form have been lost; all that has been preserved are more or less thorough Catholic revisions.

2. The first express mention of the Gnostic **Acts of Peter**, Πράξεις Πέτρου,[10] is made by Eusebius.[11] They were read not only by the Manichæans,[12] but also in ecclesiastical circles.[13] They contained 2750 *stichoi*

Contra Faustum Manichaeum, XXII, 79 [Migne, LP, XLII, 451]; *Idem*, *Contra Adimantum*, 17, 2, and elsewhere.

[1] Cf. Augustine, *Contra Faustum Manichaeum*, XXX, 4 [Migne, LP, XLII, 492–3].

[2] *Codex*, 114 [Migne, BG, CIII, 389].

[3] Lipsius, AG, I, 44–117; Zahn, *Acta Johannis*, LX–CLXXII, *Idem*, GNK, II, 856–861.

[4] *Panarion*, LI, 6.   [6] *Epist* 6, 13.

[5] *Epist.* 1, 2 [Migne, LP, XIII, 1051].   [7] *Epist.* 15, 15

[8] Cf. Photius, *loc. cit.*

[9] [Migne, PL, LIX] VI, 3–5 (6), 17 (18)

[10] Cf. Lipsius, AG, II, 1, 85–390, Egh. 34–56, Zahn, GNK, II, 832–855, Preuschen, in Harnack, LG, 131–134.

[11] *Hist. Eccl.* III, 3. 2.   [12] Faustus, see above

[13] Cf. Commodianus, *Carm. apol.* 626–630, Pseudo-Hegesippus, *De*

according to the *Stichometry* of Nicephorus. The only portion of these acts that has been preserved in the original is the Μαρτύριον Πέτρου,[1] which forms the conclusion. This is extant also in Latin in two recensions: (*a*) in the *Actus Petri cum Simone* (see below), and (*b*) in a longer form in the *Epistola Lini episcopi de Passione Petri et Pauli*.[2] A larger fragment is also extant under the title *Actus Petri cum Simone*[3] in a codex of the seventh century. The Acts relate the conflict of the Apostle with Simon and his glorious martyrdom; the true magician opposes the false, and the latter, after a futile attempt to fly up to heaven, comes to a miserable end. The date of composition is uncertain; possibly the words of Clement[4] refer to these Acts, and high antiquity is indicated by the frequent use of apocryphal passages, the origin of which can be traced only in part. It cannot be determined how many of the incidental mentions of single details in the life of Peter[5] are to be charged to the Acts, but the *Acta Nerei et Achillei*[6] apparently drew from this source.[7]

3 The **Acts of John**, Πράξεις Ἰωάννου,[8] are first men-

bello Judaico, III, 2, Ambrosiaster, on Rom. xvi. 11, Isidore of Pelusium, *Epist.* II, 99, Photius, *Codex*, 114 [Migne, BG, CIII].

[1] *Codex Patm* 48, ninth century, *Cod. Ath Vatop* 79, of the tenth or eleventh century. Reprinted by Lipsius, AA, 78-102, cf. JpTh, X, 1886, 86-106, 175

[2] Manuscript sources in Preuschen (Harnack's), LG, 133. Printed by Lipsius, AA, 1-22.

[3] *Codex Vercell* CVII, *Saec.* VII, Lipsius, AA, 45-103

[4] *Stromata*, VII, 11, 63   [5] Lipsius, AG, II, 1. 1-69

[6] Edition of Achelis, 11, 4-16, 29

[7] Lipsius, AG, II, 1, 200-206, Achelis, 57 f

[8] Printed by C. Tischendorf, *Acta Apost apocr.*, and Theo Zahn, *Acta Joannis*, Erlangen, 1880. Cf. M. Bonnet, in *Revue Crit* 1880, 449-454.

tioned by Eusebius,[1] and afterward by Epiphanius[2] as an heretical production in use among the Encratites The work was also used by the Manichæans and Priscillianists,[3] and as late as the eighth century it played a part in the Iconoclastic Controversy[4] Leucius is said by Innocent I[5] and Turibius[6] to have been its author The *Stichometry* of Nicephorus gives its length as 2500 stichoi There have been preserved.

(1) the three fragments of a discourse of John (on the nature of the body of Jesus, the parting of Jesus from the disciples, Hymn, Christophany, picture of John), which were read at the Second Council of Nicæa[7], (2) some further fragments that had already undergone Catholic redaction These relate the departure from Laodicea, the miracle of the insects, the story of Callimachus and Drusiana,[8] that of the two youths Atticus and Eugenius (showing the corruption of riches), the conversion of the high-priest of Artemis and of the proconsul,[9] and the μετάστασις (departure and death) τοῦ ἁγίου ἀποστόλου καὶ εὐαγγελιστοῦ Ἰωάν-

Cf Zahn, GNK, II, 856-865, Lipsius, AG, I, 348-542, Egh 25-28, Preuschen, in Harnack, LG, 124-127.

[1] *Hist Eccl* III, 25. 6
[2] *Panarion*, XLVII, 1.
[3] Philastrius, *De Haer* 88, Augustine, *Contra Adversarium Legis et Prophetarum*, I, 20 39, Turibius of Asturica (Astorga), *Epist ad Idacium et Ceponium*, 5 [Migne, LP, LIV, 694, and in Leo, *Opera*, Ballerini's edition, I, 713 f]
[4] Second Council of Nicæa, 787 A D , cf Mansi, *Concil collect.* XIII 168-172, Photius, *Codex*, 114, Bekker's edition, 91, 4, 5
[5] *Epist* 6, 13
[6] *Loc cit*
[7] Mansi, *loc cit* , Fragm I-III, in Zahn, *Acta Joannis*, 218-224
[8] IV, in Zahn, *Idem*, p 225, 1-234, 36.
[9] V, in Zahn, *Idem*, 234-237, cf Fabricius, II, 557-581

νου¹ Lipsius² has added other miraculous stories, an account of Zebedee's purpose to bring about the marriage of John, and others relating to the imprisonment of the Apostle, his trial before Domitian, and his banishment to Patmos The account given by Theodorus [Studita] of Studium³ was probably based upon the Gnostic Acts The date of its composition in the second century (about 160 A D, Zahn) is apparently vouched for by the antique character of the Acts, and it would be placed beyond doubt, if the mention of the martyr's ordeal by oil and of his celibacy found in Tertullian⁴ could be certainly traced back to Leucius⁵ Reference is made to the Gnostic Acts⁶ in Clement of Alexandria's⁷ *Adumbrationes in Epist Cathol* Catholic recensions are preserved (*a*) in Greek, in the so-called *Prochoros*,⁸ (*b*) in Latin, in the so-called *Abdias*,⁹ and in Pseudo-Mellitus,¹⁰ (Melito) *De Passione Joannis* ¹¹

4 The **Acts of Thomas**, Πράξεις Θωμᾶ,¹² were, according to Epiphanius, in use among the Encratites¹³ and the Apostolici,¹⁴ according to Augustine¹⁵ and Turibius,¹⁶ among the Manichæans and the Priscil-

---

[1] VI, in Zahn, *Idem*, 238-252.
[2] AG, I, 469-485, following the Codex Paris 1468, and Codex Vatican 654, cf Zahn, *Idem*, 188, 12-190, 22
[3] *Orat* VII in *Joann Ev*, Mai, NPB, V, 4 72-77.
[4] *De Praescriptione*, 36, *De Monogamia*, 17
[5] Cf also the Muratorian Fragment, 9-16
[6] Zahn, FGK, III, 87, 97   [9] Fabricius, *Cod Apocr* N. T, II, 531-590
[7] Cf § 60 5 *c*.   [10] § 40 8 *b*.
[8] Zahn, 1-192   [11] Fabricius, III, 604-623
[12] Printed by J C Thilo and M Bonnet (see above), cf Lipsius, AG, I, 225-347. Preuschen, in Harnack, LG, 123 f
[13] *Panarion*, XLVII, 1   [14] *Idem*, LXI, 1
[15] *Contra Faustum Manich* XXII, 79, etc.
[16] *Epist ad Idacium*, etc, 5 See above.

lianists.¹ Their length, given in the *Stichometry* of
Nicephorus, amounted to 1300 (1700) stichoi Considerable portions of the Gnostic original have been preserved intact in Catholic recensions.² The Acts, which
from beginning to end are a sermon on abstinence from
all sexual indulgence, relate the journey of the Apostle
to India, his residence in the city of Andrapolis, and the
occurrences at the marriage feast of the king's daughter
(I, 1-16); the building of the heavenly palace and the
conversion of the Indian king, Gundaphorus (II, 17-29);
the raising and the conversion of the wanton youth who
had been killed by a dragon (III, 30-38), the story of
the talking ass's colt (IV), the deliverance of the woman
afflicted by an unclean spirit (V, 39-47), various healings and conversions (VI, 48-58, VII, VIII), the several
imprisonments of the Apostle and his miraculous deliverances (IX), further conversions. followed finally by
that of the wife of King Mazdai (X, XI), on account
of which the Apostle was once more imprisoned and
again miraculously freed, until at last, after celebrating
the Lord's Supper with the converts (XII), he was
thrust through with lances by the king's order (Μαρτύριον). It can be shown that many of the proper names
which occur in the book are historical ³ Gundaphorus
is the Indo-Parthian king Gondaphares, who, according
to von Gutschmid, reigned from 7 to 29 A D , or, according to von Sallet and Dillmann, at the close of the first
century (died about 80 A.D) Reliable traditions may
have been at the author's service The Apocalypse of
Peter⁴ may have provided the model for the description
of Hell (VI, 52-54). The Acts must have originated

¹ Cf Photius, *loc cit.*
² *Codex Paris graec.* 1510.
³ Cf Lipsius, AG, I, 278-281
⁴ 21-34, Harris' edit.

after 232 A D. (removal of the remains of Thomas to Edessa, AG, II, 2, 425) The hymns written by Bardesanes[1] were apparently added later: (*a*) the beautiful hymn relating to the fortunes of the soul, preserved only in Syriac,[2] and (*b*) a second hymn and two prayers of consecration, which, though they may have been likewise originally Syriac, are now preserved uninterpolated in a Greek translation[3] only, the Syriac being much altered The view that the Acts were originally composed in Syriac has been maintained by Macke, but controverted by Lipsius[4]

A v Gutschmid, *Die Königsnamen*, etc , see above   F. v Sallet, *Die Nachfolger Alexanders des Grossen in Baktrien und Indien*, 1879, 157-166   A. Dillmann, in *Monatsbericht der Berliner Akademie*, 1879, 421   W Wright, *Apocryphal Acts*, II   Lond 1871, 238-245   Theo Noldeke, in *Zeitschr der deutschen morgenlandischen Gesellschaft*, XXV, 1871, 678   Idem, in Lipsius, AG, II, 2, 423-425   C Macke, in ThQu, LVI, 1874, 1-70.

5   The **Acts of Andrew**, Πράξεις 'Ανδρέου,[5] were read by the Encratites,[6] the Apostolici,[7] the Origenists,[8] the Manichæans,[9] and the Priscillianists.[10]   Only small fragments of (or references to) the original Acts have been preserved.   These relate to the story of Maximilla, the

[1] Burgess, *Hymns of Ephraem Syrus*, Lond 1853, pp xxviii-xl. Noldeke, Macke, Lipsius, AG, I, 209 f, 309-311, 318-321.
[2] Wright, German, by Macke, and Lipsius, AG, I, 292-296.
[3] Bonnet, I, 6 f , II, 27, V, 44
[4] AG, I, 345   Cf. also II, 2, 423-425.
[5] Cf Lipsius, AG, I, 543-622, Egh 28-31   Preuschen, LG, 127 f.
[6] Epiphanius, *Panarion*, XLVII, 1.
[7] *Idem*, LXI, 1   [8] *Idem*, LXIII, 2.
[9] Philastrius, *de Haer.* 88, see above   Agapius, quoted by Photius, *Codex*, 179 [Migne, PG, CIII, 521 f], Timotheus, *de acced. ad s. ecclesiam*, quoted by Fabricius, *Codex apocry.* I, 139.
[10] Turibius, *loc. cit.* No. 3, above.

wife of Egetes,[1] and to Andrew's prayer that he might not be taken down from the cross [2] Innocent I[3] names Nexocharides and Leonidas as its authors, and in this he may have been guided by trustworthy tradition [4] Of the date of composition we have no more definite indication than the fact that the book is first mentioned by Eusebius [5] Various Catholic recensions, which are divisible into several separate Acts, each with its own transmissional history, borrowed from Gnostic Acts now lost: (*a*) The Acts of Andrew and Matthew in the city of the Cannibals [6] The story, which breaks off abruptly, is continued in (*b*) the Acts of Peter and Andrew [7] These are contained in a text in which there are gaps, and they also break off abruptly The book relates the deeds of the two Apostles in the city of the barbarians Finally (*c*), Pseudo-Abdias, in the *Virtutes Andreae*,[8] relates the journey of the Apostle from Pontus to Greece, his deeds and crucifixion. The martyrdom was also the subject of later recensions [9]

[1] Evodius(?), *De Fide contra Manichaeos*, 38, in Migne, PL, XLII, 1150 [*Augustini Opera*, VIII, *App.* 31].

[2] Pseudo-Augustine, *De vera et falsa poenitentia*, 22 *Opera*, VI, *App* 716 [Migne, PL, XLI, 1120]

[3] *Epist* 6, 13

[4] Zahn, GNK, II, 858, note 1. Von Gutschmid conjectures that the name was Xenocharides, cf Lipsius, AG II, 2, p. 430

[5] *Hist Eccl* III, 25 6

[6] J C Thilo, *Acta sanct apostolorum Andreae et Matthiae, et commentatio de eorundem origine* Halle, 1846 C Tischendorf, *Acta apost apocry* XLII-LIX, 132-166

[7] C. Tischendorf, *Apocalypses apocryphae*, Lips 1856, *App* 161-167, following the *Codex Bodlei Barocc* 180 The Ethiopic version, giving Thaddeus instead of Andrew, is in Malan's *Conflicts of the Holy Apostles*, 221-229, for the Slavic, cf Bonwetsch, in ZKG, V, 1882, 506-509.

[8] Fabricius, *Cod Apocr* N T, II, 457-516.

[9] Cf. Lipsius, AG, I, 563-567.

SUPPLEMENTARY

§ 31. *Symmachus*

Harnack, LG, 112-114.

The Ebionite **Symmachus**, who was still living in the time of Septimius Severus, wrote, besides his translation of the Old Testament, a work entitled Ὑπομνήματα, which contained a polemic against the Gospel of Matthew,[1] and which may have been read even by Palladius,[2] of the fifth century. Ebed Jesu, in the fourteenth century, was acquainted with works of Symmachus in Syriac translations, and he mentions the title of one, *De Distinctione Praeceptorum*[3]

---

[1] Eusebius, *Hist. Eccl.* VI, 17.
[2] *Hist Lausiaca*, 147
[3] Assemani, *Bibliotheca orientalis*, III, 1728, 17.

DIVISION III

LITERATURE OF THE CHURCH

FIRST SECTION

PATRISTIC LITERATURE IN THE AGE OF THE APOLOGISTS AND DURING THE CONFLICT WITH GNOSTICISM

§ 32. *General*

Literature: E Rohde, *Der Griechische Roman*, Lpz 1876 (Chapter 3, *Die Griechische Sophistik*.) E Hatch, *Influence of Greek Ideas and Usages upon the Christian Church*, Lond 1890 *Griechentum und Christentum*, German translation by Pieuschen, Freib 1/B, 1892 Fourth Lecture "Greek and Christian Rhetoric" A Harnack, *Die antijudische Litteratur in der alten Kirche*, in TU, I, 3, 1883, pp 56-74 — Cf also the literature preceding § 22

1 In the second century the effort to make known the truth, purity, and excellence of the Christian religion to the civil power and to the educated part of society, led to the formation of an **Apologetic** literature Those who thus wrote had found in Christianity, in its faith and hope and love, that which they had sought in vain in the philosophy and theology of the time Their literary training was that of the Greek Sophists, whose art was in its second bloom just at that period As in their case, so in that of the Christian Sophists, it is difficult to determine where rhetoric ends and philosophy begins; and it is equally true that their works

were less adapted to quiet reading than to oral delivery. In their conception of divine things they approximately coincided with the leaders of the popular philosophy, and of this they were in part (Justin) clearly conscious Where they remained fixed in their intentional opposition to Hellenic culture (Tatian), their writings bear the stamp of their origin. Their polemic is often superficial, being directed against externalities or to knocking down men of straw After the time of Justin the chief weapon in the apologetic armory was the argument that Judaism and Christianity surpass the heathen religions in age, and, therefore, in excellence · an argument derived from Jewish apologetics, and even there supported by manifold fabrications The result of this, and of a second argument, according to which everything prophesied in the Old Testament had been fulfilled in the New, was that the Old Testament came to be held in the highest esteem, while appeal to the Gospels and the apostolic writings took secondary place

2. The controversial writings **against Judaism,** which, so far as they are known, were always in the form of dialogues,[1] were a mere supplement to the literature addressed to heathen readers It was not so much a question of serious controversy, for which there was very little occasion, as of the demonstration, interesting alike to Christians and pagans (see above), that the Old Testament had been superseded by the New It was little more than a literary artifice that a Jew was introduced into the dialogue to defend his religion, a task which he performed, for the most part, in a very inadequate manner.

3. The departures, real or supposed, from Christian

[1] Cf § 35, 36 2 *c*

belief, which were proclaimed in the Gnostic and Montanistic movements, gave rise to **Anti-heretical** writings. These, pre-eminently, became the literary monuments of the Catholic church: a church which was developing by consciously rejecting all that was foreign to itself, which had, nevertheless, learned much from its adversary, and which, on account of this very opposition, was compelled to handle the Christian truths of salvation in a scientific-theological fashion.

4. The writings that were called forth by the pastoral activity of the **Bishops** appear like echoes of the apostolic and sub-apostolic periods, and also as a presage of the future. Such they were whether they were occupied with general or special exhortations, or with the settlement of disputes which concerned the internal relations of church or churches.

CHAPTER I

APOLOGETIC LITERATURE

Editions: Pr Maranus, Par 1742   Migne, PG, V, VI   *Corpus Apologetarum Christianorum, Saec.* II, ed J C Th Eques de Otto, Vol I–V,³ Jena, 1876–81, VI–IX, 1851–72   A new and complete edition is appearing in TU   Cf also §§ 34, 36, 41
Literature: J Donaldson (§ 2 4 *b*), Vol 3   H Dembowski, *Die Quellen der christlichen Apologetik*, Lpz 1878, I *Die Apologie Tatians*   A Harnack, *Die Ueberlieferung der griechischen Apologeten des zweiten Jahrhunderts*, etc, in TU, I, 1–2, 1882, cf A Hilgenfeld, in ZwTh, XXVI, 1883, 1–45   O v Gebhardt, *Zur handschriftlichen Ueberlieferung der griechischen Apologeten* (Arethas-Codex) in TU, I, 3, 1883.

§ 33. *Quadratus*

Fragments   Otto, IX, 333–341   **Translation** P B Pratten, ANF, VIII, 749   **Literature**   A Harnack, *loc cit* 100–109   Th Zahn, in NKZ, VI, 1891, 281–287   Durr, *Die Reisen des Kaisers Hadrian*, Wien, 1881, 42 f, 69 f. — Fabricius, BG. 154 f   Richardson, BS. 109   Harnack, LG, 95 f.

Quadratus, the disciple of the Apostles, according to Eusebius[1] presented to the Emperor Hadrian, probably at Athens (125–126 A.D.), a defence of Christianity. It was still in existence when Eusebius wrote.[2] The contents of the fragment preserved by Eusebius[3] make

---

[1] *Chronicon ad Annum Abrahami* 2410, Jerome, 2142 [Migne, PG, XIX, 557]
[2] *Hist Eccl* IV, 3 1.
[3] *Idem*, IV, 3 2   Cf also, the Fragment of Papias, given by de Boor, in TU, V, 2, 1889, p. 170.

it appear possible that this "disciple of the Apostles" was identical with the early Christian prophet of the same name¹ On the other hand, identification with Quadratus, the Bishop of Athens,² is excluded by the context according to Photius,³ even Eusebius, Bishop of Thessalonica (about 600 A.D), appealed to Quadratus against the Aphtharto-docetic (monophysite) monk Andreas

§ 34 *Aristides*

Editions : (1) of the Armenian text *S. Aristides* . *sermones duo*, edd Mechitaristae, Venet 1878   P Martin, in AS, IV, 6-11, 282-287 German by F v Himpel, in ThQu, LXII, 1880, 110-122 , afterward printed by R Seeberg, *Der Apologet Aristides* (see below). 62-67   (2) of the Greek and Syriac text   J R Harris and J A Robinson, in TSt, I, 1, 1891 (cf A Harnack, in ThLZ, XVI, 1891, 301-309, 325-329)   Theo Zahn, in ThLB, XIII, 1892, 1-6   O v Gebhardt, in DLZ, XIII, 1892, 938-941   R Raabe, in TU. IX, 1, 1892 (transl from Syriac)   J Schonfelder, in ThQu, LXXIV, 1892, 531-557 (transl from Syriac)   R Seeberg, in FGK, V, 159-414 (restoration of the original text, according to the Syriac and the Greek and Armenian fragments) E Hennecke, in TU, IV, 3, 1893 (attempted reconstruction) R Seeberg, *Der Apologet Aristides*, Erlangen, 1894 (Apology, Epistle, Homily) — **Translation :** D M Kay, in ANF, IX, 259-279

Literature : The prolegomena and notes to the various editions P Vetter, in ThQU, LXIV, 1882   A. Harnack, in RE, XVII, 675-681   A Hilgenfeld, in ZwTh, XXXVI, I, 1893, 103-105 , II, 1893, 539 f   E Egli, *Idem*, I, 99-103 (date of composition)   E Nestle, *Idem*, I, 368-370   Theo Zahn, FGK, V, 415-437 (Epistle and Homily)   L Lemme, in NJDTh, II, 1893, 303-340   E Hennecke, in ZwTh, XXXVI, II, 1893, 42-126 (original form of the text). F. Lauchert, in *Revue internat de théol.* II, 1894, 278-299. G Kruger,

[1] Eusebius, *Hist Eccl* III, 37. 1. Cf. V, 17 3.
[2] Cf. Dionysius of Corinth, in Eusebius, *Hist Eccl* IV, 23. 3; Jerome, *De Viris Illust* 19, and *Epist* 70, 4.
[3] *Codex*, 162, Bekker's edit 106

in ZwTh, XXXVII, 1894, 206-223, (Aristides and Diognetus) P Pape, in TU, XII, 2, 1894 (Sermon, and fragment of the Epistle) P Vetter, in ThQu, LXXVI, 1894, 529-539 (following G Kalemkiar, refers to the acquaintance of the Armenian Esnik with the Apology of Aristides) — Fabricius, BG, 155 Harnack, LG, 96-99

1 The Apology of the Athenian philosopher, **Aristides**, which was widely circulated in the time of Eusebius,[1] has been lost in its original form. The following means are available for its reconstruction. (1) A Greek recension in the legend of Barlaam and Joasaph,[2] (2) a Syriac translation,[3] (3) a fragment of an Armenian translation, in two manuscripts[4] which contain the first two chapters The relation of these texts has not been made entirely clear, though it may be considered probable that in the Greek the original text has been much trimmed in order to adapt it to the legend, and, more especially, that it has been abridged, while the Syriac seems in general to be a true but quite paraphrastic translation, and the Armenian to be closely allied to the Syriac, though directly derived from a Greek text The statement of Eusebius,[5] not based, however, on personal inspection, that the Apology was presented to the Emperor Hadrian, probably at Athens (125-126 A D[6]) would be contradicted by the second heading in the Syriac text, if this unmistakably indicated that Antoninus Pius was the recipient Jerome[7] cannot be regarded as an independent witness.

[1] Cf *Hist Eccl* IV, 3 3
[2] Edition of Boissonade, Paris, 1832, pp 239-250.
[3] *Codex Sinait Syr* XVI
[4] *Codex Venet ann* 981, and *Codex Edschmiaz* of the eleventh century
[5] *Hist Eccl* IV, 3 3
[6] *Chron ad Annum Abrahami*, 2140, Jerome, 2142.
[7] *De Viris Illust* 20, cf *Epist* 70, 4

2. The **Apology** is simply and clearly arranged An exposition of the true idea of God (Chap I) is followed by an inquiry as to who among men have followed truth and who error in regard to God (Chap. II ff). For the purposes of this inquiry, mankind is divided into four (two) classes, — Barbarians and Greeks, Jews and Christians, and they are pictured to the emperor according to their origin (Chap. II) and character. The errors of the Barbarians are described in Chapters III–VII, and those of the Greeks in Chapters VIII–XIII. Chapter XII contains a digression on the Egyptians Chapter XIV discusses the merits and faults of the Jews, and Chapters XV–XVII constitute a fervent song in praise of Christian belief and Christian morality. The polemic against heathenism is monotonous, diffuse, and superficial The element of revelation is denied to the Jewish religion, and the arguments from antiquity and prophecy are not yet adduced. Of the Old Testament, only the Apocrypha (Tobit) are employed, and the Gospel tradition is hardly noticed On the contrary, reference is made to Paul, and possibly to the fourth Gospel [1] The *Kerygma Petri* and the *Didache* (the latter not in its present shape) appear to have been known to Aristides Apparently the Apology was little read. The resemblances found in later apologists [2] are no proof that it was used by them; [3] but Celsus may have had the writing before him The resemblances between the Apology and the Epistle to Diognetus make it conceivable that they may have been works of the same author [4]

3. Armenian tradition refers two other pieces to

---

[1] Cf II, 6, in Seeberg [3] See, however, § 36 3. *c*; 40. 7; 85. 11. *a*.
[2] Seeberg, p 232, A [4] Cf § 43.

Aristides, — an **Epistle** addressed to all philosophers (*Epistola Aristidae philosophi ad omnes philosophos*), and a **Homily** on the cry of the thief on the cross and the answer of the Crucified (Luke xxiii. 42 f.). Only an insignificant fragment of the Epistle has been preserved. In opposition to Zahn and Seeberg, Pape has shown the anti-Nestorian character of the Homily (and of the Epistle).[1]

§ 35. *Aristo of Pella*

Literature · J E Grabe, *Spicilegium* (§ 2 8 *b*), II, 2d edit. 1700, pp 127–133   Routh, RS, I, 93–109   Otto, *Corpus Apologet Christ.* IX, 1872, 349–363.   A Harnack, *Die Altercatio Simon. Jud. et Theoph Christ*, in TU, I, 3, 1883 (cf I, 1–2, 1882, 115–130). A. C McGiffert, A dialogue between a Christian and a Jew, N. Y 1889, 33 f   E Schurer, *Geschichte des judischen Volkes*, etc, I   2d edit 1890, 51–53 [English translation, Hist of the Jewish People in the Time of Christ, I, 1, pp 69–72]   P Corssen, *Die Altercatio Simon. Jud et Theoph Christ*, Berl 1890   Theo. Zahn, *Ueber die "Altercatio legis inter Simon Jud. et Theoph. Christ" des Euagrius und deren altere Grundlage*, in FGK, IV, 308–329 — Fabricius, BG, 156–158.   Richardson, BS, 109 f.   Harnack, LG, 92–96.

Origen[2] defended a little book, entitled Ἰάσονος καὶ Παπίσκου ἀντιλογία περὶ Χριστοῦ, against the reproaches of Celsus. In this work a Christian disputes with a Jew on the basis of the Jewish Scriptures, and shows that the prophecies concerning the Christ are applicable to Jesus. Of this book Celsus, the author of the letter *De Judaica Incredulitate*,[3] which has been preserved among the writings of Cyprian, states that it closed with the

---

[1] Cf. Harnack, in TU, I, 1–2, 1882, p. 114.
[2] *Contra Celsum*, IV, 51 f., edit. of Lommatzsch, XIX, 81 f.
[3] Cf. § 86. 6. *e*

conversion by the Jewish Christian of his opponent, who is characterized as an Alexandrian Jew. From one of the two passages quoted by Jerome[1] from the writing which he knew as the *Altercatio Jasonis et Papisci*, it appears that the author of the dialogue made use of Aquila's version of the Bible. Consequently, the statement of Maximus Confessor,[2] that **Aristo of Pella** was the author of the dialogue,[3] is not improbable, inasmuch as Eusebius[4] knew of a writing of Aristo, in which the war of Barcochba was mentioned. On the other hand, the assertion of Clement of Alexandria that Luke wrote the book[5] is merely a superficial conjecture. The date of composition may, accordingly, be fixed between 135 and 170 A.D. This, however, does not make it impossible that it may have been used in Justin's dialogue with Trypho (Zahn), and it is probable that it was employed by Tertullian,[6] Pseudo-Tertullian,[7] and Cyprian.[8] The hope that the 'Ἀντιλογία would be found to have been preserved in its essential features in Evagrius' *Altercatio Simonis Judaei et Theophili Christiani*[9] (written ± 430 A.D.) has been fulfilled only in a moderate degree

§ 36. *Justin*

Editions: See § 33. R. Stephanus, Paris, 1551 . C. Otto, I–V, 3d edit 1876–1881

Translations: *Sammtliche Werke der Kirchenvater*, Kempten,

[1] *Quaest. hebr. in lib. Genes*, edit of Lagarde, 3, cf also *Comm. in Gal.* iii. 13; *Opera*, edit of Vallarsius, VII, 436.
[2] *Scholia ad theol. myst. Dionys. Areop.*, Cap. 1, edit. of [Balth.] Corderius, 17.
[3] Cf. also *Chronicon Paschale ad ann.* 134; edit. Dindorf, I, 477.
[4] *Hist. Eccl.* IV, 6. 3.   [7] *Adv. Jud* 9–13.
[5] Cf. Maximus, *loc. cit.*   [8] *Testimonia*.
[6] *Adv. Praxean,* and *Adv Jud.* 1–8.   [9] Edition of Harnack, 1883, 15–49.

1830, I, II, 1-138 (*Apol*, *Dial*, *Orat*, *Cohort*) Dods and Reith in ANF, I, 163-306 (*Apol*, *Dial*, *Orat*, *Cohort*, *Monarch*, *Resurrec Fragm Martyr*) The Works now extant of Justin Martyr, translated with notes and indexes in LFC, XL, Oxf 1861 Literature. C Semisch, *Justin der Martyrer*, 2 Theile, Bresl 1840-42 C Otto in Ersch und Gruber's *Enzyklopadie*, 2 Sect, 30 Theil, 1853, 39-76 B Aubé, *Saint Justin*. Paris, 1861 (1875) M v Engelhardt, *Das Christentum Justins des Martyrers*, Erlangen, 1878, same in RE, VII, 318-321 A Harnack, *Die Ueberlieferung der griechischen Apologeten*, etc, TU, I, 1, 2, 1882, 130-195. H S. Holland in DCB, III, 560-587 Fabricius, BG, 52-75. Richardson, BS, 21-26 Harnack, LG, 99-114

1 **Justin**, philosopher and martyr,[1] was born of heathen parents[2] about 100 A.D at Flavia Neapolis, the ancient Shechem, now Nab(u)lus, in Palestinian Syria (Samaria) It is possible that he became a Christian[3] at Ephesus under Hadrian,[4] and that he there obtained a knowledge of rabbinical theology through intercourse with Jews and their associates Under Antoninus Pius he labored, not without opposition (on the part of the Cynic Crescens), as a teacher and apologist for Christianity in his own lecture room[5] The extant and apparently trustworthy "Acts" of the martyr[6] refer the date of his death to the prefecture of Rusticus, *i.e.* between 163 and 167 A D. Justin was the first and the most eminent of those who strove to effect a reconciliation between Christianity and non-Christian culture. As an author he was lovable and of broad sympathies, but his style was diffuse and frequently tedious.

[1] Tertullian, *Adv. Valent.* 5.   [2] *Dialog.* 28, Otto, 94, 18.
[3] Cf. the account in *Dialog* 2-8, *Apology*, II, 12.
[4] Eusebius, *Hist. Eccl* IV, 8. 6.
[5] Cf. Tatian, *Orat.* 19, Eusebius, *Hist. Eccl.* IV, 16. 1; Photius, *Codex*, 125.
[6] Cf. § 105, 3

Zahn in ThLZ. I, 1876, 443-446 (literature for the determination of the year of his death), and in ZKG, VIII, 1886, 37-66 (residence at Ephesus), cf § 106 4, below

2 A peculiarly evil fate has attended Justin's **literary remains**, for while his genuine works for the most part were early lost, his famous name was made to cover a number of writings which, both on internal and external evidence, cannot have belonged to him. The following are to be regarded as genuine in the order in which they are vouched for by Justin himself, or by other witnesses

(a) His Σύνταγμα κατὰ πασῶν τῶν γεγενημένων αἱρέσεων, quoted by the author himself in his Apology,[1] is no longer extant As to its contents, it is only known that it was written in opposition to Simon Magus, Menander, Marcion (perhaps also the Valentinians, the Basilidians and the Satornilians). It is at least uncertain whether it was used by later anti-heretical writers, such as Hegesippus, Irenæus, Tertullian, and Hippolytus. This writing Eusebius[2] had not seen.

Literature: at § 22.

(b) His (1) Ἀπολογία ὑπὲρ Χριστιανῶν πρὸς Ἀντωνῖνον τὸν Εὐσεβῆ, and (2) Ἀπολογία ὑπὲρ Χριστιανῶν πρὸς τὴν Ῥωμαίων σύγκλητον, are only extant in one manuscript[3] (excepting only a portion of the first **Apology** in a manuscript of the fifteenth century),[4] and singularly enough the second Apology precedes the first. The gap in the second chapter of the second Apology is covered by a citation by Eusebius,[5] who is also an im-

[1] I, 26
[2] *Hist Eccl* IV, 11. 10.
[3] *Codex Paris* 450, *anni* 1364.
[4] In *Codex Ottob Gr.* 274, *saec* XV.
[5] *Hist. Eccl* IV, 17. 2-13.

portant witness to various portions of the text The trustworthiness of the text is open to considerable question, but the genuineness of the writing is undoubted [1] There are no sufficient grounds for the assumption that the two apologies were originally one, and consequently that the one which Eusebius [2] calls the second has been lost (Harnack) Similarly the second is not to be regarded as a mere supplement to the first (Zahn) We have nothing by which we can certainly determine the date of composition of the first Apology. The usual assumption that it was written about 150 A D.[3] is contradicted by the dedication, among other things, which apparently presupposes the year 138 (139 A D) as the date As to the second Apology, Eusebius [4] asserts that it was presented to Marcus Aurelius, whereas the testimony of the writing itself [5] is to the effect that Antoninus Pius was still alive.

In the **First Apology**, Justin begins with the reflection that it is unjust to make the Christians responsible for their name, and in the first part, down to Chapter 13, he defends his brethren in the faith against the charges of godlessness and hostility to the state. He then brings forward the positive proof of the truth of his religion, based on the effects of the new faith, and more especially on the excellence of its moral teaching. To this he adds a comparison of Christian and heathen doctrines, in which the latter are represented, with naïve assurance, as the work of evil spirits. The backbone of the proof of the truth of Christianity appears in the detailed demonstration of the fulfilment in Christianity of the pre-

---

[1] Cf Justin's *Dialogue*, 120, Otto's edit 432, 13–15.
[2] *Hist*. IV, 18 2.
[3] Veil, 153–155 A.D.
[4] *Hist Eccl*. IV, 18 2.
[5] Chapter 2, Otto, 202, 4–5.

dictions of the Old Covenant prophets, who were more ancient than heathen poets and philosophers (Chaps 13-60) In the third part of the Apology it is shown from the usages of divine service that the Christians have in truth consecrated themselves to God (Chaps 61-67) The whole is closed by an appeal to the princes, in which reference is made to the edict issued by Hadrian in favor of the Christians (Chap 68) In the **Second Apology** Justin takes occasion to show from a recent proceeding against Christians in Rome, that the persecutions themselves serve to make the innocence of the Christians apparent Justin appears to have made scarcely any use of early Christian writings outside of the New Testament (*Didache ?*) Later apologists frequently took counsel of him, but subsequent to Eusebius he seems to have been little read, and only the *Sacra Parallela* show any independent acquaintance with him.[1]

Editions (besides complete editions of the Apologists and of Justin) C Gutberlet, Lpz 1883, 3d edit G Kruger in SQu, I, Freib 1891 — Translation P A. Richard in BKV, 1871. H. Veil, Strassb 1894 (with introduction and notes) Roberts and Donaldson, ANF, I, 163-193

Literature On the text, L Paul, in JclPh, CXLIII, 1891, 455-464 B Grundl, *De interpoll ex S Justin. Apol II, expungendis*, Aug Vindel 1891, On the question of the mutual relations of the two Apologies, and on the date of composition, cf F Chr Ball, in ZhTh, XII, 1842, 3-47 G Volkmar, in ThJ, XIV, 1855, 227-282, 412-467 Theo Zahn, in ThLZ, as above H Usener, *Religionsgeschichtliche Untersuchungen*, I, 1889, 101 f, 106-108 G Kruger, in JprTh, XVI, 1890, 579-593, and in ThLZ, XVII, 1892, 297-300 J A Cramer in ThSt, LXIV, 1891, 317-357, 401-436 H Veil, Strassb 1894, XXII-XXXII Relation to the *Didache*; Theo. Zahn in ZKG, VIII, 1886, 66-84

[1] Otto, II, 595 ff.

(c) The **Dialogue with Trypho**, Πρὸς Τρύφωνα 'Ιουδαίον διάλογος (*Dialogus cum Tryphone*), contained in the *Codex Paris* 450, is to be regarded as genuine on both external and internal grounds (*e g* its use by Irenæus, its likeness to the *Apology* in the exposition of Biblical passages). The text is not without mutilations. Besides the introduction to the work, and the dedication to M Pompeius,[1] a considerable part has been lost from Chapter 74 (fragments in the *Sacra Parallela ?*) Originally the work comprised two books[2] As to the date of composition, it can only be made out with certainty that it was written later than the first *Apology*[3] Unmistakable reminiscences of the author's residence at Ephesus have been incorporated in the dialogue, which is constructed with a certain graphic power and artistic grace Rabbi Tarphon probably supplied the name given to the character, Trypho[4] Justin begins by telling the story of his own conversion (Chaps. 2–8). The disputation proper is divided into two parts, the first of which contains a description of and criticism upon the Jewish law (Chaps. 8–48), while from Chapter 49 onward, objections derived from the divine adoration paid to Christ by believers are refuted by means of voluminous citations from the predictions of the prophets The *Dialogue* was much used by Irenæus and Tertullian, but otherwise it was apparently less read than the Apologies.

(d) The following writings, cited by Eusebius,[5] have been **lost**, or cannot be certainly identified with any of

---

[1] Cf. Chap 141, close
[2] *Sacra Parallela, Codex Reg. Paris* 923, fol 73.
[3] Chap 120, Otto's edit, 432, 13 f.   [5] Eusebius, *Hist Eccl* IV, 18 3 f.
[4] Zahn, ZKG, VIII, 1886, 37–66

Justin's extant writings. (1) Σύνταγμα πρὸς Μαρκίωνα, used by Irenæus, [1] (2) Λόγος πρὸς Ἕλληνας, [2] containing prolix discussions of the themes most in debate between Christian and Greek philosophers, and a description of the nature of evil spirits, (3) Ἔλεγχος πρὸς Ἕλληνας, (4) περὶ θεοῦ μοναρχίας, [3] the proof of which was derived from Biblical and Greek writers, (5) Ψάλτης, (6) Περὶ ψυχῆς [4] The possibility is not excluded that as early as Eusebius a spurious tradition obtained in regard to these writings, and Eusebius himself states that more works were current under the name of Justin than he had read

3. Reasons can be given in favor of the genuineness of the following writings, which a later tradition ascribed to Justin —

(a) Περὶ ἀναστάσεως (*De Resurrectione*), preserved in a fragmentary form in a codex of the twelfth century [5] Even Procopius of Gaza, about 500 A D, quotes from a writing of Justin which bears this title, and it can be shown to be at least credible that a work of Justin, περὶ ἀναστάσεως, may have been in the hands of Irenæus, Tertullian, and Methodius It cannot be shown that the style of the extant fragments makes it impossible that Justin may have written them The book contains a refutation of hostile objections, and a positive proof of the actuality of the resurrection, based, more especially, upon the resurrection and second coming of Christ.

[1] *Adv Haer* IV, 6 2, V, 26. 2.
[2] Cf Tatian, *Orat ad Graec*. Cap 18; Schwartz, 20, 15-17.
[3] Cf § 36, 4 *a*
[4] Harnack, LG, 110 p
[5] *Codex Rupef* of the *Sacra Parallela* (twelfth cent) Cf *Cod Coisl*. 276, fol 1-78, and *Cod Hieros* fol 80 f

Theo Zahn in ZKG, VIII, 1886, 20-37 W. Bousset, *Die Evangelienzitate bei Justin d Martyrer* Gottingen, 1891, 123-127

(*b*) The Λόγος παραινετικὸς πρὸς Ἕλληνας (*Cohortatio ad Gentiles*) which is contained in the *Codex Paris*. 451, of 914 A D., and other manuscripts, was cited as the work of Justin by Stephanus Gobarus,[1] as early as the fifth century, and in the *Sacra Parallela* of the sixth century The question of its genuineness could be more easily solved if it could be shown that the writing was already used by Julius Africanus.[2] In this case its composition might confidently be assigned to the second century In its style and language, as in its dogmatic contents, it differs considerably from those works of Justin which are recognized as genuine. Yet it still remains possible that the writing was identical with one of those mentioned by Eusebius The author was acquainted with Egypt and Italy (cf. Chapters 19 and 37) Volter's attempt to discover its author in Apollinaris of Hierapolis[3] is as little convincing as that of Draeseke and Asmus to show that Apollinaris of Laodicea was the author, and that the work was directed against the edict of Julian in 362 A D The essential content of the book consists in the proof that the truth was not known to the Greek poets and philosophers, and that whatever of good may be found in their writings was derived from the prophets. It can be easily imagined that the appearance of the *Cohortatio* was occasioned by the Pseudo-Plutarchian extract from the *Placita* of Aetius[4] (made about the middle of the

[1] Photius, *Codex*, 232, Bekker, 290
[2] Thus von Gutschmid, the opposite view, Schürer, Neumann, and Draeseke
[3] Cf. § 39.   [4] So Diels

second century), which was probably widely circulated as a convenient manual, and which was evidently attacked in this treatise [1]

C Ashton, *Justini philosophi et martyris Apologiae pro Christianis*, 1768, p 293   A von Gutschmid in JclPh, LXXXI, 1860, 703-708 (*Kleine Schriften*, II, 1890, 196-203)   E Schurer in ZKG, II, 1878, 319-331   D Volter in ZwTh, XXVI, 1883, 180-215   C J Neumann in ThLZ, VIII, 1883, 582-585   J Draeseke in ZKG, VII, 1885, 257-302, and *Apollinarios von Laodicea* in TU, VII, 1892, 83-99, cf A Julicher in GGA, 1893, 82-84 — H Diels, *Doxographi graeci*, Berol. 1879, 17, cf 66   J. R. Asmus in ZwTh, XXXVIII, 1895, 115-155

(c) Πρὸς Ἕλληνας (*Oratio ad Graecos*) has been transmitted in Greek in the *Codex Argent. Gr.* 9, of the thirteenth or fourteenth century (burned in 1870), and in an extended Syriac recension in a codex of the sixth or seventh century,[2] in the British Museum   In the latter, however, it is attributed, not to Justin, but to a certain Ambrosius, who is described as an eminent Greek   This powerful little treatise cannot be identical with any of the writings mentioned by Eusebius, and can hardly be the work of Justin   It is not necessary, however, on this account, to suppose that it was written after the second century.   It appears to stand in close relationship (common source for both?) to the *Oratio* of Tatian, and it contains some noteworthy parallels to the *Apology* of Aristides

E B Birks, in DCB, II, 162-167 (Ambrosius, author of Πρὸς Ἕλληνας, and of the Epistle to Diognetus).   J Draeseke in JprTh, XI, 1885, 144-153 (author, Apollonius)

(d) The tradition as to certain **Fragments** of writings ascribed to Justin, is either confused, obscure, or corrupt.

[1] Cf also § 44   [2] *Codex Nitr Mus. Brit.* 987 add. 14658, *saec.* VI-VII.

They have been variously supposed to belong to an Apology,[1] or to a writing, Πρὸς "Ελληνας,[2] or Κατὰ 'Ελλήνων,[3] or, finally, to be of unknown origin [4]

(*e*) It cannot be finally determined what work we are to understand by the 'Απολογία ὑπὲρ Χριστιανῶν καὶ κατὰ 'Ελλήνων καὶ κατὰ 'Ιουδαίων, which Photius [5] mentions as composed by Justin (together with two other writings [6]), but distinct from the Apologies known to us. It is quite uncertain whether Photius had any independent acquaintance with the genuine works of Justin which he enumerates in conformity with the list given by Eusebius.

4. The following writings are certainly **spurious**: —

(*a*) The writing Περὶ θεοῦ μοναρχίας (*de Monarchia*) (preserved in the *Codex Paris* 450, 1364 A D.)[7] does not correspond to the description given by Eusebius (see above, 2 *d*), inasmuch as it brings forward its proofs solely from a number of expressions of Greek poets (for the most part forged), without any regard to the Bible. The style also differs in a marked way from that of Justin. The *terminus ad quem* of the date of its composition is determined by the date of the archetype of *Codex Paris* 450, which must have been written considerably before 1364 A D. (Harnack)

(*b*) The 'Ανατροπὴ δογμάτων τινῶν 'Αριστοτελικῶν

---

[1] *Sacra Parallela*, Otto, *Frag* X, possibly belonging to Gregory of Nyssa, *Sacra Parallela*, Otto, *Frag* XIII
[2] *Sacra Parallela*, Otto, *Frag* XIV, *Cod Paris*, 450 *bis*, Otto, IV, 214-223
[3] Leont Byz *Adv. Eutychian et Nestor* lib II, *Cod Bodl* A, 33, Otto, V.
[4] *Sacra Parallela*, Otto, *Frag* VI and VII, Antonius Melissa, I 19, II, 6 43. Otto, *Frag* XV-XVIII.
[5] Photius, *Codex*, 125
[6] Cf § 36. 4. *b–d.*
[7] *Codex Argentor* 9 *saec* XIII-XIV Cf. § 36. 3 *c.*

(*Confutatio dogmatum Aristotelis*), contained in the *Codex Paris* 450 (A D 1364), and possibly identical with the writing mentioned by Photius,[1] is a purely philosophical work, addressed to a certain Presbyter Paul, and was probably not written earlier than the sixth century.

(*c*) and (*d*) The Ἐρωτήσεις Χριστιανικαὶ πρὸς τοὺς Ἕλληνας (*Quaestiones Christianorum ad Gentiles*), and the Ἐρωτήσεις ἑλληνικαὶ πρὸς τοὺς Χριστιανοὺς περὶ τοῦ ἀσωμάτου καὶ περὶ τοῦ θεοῦ καὶ περὶ τῆς ἀναστάσεως τῶν νεκρῶν (*Quaestiones Gentilium ad Christianos*), contained in the *Codex Paris*. 450, were apparently written by the same author, certainly not before 400 A D Ἀποκρίσεις πρὸς τοὺς ὀρθοδόξους περὶ τινῶν ἀναγκαίων ζητημάτων (*Quaestiones et responsiones ad orthodoxos*) are a scholarly repertory touching important theological and ecclesiastical questions. In it Irenæus, Origen, and others are cited. The work presupposes the activity of the Antiochian school, though it dates from the fifth century.[2] The work cited by Photius, Ἀποριῶν κατὰ τῆς εὐσεβείας κεφαλαιώδεις ἐπιλύσεις, may be identical with or related to one of the writings at the head of this section (*c* and *d*)

(*e*) The Epistle to Zenas and Serenus, ascribed to Justin, and contained in the *Codices Paris* 451, 450, and many other manuscripts (also in Syriac recension), is of indeterminable origin. The statement that it was the work of a certain Justin of the seventh century, who was superior of the monastery of Anastasius, near Jerusalem, cannot be verified The Epistle contains rules for Christian conduct according to the ascetic

---

[1] Photius, *Codex*, 125
[2] *Quaest* 71 Cf W Gass, in ZhTh, XII, 1842, 4, 35–154

ideal, and its author possessed knowledge of Greek comedy and tragedy, apparently at first hand [1]

(*f*) While the foregoing writings have been merely ascribed to Justin without originally professing to be his work, the Ἔκθεσις περὶ τῆς ὀρθοδόξου πίστεως ἢ περὶ τριάδος (*Expositio rectae fidei*) is a forgery It is extant in twenty-three manuscripts,[2] and in a Syriac recension. This work has been transmitted in two forms, the shorter of which appears to have been the original (Harnack thinks otherwise) As early as Leontius of Byzantium, in the sixth century, the longer form was cited as the work of Justin, and since it is an attack on the Nestorians and Eutychians, the date of its composition may be fixed at about 500 A D Draeseke has sought to show that the shorter form represents the writing of Apollinaris of Laodicea Περὶ τριάδος, but his hypothesis is open to grave doubt.

J. Draeseke, in ZwTh, XXVI, 1883, 481-497, ZKG, VI, 1884, 1-45, 503-549, also his *Apollinaris von Laodicea*, in TU, VII, 1892, 158-182, cf A Julicher, in GGA, 1893, 85-86 F X Funk, in ThQu, LXXVIII, 1896, 116-147, 224-250

5. Of the Πρὸς Εὐφράσιον σοφιστὴν περὶ προνοίας καὶ πίστεως λόγος nothing further is known than that it was ascribed to Justin by Maximus Confessor.[3] According to Photius,[4] a writing entitled Περὶ τοῦ παντός [5] was said by some to be the work of Justin Jerome,[6] probably merely on the authority of Eusebius,[7] asserts that Justin interpreted the *Apocalypse*

[1] P Wendland, *Quaestiones Musonianae*, Berol. 1886, 45-48
[2] *Sacra Parallela, Codex Paris* 451 The title is variously given
[3] *Diversae definitiones*, II, 154, Combefis. [Migne, PG, XCI, 279, *Opuscula theologica et polemica*]
[4] *Codex*, 48
[5] Cf § 91 5 *a*
[6] *De Viris Illust* 9
[7] *Hist Eccl* IV, 18 8, V, 8

6. On the Epistle to Diognetus, see below.¹

§ 37 *Tatian*

Literature H A Daniel, *Tatianus der Apologet*, Halle, 1837
W. Moller, in RE, XV, 212-214   J M Fuller, in DCB, IV, 782-804. — Fabricius, BG, 87-95   Richardson, BS, 33-35.   Harnack, LG, 485-496

1. Tatian was born in the country of the Assyrians,² that is, east of the Tigris, and, according to Clement³ and Epiphanius,⁴ was of Syrian nationality. He was educated, however, as a Hellenist,² and had already acquired reputation as a rhetorician,⁵ when, at Rome, he abandoned Greek views and became a Christian.⁶ A pupil of Justin, he lived and taught as a member of the Roman church, till his master's death (167 A.D., at the latest). Probably at 172 A.D.,⁷ he broke with the church, joined the Encratites, and defended the doctrinal views of the Gnostics.⁸ He left Rome, and betook himself to the East. The place and date of his death are unknown. In the West, the recollection of him as a heretic obscured his fame as an apologist;⁹ but Tertullian¹⁰ and Jerome¹¹ had independent knowledge of him. Clement¹² esteemed his teacher highly, copied from his *Oratio* again and again, and waged polemic against his heretical writings. Julius Africa-

¹ Cf. § 43.
² *Orat.* 42
³ *Stromata*, III, 12 81.
⁴ *Panarion*, XLVI, 1.
⁵ *Orat* I, Schwartz, 2, 9.
⁶ Before 152 A.D , Eusebius, *Chron.*
⁷ Eusebius, *Chron*
⁸ Irenæus, *Adv Haer.* I, 28. 1.
⁹ Cf *Idem*, III, 28 8.
¹⁰ *Jejun* 15 Cf the *Apologeticus.*
¹¹ *Praef Com Tit.*, Vallarsius, VII, 1. 686, *Com in Amos*, 2, 12, Vallarsius, VI, 247, etc.
¹² Cf. *Stromata*, I, 1. 11.

nus made use of his chronological data,[1] he was read even by Eusebius,[2] and Epiphanius[3] had at least heard of him   He continued to be held in high esteem in the Syrian church on account of his *Harmony of the Gospels*

2 According to Eusebius,[4] Tatian left behind him a large number of writings   To-day we can only judge of his literary peculiarities by his apologetical works   The Λόγος πρὸς ″Ελληνας (**Oratio ad Graecos**), which once existed in the *Codex Paris* 451 (914 A D), is now only preserved in manuscripts derived from this source. It belonged to Tatian's Catholic period, and was therefore written in Rome between 152 and 172 A D, or possibly before the death of Justin (Harnack holds a different view)   The writing contains a sharp and bitter criticism of Greek religion, ethics, philosophy, and art   It is interesting, though frequently unjust and one-sided. Its positive portions are distinguished by the originality of their theological and psychological views, and the chronological data upon which the arguments for Christianity, because of its antiquity, are based, give evidence of honest endeavor   But the impression of great erudition made by the citation of so many sources is destroyed when we consider that Tatian was acquainted with very few of these at first hand, but had obtained most of his quotations by means of compends which he used very uncritically   Occasional expressions recall those of the New Testament scriptures (John, Romans, Corinthians, Colossians, and Ephesians), and use was made of the works of Justin (Dembowski holds a different view)   Tatian's style was hard, abrupt,

---

[1] Cf § 82   [3] *Panarion*, XLVI.
[2] vv. ll.   [4] *Hist Eccl.* IV, 29. 7.

and obscure; but all that he says gives evidence of a remarkable personality.

Editions Compare citations at § 33; also J Frisius-Gesner, Tigur, 1546 W Woith, Oxon 1700 C Otto, *Corpus apol Christ* VI, 1851 E Schwartz, in TU, IV, 1, 1886 — **Translations** V Grone, in BKV, 1872 A Harnack, Giessen, 1884 J. E. Ryland, ANF, II, 65–83
Literature A v Gutschmid (§ 36 3 *b* Justus of Tiberius as the source of chronological data) Bluemner, in *Archaolog. Zeitung*, XXVIII, 1871, 86–89 (remarks on history of art) H Dembowski, *Die Quellen der christlichen Apologetik*, Lpz 1878 A Harnack, in TU, I, 1, 2, 1882, 196–232. A Kalkmann, in RhM, XLII, 1887, 489–524 (remarks on works of art) M Kremmer, *De Catalogis Heurematum*, Lips. 1890 A Ponschab, Metten, 1894–95.

3. The following writings of Tatian are only **known by title**: —

(*a*) Περὶ ζῴων, cited in *Orat.* 15.[1]

(*b*) Πρὸς τοὺς ἀποφηναμένους τὰ περὶ θεοῦ, mentioned (as though still in its genesis) in *Orat* 40.[2]

(*c*) Προβλημάτων βιβλίον, cited by Rhodo,[3] Tatian's pupil. The author tried to prove contradictions in Holy Scripture (cf. the attempt of Apelles, § 27. 4).

(*d*) Περὶ τοῦ κατὰ τὸν σωτῆρα καταρτισμοῦ, cited by Clement,[4] who quotes from it a passage referring to the exposition of 1 Cor vii. 5 Eusebius[5] tells us that paraphrases of the Pauline Epistles were attributed to Tatian, and Tatian[6] himself mentions a writing in which he treated of the nature of demons This can scarcely be identical with the book Περὶ ζῴων.

4. It was apparently in the latest period of his life-

[1] Schwartz, TU, IV, 1, 16. 13; cf. Kalkmann, 516.
[2] Schwartz, *Idem*, 41 13 f.
[3] Eusebius, *Hist Eccl.* V, 13. 8.
[4] *Stromata*, III, 12. 81.
[5] *Hist Eccl.* IV, 29. 6
[6] *Orat.* 16, Schwartz, 17 11

time (Harnack and Moller think differently) that Tatian undertook to amalgamate the various Gospel accounts in a compendious and harmonious form, in order to avoid repetitions and contradictions. In so doing, he handled the text with great freedom, omitted both genealogies of Jesus, and arranged the pericopes in an order which suited his own purposes, the whole beginning with the first verses of the Fourth Gospel. This Diatessaron, Εὐαγγέλιον διὰ τεσσάρων,[1] written in Syriac (Greek?), passed current in the Syrian church for two centuries as the only book of the Gospels, and was used as such in the homilies of Aphraates (between 336 and 346 A.D.) and in the *Doctrina Addai*.[2] Not till the second half of the fourth century were successful efforts made to displace it by the separate Gospels. The traces of this struggle are recognizable in the Commentary (theological scholia) written by Ephraem Syrus (+378 A.D.) to the Diatessaron.[3] Theodoret of Cyrrhus was compelled to confiscate (about 450 A.D.) hundreds of copies of the work in his congregations;[4] and even in the fourteenth century it found honorable mention.[5] The Syriac Text (preserved in an Armenian translation), which is woven into the commentary of Ephraem, offers a good though inadequate clue for its reconstruction. An Arabic translation from the twelfth century, made from a Syriac copy of the ninth, has been preserved. It corresponds in all essential points with the order of Ephraem's text, and appears to be nearer to

---

[1] Eusebius, *Hist. Eccl.* IV, 29 6.
[2] Cf. 101
[3] Cf also Dionysius Bar-Salibi, Assemanni (§ 2. 8. *b*) I, 57, II, 159,
[4] *Haereticarum fabularum Compendium*, I, 20.
[5] Ebed-Jesu, *Praefat. Nomocan.*

the original than the post-Hieronymian Gospel-harmony which Victor of Capua, between 541 and 547 A D, caused to be incorporated with the Vulgate text in the *Codex Fuldensis.*

Editions: E. Ranke, *Codex Fuldensis*, Marb 1868 J. Aucher and G Moesinger, *Evangelii concordantis expositio facta a S Ephraemo*, Venet 1876. The reconstruction of the text, Zahn, FGK, I, 112-219 A Ciasca, *Tatiani evangeliorum harmoniae arabice*, Rom. 1888 [J H Hill. *The Diatessaron of Tatian*, Edinb. 1894] H. W Hogg, ANF, IX, 35-138 Literature. A Harnack, in ZKG, IV, 1881, 471-505 Theo Zahn, FGK, I, 1881 (cf Frz. Overbeck, in ThLZ, VII, 1882, 102-109); II, 1883, 286-299, GNK, II, 2, 530-536, and in NKZ, IX, 1894, 85-120 J P P Martin, in RQuH, XLIV, 1888, 5-50 J R Harris, The Diatessaron of Tatian, Lond 1890, cf A Harnack, in ThLZ, XVI, 1891, 355 f. J R Harris, Fragments of the Commentary of Ephraim Syrus upon the Diatessaron. S Hemphill, The Diatessaron of Tatian, Lond. 1888 Th Zahn, NKZ, V, 1894, 85-120; cf. ZKG, XVI, 1895, 166 f H Goussen, *Studia Theologica* (some new fragments of the Diatessaron), Lpz 1895, 62-67; cf. Th Zahn, in ThLB, XVI, 1895, 497-500

§ 38. *Miltiades*

Literature: C Otto, *Corpus Apologetarum Christianorum*, IX, 1872, 364-373 (earlier works are noted there) A Harnack, TU, I, 1882, 278-282 R Seeberg, in FGK, V, 237-240 — Fabricius, BG, 165 f. Harnack, LG, 255 f

Miltiades, the rhetorician,[1] probably a native of Asia Minor, wrote during the reigns of Antoninus Pius and Marcus Aurelius. He is mentioned by Tertullian[1] as an anti-Gnostic writer between Justin and Irenæus; and by the author of *The Little Labyrinth*,[2] as an orthodox writer between Justin and Tatian Of his **writings,**

[1] Tertullian, *Valent.* 5.   [2] Eusebius, *Hist Eccl.* V, 28. 4.

nothing has been preserved. The following are known only by their titles or subject matter: —

(a) An anti-Montanistic writing,[1] Περὶ τοῦ μὴ δεῖν προφήτην ἐν ἐκστάσει λέγειν, which is cited by the anonymous anti-Montanistic writer in Eusebius.[2]

(b) An anti-Gnostic (anti-Valentinian) writing.[3]

(c) Two books Πρὸς Ἕλληνας.

(d) Two books Πρὸς Ἰουδαίους.

(e) An Apology for Christianity (Ὑπὲρ τῆς κατὰ Χριστιανοὺς φιλοσοφίας), addressed to secular rulers. This apology may even have been presented to Antoninus Pius On the possibility of identifying it with the Apology of Pseudo-Melito (as Seeberg suggests), see below.[4] The writings mentioned under c–e were in the hands of Eusebius [5]

§ 39 Apollinaris

Literature: Routh, RS, I, 157–174 C Otto, *Corpus Apol. Christ.* IX, 1872, 479–495. A. Harnack, TU, I, 1882, 232–239, *Idem*, RE (2d edit) I, 529 — Translation: B P Pratten, ANF, VIII, 772–773 Fabricius, BG, 160–162. Richardson, BS, 113 Harnack, LG, 243–246.

Apollinaris, Bishop of Hierapolis,[6] wrote during the reign of Marcus Aurelius, not long after the formation of the Phrygian (Montanistic) sect.[7] The following **writings** are mentioned as his work: —

(a) One or several anti-Montanistic tracts, with which Serapion,[8] Bishop of Antioch, and Eusebius [9] were acquainted.[10]

[1] Cf. § 53 2 c
[2] Eusebius, *Hist Eccl.* V, 17. 1.
[3] Tertullian, *Valent* 5.
[4] § 40 7.
[5] *Hist. Eccl* V, 17. 4.
[6] Eusebius, *Chron.*, 170 A.D.
[7] Eusebius, *Hist. Eccl* IV, 27.
[8] *Idem*, V, 19. 2
[9] *Idem*, IV, 27, V, 16. 1. .
[10] Cf § 53 2. c,

(*b*) Ὁ πρὸς Ἀντωνῖνον λόγος ὑπὲρ πίστεως The title is given by Nicephorus Callistus,[1] and, according to Eusebius,[2] the writing was presented to Antoninus in the year 170 A D

(*c*) Πρὸς Ἕλληνας συγγράμματα πέντε [3] Nicephorus[1] remarks that this writing was in the form of a dialogue

(*d*) Περὶ ἀληθείας in several books, two of which were known to Eusebius [3]

(*e*) Περὶ εὐσεβείας · attested only by Photius [3]

(*f*) Περὶ τοῦ πάσχα, only mentioned in the *Chronicon Paschale*,[4] where two small fragments are given, the genuineness of which there is no reason to doubt

§ 40 Melito

Fragments: Routh, RS, I, 111-153   Pitra, SpS, I, II, III   C Otto, *Corpus apol Christ* IX, 1872. 374, 478, 497-512   Pitra, AS, II, III (cf below)   Cf Loofs, in ThLZ, IX, 1884, 407 f —
Translation B P Pratten, in ANF, VIII, 750-762
Literature P. Halloix. *Ill eccl Orient scriptorum vitae et documenta*, II, Duaci, 1636, 817-839   C Chr Woog, *de Melit Dissert* II, Lips 1744, 51   F Piper, in StKr, XI, 1838, 54-154   A Harnack, TU, I, 1882, 240-278   C Thomas, *Melito von Sardes*, Osnabr 1893, cf G Kruger, in ThLZ, XVIII, 1893, 568-571 — Fabricius, BG, 149-151. Richardson, BS, 110 f   Harnack, LG, 246-255.

1 **Melito,** Bishop of Sardis,[5] may have already been active as an author[6] when Antoninus Pius issued his edict of toleration (158 A D)   He flourished at the time when Soter became Bishop of Rome (166-167),[7] and died

---
[1] *Hist Eccl* X, 14, cf Eusebius, *Hist Eccl.* IV, 27, V, 5 1-4
[2] Eusebius, *Chron* , *Chronicon Pasch* , 169 A D.
[3] Eusebius, *Idem*, Photius, *Codex*, 14
[4] *Chronicon Pasch* , edit Dindorf, 13 f   [6] *Idem*, IV, 13 8
[5] Eusebius, *Hist Eccl* IV, 13 8, 26. 1   [7] *Idem*, IV, 21, cf IV, 26. 1.

some time before 194–195.¹ He himself² tells us that he undertook a journey to Palestine He played a great part in the ecclesiastical life of Asia Minor, and interested himself much in the controversies of the church (*e g* the Paschal, Marcionite, Montanist, see below) He was a man of prophetic gifts and of strict ascetic practice ³

2 Melito was a prolific and many-sided writer The long **list** given by Eusebius⁴ does not, according to his own statement, exhaust the number of Melito's books and tracts, and the extant titles of these works warrant the conclusion that his activity was not confined to apologetics and polemics, but extended also into the theological and didactic field His name remained famous, but his writings became unknown to following generations Tertullian made much use of them (Harnack), and the Alexandrians, Clement, Origen, and Alexander read one or more of them. A knowledge of Melito's writings is betrayed not only by Eusebius, but by Anastasius Sinaita, by the compiler of the *Chronicon Paschale*,⁵ and in the *Catenae* In the Syrian church also they did not entirely disappear.

3 The following **writings** of Melito, enumerated by Eusebius, have been lost excepting only some small **fragments** The titles, in some cases, have been handed down in uncertain form. There is no reason to suppose that Eusebius enumerated them in a fixed order

(*a*) Περὶ τοῦ πάσχα δύο (λόγοι) was known to Clement of Alexandria, who took occasion by it to write

---

¹ Polycrates, in Eusebius, V, 24. 5   ² *Idem*, IV, 26. 14
³ Polycrates, in Eusebius, *Hist Eccl* V, 24 5. Tertullian, in Jerome, *De Viris Illust* 24
⁴ Eusebius, *Hist Eccl* IV, 26 2   ⁵ Dindorf's edition, 482 ff

his own treatise on the Passover¹ Eusebius has preserved a fragment, from which it appears that this book may be referred to the proconsulate of Servilius Paulus (according to Rufinus, Sergius Paulus); that is, probably before 168 A D ²

(*b*) Περὶ πολιτείας καὶ προφητῶν:³ perhaps an anti-Montanistic treatise.

(*c*) Περὶ ἐκκλησίας.

(*d*) Περὶ κυριακῆς.

(*e*) Περὶ φύσεως ἀνθρώπου.⁴

(*f*) Περὶ πλάσεως

(*g*) and (*h*) Περὶ ὑπακοῆς πίστεως αἰσθητηρίων⁵ This title is evidently incorrect, and probably should be divided into two : Περὶ ὑπακοῆς πίστεως and Περὶ αἰσθητηρίων

(*i*) Περὶ ψυχῆς καὶ σώματος (ἢ νοός should be omitted).⁶

(*k*) Περὶ λούτρου; an interesting fragment. The same fragment which Pitra found in a Vatican Codex⁷ has been shown by J M. Mercati⁸ to exist in a Codex at Florence⁹ It is given by Pitra in his *Analecta Sacra*¹⁰ In this writing analogies to baptism are drawn from artisan and natural life, and the baptism of Jesus is compared to the dipping of sun, moon, and stars into

---

[1] Eusebius, *Hist Eccl* IV, 26. 4   Cf. VI, 13 9.

[2] Cf G Voigt, *Eine verschollene Urkunde des antimontan Streits* Lpz. 1891, 84–88 Theo. Zahn, FGK, V, 1893, 26, and the literature discussed by each.

[3] Jerome, *De Vita Prophetarum*, so also Otto, 376, No. 5.

[4] So Rufinus and Syriac   Some MSS. of Eusebius give πίστεως.

[5] Jerome gives *De Sensibus* and *De Fide*, Rufinus, *De Oboedientia Fidei* and *De Sensibus*

[6] For title, see No. 6 below.   [9] *Codex Ambros* I, 9 Supp ann 1142.

[7] *Codex Vatican. graec* 2022.   [10] *Analecta Sacra*, II, 3–5.

[8] ThQu, LXXVI, 1894, 597–600.

the ocean. It was probably directed against the Marcionites (Thomas).

(*l*) Περὶ ἀληθείας.

(*m*) Περὶ κτίσεως καὶ γενέσεως Χριστοῦ.

(*n*) Λόγος αὐτοῦ περὶ προφητείας [1] The construction of αὐτοῦ is uncertain; it is not impossible to construe it with λόγος (Otto, Harnack).

(*o*) Περὶ φιλοξενίας.

(*p*) Ἡ κλείς. A "glossary to Biblical conceptions and words, collected from the Latin Fathers" (Harnack, LG, 254) It is contained in eight manuscripts, transmitted under various titles and for the most part anonymously. It was wrongly attributed by Pitra, as *Clavis Scripturae*, to Melito [2] On the contrary, O. Rottmanner and L. Duchesne [3] have shown that the writing was dependent upon Augustine

(*q*) and (*r*) Τὰ περὶ τοῦ διαβόλου καὶ τῆς ἀποκαλύψεως Ἰωάννου [4] (perhaps Περὶ τοῦ διαβόλου and Περὶ τῆς ἀποκαλύψεως Ἰωάννου) The fragment preserved by Origen,[5] in which Absolom is made to typify the Devil (Antichrist), may belong to the former writing

(*s*) Περὶ ἐνσωμάτου θεοῦ (Origen : Περὶ τοῦ ἐνσώματον εἶναι θεόν). It is possible (?) that to this belonged the fragment from Origen,[6] preserved by Theodoret, which attempted to prove the corporeality of God Perhaps even Gennadius [7] was acquainted with the work.

---

[1] Jerome and Syriac, as *de prophetia sua*, Rufinus, *de prophetia ejus*.
[2] Cf SpS, III, 1–308, AS, II, 6–154, 585–623
[3] Rottmanner, in *Bull. Crit.* 1885, 47–51, Duchesne, *Idem*, p 196 f.
[4] Jerome, *De Diabolo, de Apocalypsi Joannis*, Rufinus, *De Diabolo; de Revelatione Joannis*
[5] *Ad Psal iii. inscrip*, edit Lommatzsch, XI, 411.
[6] *Select in Genes.*, edit. Lommatzsch, VIII, 49 f.
[7] *De Eccl dogm.* 4, edit. Oehler, in *Corpus Haereseol.* I, Berl. 1856, 337.

(*t*) Πρὸς 'Αντωνῖνον (βιβλίδιον·[1] πρὸς αὐτοκράτορα Οὐῆρον ὑπὲρ τοῦ καθ' ἡμᾶς δόγματος ἀπολογία) According to Eusebius[2] this writing was presented to Marcus Aurelius in 170 A D (*Chronicon Paschale*, 169), and no conclusive objection can be made to this date The extant fragments[3] show that Melito tried to win the favor of the Emperor to Christianity by referring to the blessing which it had brought and was still bringing to the Roman Empire, and by appealing to the example of his predecessors, of whom only Nero and Domitian had shown themselves enemies of the new religion The *Chronicon Paschale* asserts that the Apology was dependent on Justin.

(*u*) 'Εκλογαί, in six books, containing extracts from the Old Testament Scriptures collated at the request of Onesimus. The dedication, which is still extant, relates the circumstances which gave rise to the book, and contains a list of the Old Testament Scriptures made by Melito on the basis of his own inquiries in Palestine.

4. Anastasius Sinaita[4] cites some words from a writing Εἰς τὸ πάθος, which, there is no reason to doubt, was the work of Melito[5] The same Anastasius[6] gives a fragment of the third book of a writing, Περὶ σαρκώσεως Χριστοῦ, which was directed against Marcion. The objections to its genuineness brought forward on the ground of the theological views contained in the fragment are not conclusive[7]

[1] Eusebius, *Hist Eccl* IV, 13 8
[2] *Chron. ad ann* 2186 = 170.
[3] Eusebius, *Hist Eccl* IV, 26 5-11, *Chron. Pasch. ad ann*. 164-165, edit Dindorf, 483
[4] *Hodegos*, Chap. 12. Migne, PG, LXXXIX, 197
[5] Cf No. 6, below   [6] *Hodegos*, Chap 13 229
[7] See, however, Hilgenfeld, in *Allgem Lit Zeits* 1847, I, 668

5. Of the four "Melitonian" fragments[1] preserved in several manuscript *Catenae*, among the explanations on Genesis, one belonged possibly to Eusebius of Emesa,[2] while the others may very well have belonged to one (which?) of Melito's works

6 Four fragments have been preserved in Syriac, and from the complicated history of their transmission it would appear possible that they all belonged to a work of Melito Περὶ ψυχῆς καὶ σώματος καὶ εἰς τὸ πάθος,[3] which was used by Hippolytus[4] and worked into a sermon by Alexander of Alexandria.

Mai, NPB, II, 1854, 529, 540, SpR, III, 1840, 699–705 W. Cureton, *Spicilegium Syriacum*, Lond 1855, 52–54 SpS, I, 3–5, II, IX, and LVI f III, 417 P de Lagarde, *Anal Syr* Lips et Lond 1858, 189 Otto, 419–423 AS, IV, 197, 323 f, 432 Cf G Kruger, in ZwTh, XXXI, 1888, 434–448, and the literature there cited and discussed Cf § 69 a

7 The Syriac **Apology**, contained in a codex in the British Museum[5] and ascribed in its heading to Melito, cannot be identified with this writer's Apology, since the passages attested by Eusebius (and the *Chronicon Paschale*) are not to be found in it (Jacobi) Neither are there any grounds for identifying it with the Melitonian writing Περὶ ἀληθείας (Ewald holds the opposite view) The writing was addressed (see the close) to Antoninus, a name which may be understood to mean Antoninus Pius, or perhaps even Caracalla or Heliogabalus It remains possible that the Syriac scribe wrote Melito by mistake for Miltiades[6] (note, however, his

[1] Pitra, SpS, II, LXIII f Otto, 416–418 [3] See above, 3. 1. and 4.
[2] *Scholia* on Gen xxii 13 Cf Piper, 65–68. [4] *De paschate*
[5] *Cod Nitr Misc. Mus Britt nunc* 14658, *saec* VI v. VII
[6] Seeberg's view Cf § 38

intimate acquaintance with Syrian conditions), or that, since the work is composed in excellent Syriac, it may not be a translation at all (Noldeke) The Apology exhibits a plain connection with that of Aristides (whether with Justin's also, is doubtful); the idolatry of those who worship the elements and pray to many gods is contrasted with the true idea of God (truth and error in contrast).

Editions Syriac and English W Cureton, *Spicil Syr.* 1855, 41–51 (22–31)   Syriac and Latin   Otto, 423–432, 497–512   German Welte, in ThQu, XLVI, 1862, 392–410   V Grone, in BKV, 1873   P B Pratten, ANF VIII, 751–62
Literature: J. L Jacobi, in *Deutsch. Zeitschr f chr. Wissensch und chr Leben*, VII, 1856, 105–108   G H A Ewald, in GGA, 1856, ni 658   Th. Noldeke, in JprTh, XIII, 1878, 345 ff   R Seeberg, in FGK, V, 237–240

8 (*a*) The fragment of an Epistle of Melito to Eutrepius, edited by Pitra,[1] from an Armenian codex, has no connection with the bishop of Sardis.

(*b*) The name of Melito may be concealed in that of Mellitus, who is mentioned as the author of a book *De Passione S. Joannis Evangelistae* (of the fourth century?)

(*c*) In the prologue to a recension of the book *De transitu beatae Mariae* (*virginis*), the author calls himself Melito, *servus Christi, episcopus ecclesiae Sardensis* The prologue is of post-Augustinian origin.

(*d*) Melito (Milotho, Milito) is named in one manuscript as the author of a *Catena in Apocalypsin*, which was made about 1300 A.D. by an anonymous writer.[2]

---

[1] AS, IV, 16, 292
[2] Following Harnack, LG, 252–254   Cf literature cited there

§ 41. *Athenagoras*

Editions: Cf. citations preceding, § 33. P. Nannius, Paris and Lovan 1541 (*De Resurrectione*); C. Gesner, Tiguri, 1557 (*Supplicatio*); Otto, *Corpus apol* VII, 1857; E. Schwartz, in TU, IV. 2, 1891; Cf. E. Preuschen, in ThLZ, XVII, 1892, 543–546. — **Translations** A. Bieringer, in BKV, 1875; B. P. Pratten, in ANF, II, 129–162 (Plea for the Christians; Resurrection). **Literature** C. Otto, in ZhTh, XXVI, 1856, 637–644; Markel, *De Athenag libro apologetico qui* Πρεσβ π Χριστ *inscr.* Konigsb 1857. Forster, *Ueber die Glaubwurdigkeit der von Athenagoras uberlieferten kunstgeschichtlichen Notizen*, in the *Gymnas Programme* on the earliest pictures of Heia, Breslau, 1868, 29 ff. H. Diels, *Doxographi graeci*, Berol 1879, 90; G. Loesche, in JprTh, VIII, 1882, 168–178; A. Harnack, TU, I, 1–2, 175–189; Theo. Zahn, FGK, III, 60. — Fabricius, BG, 95–101; Richardson, BS, 36–38; Harnack, LG, 526–558.

1. **Athenagoras**, first called the Athenian in a late manuscript tradition (by an emendator of the Paris Codex 451 of the eleventh century), wrote during the reign of Marcus Aurelius. He may have been the same person as the Athenagoras to whom the Alexandrian Boethus[1] (after 180 A.D.) dedicated his book Περὶ τῶν παρὰ Πλάτωνι ἀπορουμένων (Zahn). The particulars about him given by the compiler who made excerpts from Philip of Side[2] [Pamphylia], are for the most part worthless, and the statement that he was the leading superintendent or teacher in the Alexandrian catechetical school may be doubted.

2. Two **works** of Athenagoras have been preserved.[3] (*a*) Πρεσβεία περὶ Χριστιανῶν (*Supplicatio, legatio pro*

---

[1] Photius, *Codex*, 154, 155
[2] Cf. Dodwell, *Dissertat in Irenaeum* 1689, App. 488 f
[3] In the *Codex Paris* 451, of 914 A.D., and numerous manuscripts dependent on it

Christianis), addressed to the Emperor Marcus Aurelius and L. Commodus, and consequently written later than 176, and previous to 180, probably in 177. The address has not been preserved complete, and the name of the author was unknown to the transcriber of the Paris Codex 451. After an introduction, in which he exposes the difference between the treatment of Christians and the justice exercised by the rulers in other cases (Chaps. 1-3), the apologist defends his fellow-believers against accusations of atheism (Chaps. 4-30), and immorality (Thyestian banquets and Oedipean nuptials; Chaps. 31-36). The work ends with a reiterated appeal to the emperors.

(*b*) The Περὶ ἀναστάσεως (*de Resurrectione*), attested by Athenagoras himself,[1] contains, after the introduction, a refutation of hostile objections to the resurrection of the body (Chaps 2-10), and a philosophical proof of it based upon the purpose of man's creation (Chaps. 12-13), his nature (Chaps. 14-17), and destiny (Chaps. 18-25). There is no reason to doubt that both writings were by the same hand. Each proclaims the Christian Platonist who, in spite of the stress he lays on the revealed character of Christianity, makes a greater use of philosophical material than Justin. Athenagoras was a writer of taste, and, compared with Justin and Tatian, he was distinguished by a clear and simple method of arrangement. He differs from the latter author, more especially in subordinating controversy to positive argument, and in not laying himself open to the reproach of an inadequate comprehension of his opponent's views. Thus the first part of his Apology

[1] *Supplicatio*, at the close of Chap. 36 in Otto's edition; and at the beginning of Chap. 37 in that of Schwartz

contains an occasional brilliant exposition of the Christian belief in God, in philosophical form, and the last part sets forth most admirably, over against silly calumnies, the endeavor of Christians after morality. Athenagoras' work on the Resurrection is distinguished more especially from that of Justin(?) by the absence of any reference to Christ's resurrection as an argument. Athenagoras displays acquaintance with classical writers, but like Tatian he mistreats the history of art (Forster). There are resemblances to Old and New Testament passages; Justin's Apology was used (there is doubt with regard to that of Aristides), but no use of Tatian's *Oratio* can be proved. Athenagoras was read but little, partly on account of his strictly philosophic attitude. It is possible (as Ebert, Bieringer, Loesche, and Harnack maintain) that Minucius Felix was acquainted with his writings, but this is not capable of proof. Methodius of Olympus cited a passage from the *Supplicatio*, naming the author [1] On the other hand, to men like the Alexandrians, his crass doctrine of the resurrection may have been offensive.

§ 42. *Theophilus*

Editions See references preceding, § 33 J. Frisius-Gesner, Tiguri, 1546 C Otto, *Corpus*, VIII, 1861 — **Translations** J Leitl, in BKV, 1872 Marcus Dods, in ANF, II, 89–121 (to Autolycus)

Literature L Paul in JclPh, CXIII, 1876, 114–116 (Text). A Harnack, *Die Zeit des Ignatius von Antiochien*, Lpz 1878, 42–44, *Idem*, TU, I, 1–2, 1882, 282–298, ZKG, XI, 1889, 1–21. C Erbes, in JpiTh, V, 1879, 464–485, 618–653, XIV, 1888, 611–632 A B. Cook, *Theophilus*, etc, II, 7, in *The Classical Review*, 1894, 246–248 Fabricius, BG, 101–106 Richardson, BS, 35 f Harnack, LG, 496–502.

[1] Edition of Bonwetsch, I, 129 f, cf Epiphanius, *Panarion*, LXIV, 20 f.; Photius, *Codex*, 234, edition of Bekker, 293

1. The three books, Θεοφίλου πρὸς Αὐτόλυκον, which are preserved in a manuscript[1] of the eleventh century and in others which depend on it, were known, possibly, to Tertullian,[2] Minucius Felix,[3] and Julius Africanus,[4] probably, also, to Novatian,[5] and certainly to Lactantius,[6] Eusebius,[7] and to the writer of the *Sacra Parallela*[8] There is confusion as to the author[9] Eusebius alone attributes the **Ad Autolycum** to Theophilus, who, according to the *Chronicon (ad annum Abrahami* 2185, 2193), is said to have been the (sixth) bishop of Antioch, from 169–177 A D If Eusebius is correct in regard to the author (the opposite position is taken by Erbes, though without sufficient reason), the statement of the Chronicle is erroneous, since the death of Marcus Aurelius (180 A D) is mentioned[10] in the third book The **author** was an Oriental, born not far from the Euphrates and the Tigris,[11] educated as a Hellenist, but possessed of Hebrew knowledge,[12] and not till manhood converted from heathenism to Christianity[13] That he wrote during the reign of Commodus appears from the fact that the death of this emperor is not mentioned in the chronological survey in the third book

2 The **three books** are mutually independent of each other The first is the record of a disquisition on the Christian doctrine of God and the resurrection, for

---

[1] *Codex Marcian* 496. *saec.* XI.   [3] Edition of Dombart, XII, N 1, 133.
[2] Cf Otto, 360   [4] Gelzer, I, 22–23
[5] Cf. *Ad Autolycum*, I, 1, Otto, 10, 3 ff, with *De Trinitate*, 2
[6] *Div Instit* I, 23.
[7] *Hist Eccl.* IV, 21 1, and following Eusebius, Jerome, *De Viris Illust* 25.
[8] Le Quien, I, 787, cf 785.   [11] *Ad Autol* II, 24.
[9] E g Gennadius, *Viri Illust* 34   [12] *Idem*, II, 12, 24, III, 19
[10] Otto, III, 27.   [13] *Idem*, I, 14

the benefit of an otherwise unknown person, Autolycus The second, prepared at the request of Autolycus, is an elaboration and amplification of the same, in that it gives a survey of the "creation, and of all other things,"[1] as they were foretold by the prophets The third is a treatise presenting the argument for Christianity and its sacred writings, drawn from their antiquity This last was possibly circulated separately[2] Original thought is wanting in the work of this author: he confined himself strictly to the arguments of his older prototypes (Justin) His language and statement seldom rise above the level of the pedantic The way in which the New Testament writings are used[3] evinces an advanced stage in the formation of the canon

3 The following writings have been lost:—

(*a*) A work, the first book of which was entitled Περὶ ἱστοριῶν, cited elsewhere by the author himself (vv. ll) The citations made by John Malalas[4] from a chronographer, Theophilus,[5] were derived, possibly, from this book,

(*b*) A Σύγγραμμα πρὸς τὴν αἵρεσιν Ἑρμογένους,[6] which, possibly, was employed by Tertullian and Hippolytus (so Harnack),

(*c*) A Λόγος κατὰ Μαρκίωνος,[6] possibly known to Irenæus (so Harnack), Tertullian, and Adamantius,[7]

(*d*) Κατηχητικὰ βιβλία,[6]

(*e*) A commentary on Proverbs, the existence of which is attested only by Jerome,[8]

[1] Otto, 78 1 [2] Lactantius, *loc. cit.*
[3] Cf citations from John (*Ad Autol.* II, 22) and Paul (*Idem*, III, 14)
[4] Edit of Dindorf, 29 4, etc [5] Zahn, FGK, II, 6
[6] Eusebius, *Hist Eccl* IV, 24 1
[7] Zahn, in ZKG, IX, 1888, 235, GNK, II, 420
[8] *Viri Illust* 25

(*f*) Jerome[1] was acquainted with a commentary on the Gospel, written by Theophilus Zahn and Hauck[2] maintain that the Gospel commentary attributed to Theophilus (which was first edited by De la Bigne, and afterwards proved by Harnack to exist in a manuscript of the seventh century at Brussels, and found by Pitra in two other manuscripts) is, in general, identical with the work mentioned by Jerome, and it was already in the hands of Commodianus. Zahn considers that he has proved it to have been the work of Theophilus of Antioch; whereas Harnack, on the contrary, defends the view that the commentary is a conglomerate from the works of the earlier Latin Fathers, composed in the West about 500 A D. (Bornemann: between 450 and 700 A D.) In its present form the work is not a unit

Editions De la Bigne, *Sacra bibliotheca* (§ 2 8. *a*), V, 1575, 169–196   C Otto, *Corpus Apol Christ.* VIII, 278–324. Theo Zahn, FGK, II, 1883, 29–85, cf A Harnack, in TU, I, 4, 1884, 164. J B Pitra, AS, II, 624–634

Literature: Theo. Zahn, FGK, II, 1883; III, 1884, 198–277; ZkWL, V, 1884, 626–628   A Harnack, in TU, I, 4, 1883, 97–175; ThLZ, XI, 1886, 404, 405   A Hauck, in ZkWL, V, 1884, 561–568 W Sanday in *Studia Biblica*, etc I, Oxf 1885, 89–101   W Bornemann, in ZKG, X, 1889, 169–252

SUPPLEMENTARY

§ 43   *The Epistle to Diognetus*

Editions: See citations preceding, § 33 and 36. H. Stephanus, Paris, 1592   C Otto, *Corpus Apol. Christ.* III, 158–211   O v Gebhardt, in *Patr Apost Opera*, I, 2, 2d edit, Lpz. 1878, 154–164

[1] *De Viris Illust* 25   *Epist* 121, 6, Vallarsi, I, 866. *Praef Comm. ad Matth*

[2] Against Hauck, see Bornemann.

F. X Funk, in *Opera Patr. Apost* I, Tubingen, 1881, 310-333 — Translations · J C Mayer, in BKV, 1869 H Kihn (see below), 155-168 Roberts and Donaldson, ANF, I, 25-30. Literature See citations preceding, § 36. C. Otto, *De Epist ad Diognet* Jena, 1852 J Donaldson (cf § 2. 4 *b*), II, 1866, 126 ff Frz Overbeck, *Ueber den pseudo-justin. Brief an Diognet* (Basel, *Universitats-Program*, 1872), in *Studien zur Geschichte der alten Kirche*, I, Chemnitz, 1875, 1-92, cf. Theo Zahn, in GGA, 1873, 106-116. A Hilgenfeld, in ZwTh, XVI, 1873, 270-286 R A Lipsius, in LCB, 1873, 1249-51 Theo Keim, in PKZ, 1873, 285-289, 309-314. A Harnack, in *Prolegomena* to von Gebhardt's edition, 1878 E B Birks, in DCB, II, 162-167 K J. Neumann, in ZKG, IV, 1881, 284-287 H Doulcet, in RQuH, XXVIII, 1880, 601-612 J Draeseke, in JprTh, VII, 1881, 213-283, 414-484 (Apelles, the author); cf F Overbeck, in ThLZ, VII, 1882, 28-33 H Kihn, *Der Ursprung des Briefs an Diognet*, Freib 1882; cf A Harnack, in ThLZ, VIII, 1883, 100-102. J A Robinson, in TSt, I, 1, 1891, 95-97 R Seeberg, in FGK. V, 240-243 G. Kruger, in ZwTh, XXXVII, 1894, 206-223 Fabricius, BG, 65 f. Richardson, BS, 3-5. Harnack, LG, 757 f.

The Strassburg codex [1] of the thirteenth or fourteenth century, which was burned in 1870, contained a writing (**Epistle**) Πρὸς Διόγνητον, which it ascribed to Justin,[2] the author of the treatise Πρὸς Ἕλληνας, which preceded it in the manuscript. The attempt to defend the attestation given by the manuscript (Otto) may be regarded as abortive, but just as little has it proved possible to make the Epistle intelligible as a product of the third century (Zahn, Harnack, and Seeberg), or of the period following Constantine (Overbeck), or as a humanistic attempt "to write a good declamation in the old style" (Donaldson, p 142). Very probably the Epistle belongs to the second century, and on internal evidence it is possible that it was written before the war

---

[1] *Codex Argent.* 9, *saec.* XIII-XIV.   [2] Cf. § 36. 3. *c*.

of Barcochba (before 135 A D) The striking resemblance between the Apology of Aristides and the Epistle has led to the assumption of an identity of authors Doulcet, Kihn, and Kruger). On this supposition we may recognize in the person addressed the teacher of Marcus Aurelius. The author's purpose was to answer certain precisely formulated questions raised by Diognetus as to the character and essence of the Christian worship of God and love of one's neighbor, and to remove his doubts as to why Christianity had come into the world now for the first time. After a superficial treatment of Greek idolatry (Chap 2) and of the perverted form in which the Jews worship the one God Chaps 3, 4), there follows a touching description of Christian belief and of Christian practice, which is everywhere interwoven with reminiscences of Pauline and Johannine thoughts The two final chapters (11, 12) do not belong to the Epistle, but were added later by another hand.

§ 44 *Hermias*

Editions · See citations preceding, § 33 J Oporinus, Basil, 553, 402–406 W F Wenzel, Lugd Bat 1840 C Otto, *Corpus Apol Christ* IX, 1872, 1–31 , cf XI–LI H Diels, *Doxographi Graeci*, Berl 1879. 649–656 , cf 259–263 — Translations J Leitl, in BKV, 1873 Fabricius, BG, 114–116 (119) Harnack, LG, 782 f

A short treatise entitled Ἑρμείου φιλοσόφου διασυρμὸς τῶν ἔξω φιλοσόφων has been preserved in thirteen manuscripts[1] (some of them worthless, however) In it the contradictory statements of the philosophers as to the human soul, God, the world, and, more especially, the ultimate principles of things, are satirized with cheap

[1] *Codex Patmens.* 202 σβ', *saec.* X , *Codex Monac.* 512, *saec* XV *al*

but amusing wit It is impossible to make any positive statement as to the **date of composition**, since the writing is not mentioned in the works of Christian antiquity. But the supposition that it was written in the second century is not contradicted either by the manuscript transmission,[1] by the high probability that in one place, at least,[2] use was made of the *Cohortatio ad Gentiles*,[3] or, finally, by the general character of the little treatise, the banal polemic of which is not necessarily out of place in the work of a Christian sophist. It must remain an open question whether its composition was occasioned by the appearance or circulation (though in a form different from that attacked in the *Cohortatio*) of the *Placita* of Pseudo-Plutarch In any case it is not made any more intelligible by being transferred to a later century, even the fifth or sixth (thus Menzel, Diels, and Harnack).

§ 45. *Minucius Felix*

Editions: F Sabaeus-Brixianus, Rom. 1543 (as 8th book of Arnobius) F Balduinus, Heidelberg, 1560 (first separate edition) Migne, PL, III, 239-376 C Halmius, in CSE, II, Vindob. 1867, cf H Usener, in JclPh, XCIX, 1869, 393-416 J. J Cornelissen, Lugd Bat 1882 Aem Baehrens, Lpz 1886

Translations. A Bieringer, in BKV, 1871 B Dombart, Erlangen, 1881 (2d edit, with reprint of Halmius' text). Robert E. Wallis, in ANF, IV, 173-198 (*Octavius*)

Literature · A Ebert, *Tertullians Verhaltniss zu Minucius Felix*, in ASGW, V, 1870 (1868), 319-386, and his *Allgem. Geschichte* (§ 2 5), 1889, 25-32. W Hartel, in *Zeitschr. f d. osterr. Gymn* XX, 1869, 348-368 E. Behr, *Der Octavius des Minucius Felix in*

---

[1] Cf *Codex Ottob* 112 (and 191)

[2] Cf. § 2 with *Cohortatio*, 7

[3] See above, § 36 3 *b*. On Herm 11, cf. with *Cohortatio*, 31. See Pseudo-Plutarch, *Placita*, I, 7 4, Diels, 299.

seinem Verhaltnisse zu Ciceros Buchern de natura deorum, Gera,
1870   Theo Keim, Celsus wahres Wort, Zurich, 1873, 151-168
H. Dessau, in Hermes, XV, 1880, 471-474   P de Félice, Blois,
1880, cf K J Neumann, in ThLZ, VI, 1881, 421-424   V Schultze,
in JprTh, VII, 1881, 485-506, cf. W Moller, Idem, 757-759
G. Salmon, in DCB, III, 920-924   G. Loesche, in JprTh, VIII,
1882, 168-178   P Schwenke, Idem, IX, 1883, 263-294   Reck, in
ThQu, LXVIII, 1886, 64-114   L. Massebieau, in Rev de l'hist des
relig XV, 1887, 316-346. F Wilhelm, in Breslau Philol Abhandlungen, Breslau (Vratisl), 1887, cf Harnack, in ThLZ, XI, 1887, 422,
423. K. J Neumann, Der romische Staat und die allgem. Kirche,
I, Lpz 1889, 241-245   B Seiller, De sermone Minuciano, August.
Vindel. 1893   J Vahlen, Quaestiones Minucianae, Ind Lect.
Berol 1894 (criticism of the text)   M Schanz, in RhM, L, 1895,
114-136   W. Teuffel (§ 2 5) II, 927-931, 5th edit   Schoenemann,
BPL, 58-77   Richardson, BS, 47-50. Harnack, LG, 647.

1. In a Parisian codex[1] of the ninth century and in a copy therefrom,[2] possibly of the sixteenth, there is preserved in Latin a discussion as to the worth or worthlessness of Christianity. It is written in the form of a dialogue (held at Ostia) between the heathen Cæcilius and the Christian Octavius, in which **Minucius Felix,** a Roman advocate (concerning whom further information is wanting) plays the part of umpire. After an introduction, in which the situation is graphically depicted (Chaps. 1-4), there follows the attack of Cæcilius (Chaps. 5-13), who, from the standpoint of the Academic, rejects the theoretical bases of Christianity, and, from that of the conservative politician and moralist, the practical piety and conduct of Christians. After some digressions (Chaps. 14, 15), Octavius replies (Chaps. 16-38), following up his opponent point by point, and theoretically defending a Christianized stoi-

[1] Codex Paris. 1661, saec. IX.   [2] Codex Dijon. 6851.

cism, while warmly returning his adversary's reproaches. At the close, Cæcilius confesses himself vanquished. The dialogue, which is called **Octavius** from the name of the victor, is excellently arranged, its train of thought is everywhere clear, while much taste is shown in its execution. The whole is an admirable specimen of the manner in which an educated Roman was able to expound the new religion.

2 The book was written in unmistakable [1] dependence upon Cicero's dialogue, *De Natura Deorum*, though the author's ability to think and write independently (note particularly the latter portion) cannot be denied. He was acquainted also with other writings of Cicero, and with other Latin classics, at first hand, though he may not have read any Greek authors (Plato). Similarity to the New Testament Scriptures is restricted to current phrases. A knowledge of Justin's Apology [2] may be assumed, though relationship to the works of Aristides, Athenagoras, and Theophilus consists in part in generalities, and is explicable in part without the assumption of any dependence. It cannot be proved that the polemic of Cæcilius was patterned after that of Celsus, as Keim holds, but, on the other hand, use may have been made of rhetorical expressions of M. Cornelius Fronto of Cirta [3] (died about 170 A.D.).

3. The date of **composition** is disputed. Even the *terminus ad quem* cannot be fixed so long as there is any doubt as to the authenticity of the treatise, *Quod Idola Dii non sunt* [4] (attributed to Cyprian), in which

---
[1] See, however, Wilhelm.
[2] Cf. especially, Chap. 29, 6–8, with Justin's *Apology*, I, 55.
[3] Cf. Chap 9, 15; 31, 2.
[4] Cf § 86. 3 n.

excerpts were made from the *Octavius* Lactantius[1] places Minucius before Tertullian, but Jerome[2] reverses the order. The literary relationship between the *Octavius* and Tertullian's *Apologeticus* is explained variously, but nothing appears to favor the assumption of the dependence of Minucius upon Tertullian (against the view of Massebieau), little can be said in favor of a common source (against the view of Wilhelm), and very much can be adduced pointing to the dependence of Tertullian upon Minucius (so Ebert, Schwenke, and Reck) The character of the accusations made by the heathen, and the situation of the Christians with regard to the state and society,[3] is easily intelligible in the second century, but not at all in the time of the Syrian emperors, and scarcely so under Philip the Arabian (Neumann) The way in which Fronto is mentioned, and the victory over the Parthians in 162-3 A.D.,[4] spoken of as though it were an occurrence in the near past (reading of the manuscript), apparently makes the assumption almost certain that the dialogue was written during the reign of Marcus Aurelius. Schanz, indeed, places it before 161 A D The inscription found at Cirta, dated 210 A D, and engraved by a certain M Cæcilius Natalis,[5] may have been the work of a son of the participant in the dialogue, whose full name is unknown [6]

4 Jerome[7] was acquainted with a writing alleged to have been written by Minucius Felix, entitled *De Fato vel Contra Mathematicos*, but he had doubts as to its

---

[1] *Div. Inst.* V, 1. 22-23, cf. also I, 11. 55.
[2] *De Viris Illust.* 58, cf. 53, see also *Epist.* 70. 5.
[3] Cf *e g* 28, 3
[4] Chap 7, 4.
[5] Cf. *Corpus Inscript Latin* VIII, 6996.
[6] Cf, however, the conjecture of Baehrens on 1, 5.
[7] *De Viris Illust* 58, cf. *Epist.* 70, 5.

genuineness Presumably it was a forgery, suggested by the statement made in the *Octavius*,[1] that the author intended to write more at length concerning Fate, in another place

[1] 36, 2

CHAPTER II

ANTI-HERETICAL LITERATURE

Cf the literature cited before § 22, and the writings mentioned at §§ 36. 2 a, d 1, 38 b, and 40 3 k.

§ 46 *Agrippa Castor*

Routh, RS, I, 85-90 — Fabricius, BG, 155 f Harnack, LG, 114 f

Eusebius[1] had read a work by **Agrippa Castor**, entitled Ἔλεγχος κατὰ Βασιλείδου, a fragment of which he gives[2]

§ 47. *Rhodo*

Routh, RS, I, 437-446. B P Pratten, in ANF, VIII, 766 H Voigt, *Eine verschollene Urkunde* (§ 40 3. a), 224-233 — Fabricius, BG, 164. Harnack, LG, 599

Rhodo,[3] of Asia Minor, was a disciple of Tatian at Rome. Eusebius mentions three of his **writings**, two of which he had read : —

(a) A work, dedicated to Callistio, and directed against Marcion, his school, and Apelles. The two interesting fragments preserved by Eusebius treat of the divisions among the Marcionites, and of a controversy between Rhodo and Apelles which is very characteristic of the contrast between apologetic and Gnostic theology.

[1] *Hist. Eccl.* IV, 7. 6 f.
[2] Cf. Jerome, *De Viris Illust.* 21, and Theodoret, *Haer fab.* I, 4
[3] Eusebius, *Hist. Eccl* V, 13

(b) Ὑπόμνημα εἰς τὴν ἐξαήμερον.
(c) A writing directed against Tatian's *Problemata*.

Jerome[1] asserts, without reason, that Rhodo was the anonymous anti-Montanistic writer cited by Eusebius[2] Voigt attempts to prove that Rhodo was the author of the anti-Montanistic source used by Epiphanius.[3]

§ 48 *Musanus*

Theo Zahn, FGK. I, 287, GNK, II, 2, 438. — Fabricius, BG, 164 f Harnack, LG, 760

According to Eusebius,[4] **Musanus**, a contemporary (and fellow-countryman?) of Apollinaris, Melito, Modestus, and Irenæus,[5] wrote a work against the Encratites, which no one besides Eusebius appears to have seen.[6]

§ 49 *Philip of Gortyna*

Fabricius, BG, 168. Harnack, LG, 237.

Philip, Bishop of Gortyna, in Crete, wrote, in the time of Marcus Aurelius (or Commodus?), a book against Marcion, of which Eusebius[7] alone appears to have possessed any independent knowledge.[8]

§ 50 *Modestus*

Fabricius, BG, 165 Harnack, LG, 759.

According to Eusebius,[9] a certain **Modestus**, a contemporary of Philip and Irenæus, wrote a book against Marcion.[10]

---

[1] *De Viris Illust* 37, cf. 39.
[2] *Hist Eccl* V, 16
[5] *Idem*, IV, 21 Otherwise *Chron. ad ann. Abrahami* 2220. Sever. XI.
[6] Cf Jerome, *De Viris Illust.* 31, and Theodoret, *Haer. fab.* I, 21.
[7] *Hist Eccl.* IV, 25, cf. 21 and 23. 5
[8] Jerome, *De Viris Illust* 30
[3] *Panarion*, XLVIII, 2–13.
[4] *Eccl. Hist.* IV, 28.
[9] *Hist. Eccl.* IV, 25, cf. 21.
[10] Jerome, *De Viris Illust.* 32.

§ 51 Hegesippus

Routh, RS, I, 205-284   B P Pratten, in ANF, VIII, 762-765
A Hilgenfeld, in ZwTh, XIX, 1876. 177-229   Theo Zahn, in ZKG,
II, 1878, 288-291, and ThLB, XIV, 1893, 495-497   C Weizsacker,
in RE, V, 695-700   C de Boor, in TU, V, 2, 1889, 165-184
Ph Meyer, in ZKG, XI, 1889, 155-158   Fiz Overbeck, *Ueber die
Anfange der Kirchengeschichtsschreibung*   Basel, 1892, 6-13, 17-22
E Biatke, in ThLB, XV, 1894, 65-67 — Fabricius, BG, 158-160
Richardson, BS, III f   Harnack, LG, 483-485

1. **Hegesippus**, an Oriental, probably a Jew, and at all events well acquainted with Syriac and Hebrew, stopped[1] in Corinth and in Rome, while travelling in the West, in the time of the Bishop Anicetus, 154 (156)-166 (167) A D. According to his own statement,[2] he was still living at the time of Eleutherus, Bishop of Rome, 174 (175)-189 A D   The statement of the *Chronicon Paschale*,[3] that he died during the reign of Commodus (180-192 A D) is perhaps a mere combination of the accounts given by Eusebius

2   Hegesippus wrote a work, probably entitled Ὑπομνήματα,[4] which consisted of five books from which Eusebius[5] has given some extensive **fragments**   The one conjecture, that this work was a sort of church history, is as untenable[6] as the other, that Hegesippus intended to give statistics of his time, or an account of his travels   The fragments make it appear quite likely that Hegesippus' purpose was to give the true tradition of the apostolic preaching in its simplest form,[7] in opposi-

---
[1] Eusebius, *Hist Eccl* IV, 22   [2] *Idem*, § 3.
[3] Edition of Dindorf, 490
[4] Eusebius, *Hist Eccl.* IV, 22 1, cf II 23 4.
[5] *Idem*, II, 23   III, 11, 16, 20, 32   IV, 8, **22.**
[6] Cf Weizsacker and Overbeck
[7] Eusebius, *Hist Eccl* IV, 8, 2

tion to the doctrine of Gnosis. The historical sections introduced into the work were also meant to serve the purpose of this demonstration. The fragments give no occasion for the assumption that Hegesippus either belonged to, or was closely connected with, a Jewish-Christian sect; they rather show him to have been a forerunner of Irenæus. Eusebius[1] is almost the sole witness to his work. Besides Eusebius, only Philippus of Side[2] and Stephanus Gobarus[3] are to be so considered, although we need not suppose that even they had seen the complete work. On the possibility that the entire writings of Hegesippus were extant in the sixteenth century, see the remarks of Zahn, Meyer, and Bratke.

§ 52 *Irenæus*

Editions. D. Erasmus, Basel, 1526, and after (Latin). N. Gallasius, Genev. 1570 (contains also the Greek fragments). F. Feuardentius, Paris, 1576, and later. J. E. Grabe, Oxon 1702. R. Massuet, Paris, 1712, 34. A. Stieren, 2 vols Lips 1848-53. Migne, PG, VII, 433-1322. W. W. Harvey, 2 vols Camb 1857, cf *Monumenta syriaca*, edit G. Moesinger, II, 8 f (Syriac), 10 f (Latin text). Pitra, AS, II, 188-217. — **Translations**. H. Hayd, 2 vols in BKV, 1872-73. Roberts and Donaldson, ANF, I, 315-578 (Against Heresies, and Fragments). J. Keble, in LFC, XLII, Oxf 1872 (Extant Works).

Literature. A. Stieren, in Ersch and Gruber's *Allgem Enzyklop*, etc., 2d section, 23d part, Lpz 1844, 357-386. H. Ziegler, *Irenäus der Bischof von Lyon*, Berl 1871. R. A. Lipsius, in HZ, XXVIII, 1872, 241-295, and in DCB, II, 252-279. C. Leimbach, in *Zeitsch. f. Luth. Theol und Kirche*, XXXIV, 1873, 614-629. O. v Gebhardt, in ZhTh, XLV, 1875, 368-370. Theo Zahn, in ZKG, II, 1878, 288-291; RE, VII, 129-240; FGK, IV, 249-283; ThLB, XIV, 1893, 495-497. F. Loofs, *Irenaushandschriften*, Lpz. 1888. Ph.

[1] Jerome, *De Viris Illust.* 22
[2] Cf De Boor, 169.   [3] Cf Photius, *Codex*, 232, Bekker, 288.

IRENÆUS

Meyer, in ZKG, XI, 1889, 155-158 A Papadopulos-Kerameus, 'Ανάλεκτα Ἱεροσολυμιτικῆς Σταχυολογίας I, Petersb 1891, 387-389, cf J Haussleiter, in ZKG, XIV, 1893-94, 69-73. Fabricius, BG, 75-87 Richardson, BS, 26-29 Preuschen, in Harnack's LG, 263-288.

1 **Irenæus** was born in Asia Minor, at a date that can scarcely be fixed earlier than 120 A.D, and certainly not later than 130 [1] According to his own statement, he was a disciple of Polycarp (died 155) and of other presbyters, "who had seen John, the disciple of the Lord" [2] We are credibly informed that he was in Rome in 155 [3] At the time of the persecution of the Christians in Lyons and Vienne (177 A D), he was a presbyter in Lyons Having been commissioned by the Confessors, he journeyed to Rome to see Bishop Eleutherus upon matters relating to the Montanists After his return he became bishop, succeeding Pothinus, who had perished in the persecution. In this capacity he wrote to Victor, Bishop of Rome (that is, after 189 A.D.), in connection with the controversies in regard to the date of Easter The date of his death is unknown: the statement that he died a martyr's death originated in the fifth century.[4]

2. Irenæus never devoted himself to a scholastic pursuit of heathen or Christian philosophy, and he felt that he was not a born author [5] Although, in his position

---

[1] Zahn, 115, Leimbach, 126, v Gebhardt, 126-130, Lipsius, 130 A D
[2] *Adv Haer* II, 22. 5, Stieren's text Cf also III, 3, 4, V, 5. 1, 30 1; 33 3, 36 2, and Eusebius, *Hist Eccl* V, 20.
[3] Supplement of Martyrdom of Polycarp in *Codex Mosqu*
[4] Jerome, *Comm in Isa* 64 (410 A D), but not yet in *De Viris Illust.* 35 (392 A D) Pseudo-Justin, *Quaest et Respon* 115, Otto, 188 Gregory of Tours, *Hist Francorum*, I, 29 (27)
[5] I, *Praef*

as bishop, occasion was not wanting for his taking up the pen, he himself disclaims all readiness in expressing himself[1] His principal work was his book against the heretics, under the title Ἔλεγχος καὶ ἀνατροπὴ τῆς ψευδωνύμου γνώσεως.[2] The shortened title, πρὸς αἱρέσεις, is given by Cyril of Jerusalem,[3] **Adversus Haereses**, by Jerome[4] Numerous and extensive fragments of the original have been preserved by Hippolytus, Eusebius, Epiphanius, and others On the possibility that the original was extant as late as the sixteenth century, see Zahn The work is extant as a whole only in a Latin translation (in nineteen manuscripts of very varying value · Loofs), which probably was known to Tertullian. The slavish fidelity of this version compensates to a certain degree for the loss of the original text. It is uncertain whether the fragments preserved in Syriac[5] justify the conclusion that there was a complete Syriac version made. The work was written in Gaul when Eleutherus was bishop of Rome,[6] that is, between 174 (175) and 189 A D, but probably not till after 180 A D. The author's original intention was to expose (ἔλεγχος) in two books, to a friend unnamed, the errors of the heretics (especially those of the Valentinians), and to refute them (ἀνατροπή) At the close of the second book[7] a still more elaborate refutation, based on Holy Scripture, appeared desirable, to which he devoted a third (doctrine of the Evangelists and Apostles), then

---

[1] I, *Praef*
[2] II, *Praef*, IV, *Praef* 1 and 12. 4, V, *Praef*. Cf. Eusebius, *Hist. Eccl* V, 7 1
[3] *Catech* 16, 6.
[4] *De Viris Illust* 35
[5] Harvey, II, 431-453
[6] *Adv Haer* III, 3. 3
[7] *Idem*, II, 35. 4

a fourth (discourses of Jesus), and finally a fifth book. The last was meant to give, besides the discourses of Jesus, an explanation of the true doctrine of Paul in opposition to the misrepresentations of heretics, but in point of fact it pursued entirely different trains of thought (resurrection of the flesh; chiliastic hopes) Consequently the book as a whole lacks a satisfactory conclusion In his portrayal of the erroneous doctrines of the Valentinians, Irenæus may have relied upon personal acquaintance with disciples of Valentinus and upon knowledge of his opponents' writings. He was also acquainted with earlier controversial writings against the heretics, such as the two books of Justin and the writings of Hegesippus [1] He took his materials for positive proof in the first place from the Holy Scriptures, the New Testament taking its place as of equal authority with the Old Associated therewith was an appeal to the uncorrupted apostolic tradition which alone ensured a correct understanding of Scripture [2] He himself acknowledged his indebtedness to "presbyters" of Asia Minor for many direct communications of apostolic doctrine [3] He was acquainted with the work of Papias,[4] and had read Ignatius' Epistle to the Romans,[5] Polycarp's Epistle to the Philippians,[6] and Justin's *Syntagma* against Marcion,[7] and his first Apology.[8] His work was much used both in the West and in the East,[9] and remained the classic anti-heretical writing. Tertullian

---

[1] IV, *Praef*. Cf IV, 6. 2
[2] Especially III, 2 and 3.
[3] Cf. § 52. 1, above.
[4] V, 33. 3 f.
[5] V, 28. 4.
[6] III, 3. 4
[7] IV, 6 2; V, 26 2
[8] II, 30. 5 (*Apol*. I, 22); II, 32. 1 (15); III, 2. 3 (12); III, 4 (60); IV, 37. 6 (43), V, 3. 2 (19).
[9] Cf. Preuschen, 266 f.

copied the first book in his treatise against the Valentinians[1]

3 The **remaining writings** of Irenæus have been lost. The following are known by title or from fragments: —

(*a*) Περὶ μοναρχίας ἢ περὶ τοῦ μὴ εἶναι τὸν θεὸν ποιητὴν κακῶν ἐπιστολή, which was addressed to the Roman presbyter Florinus,[2] who was inclined toward Valentinian errors Eusebius[3] has preserved a fragment which is important on account of its historical statements[4] On the possibility that Philaster[5] had knowledge of this writing, see remarks of Theo Zahn[6]

(*b*) Περὶ ὀγδοάδος σπούδασμα was directed against this same Florinus after his rupture with the church. A fragment, which formed the conclusion, is preserved by Eusebius,[7] and possibly a Greek fragment is extant.[8]

(*c*) Περὶ σχίσματος ἐπιστολή, addressed to the Roman Blastus,[9] in the Easter controversy. Blastus was a Quartodeciman[10]

(*d*) Πρὸς Βίκτωρα ἐπιστολή,[11] addressed to the Roman bishop Victor (189–198/99 A D), warning him against taking extreme measures in the Easter controversy. A

---

[1] Cf *Opera* of Tertullian, J. S. Semler's edit. V, 1773, 300–351, Oehler, III, 658–681.
[2] Eusebius, *Hist Eccl* V, 20. 1 Cf. Harnack, LG, 593 f.
[3] *Idem*, 4–8.
[4] In Armenian, AS, II, 200 f
[5] Philaster, *De Haer* 79 Migne, PL, XII, 1190. Cf. Augustine, *De Haer* 67 Migne, PL, XLII, 42.
[6] Zahn, FGK, IV, 306.
[7] *Hist. Eccl* V, 20. 2.
[8] *Frag Graec.* VIII, Harvey, II, 479.
[9] Eusebius, *Hist.* V, 20. 1. Cf. 15. Harnack, LG, 594 f.
[10] Pseudo-Tertullian, 22.
[11] Maximus Confes. *De Quaestione Paschae epistola Hieron* 35: ὁ περὶ τοῦ πάσχα λόγος. Pseudo-Justin, *Quaest.* etc. Otto, 188 (?).

further extract is given by Maximus Confessor,[1] and a Syriac fragment by Harvey [2] Preuschen takes another view.[3]

(*e*) Another letter relating to the Easter controversy [4] must have been sent by Irenæus to an Alexandrian (bishop?)

(*f*) and (*g*) Eusebius [5] was acquainted with an apologetic writing, Πρὸς Ἕλληνας λόγος περὶ ἐπιστήμης, and an exposition of the rule of faith, λόγος πρὸς Μαρκιανὸν εἰς ἐπίδειξιν τοῦ ἀποστολικοῦ κηρύγματος.

(*h*) Eusebius [6] mentions a Βιβλίον διαλέξεων διαφόρων That this writing contained Sermons seems to be proved by the fragments in the *Sacra Parallela* [7] and in a Catena [8]

(*i*) Some fragments of his Λόγοι πρὸς Δημήτριον διάκονον Βιαίνης περὶ πίστεως, attested by Maximus Confessor,[9] have been preserved [10]

(*k*) According to the heading of a Syriac fragment,[11] Irenæus wrote a Commentary on the Song of Songs in several parts.

(*l*) A book, Περὶ τῆς ἁγίας τριάδος, has been ascribed to Irenæus, but probably only by mistake [12]

(*m*) Irenæus intended to write a special treatise

[1] *Sermo* VII, *De Eleemos* Combefis II, 554 *Frag. Graec*. IV, Harvey Cf also AS, II, 197, N 3
[2] *Syr Frag* XXVIII, Harvey Cf. AS, IV, 27, 300.
[3] Preuschen, LG, 593 f Cf Theo Zahn, FGK, IV, 283-308
[4] Cf *Frag Syr* XXVII, Harvey.
[5] *Hist Eccl* V, 26
[6] *Hist* V, 26. Cf Jerome, *De Viris Illust*. 35.
[7] Harvey, *Frag Graec*. XI.
[8] Harvey, *Frag* XLI. [9] Combefis. II, 72
[10] Harvey, *Frag Graec* V, *Lat* VI; AS, II, 202.
[11] Harvey, *Frag. Syr* XXVI
[12] *Sac. Parallela*, *Codex Coisl* 276 f., 138 a.

against Marcion,¹ but it is not known whether he executed his plan²

4. The origin of the four fragments³ published by Pfaff as the work of Irenæus is uncertain While the third might have been by Irenæus (Zahn), the supposition that he wrote the second is excluded by the fact that the Epistle to the Hebrews is cited as Pauline⁴ It is not impossible that all four fragments belong to the second century, though Funk⁵ defends the view that the second fragment was written after 400 A.D.⁶

Ch M Pfaff in the *Giornale de Letterati d'Italia*, XVI, 1714, 228–245, and in *Syntagma dissert. theol* 1720, 573 f A Stieren, *Opera Irenaei*, II, 381–528. Theo Zahn, FGK, III, 1884, 280 f.; IV, 1891, 285, 4. — Harnack, LG, 760 f.

§ 53. *Montanists and Anti-Montanists*

Routh, RS, I, 465–485, II, 183–217. G. N Bonwetsch, *Die Geschichte des Montanismus*, Erlangen, 1881, 197–200. Theo Zahn, *Die Chronologie des Montanismus*, in FGK, V, 1–57 *passim*. — Fabricius, BG, 164, 180 f Harnack, LG, 238–243.

1 Our knowledge of **Montanistic** writings is limited to the following. In the Decretal of Gelasius,⁷ certain *Opuscula Montani, Priscillae et Maximillae* were interdicted By these were meant, possibly, "Oracular Sayings" such as have been preserved singly by various writers, *e.g* Tertullian, Eusebius, Epiphanius, and Didymus⁸ It is possible that the Montanist Asterius Ur-

[1] I, 27. 4, III, 12 12, edit. of Stieren.
[2] Cf Eusebius, *Hist* IV, 25, and Theodoret, *Haer. fab* I, 25. Cf. (*g*) above.
[3] Harvey, *Frag*. XXXV–XXXVIII.
[4] Cf. Quotation from Irenæus by Stephanus Gobarus (Photius, *Codex*, 232. Bekker's edit. 291).
[5] ThQu, LXXVI, 1894, 702 f.
[6] See also his edition of the *Didache* (XIV).
[7] VI, 43.   [8] Cf. Bonwetsch, and LG, 238 f.

banus¹ prepared a collection of such oracles. Themison,² the Montanist, wrote a catholic epistle after the manner of the Apostles³ The writing of Miltiades against the Montanists called forth a rejoinder.⁴

2. Not much is known, either, concerning anti-Montanistic writings.

(*a*) Eusebius⁵ preserved nine fragments — some of them extensive — from the work of a man (*Anonymus Eusebianus*) who wrote thirteen or fourteen years after the death of Maximilla (197 A.D.), but whose identity cannot be established. Jerome⁶ conjectured that the author was Rhodo; Rufinus, that he was Apollinaris of Hierapolis.

(*b*) Eusebius⁷ has preserved six fragments, and gives certain notes from a work of Apollonius, who wrote forty years after the appearance of Montanus (197?). According to Jerome,⁸ Tertullian directed the seventh book of his work Περὶ ἐκστάσεως ⁹ against this Apollonius.

(*c*) Concerning the anti-Montanistic writings of Miltiades and Apollinaris, see below.¹⁰

(*d*) According to a remark by Prædestinatus,¹¹ which cannot now be further verified, Soter, Bishop of Rome,¹² is said to have written against the Montanists, and Ter-

---

[1] Anti-Montanist, in Eusebius, *Hist* V, 16–17, ANF, VII, 335–337.
[2] Anti-Montanist, in Eusebius, V, 16–17.
[3] Apollonius, in Eusebius, *Hist.* V, 18. 5.
[4] Anti-Montanist, in Eusebius, *Hist.* V, 17. 1, cf. also Jerome, *Ep* 41 (133. 4).
[5] Eusebius, *Hist. Eccl.* V, 16–17.
[6] Jerome, 39, cf. 37, Eusebius, *Hist.*, *loc cit*
[7] Eusebius, *Hist* V, 18
[8] *De Viris Illust* 40.
[9] Cf. § 85. 10. *a*.
[10] Cf § 38. *a*; 39. *a*.
[11] 26.
[12] § 54.

tullian is said to have opposed him as he did Apollonius.

(*e*) The *Alogi*, so called by Epiphanius, also wrote against the Montanists and the Gnostics, and he made extracts from their writings in his *Panarion*.[1]

(*f*) Epiphanius[2] made use of an anonymous anti-Montanistic writing Among the various hypotheses[3] as to its author, the best founded is that of Voigt, who claims the book for Rhodo.[4] It is possible that Epiphanius made use of still another ancient source.[5]

(*g*) Didymus[6] made use of an ancient writing in opposition to Patripassian Monarchianism, which is attributed by Voigt to Hippolytus (περὶ χαρισμάτων), and by Harnack to Clement (περὶ προφητείας).

[1] Cf *Haer*. II
[2] *Panarion*, XLVIII, 2-13
[3] Bonwetsch, Hippolytus, Hilgenfeld, Apollonius; Lipsius, the anonymous writer mentioned by Eusebius.
[4] Cf. § 47
[5] *Haer* XLIX, 1.
[6] *Trinitat* III, 41; Cf. II, 15, III, 18, 19, 23, 38.

CHAPTER III

EPISCOPAL AND SYNODAL WRITINGS

§ 54. *The Roman Bishops*

C. P. Caspari, *Ungedruckte Quellen* (§ 18), pp. 31-35.
A. Harnack, *Der pseudocyprianische Traktat de aleatoribus*, in TU, V, 1, 1888. P de Lagarde, *Septuagintastudien*, in *Abhandlungen der kon. Gesellschaft der Wissenschaften zu Gottingen*. XXXVII, 1891, 85 —Fabricius, BG, 162 Harnack, LG, 589 f , 591 f., 595 f.

Among the Roman bishops of the first century, only Victor attempted authorship **Soter** (166/167-174 or 175 A.D.)[1] was probably the author of the writing mentioned by Dionysius[2] as sent from the Roman congregation to the Corinthians. **Eleutherus** (175-189 A D.) was author of the pacific epistles addressed to Montanistic congregations, which Tertullian[3] mentions. Of **Victor**, (188-99), an African, Jerome[4] observes that, with Apollonius,[5] and before Tertullian, he was the first Latin writer of Christendom. Eusebius was acquainted with a letter of the Roman congregation in the Paschal controversy, which is said to have exhibited Victor's characteristics.[6] The writing in question was a circular letter (with which the writing of Victor mentioned by Polycrates[7] probably was identical; Caspari holds a different view), and the

---

[1] Cf. § 53. 2. *d.*
[2] In Eusebius, *Hist.* IV, 23 11.
[3] *Adv. Praxean*, 1
[4] *De Viris Illust*. 53.
[5] § 105 6
[6] Eusebius, *Hist. Eccl.* V, 23. 3 (2)
[7] Eusebius, *Hist Eccl.* V, 24. 8.

Epistle by which Victor excluded the Asiatic churches from communion was also a circular letter. Even in the time of Jerome, certain *mediocria de religione volumina*, written by Victor, are said to have been extant[1] Harnack is inclined to recognize in him the author of the pseudo-Cyprianic tractate *De Aleatoribus*,[2] and Lagarde considers it possible that the fragment of a Latin apology in the *Codex Fuldensis* of Tertullian's *Apologeticus*,[3] was by him.

§ 55 *Dionysius of Corinth*

Routh, RS. I, 177-201 — Fabricius, BG, 162 f Richardson, BS, 112 Harnack, LG, 235 f

Dionysius, bishop of Corinth, a contemporary of Soter of Rome, wrote a number of **Epistles** to various churches. They were early collected, perhaps by himself, and Eusebius,[4] who had read them, gives a detailed account of them. They were as follows: (1) To the Lacedæmonians,[5] (2) to the Athenians,[6] (3) to the Nicomedians,[7] (4) to the church of Gortyna and the other churches in Crete,[8] (5) to the church of Amastris and the remaining churches of Pontus,[9] (6) to the Cnossians,[10] and to the Romans[11] The Epistle to Chrysophora[12] appears to have stood apart from this collection. Eusebius gives four small pieces

---

[1] *Chron. ad ann.* 2209 *Abr Pert.* I = 193; cf also Jerome, *De Viris Illust* 34.
[2] § 86. 6. *c.*
[3] § 85. 5 *a.*
[4] Eusebius, *Hist Eccl* IV, 23.
[5] *Idem*, § 2.
[6] *Idem*, § 2.
[7] *Idem*, § 4.
[8] *Idem*, § 5.
[9] *Idem*, § 6.
[10] *Idem*, §§ 7-8.
[11] *Idem*, §§ 9-12.
[12] *Idem*, § 13

from the Epistle to the Romans,[1] which was a letter of thanks. The bishops (?) of Pontus, Bacchylides, and Elpistus,[2] and also Pinytus, bishop of Cnossus,[3] replied to the letters addressed to their churches.[4]

§ 56. Serapion of Antioch

Routh, RS, I, 449-462. A. Harnack, *Die Zeit des Ignatius*, etc., (§ 9), 46 f — Fabricius, BG, 166 f Richardson, BS, 114. Harnack, LG, 503 f

Eusebius[5] was acquainted with the following writings of **Serapion,** bishop of Antioch (perhaps [189] 192-209 A.D)[6]

(*a*) An Epistle to Domninus, who had fallen away into Judaism.

(*b*) An Epistle relating to Montanism, addressed to the " ecclesiastical men," Pontius and Caricus.[7]

(*c*) Other Epistles to various persons.

(*d*) A Λόγος περὶ τοῦ λεγομένου κατὰ Πέτρον εὐαγγελίου, addressed to the Church at Rhos(s)us, in warning against the Docetic contents of this Gospel of Peter. An extract from it is given by Eusebius [8]

The remark of Socrates [9] that Serapion, in one of his writings, had described Christ as ἔμψυχον, appears to be independent of Eusebius.

---

[1] Cf Eusebius, *Chron Sync* 665 13, Jerome, *Ad ann Abrahami* 2187, Commodus' eleventh year, A D. 173, and Jerome, *De Viris Illust* 27, *Epist* 70. 4.

[2] LG, 236   [4] Eusebius, IV, 23. 6-7.
[3] BG, 164, LG, 237.   [5] *Hist Eccl* VI, 12.
[6] Eusebius, *Chron. ad ann. Abrahami* 2206, the eleventh year of the Emperor Commodus, cf. Eusebius, *Hist. Eccl.* V, 22, VI, 11. 4.
[7] *Hist Eccl.* V, 19.
[8] *Hist Eccl* VI, 12. 3-5, cf § 16 2.
[9] *Hist Eccl.* III, 7.

§ 57. *Writings in the Paschal Controversy*

The Paschal controversy occasioned some **correspondence** between bishops and the churches. The following may be mentioned: —

(*a*) Letters by the bishops Theophilus of Cæsarea and Narcissus of Jerusalem at the head of the Palestinian bishops,[1]

(*b*) by Victor of Rome;[2]

(*c*) by Palmas, bishop of Amastris, at the head of the bishops of Pontus,[3]

(*d*) by the congregations of Gaul, under the leadership of Irenæus,[4]

(*e*) by the bishops of Osrhoene,[5]

(*f*) by Bacchylus, bishop of Corinth;[6]

(*g*) by Polycrates, bishop of Ephesus, two extracts of which, addressed to Victor of Rome, have been preserved[7]

(*h*) Letters of protest by various bishops against the excommunication of the Asiatics by Victor.[8]

---

[1] Eusebius, *Hist Eccl* V, 23 3 (2), LG, 503.
[2] Cf § 54
[3] Eusebius, *loc cit* , BG, 169, LG, 237
[4] Eusebius, *loc. cit* , cf § 52. 3 *d*
[5] *Loc cit* 4 (3), LG, 503
[6] *Loc. cit* , BG, 168 f , LG, 261.
[7] Eusebius, V, 24. 2–7, 8, RS, II, 11–36, BG, 169 f ; LG, 260.
[8] Eusebius, V, 24 10, LG, 260.

SECOND SECTION

PATRISTIC LITERATURE IN THE AGE OF THE RISE OF THEOLOGICAL SCIENCE

§ 58. *General*

H E. F. Guerike, *De schola quae Alexandriae floruit catechetica commentatio*, I, Hal Sax 1824 (The second part, *De interna scholae historia*, contains an account of its theological achievements) C F W Hasselbach, *De schola quae Alexandriae floruit catechetica*, I, Stettin, 1826 (against Guerike) E. R Redepenning, *Origines*, 2 vols Bonn, 1841, I, 57–83 E Vacherot, *Histoire critique de l'école d'Alexandrie*, 2 vols, Lyon, 1846, 51. Ch Bigg, The Christian Platonists of Alexandria, Oxf 1886, *passim* A Harnack, *Lehrbuch der Dogmengeschichte*, I, 501–506 (3d edit 591–596) A Ehrhard, *Die griechische Patriarchalbibliothek von Jerusalem*, in *Romische Quartalschrift*, IV, 1891, 217–265, 329–331, 383 f

1. The scientific exploitation of the sources and doctrines of Christian faith by the media and in the forms of current science, for the deepening of Christian knowledge, was a project which possibly was not entirely foreign to the ecclesiastical writers of even the second century, but in their literary productions, even those of Irenæus, it holds a subordinate place Among the Gnostics alone was it actively pursued, and their method was placed at the service of the church after the close of the second century

2. It is in the patristic literature of the East more especially that interest in such scientific work appears

It was particularly in the **Catechetical School of Alexandria**[1] that it was fostered. This school was not intended for the instruction of catechumens, nor was it a theological seminary, but it stood open to all members of the church whose horizon was wide enough and whose desire for knowledge was active enough to make them feel the need of deeper study or able to bear it It was not closed to the heathen either, so far as they were really desirous to understand Christian thought. The origin of the institution and also its early history are obscure, but nothing forbids the supposition that it was founded or attached to the church on account of dangers threatened by Gnosticism About the year 180 it had long existed as an ecclesiastical institution[2] It is more than doubtful whether Athenagoras, the Apologist, ever stood at its head,[3] though this was certainly true of Pantænus.[4] But the school owed its special reputation to the activity of Clement[5] and Origen,[6] which marked an epoch in the history of Christian literature Both of them, while loyal to the church, nevertheless in their whole method aspired beyond the limits set to Christian Gnosis by the Rule of Faith Their tradition was long maintained in the Catechetical School

3. Scientific aspirations did not remain limited to Alexandria and its school It is possible that even Bardesanes[7] founded a school in Christian **Edessa**; a school which was at its best in the third century, and possessed a celebrated teacher in the presbyter Maca-

---

[1] Eusebius, *Hist. Eccl.* V, 10. 1, 4; VI, 3. 3; 6 1.
[2] *Idem*, V, 10 1.
[3] § 41 1
[4] § 59
[5] § 60.
[6] § 61.
[7] § 25.

rius.¹ Alexander, bishop of Jerusalem,² laid the foundation of a theological library,³ both he and his colleague Theoctistus of Cæsarea were favorably inclined to learning. A notable rival of the Alexandrian Catechetical School arose in the school founded by Origen at **Cæsarea** in Palestine,⁴ the library of which, founded by Pamphilus,⁵ was renowned for centuries.⁶ The influence of the great Alexandrian, however, became dominant in Eastern theological literature, which was dependent upon him wherever an author's subject admitted. Even those who, like Methodius,⁷ were opposed to the results, were nevertheless indebted to it at least for their form. The unique independence of Julius Africanus⁸ was only an exception that proved the rule.

4. The Latin element became more and more the leading one in **Western** patristic literature from the third century onward, and two centuries later a knowledge of Greek had become the mark of unusual erudition.⁹ With Western writers of the third century the interests of learning were subordinated to those of apologetic, polemic, and ecclesiastical questions. Only the literary work of Hippolytus,¹⁰ who wrote in Greek, can be compared with that of the Alexandrians or of Julius Africanus.

¹ LG, 533.
² § 81
³ Eusebius, *Hist.* VI, 20. 1.
⁴ § 61. 2.
⁵ § 83

⁶ LG, 543-545
⁷ § 76
⁸ § 82.
⁹ Celestine I. *Epist.* VIII, 9.
¹⁰ § 91.

CHAPTER I

THE ORIENTALS

I. The Alexandrians

§ 59. *Pantænus*

Routh, RS, I, 375–383   Migne, PG, V, 1327–1332   Theo Zahn, FGK, III, 156–174   B P Pratten, in ANF, VIII, 776–777   Fabricius, BG, 167 f   Richardson, BS, 115 f.   Harnack, LG, 291–296

Pantænus, the Sicilian,[1] according to Eusebius,[2] was active as master of the Catechetical School of Alexandria as early as the beginning of the reign of Commodus (180 A D), and he died about 200 A D or shortly before   He is said to have expounded the treasures of divine teaching not only in his lectures but in his writings[3]   This statement, which is scarcely correct, was enlarged by Jerome[4] and later writers (Anastasius Sinaita, Maximus Confessor), who tell us, apparently without reason, that Pantænus was the author of exegetical works upon Holy Scripture.

§ 60   *Clement*

Editions: P Victorius, Florent 1555   F Sylburg, Heidelb 1592 and after   J Potter, 2 vols Oxf 1715   R S Klotz, 4 vols Lpz 1831–1834   Migne, PG. VIII–IX   W Dindorf, 4 vols Oxf 1869, cf Lagarde, in GGA, 1870, XXI, 801–824 (*Symmicta*, I, Gottingen, 1877, 10–24)   A critical edition by E Hiller (†) and

---

[1] Clement, *Stromata*, I, 1 11.
[2] *Hist. Eccl.* V, 10. 1.
[3] *Idem*, V, 10 4
[4] *De Viris Illust* 36.

K J Neumann is announced (ThLZ, 1885, 535) On the text, cf.
C G Cobet, Διορθωτικὰ εἰς τὰ Κλήμεντος τοῦ ʼΑλεξανδρέως, in
Λόγιυς Ἑρμῆς, I, Lugd Bat 1866, 166–197, I, 2, 1867, 201–287, 425–
534 A Nauck, critical observations, in *Bull de l'acad impér de
St Petersbourg*, XII, 1868, 526–528, XVII, 1872, 267–270, XXII,
1877, 700 U de Wilamowitz-Moellendorff, *Commentariolus grammaticus*, II, Ind Schol Gryphisw 1880, 6–16 O Stahlin, *Observationes criticae in Clem Alex* Erlangen, 1890
Translations· L Hopfenmuller and J Wimmer, in BKV, 1875
(*Quis dives Protrepticus Paedagogus*) Alex Roberts, Jas Donaldson, W L Alexander, and William Wilson, in ANF, II, 163–
604 (Exhortation, Instr, Stromata, Fragm, and *Quis dives*)
Literature H J. Reinkens, *De Clem Presb Alex* Vratisl 1851
B F Westcott, in DCB, I, 559–567 Theo Zahn, *Supplementum Clementinum*, FGK, III, 1–176, 319–321 (cf ZkWL, VI, 1885,
24–39) Cf R A Lipsius in LCB, 1885, No 8, and K J Neumann, in ThLZ, X, 1885, 533–535 O Stahlin, *Beiträge zur Kenntniss der Handschriften des Clemens Alex* Nuremb 1895,
Fabricius, BG, 119–149. Richardson, BS, 38–42. Preuschen, LG, 296–327.

1. **Titus Flavius Clement**[1] was probably born of heathen[2] parents, possibly in Athens,[3] about 150 A D.; became a Christian, and enjoyed the society and instruction of prominent teachers while journeying in Greece, lower Italy, and the East. He finally settled[4] with Pantænus[5] in Alexandria. It is possible that from 190 A D onward he was associated with Pantænus as a teacher in the Catechetical School, and that after the death of Pantænus he became its principal, and at the same time presbyter of the Alexandrian church[6] The persecution of the Christians (202 or 203 A.D.)

[1] Eusebius, *Hist. Eccl* VI, 13. 1.
[2] *Paedagog.* I, 1 1, cf II, 8. 62
[3] Epiphanius, *Panarion*, XXXII, 6, cf. also the arguments based upon his "Attic" Greek given by Dindorf and. Cobet
[4] *Stromata*, I, 1. 11.   [5] § 59.   [6] *Paedagog.* I, 6. 37.

drove him from Alexandria, whither he never returned. Before 211 A D. he was with Bishop Alexander[1] in Cicilia or Cappadocia. This same Alexander, in a letter to Origen,[2] about 215 or 216 A.D., mentions Clement as deceased.

2 Judgment of Clement as a **writer** must not be biassed by the statement, true though it be, that he "belongs among those mosaic-writers who gather and piece together without being capable of independently comprehending the authors whom they misuse "[3]

Undoubtedly Clement derived his knowledge of the numerous authors whom he cited, from anthologies and not at first hand, and in his use of them he proceeded uncritically and credulously (Jewish forgeries), and if he actually copied from Musonius, the tutor of Epictetus, in large sections of his *Paedagogus* and of the *Stromata*, as contended by Wendland, this fact must considerably shake our confidence in the independence, not only of the apologetic and polemic, but also of the practical and didactic details of his great work But still Clement often enough shows himself to be a writer of elevated thought, and captivating eloquence which occasionally[4] rises to a poetic height, and gives evidence of the most ardent devotion to a purpose ideally conceived, and executed with genuine intelligence. At all events his work has not a parallel of equal worth in the Christian literature of the first centuries In spite of his ostensible aversion to the arts of the Sophists,[5] Clement

---

[1] § 81
[2] Eusebius, *Hist. Eccl* VI, 14 9
[3] Bernays, 312 (see below)
[4] Cf the beginning and close of the *Protrepticus*, and more especially the seventh book of the *Stromata*
[5] *E g Stromata*, I, 10. 47 sq

delighted to write in soaring and rhetorical language. His style has been praised for its comparative purity,[1] and it is everywhere obvious that he had read the works of Plato. He was well acquainted with early Christian literature,[2] and he displayed candid judgment in his estimate of even heretical works He had read the writings of Tatian, Melito, and Irenæus His great work was often mentioned with praise by later writers,[3] and it was occasionally copied without acknowledgment (*e g* by Hippolytus, in his *Chronicon*, by Arnobius, and by Theodoret of Cyrrhus) Whether and to what extent it was copied by Tertullian is uncertain.

V Rose, *Aristoteles pseudepigraphus*, Lips 1863, *passim* J. Bernays, *Zu Aristoteles und Clemens* in *Symbola Philologorum Bonn in hon Fr Ritschelii coll* I, Lips 1864, 301-312, again reprinted in *Gesam Abhandlungen*, I, 151-164 Bernays, in SBBA, 1876, 607 (*Strom* II, 21 137-146) C Merk, *Clem Alex in seiner Abhangigkeit von der griechischen Philosophie*, Lpz 1879 H Diels, *Doxographi graeci*, Berl 1879, 129-132, 244 f E Maass, *De biographis graecis quaestiones selectae* (Favorinus as the source of *Strom* I, 14. 59-65), in *Philolog Untersuchungen*, edited by A Kiessling and U v. Wilamowitz-Moellendorf, III, Berol. 1880, *passim* (cf. also opinion of Wilamowitz, *Euripides Herakles*, I, Berl 1889, 171). F Overbeck, *Ueber die Anfange der patristischen Litteratur*, in HZ, XLVIII (XII), 1882, 454-472 P Wendland, *Quaestiones Musonianae*, Beil 1886 E Hiller, *Zur Quellenkritik des Clem Alex* in *Hermes*, XXI, 1886, 126-133 A Scheck, *De fontibus Clem. Alex* Aug Vindel [Augsburg], 1889 M Kremmer, *De catalogis heurematum*, Lips 1890 (*Strom* I, 74-80) Aem Wendling, *De Peplo Aristotelico Quaestiones selectae*, Argentor. 1891 (*passim*) — E Noeldechen, *Tertullians Verhaltniss zu Clem von Alex* in JprTh, XII, 1886, 279-301 (Opposite view, P. Wendland,

---

[1] Dindorf (see above), XXVII.
[2] Cf. the list given by Bigg, *Christian Platonists*, p. 46.
[3] Cf particularly Photius, *Codex*, 109-111.

l c , 48-54, cf also P de Lagarde, § 54, above) *Chronica minora*, ed C Fiick, I, Lips 1893, V–XXV (§ 91, 7 *c*) R Roehricht, *De Clem Alex Arnobii in irridendo gentilium cultu deorum auctore*, Hamb 1893 C Roos, *De Theodoreto Clem et Eusebii compilatore*, Hal Sax 1883 Cf also A Schlatter, TU, XII, 1, 1894 (§ 71, below), on *Strom* I, 21 109-147 Attestations are given by Dindorf and Preuschen

3 The **principal work** of Clement consists of three writings which are connected, not indeed by a common title, but by the unifying fundamental idea of a progressive introduction to Christianity.[1]

(*a*) The ["**Exhortation** to the Heathen"], Προτρεπτι- κὸς πρὸς Ἕλληνας,[2] which is preserved in a manuscript in the National Library in Paris,[3] was written, perhaps, previous to 189 A D ,[4] or possibly not till the author was engaged in teaching (195–200? A D)[5] In form and contents it belongs among apologetic works, but it is often superior to them in its construction as well as in the energy of its diction After a most effective introduction (1 1–10), he shows the folly and worthlessness of the religious doctrines and practices of the heathen, and the untrustworthiness of their philosophical and poetical wisdom (2 11–7 76) Reference is then made to the prophets as the primary witnesses to the truth; and the goodness and mercy of God are proved from Scripture (8 77–9 88). He then proceeds to refute the objection that it is wrong to reject the practices handed down from the Fathers (10. 89–110) The divine revelation in the Logos is extolled in its several mani-

[1] *Paedagog.* Introd., cf *Strom* VI, 7. 1.
[2] On the title, see *Paedagog.* I, 1. 1–3, *Strom.* VII, 4. 22. Potter, on *Protrep* 1.
[3] *Codex Paris.* 451, *Ann.* 914   [5] Demetreskos.
[4] Zahn, cf Eusebius, *Hist Eccl.* V, 28. 4.

CLEMENT OF ALEXANDRIA 167

festations, and the work ends with a description of the God-fearing Christian (II. 111-12. 123)

O Hartlich, *De exhortationum a Graecis Romanisque scriptorum historia et indole*, in the *Leipz Stud zur classischen Philologie*, Lpz 1889, 332 f. Δ Δημητρέσκος, Κλήμεντος Ἀλεξανδρέως ὁ προτρεπτικὸς πρὸς Ἕλληνας λόγος, Βούκουρεστιῶν, 1890

(b) The **Instructor**, Παιδαγωγός, in three books, is preserved in several manuscripts [1] It was written after the Προτρεπτικός,[2] and before the Στρωματεῖς [3] It was intended so to prepare the souls of those enrolled in the number of (ripe Christian) men, as to make them capable of receiving gnostic knowledge [4] After a characterization of the Logos as a "Pedagogue" (I, 1 1-3 9), and the children of God as the subjects of education (4. 10-6. 52), the method of education is unfolded (7 53-61), and the doubts of the Gnostics (Marcionites) as to the unity of the divine principle and, consequently, as to the possibility of a unified education, are refuted by pointing out the necessity not only of mercy in all sound education, but also of retributive and penal justice (8 62-13 103). The second and third books portray the proper character of the Christian life and its various details (*e g*. eating and drinking, dwellings, pleasures, sleep, recreations, relations of the sexes, clothes, ornaments, etc.) Worthy of special mention are the spirited introduction to the third book (on the idea of true beauty), and the description of the ideal of the Christian life, in the closing chapters The second of the two

[1] *Codex Paris* 451, *ann* 914 (begins, however, at I, 96 155, Potter's edition), *Codex Mutin*. III, D. 7, *saec* XI, *Codex Medic. Laur. plut.* V, c. 24, *saec* XI, etc.
[2] *Paedagog.* I, 1. 1. [4] *Stromata*, VI, 1. 1.
[3] *Stromata*, VI, 1 1.

Hymns appended to the *Paedagogus* in many manuscripts (Εἰς τὸν παιδαγωγόν) was certainly not the work of Clement, but appears rather to have been the effusion of a later writer inspired by the *Paedagogus*; while the first (Ὕμνος τοῦ ἁγίου σωτῆρος Χριστοῦ, — τοῦ ἁγίου Κλήμεντος) is not necessarily spurious, though it is rendered doubtful by the introduction, which was not by Clement.

(*c*) The third writing, Κατὰ τὴν ἀληθῆ φιλοσοφίαν γνωστικῶν ὑπομνημάτων (ὀκτώ) Στρωματεῖς [1] [**Stromata**], preserved in a manuscript of the eleventh century,[2] was intended to complete and to crown,[3] by means of the λόγος διδασκαλικός,[4] the propædeutic purpose embodied in the first two works. This plan was not strictly adhered to, for Clement frequently fell back into exoteric and apologetic lines of thought, particularly in his discussions of marriage and martyrdom in the third and fourth books. The whole is wanting in clearness; and this fault is not sufficiently atoned for by reiterated reference to the title.[5] At the end of the seventh book, the author is not much further advanced than at the beginning of the first.

Clement takes as his starting-point the importance of philosophy for the pursuit of Christian knowledge (I, 2.19–13 58). In another place,[6] he indicates that the chief aim of his treatise is to prove that the true Gnostic (whose character is described in the sixth and seventh books) is he who truly fears God. The work

---

[1] Cf. I, 29. 182, III, 18. 110; IV, 1. 1. Also Euseb. *Hist. Eccl.* VI, 13. 1, and Photius, *Codex*, 111.
[2] *Codex Medic. Laur. plut* V. c. 3, *saec* XI (commencement wanting).
[3] VI, 1. 1.   [5] *Eg.* IV, 2. 4; VI, 1. 2. VII, 18. 111.
[4] *Paedagog.* I, 1 2.   [6] VI, 1. 1.

thus becomes a defence of the scientific labors of the Catechetical School. The superiority of revelation to philosophy is specially emphasized,[1] and the principles of the συμβολικὸν εἶδος [2] in the presentation of religious truths, are explained.[3] Considerable space is taken up with discussing the plagiarisms (κλοπή)[4] of Greek poets and philosophers from Jewish, and consequently from Christian, wisdom.[5] In what way Clement carried out the projected continuation, announced in the close of the seventh book, cannot be stated with entire certainty. Eusebius,[6] the *Sacra Parallela*,[7] and Photius[8] certify that an **eighth Stroma** existed. A fragment of a treatise on questions of logic is preserved in the *Codex Lauren.* as the eighth *Stroma*. Zahn thinks that this fragment, as well as the other two pieces which follow it in the manuscript, Ἐκ τῶν Θεοδότου καὶ τῆς ἀνατολικῆς καλουμένης διδασκαλίας κατὰ τοὺς Οὐαλεντίνου χρόνους ἐπιτομαί and Ἐκ τῶν προφητῶν ἐκλογαί,[9] in fact belonged to the eighth *Stroma*, from which they were excerpted by an unknown hand. Von Arnim contends that all three pieces represent simply preliminary work, possibly, though not probably, intended for the unfinished eighth *Stroma*, in the form of excerpts from the works of heathen philosophical (sceptic, Stoic), and Gnostic (Valentinian) writers, and with hardly any original additions of his own.

On the meaning of the title, cf. Aulus Gellius, *Noctes Atticae Praef.* 6-8, edition of M. Hertz, I, 1883, 3. J. von Arnim, *De octavo*

[1] Book II.
[2] VI, 2. 4.
[3] Book V.
[4] VI, 2. 4, etc.
[5] I, 15. 66-18. 90; 25. 165-166; V, 14. 89-141; VI, 2. 4-4 38, and *passim*.
[6] *Hist.* VI, 13. 1.
[7] *Codex Rupef.*
[8] *Codex*, 111.
[9] § 24. 3

Clementis Stromateorum libro. *Ind Schol* Rostock, 1894 The citations from the *Stromata* made by later writers are collected by Zahn (21–30), and Preuschen (313–315) T B Mayor, *Critical Notes on Clement of Alexandria's Stromata I–II*, in *Class Rev*. 1894 9, 385-391

4 In the little book Τίς ὁ σωζόμενος πλούσιος [1] [**Quis Dives**] Clement illustrates his conception of riches [2] by an exposition of Mk x 17–31, in which the hidden sense,[3] not the literal meaning of the words, is decisive: the question being determined, not by riches in themselves, but by their proper or improper use. The whole concludes [4] with the narrative of the Apostle John and the youth who was baptized, lost, and again rewon. The second *Similitude* of Hermas is used in Chapters 11–19 without acknowledgment The date of composition cannot be determined in spite of Zahn's view [5]

Editions · M Ghislerius, *Commentarii in Jeremiam* III, Lugd 1623, 262–282 (under the name of Origen, but see the preface). F Combefisius, *Auctarium patrum novissimum*, I, Paris, 1672, 163–194 J Fell, Oxon 1683. C Segaar, Traj Rhen 1816 K Koster, in SQu, VI, 1893.

5. **Fragments** of the following have been preserved: —

(*a*) Περὶ τοῦ πάσχα, directed against the Quartodecimans, and called forth by a work of Melito [6] with the same title. Fragments of it are found in the *Chronicon Paschale*,[7] in the Ἱερά of Leontius and John,[8] and in a

---

[1] *Codex Vatic*. 623, of the fifteenth century. The archetype of this manuscript is the *Codex Escurial* Ω, III, 19, of the eleventh century So Stahlin. For Chap. 42, cf Eusebius, *Hist*. III, 23, and later manuscripts.
[2] *Paedagog*. III, 6. 34-46.
[3] Cf Chaps. 5 (beginning) and 20 (beginning).
[4] Chap. 42   [5] Zahn, 37 f See below, No. 7 *a*.
[6] Eusebius, *Hist. Eccl* IV, 26 4 Cf also VI, 13. 3, 9.
[7] Dindorf, I, 14
[8] *Lib*. II *rerum sacrar*. (Mai, NC, VII, 94, 98 f).

work of Nicephorus.¹ All the fragments are given by Zahn,

(*b*) Κανὼν ἐκκλησιαστικὸς ἢ πρὸς τοὺς ἰουδαΐζοντας, which was dedicated to Alexander, bishop of Jerusalem.² A fragment is contained in the supplement to Nicephorus,³

(*c*) The Ὑποτυπώσεις,⁴ in eight books,⁵ described by Photius,⁶ appear to have been a brief commentary on the whole Bible, including some portions of the early literature (Barnabas, Apocalypse of Peter) which did not become part of the canon. Into this work dogmatic and historical disquisitions may have been introduced Numerous fragments from it have been preserved by Eusebius,⁷ Œcumenius,⁸ Photius,⁹ and others According to Zahn, the *Adumbrationes Clementis Alexandrini in epistolas canonicas*,¹⁰ which have been preserved only in a Latin translation, formed part of the *Hypotyposes*. Bunsen contended that these themselves constituted the eighth book of the *Stromata*, and that consequently the fragment¹¹ assigned to this book by Zahn belonged to the *Hypotyposes*.¹²

---

¹ *Antirrhet adv Constant Copronym* III, 26 (Mai, NPB, VI, 1. 91). Cf also J. B Pitra, *Jur. Eccl Graec Hist monum* I, 299 Zahn, 32–36.
² Eusebius, *Hist. Eccl.* VI, 13. 3. Jerome, *De Viris Illust* 38.
³ *Antirrhet. adv. Constant. Copronym* III. Cf. D. N Le Nourry, *Apparatus* (§ 2. 3. *a*), I, 1334 Pitra, SpS, I, 351, and LXXI. J A Fabricius, *Opera Hippolyti* (§ 91), II, 73. Zahn, 35–37.
⁴ On the title, see BG, V, 529. Zahn, 130.
⁵ Eusebius, *Hist Eccl.* VI, 13. 2   ⁶ *Codex*, 109.
⁷ *Hist Eccl* I, 12. 1 sq., II, 1. 3–5; 9. 2 sq ; 15, VI, 14. 2–4
⁸ *Commentarii in Acta Apostolorum, in omnes Pauli epistolas, in epistolas catholicas omnes*, edit. F. Morellus, Paris, 1631. Potter, 1014 sq
⁹ *Loc cit.*
¹⁰ *Codex Laudun.* 96, *saec.* IX; *Berol Phill.* 1665, *saec* XIII.
¹¹ See No. 3. *c*, above.   ¹² Similarly, Westcott, DCB, I, 563.

The *Adumbrationes* are reprinted by Zahn, 64–103. Cf. the collation of the *Codex Berol* by Preuschen, 306 f. C. C. J. Bunsen, *Analecta Ante-Nicaena*, I, 1854, 157–340.

6. The following are only known by their titles: —

(a) Διαλέξεις περὶ νηστείας καὶ περὶ καταλαλίας, which is mentioned by Eusebius,[1] and was possibly the same kind of work as the *Quis dives*,[2]

(b) Προτρεπτικὸς εἰς ὑπομονὴν ἢ πρὸς τοὺς νεωστὶ βεβαπτισμένους, also mentioned by Eusebius,[3] may have belonged to the same category as the Διαλέξεις,[4]

(c) Περὶ προνοίας, not mentioned by Eusebius. The fragments given by Maximus Confessor[5] and the statement of Anastasius,[6] lead to the conclusion that the writing, which consisted of at least two books, contained philosophical definitions. It is not settled beyond all doubt that Clement was the author.[7]

7. (a) It cannot be inferred with certainty from his own words[8] whether Clement really wrote a treatise, Περὶ ἀρχῶν καὶ θεολογίας, or whether he simply intended to do so.[9]

(b) Neither can it be certainly determined whether Clement composed a book Περὶ ἐγκρατείας and (or) a Λόγος γαμικός,[10] or whether, in the passages cited, he simply copied in an unskilful fashion the title of one (or several) treatises of Musonius.[11]

---

[1] Eusebius, *Hist. Eccl.* VI, 13. 3.
[2] Zahn, 44
[5] Combefisius, II, 144 (146), 152 (176).
[6] *Quaest.* 96 (PG, LXXXIX, 741).
[7] Zahn, 39–44. Preuschen, LG, 302 f
[8] *Stromata*, IV, 1. 1, and *Quis dives*, 26 (end), Potter's edit. 950.
[9] Cf against Zahn, 38 f, Von Arnim (cf No. 3. c), 13 f.
[10] So most scholars, following *Paed.* II, 6. 52; 10. 94; III, 8. 41.
[11] Wendland, 36 sq.
[3] Eusebius, *loc. cit.*
[4] Zahn, 44.

(c) According to Palladius,[1] Clement[2] wrote a σύγγραμμα εἰς τὸν προφήτην Ἀμώς

(d) The following works were projected by Clement, but nothing is known as to the execution of his plan:—

(1) Περὶ προφητείας, which was intended[3] to vindicate the inspiration of the books of the Old and New Testaments against the attacks of the Gnostics, and to set forth the nature of prophecy as against the objections of the Montanists,[4]

(2) Περὶ ψυχῆς[5] The two fragments referred to this writing by Grabe[6] are spurious;

(3) Περὶ ἀναστάσεως,[7]

(4) Εἰς τὴν Γένεσιν.[8]

§ 61. Origen

Editions: J Merlinus (and Guil Paroy), 4 vols. Parhis. 1512 and after D Erasmus, Basil 1536 and after Following these, J J. Grynæus, 2 vols Basil. 1571 G Genebrardus, 2 vols Paris, 1574 and after First complete edition, C and C V de la Rue, 4 vols Paris, 1733–59 (without the fragments of the *Hexapla* and the *Philocalia*) Again reprinted by F Oberthur, 15 vols Viceb 1785 C H E Lommatzsch, 25 vols Berol 1831–48 (containing also the *Philocalia*). Migne, PG, XI–XVIII (enlarged by the portions given by Gallandi (cf § 2. 8 a) XIV, App ; most of those in Mai, NPB, VII, 1854, and a fragment from Cramer) On the fragments of *Catenae*, cf J. A Cramer, *Catenae in NT*, 8 vols Oxon 1838–44 — **Translations·** F Crombie, in ANF, IV, 237–669 (Prolog of Rufinus, De Princip. Celsus); and A. Menzies, ANF, IX, 295–

[1] *Hist Lausiaca*, 139 (PG, XXXIV, 1236)   [2] *Loc. cit.* No. 2.
[3] *Stromata*, I, 24. 158, IV, 1. 2, IV, 13. 91, 93; V, 13. 88.
[4] Preuschen, LG, 308 Cf Zahn, 45 f
[5] Cf *Stromata*, II, 20. 113, III, 3. 13; V, 13 88.
[6] Potter, 1020.   [7] Cf I, 6. 47, II, 10. 104.
[8] Cf. Eusebius, *Hist.* VI, 13. 8, *Strom* III, 14 95; VI, 18. 168 Zahn, 45. Preuschen, 309.

408 (Letter to Gregory, Comm. on John). J. Patrick, *Idem*, 413-512 (Comm. on Matt)

Literature: P D Huetius, *Origeniana, seu de vita, doctrina et scriptis Origenis libri*. III, in *Origenis in s Scripturas Commentaria* I, Rothomagi, 1668, 1-278; reprinted by De la Rue, IV, 2, 79-338, Lommatzsch, XXII-XXIV, 262, PG, XVII, 633-1284 E R Redepenning, *Origines*, 2 vols Bonn, 1841-46 W Moeller, in RE, XI, 1877, 92-109 B F. Westcott, in DCB, IV, 96-142 — Fabricius, BG, 201-449 Richardson, BS, 50-55. Preuschen, LG, 332-405.

1. Next after Paul, Origen was the first Christian writer as to whose life and work we have any detailed information. To be sure, the collection of Origen's letters made by Eusebius[1] has been lost, and of the Ἀπολογία Ὠριγένους, in six books, written by the presbyter Pamphilus of Cæsarea, with the assistance of his friend Eusebius, only the first book has been preserved in Rufinus'[2] Latin version. But Eusebius devoted the greater part of the sixth book of his Ecclesiastical History to the memory of the great theologian, whose experiences from his cradle appeared to him remarkable.[3] The Panegyric of Gregorius Thaumaturgus[4] is a particularly valuable document relating to his honored teacher's method of teaching and his success as an instructor. Jerome,[5] and particularly Photius,[6] show independent acquaintance with this Apology.

2. **Origen**, surnamed Adamantius,[7] was born of Christian parents, at Alexandria,[8] in 185 or 186 A.D.[9] His

[1] *Hist. Eccl.* VI, 36. 3.
[2] § 83.
[3] *Hist Eccl* VI, 2. 2.
[4] § 75. 3. a.
[5] *De Viris Illust* 54, 62, etc.
[6] *Codex*, 118.
[7] Eusebius, *Hist. Eccl.* VI, 14. 10. Epiphanius, *Panarion*, LXIV, 1. Cf. A. Boeckh, *Corp Inscrip Graec.* 9373. Arbitrary meanings were given to this name by Jerome (*Epist* 33, 3), and Photius (*Codex*, 118)
[8] See, however, Epiphanius, *Panarion*, LXIV, 1.
[9] Eusebius, *Hist Eccl.* VI, 2. 12, 36. 1, compared with VII, 1.

father, Leonides,[1] gave the precocious boy his first instruction in religion and in the encyclical sciences,[2] and while still young, Origen became a pupil of Clement in the Catechetical School.[3] By the death of his father in the persecution of 202 (203) A.D., the boy (whom his mother's craft alone had saved from a like fate)[4] was compelled, before his seventeenth year, to support himself and the numerous family by private teaching Soon afterward, however (203), he was appointed by Bishop Demetrius[5] (189–232 A.D) head of the Catechetical School as the successor of Clement In this capacity for thirteen years, only interrupted by occasional journeys to Rome and Arabia, he exercised a profound influence. He also engaged in literary labors, and studiously extended his knowledge.[6] Youthful enthusiasm and a literal interpretation of the words of Scripture led him into an exaggerated asceticism which went to the length of voluntary emasculation.[7] The bloody persecution under Caracalla, 215 (216) A.D., compelled him to flee to Palestine, where he resumed his old relations with Alexander, bishop of Jerusalem, and entered upon new ones with Theoctistus of Cæsarea The circumstance of his preaching in Cæsarea while still a layman occasioned his recall to Alexandria by Demetrius. For a decade and a half he labored with the utmost activity both as a teacher and an author,

---

[1] *Idem*, VI, 1.
[2] *Idem*, VI, 2. 7.
[3] *Idem*, VI, 6.
[4] *Idem*, VI, 2. 5
[5] BG, 298, LG, 330–332.
[6] Hebrew cf Jerome, *De Viris Illust* 54, and *Epist*. 39, 1, also Origen, *Princip* I, 3. 4, IV, 22. *Frag Graec* 7, philosophical studies with Ammonius Saccas (the sack-bearer, or porter?).
[7] Eusebius, *Hist. Eccl.* VI, 8. 2.

encouraged and urged on by his friend Ambrosius.¹ His increasing celebrity as a scholar rendered the jealousy of the bishop more and more bitter. A journey to Achaia (231 A.D), undertaken with the permission of Demetrius,² took him through Palestine, where he was ordained presbyter by the united bishops.³ Demetrius caused a synod of bishops and presbyters to proscribe his residence in Alexandria on account of his irregular ordination and heterodox tendencies, and this sentence he intensified to deposition at a synod composed of bishops alone (231 or 232 A D) Origen betook himself to Cæsarea in order to found there a school constituted like that of Alexandria. It soon became a centre for the scientific study of Christian theology.⁴ Besides his lectures and literary work, he continued, with the greatest zeal, his popular expositions of Scripture in public worship. The statement that he escaped the persecution under Maximus Thrax by flight, is a supposition based merely upon the account of Palladius⁵ His residence in Cæsarea was probably only interrupted by journeys in Palestine, and to Sidon, Athens, Arabia (and Cappadocia?) Under Decius he suffered frequent torture in prison and died soon afterward (probably in 254 A.D) at Tyre, where, till late in the Middle Ages, his memory was still fresh.

On Ammonius and Origen, see L. Kruger, in ZhTh, XIII, 1843, 46–62, and E Zeller, *Die Philosophie der Griechen*, III, 2 (3d edit), 459–463

It is regarded by Kruger as certain, and by Zeller as at least very improbable, that Origen had heard Ammonius. For an account of

¹ BG, 288 f   RS, III, 3–9   DCB, I, 90 f.   LG, 328–330.
² Jerome, *De Viris Illust* 54.   ⁴ Gregorius Thaumaturgus.
³ Eusebius, *Hist Eccl* VI, 23 4   ⁵ *Hist Laus* 147   PG, XXXIV, 1250

the events of 231 A D and the following years, see A. C McGiffert, *The Church History of Eusebius* (§ 2 1), pp 394-397

3 Origen's **literary fertility** would still remain almost unexampled, even if Epiphanius' estimate of six thousand books[1] were a mere exaggeration.[2] According to Jerome,[3] he wrote, in any case, more than other people usually read But this fecundity is explicable when it is considered that many of his works were products of the moment, which, like his later homilies, were taken down by others or dictated by himself,[4] and that he is diffuse even where he thought it necessary to excuse himself for his diffuseness[5] He was neither a brilliant nor a good stylist, but he was, however, a gifted scholar, who was capable of producing effects wherever his personality rose victorious above learned trifles. None among the later Fathers equalled him in originality of thought, and the church has always been compelled to recognize, even though unwillingly, the genius of the greatest theologian before Augustine.

4. The list of Origen's writings, made by Eusebius and incorporated in his life of Pamphilus,[6] has been lost; and Jerome's list (borrowed from Eusebius ?), which has been preserved by chance, offers only an incomplete and not thoroughly reliable substitute The decision of the decretal of Gelasius as to the writings of Origen — also his condemnation by Justinian (543 A D) and by the fifth general council (553 A.D.) — aided

[1] Epiphanius, *Panarion*, LXIV, 63.
[2] Cf., on the other hand, Jerome, *Adv. Rufin.* II, 22
[3] *Idem*, IV.
[4] Cf the ταχυγράφοι, Eusebius, *Hist Eccl.* VI, 23 2.
[5] *Fragm ex Comm Joh* V. *Philoc. cap* 5
[6] Eusebius, *Hist. Eccl.* VI, 32. 3.

in decimating his **literary remains.** Only the smallest portion of his works is now extant, and of these not half are preserved in the original, but in Latin translations, of which those by Rufinus of Aquileia are only paraphrases or excerpts,[1] and not free from arbitrary alterations of passages which were suspicious from a dogmatic point of view [2] While the translations have reached us in numerous manuscripts, the manuscript transmission of the works preserved in the original is (with the exception of the books against Celsus) very scanty. The *Philocalia* of Gregory Nazianzen and Basil of Cæsarea (about 382 A D) is an anthology from the works of Origen, made with taste and insight. This work is a systematic grouping of the material in twenty-seven chapters, and is important as an aid for textual criticism, and suited for an introduction to a study of the author.

The list of Jerome is given by R Redepenning in ZhTh, XXI, 1851, 66 (76)–79, and Pitra, SpS, III, 313–317 Thence reprinted by E Preuschen, LG, 334 f , with a list of manuscripts so far as known, *Idem*, 390–403 The manuscripts of the *Catenae: Idem*, 404 f , cf also 835–842 — Editions of the *Philocalia:* J Tarinus, 1618 sq (1624) Guil Spencerus, Cantab. 1658 (1677) J A. Robinson, Cambridge, 1893.

5. The work of Origen was epoch-making in the field of Biblical textual criticism and exposition. Although his efforts to establish a **Bible text,**[3] purified from the results of carelessness, subjective conjectures, and intentional alterations, were not prompted by a genuinely

---

[1] *Perorat in Origen. Comm in Epist. ad Rom.,* Lommatzsch, VII, 458 *sq*
[2] *Proleg. in libr.* περὶ ἀρχῶν, *Idem*, XXI, 12
[3] *Comm in Matt* XV, 40, Lommatzsch, III, 357

critical motive, and although he exhibited bias and indifference in his choice of readings,[1] nevertheless his text of the New Testament (and the copies that were made from it) possessed an authoritative character,[2] and it has not yet lost its importance as a witness to the text. The edition of the Old Testament, which he prepared with the aim of producing an accurate text of the Septuagint, is called the **Hexapla** (τὰ ἑξαπλᾶ scil. γράμματα) because it was arranged in six parallel columns (1) the original text in Hebrew characters, (2) in a Greek transliteration, (3) the version of Aquila, (4) Symmachus, (5) Septuagint, (6) Theodotion In the case of certain books, a previously unknown translation, discovered by Origen, was added, in a seventh column, and in the case of the Psalms there were two further columns with a sixth and seventh translation[3] The value even of this gigantic undertaking was limited not only by a superstitious veneration for the Septuagint, but also by its originator's inadequate knowledge of Hebrew. The work was begun in Alexandria, and completed in Tyre twenty-eight years later.[4] Copies of it were not multiplied, on account of its huge compass, and it has therefore perished Only the Septuagint portion of the Hexapla, which was frequently copied, has been preserved, though in an incomplete form, in fragments and in the Syriac translation of Paul, bishop of Tella (617–618 A.D.). Origen himself

[1] *E g Comm. Joh.* I, 40; Lommatzsch, I, 79
[2] *Exemplaria Adamantii*, in Jerome's *Comm. ad Gal* III, 1; *ad Matt.* XXIV, 36. Cf. *Codex Coisl* 202, *Subscr*
[3] Cf Eusebius, *Hist Eccl* VI, 16 Jerome, *Comm Tit.* III, 9 Inexactly, Epiphanius, *De mens et ponderib* 7
[4] Epiphanius, *Idem*, 18, see, however, Field, XLVIII sq

made¹ a separate edition of the four principal versions, the *Tetrapla*, which likewise has been lost.

On works on N T. textual criticism, see the *Prolegomena* of C R Gregory, to Tischendorf's edition, and the *Prolegomena* of Westcott and Hort   The best edition of the remains of the Hexapla is that of F F.eld, 2 vols, Oxf 1875   See also Migne, PG, XV, XVI, 1, 2, 3, Paris, 1857-63   A Ceriani, *Monum sacra et profana*, VII, Mediol 1874   P de Lagarde, *Veteris Testamenti ab Origene recensiti fragmenta apud Syros servata*, Gottingen, 1880   G Morin, in his edition of Jerome's *Excerpta in Psalterium*, in *Anecdota Maredsol* III, 1. 95   C H Taylor, in DCB, III, 14-23   F Bleek, *Einleitung in das A. T.*; sixth edition by J Wellhausen, Berl 1893, § 254

6 Origen was the first important **exegete** in the history of the church. At least, it is no longer possible — Clement's writings excepted — to lay our hands upon the works of his predecessors, whom he himself occasionally mentioned² Heracleon, whose exposition of the Gospel of John Origen often attacked without justification and with ill-applied severity,³ belonged to the Valentinian school. Origen, however, became (not always to the advantage of the cause) the most influential of all early ecclesiastical exegetes, a whetstone for those who followed him;⁴ and traces of his influence may be found even down to the period of Humanism (Erasmus)

¹ Eusebius, *Idem*, VI, 16. 4.   Epiphanius, *Idem*, 19.
² *Homil. in Gen.* V, 5; XV, 7; *in Exod.* XIII, 3; *in Levit.* VIII, 6, *in Num.* IX, 5; XXVI, 4, *in Josh.* XVI, 1, 5, *in Jud* VIII, 4, *in Jerem.* XI, 3, XIV, 5, *in Luc* XXXIV.   *Comm in Matt.* X, 22, XIV, 2, XV, 1, XVII, 17, 28, *in Matt. Comm. Ser* 31, 69, 75, 126; *in Rom.* IV, 10 (Lommatzsch, VI, 304), VI, 7 (Lommatzsch, VII, 40).
³ *In Joh* II, 8, etc.
⁴ Gregorius Nyss., in Suidas' *Lexicon*, under "Origen."

J A Ernesti, *De Origene interpretationis librorum SS. Grammaticae auctore* [Lips 1756], in *Opuscula philologica et critica*, Lugd Batav 1776, 288-323 See, on the other hand, J G Rosenmuller, *Historia interpretationis libror. sacror* III, Lips. 1807, particularly, 151-156, 161

1. Three groups are to be distinguished[1] among his **exegetical works**. Scholia, Homilies, and Commentaries.

(*a*) Σχόλια, **Excerpts**, probably identical with the Σημειώσεις,[2] or scarcely distinguishable from them, are brief exegetical remarks on difficult passages.[3] Whatever is now extant, chiefly in *Catenae* drawn from this source,[4] requires further critical sifting. The list of Jerome mentions *Excerpta* on Exodus, Leviticus, Isaiah, Psalms, and Ecclesiastes

(*b*) Ὁμιλίαι, **Homilies**,[5] were discourses during public worship,[6] addressed both to the baptized and the unbaptized. Their subjects were usually suggested by the lesson, or were sometimes selected at the particular desire of members of the congregation,[7] or of the one in charge of the service[8] They were not all literary productions in the proper sense (like Song of Songs, or Luke), many of them having been taken down by others from his *extempore* discourses.[9] The author did

---

[1] Jerome, *Prolog interpret Origenis hom. in Ezech.* Lommatzsch. XIV, 4 sq
[2] Jerome, *Prooem in prim libr. Comm in Isai.*
[3] *Commaticus sermo*, Jerome, *Prefat. Comm in Gal.*
[4] LG, 403-405
[5] On the name, see Redepenning, II, 241.
[6] *In Ezech.* VI, 5, Lommatzsch, XIV, 86.
[7] *Num.* XV, 1, *Idem*, X, 168.
[8] *I Sam.* II, *Idem*, XI, 318 *Ez* XIII, 1, *Idem*, XIV, 160.
[9] *Pentateuch. Jeremiah* Cf. Eusebius, *Hist Eccl* VI, 36. 1 Rufinus, *Perorat in Orig Comm in Ep ad Rom.* Lommatzsch, VII, 458 sq.
P. Koetschau (in the *Festschrift des Jenaer Gymnasiums zur 350jahriger*

not regard these writings as products of rhetorical art,[1] but rather as intended for the instruction and edification of the entire congregation,[2] and on this very account he did not profess to have treated the divine mysteries either scientifically or exhaustively,[3] being conscious that sacred and sublime truths may not be unveiled to every man. The homilies lack orderly arrangement, and their unity lies in the text treated.[4] Typology and allegory predominate;[5] the doctrine of the threefold sense of Scripture is frequently applied,[6] and historical interpretation is absent[7] The style is "simple, without any ornamentation, sometimes diffuse, indeed, but nowhere prosy or dull"[8] The homilies were imitated frequently in both the Greek and Latin church. They remain significant, also, in literary history, as the first actual examples of an orderly Christian discourse connected with divine worship. The following have been preserved:[9]—

1. *Genesis:* delivered after 244 A D. Two Greek fragments from the second homily,[10] and seventeen in the translation of Rufinus,[11]

Jubelfeier des Eisenacher Gymnasiums am 18 Okt. 1894, 51–58), has shown that the long fragment in the *Philocalia* (XV, 19, Robinson, 84 19–86. 3), which was suspected by himself (TU, VI, 1, 1889, 133) and Robinson (*Philocalia*, LII), certainly belongs to Origen, and he has made it probable that the fragment formed the second part of the exposition in the *Contra Celsum*, VI, 77, where it certainly does not now occur.

[1] *Rom* IX, 2, Lommatzsch, VII, 292.
[2] *Lev* I, 1, *Idem*, IX, 173 sq
[3] *Lev.* IX, 4 and 10, *Idem*, IX, 222 and 364; *Rom.* X, 11, *Idem*, VII, 408
[4] Cf *Contra Celsum.* III, 52   [5] *Song of Songs*, cf also *Joshua*
[6] Cf particularly, *Gen* II, Lommatzsch, VIII, 130–147
[7] Cf. particularly, *Jeremiah.*   [10] Lommatzsch, VIII, 100–104.
[8] So Redepenning   [11] *Idem*, VIII, 105–298
[9] Cf. Westcott, DCB, IV, 96–142.

ORIGEN   183

are extant   Contents. (1) Chap 1 Creation, (2) vi 13-16, construction of the ark,¹ (3) xvii 1-14, circumcision of Abraham, (4) xviii 1-21 visit of the three men to Abraham, (5) xix. Lot and his daughters, (6) xx Abimelech, (7) xxi birth of Isaac, ejection of Ishmael, (8) xxii 1-14, offering of Isaac, (9) xxii 15-17, renewed promise to Abraham, (10) xxiv Rebecca at the well, (11) xxv 1-11, Abraham and Keturah, Isaac at the Well of the Living, (12) xxv 21-26, xxvi 12, birth of Esau and Jacob, (13) xxvi 14-22, Isaac's well, (14) xxvi 23-30, Isaac and Abimelech, (15) xlv 25 f, return of the sons of Jacob from Egypt, (16) xlvii 20 f, Joseph and Pharaoh, (17) xlix. Jacob's blessing (ending is lost)   Jerome's list also mentions *Localium (moralium) homiliarum*, II ²

2 *Exodus*: delivered after 244 A D, two Greek fragments from the eighth homily, and thirteen in Rufinus' translation.³ *Contents*: (1) Chap 1 1-10, multiplying of the children of Israel, the new king, (2) 1 15-22, the midwives, (3) iv 10-v mission of Moses, (4) vii-x the seven plagues, (5) xii 37-xiv Exodus from Egypt, (6) xv 1-22, the song of Moses, (7) xv. 23-xvi 12, the water of Marah and the manna, (8) xx 1-6. the first two Commandments; (9) xxv the Tabernacle, (10) xxi 22-25, miscarriage, (11) xvii - xviii Rephidim, Amalek, Jethro; (12) xxxiv 33 ff, the veil on Moses' face, (13) xxxv gifts for the tabernacle

3 *Leviticus*. delivered after 244 A D, one Greek fragment from the second homily,⁴ two from the eighth,⁵ and sixteen in Rufinus' translation ⁶   Almost the entire eighth homily is found in Procopius of Gaza (so Klostermann, 12)   *Contents:* (1) Chap 1. 1-9, burnt offering, (2) iv 3, 27 f, law of the trespass offering, (3) v. 1 ff., trespass offering, (4) vi 1-23 (v 20-vi 23), guilt offering, burnt offering, meat offering, (5) vi 24-vii. 34 (vii 1-34), trespass offering, and peace offering, (6) vii 35-viii 13, consecration of Aaron and his sons, (7) x 8-xi rules for the priests, clean and unclean animals, (8) xii 2-xiii. xiv leprosy and its cleansing, two Greek fragments, (9) xvi 1-17, the great day of Atonement; (10) xvi.

[1] Procopius, 273 a-277 c, extract from *Hom.* II.
[2] Cf Rufinus, *Apol* II, 20.
[3] Rue, II, 158, Lommatzsch, IX, 1-162.
[4] Lommatzsch, IX, 171 (?)
[5] A. Mai, *Class. Auct.* X, 600.   [6] Lommatzsch, IX, 172-446.

the fast on the day of Atonement, and the scape-goat, (11) xx. 7, cf xxvi sanctification, (12) xxi 10, the high-priest, (13) xxiv. 1–9, lamps, shewbread, etc , (14) xxiv. 10–14, blasphemy, (15) xxv. Sabbatical and Jubilee years; (16) xxvi 3–13, the blessing.

4 *Numbers*: delivered after 244 A D One Greek fragment from the thirteenth homily,[1] and twenty-eight in Rufinus' translation [2] *Contents*. (1) Chap i 1–3, the first numbering, (2) ii 1 f, order of encampment, (3) iii 11–13, separation of the Levites; (4) iii 39, numbers of the Levites, (5) iv 18 f, 47, offices of the Levites, (6) xi 24 ff, xii 1 ff, the seventy elders, the Ethiopian wife of Moses, (7) xii 5–10, leprosy of Miriam, (8) xiv 8 ff, the spies, murmuring of the people, (9) xvi –xvii company of Korah, Aaron's rod, (10) xviii 1 ff, duties and portions of the priests; (11) xviii tithes, (12) xxi 16–24, the song of the well, (13) xxi. 24 ff, xxii defeat of Sihon and Og, Balaam's ass, (14) xxii Balaam; (15) xxiii 1–10, Balaam's first prophecy, (16) xxiii 11–24; second prophecy; (17) xxiii. 27–xxiv. 9, third prophecy, (18) xxiv 10–19, fourth prophecy, (19) xxiv. 20–24, fifth prophecy, (20) xxv. Israelites' worship of Baal, (21) xxvi second numbering, (22) xxvii 1 ff, the daughters of Zelophehad, appointment of Joshua, (23) xxviii. various feasts, (24) xxx offerings, (25) xxxi vengeance on the Midianites, (26) xxxi 48 ff xxxii number of the children of Israel, (27) xxxiii encampments of the Israelites, (28) xxxiv. borders of the promised land

5 *Deuteronomy*: delivered before the homilies on Luke,[3] that is, possibly before 235 A D. Jerome's list speaks of thirteen homilies none of them is now extant.

6 *Joshua*. delivered after 244 A D, later than those on Jeremiah,[4] and during a severe persecution,[5] that is, probably, not earlier than 251 A D One Greek fragment, from the twentieth homily, has been preserved in the *Philocalia*,[6] and twenty-six fragments, in Rufinus' translation [7] Homilies 1–4 and 16–26 were used by Procopius *Contents*. (1) Introduction; (2) Chap. 1 1–14, the appointment of Joshua, (3) 1. 16 f, ii. the preparation, (4) iii the crossing of the

---

[1] Lommatzsch, X, 156, N 2. [4] *Homily* XIII, 3.
[2] *Idem*, X, 9–370. [5] *Idem*, IX, 10.
[3] *Homil in Luc.* VIII
[6] *Philocalia*, 12, Lommatzsch, XI, 167–169.
[7] Lommatzsch, XI, 6–214.

Jordan, (5) iv.–v. 9, renewal of the covenant, (6) v 8–15, Passover at Gilgal, (7) vi taking of Jericho, (8) vii –viii 29, defeat before Ai, taking of the city; (9) viii. 30, altar on Mount Ebal, (10) ix stratagem of the Gibeonites, (11) x battle at Gibeon, (12) x spiritual explanation of the wars of Joshua, (13) x 28 ff, taking of Libnah and other cities; (14) xi. 1 ff, Jabin, (16) xiii 1 ff, age of Joshua, command for partition, (17) xiii 14, the Levites without inheritance; (18) xiv 6 ff, the request of Caleb; (19) xv 1, the borders of Judah, (20) xv. 13–20, Caleb's daughter, (21) xv 63, the unconquered Jebusites, (22) xvi 10, Ephraim and the Canaanites; (23) xviii 8, partition, (24) xix 47 ff (LXX), the Amorites, Joshua's inheritance, (25) xxi 2–7, the cities of the Levites, (26) xxi 42 (LXX), the stone knives, and the altar of the tribes beyond Jordan.

7. *Judges* delivered and written down by Origen himself before the commentary on the Song of Songs,[1] perhaps in 235 A D Nine are contained in Rufinus' translation [2] *Contents:* (1) Chap ii 7, Israel serves the Lord, (2) ii 8–14, death of Joshua, (3) iii 9–16, Othniel, Ehud, (4) iii 31, iv 1–3, Shamgar, Jabin, Sisera, (5) iv 4 ff, Deborah, Barak, Joel, (6) v. the Song of Deborah, (7) vi 1 ff, the Midianites, (8) vi 33 ff, Gideon, (9) vii victory of Gideon.

8 *Samuel* and *Kings:* delivered after 244 A D Jerome's list gives four homilies on 1 Kings,[3] one on 2 Kings. One homily on 1 Sam i 11 (Elkanah, Peninnah, Hannah, Samuel) in a Latin translation is of unknown origin [4] In the original there is one homily on 1 Sam. xxviii Ὑπὲρ τῆς ἐγγαστριμύθου (Witch of Endor) [5] The homily was severely attacked from various quarters, particularly by Eustathius of Antioch

· 9. *Job:* The list of Jerome gives the number of homilies as twenty-two [6] A fragment of a homily in the (lost) translation of Hilary of Poitiers [7] is preserved in Augustine's book *Contra Julian* [8]

10 *Psalms:* delivered between 241 and 247 A D (See Homily I, on Ps. xxxvi 2, II, on Ps xxxvii 1) Jerome's list gives at least

[1] *Prol ad Cant Cantic,* Lommatzsch, XIV, 317
[2] *Idem*, XI, 217–284.   [4] Lommatzsch, XI, 289–316.
[3] Cassiodorus, *Inst div. litt* I, 2.   [5] Lommatzsch, XI, 317–332.
[6] Cf *in Ezech* VI, 4, and Eustathius, *De Engastrim.* 21, Jahn, 59.
[7] Jerome, *De Viris Illust* 100
[8] Augustine, *Contra Julian* II, 27; Lommatzsch, XI, 333 sq.

one hundred and thirteen on sixty Psalms   In the *Catenae* are numerous fragments. In Rufinus' translation there are nine: five on Ps xxxvi, two on Ps xxxvii, and two on Ps xxxviii [1]

11. *Proverbs:* Jerome's list gives seven, of which none is extant.

12. *Ecclesiastes:* the list of Jerome gives eight, of which none is extant [2]

13 *Song of Songs:* delivered before 244 A D. Two are contained in Jerome's translation [3] They were much read in the Middle Ages and therefore have been preserved in numerous manuscripts.

14 *Isaiah.* their date is uncertain 235 A.D. (?) after 244 A.D. (?). Jerome's list gives thirty-two, and Jerome himself was acquainted with twenty-five [4] In Jerome's translation are nine [5] (purged of trinitarian heresies)   *Contents:* (1) Chap. vi 1–7, the vision; (2) vii 10–16, the reward of the Virgin; (3) iv 1, the seven women, (4) vi 1–7, the vision; (5) xli 2, vi. 1–7; (6) vi. 8–10, the commission, (7) viii 18–20, the prophet and his children; (8) x 10–13, (9) vi 8–vii. 11 (fragment).

15 *Jeremiah:* delivered after 244 A D, in a time of peace.[6] Jerome's list is probably incorrect in giving twenty-four homilies.[7] In the original there are nineteen attributed to Cyril,[8] twelve of which [9] are preserved also in Jerome's [10] translation · order confused. Two additional homilies [11] are contained in the same translation.[12] A fragment of the thirty-ninth homily is found in the *Philocalia*.[13] *Contents.* (1) Chap. i. 1–10, the commission, (2) ii 21 f., the wild vine, (3) ii 31, the goodness of God, (4) iii 6–10, dangers of apostasy, (5) iii 22–iv 8, call to repentance; (6) v 3–5, lack of understanding; (7) v 18 f., chastisement; (8) x. 12–14, God's

---

[1] Lommatzsch, XII, 152–306.   ([2] See, however, Gallandi
[3] Lommatzsch, XIV, 235–278
[4] Jerome, *Praef. in Comm ad Isai., Adv Rufin.* I, 13.
[5] Cf Rufinus, *Adv Hieronym* II. Lommatzsch, XIII, 235–301.
[6] *Homily* IV, 3
[7] Cassiodorus, *Inst div. litt* I, 3 gives 45, cf. *Philocalia*, 10
[8] *Codex Scorialens.* Ω, marked as by Cyril, *Codex Vatican.* 623
[9] *Homilies*, 1, 2, 4, 8–14, 16, and 17
[10] *Praef in Hom. in Jer. et Ezech.*   [11] *Hom.* 20 and 21
[12] Lommatzsch, XV, 109–388, 389–417.
[13] *Philocalia*, 10, Lommatzsch, XV, 418–420; cf. also the *Excerpta, Idem*, XV, 421–480.

work upon men, (9) xi 1-10, God's message to his people, (10) xi 18-xii 9, apostasy of the Jews, (11) xii 11-xiii 11, rejection of the Jews, (12) xiii. 12-17, righteous judgment, (13) xv 5-7, punishment of the impenitent, (14) xv 10-19, lot of the rejected prophets, (15) xv 10-12, xvii 5; no reliance upon man, (16) xvi 16-xvii 1, fishers for souls sin of Judah, (17) xvii 11-16, parable of the partridge (incomplete), (18) xviii 1-16, xx 1-6, the potter punishment of the impenitent Pashur, (19) xx 7-12, trial, and trust in God, (20) Latin 1 23-29, the hammer that smote the earth, (21) Latin li 6-9, flight from Babylon, (22) *Philocalia*, xliv 22

16 *Ezekiel* delivered after 244 A D. Jerome's list is incorrect, giving twelve homilies there are fourteen in Jerome's translation [1] *Contents* (1) Chap 1 1-16, the first vision, (2) xiii 2-9, against the false prophets, (3) xiii 17-xiv 8, gravity of the prophetic office, (4) xiv 13 f, deliverance of pious individuals, (5) xiv xv 2, judgments of God, (6) xvi 2-15, Jerusalem's faithlessness, (7) xvi 16-29, false doctrine, (8) xvi 30-33, results of false doctrine, (9) xvi 45-52, arrogance, (10) xvi 52-60, fruit of chastisement, (11) xvii 2, 3, parable of the eagle, (12) xvii 12-24, judgment and promise, (13) xxviii 12 f, concerning the King of Tyre; (14) xliv 2, the closed gate

17 *Luke*: delivered before the commentary (xxxii) on John [2] In Jerome's translation there are thirty-nine homilies, probably much abridged [3] On the possibility of the existence of more, see the remarks of Huet [4] *Contents*: (1) Chap 1 1-3, the four Gospels, (2) 1 6, piety of Zacharias and Elizabeth, (3) 1 11, the appearance of the angel, (4) 1 13-17 *a*. the promise to Zacharias, (5) 1 22, Zacharias' dumbness, (6) 1 24-32 *a*, Mary and the angel, (7) 1 39-45, Mary and Elizabeth, (8) 1 46-51 *a*, the song of Mary, (9) 1 56-64, birth of the Baptist, (10) 1 67-76, song of Zacharias, (11) 1 80-ii 2, growth of John, (12) ii 8-10, the angel and the shepherds, (13) ii 13-16, song of the angels, (14) ii 21-24, circumcision and purification, (15) ii 25-29, Simeon, (16) ii 33 f, Simeon's prophecy, (17) ii 33-36, Hannah; (18) ii

[1] Lommatzsch, XIV, 4-178 [3] Lommatzsch, V, 85-236
[2] Cf Chap ii, Lommatzsch, II, 378
[4] Huet, *Origeniana*, etc (see above), III, 2, 2 7, Lommatzsch, XXIV, 138 sq

40-49, Jesus in the temple, (19) ii 40-46, Jesus in the temple, (20) ii 49-51, obedience of Jesus, (21) iii 1-4, call of the Baptist, (22) iii 5-8, call to repentance, (23) iii 9-12, tax-gatherers, (24) iii 16, baptism of water and fire, (25) iii 15, the people regard the Baptist as the Messiah, (26) iii 17, the winnowing, (27) iii 18, the work of the Baptist, (28) iii 23 ff, genealogy (cf Matthew), (29) iv 1-4, the first temptation, (30) iv 5-8, second temptation, (31) iv 9-12, third temptation, (32) iv 14-20 and (33) iv 23-27, Jesus in Nazareth, (34) x 25-37, the Samaritan, (35) xii 58 f, peace with thine adversary, (36) xvii 33-21 (inverted order). the kingdom of God is within you, (37) xix 29 ff, the ass's colt, (38) xix 41-45, the cleansing of the temple, (39) xx 27 ff, 20 ff The questions of the high priests and the scribes

18 *Acts of the Apostles* date uncertain. Twenty-seven (seventeen) homilies according to Jerome's list A Greek fragment of the fourth homily, on i 16, is contained in the *Philocalia* [1]

19 *Corinthians*: Jerome's list gives eleven homilies on 2 Cor Apparently nothing has been preserved [2] They appear to have been delivered before the seventeenth homily on Luke,[3] and after the *Contra Celsum*,[4] i e after 248 A D [5]

20 *Galatians* · seven homilies according to Jerome's list, nothing preserved

21. *Thessalonians* two homilies according to Jerome's list, nothing preserved

22 *Titus*. one homily according to Jerome's list, nothing preserved

23 *Hebrews*: eighteen homilies according to Jerome's list, two fragments given by Eusebius [6]

Editions · *Origenis Homiliae*, 1475, published without the name of editor or place of publication The Homilies on the Pentateuch, Joshua, and Judges, at Venice, 1503 and 1512 The Homilies on the Song of Songs, Isaiah, Jeremiah, Ezekiel, Matthew (16 homilies), Luke (6), John (2), at Venice, 1513 The seven Homilies on Jere-

---

[1] *Philocalia*, 7, Lommatzsch, V, 245 sq.
[2] See Cramer, however   [3] Lommatzsch, V, 151.
[4] Cf. VIII, 24, Lommatzsch, XX, 142
[5] Westcott, *loc cit* 118 a, Preuschen, LG, 374.
[6] Eusebius, *Hist. Eccl* VI, 25. 11 sq, 13 sq.

miah, not translated by Jerome, were published by M Ghislerius (Greek — *Codex Vatic* — and Latin) in *Comm in Jerem* III, Lugd 1623 The nineteen Homilies on Jeremiah, bearing the name of Cyril, were published by B Coiderius (Greek — *Codex Scorial* — and Latin), Antveip 1648 The first edition of the homily ὑπὲρ τῆς ἐγγαστριμύθου, was published by L Allatius. Lugd 1629, 328-344, the latest, by A Jahn, in TU, II. 4, 1886, together with the reply of Eustathius — **Translations**. *Homiliensammlung aus den ersten sechs Jahrhunderten der christlichen Kirche*, by L Pelt, and H Rheinwald, I, 1. Berl 1829 (Hom 15 and 16 on Jeremiah, Hom 2 and portions of 9 and 39 on Luke) J C. W Augusti, *Predigten. auf alle Sonn- und Festtage aus den Schriften der Kirchenvatern*, new edit, I, 2, Coblence, 1833, II, 1, Cobl 1846 H Holtzmann, in Bunsen's *Bibelwerk*, VI, 1870, *Bibelurkunden*, II, 805–816 *Die Predigt der Kirche*, edited by G Leonhardi, Vol 22, edited by F. J Winter, Lpz 1893 (homilies 2 and 5 on Genesis, 2 on Leviticus, 1 on Song of Songs, 15, 16, and a part of 39 on Jeremiah, and 2, 7, and 8 on Luke) — Literature · See handbooks on the history of preaching Redepenning, *Origenes*, II, 212–261 Westcott, DCB, IV, 104–118 E Klostermann (*Griechische Excerpte aus Homilien des Origenes*) has proved in TU, XII. 3, 1894, that Procopius of Gaza copied the first four and the last eleven of Origen's Homilies on Joshua, in his ἐκλογαί (cf § 2, 1).

(*c*) The Τόμοι[1] were elaborate **commentaries**, which, in contrast with the more popular expositions in the homilies, were intended to make the contents of Holy Scripture intelligible to the educated and to those who desired profounder knowledge Their exegetical method, nevertheless, did not differ fundamentally from that of the homilies While painfully scrupulous in ascertaining the literal sense of the words, the author was indifferent to the wider context, and was altogether dominated by a conception that was based upon dogmatic assumptions, of which the chief was a belief in

[1] Th Birt, *Das antike Buchwesen*, 27 f.

the inspiration of the very letters. The following have been preserved: —

1 *Genesis:* The first eight books were written while Origen was still in Alexandria,¹ the remainder in Cæsarea. According to Eusebius² there were twelve books in all, according to Jerome,³ thirteen. Jerome's list gives fourteen. Two fragments in Latin, taken from the introduction, are given by Pamphilus,⁴ and one fragment from the first book, by Eusebius in his work against Marcellus of Ancyra.⁵ Fragments from the third book are as follows (*a*) in the *Philocalia*,⁶ and a short piece in Eusebius' *Præparatio Evangelica*;⁷ (*b*) *Philocalia*;⁸ (*c*) Eusebius' *History*.⁹ It is uncertain whether the last is a literal citation.¹⁰ According to a statement of Origen,¹¹ the commentary extended to Chapter V, 1. On its contents see Origen, *Contra Celsum*.¹² Harnack¹³ has shown that probably Ambrosius made use of the commentary in his *de Paradiso*.

2 *Exodus:* written before the commentary on the Song of Songs,¹⁴ that is, before 240 A D. The name Σημειώσεις is applied to them in the *Philocalia*,¹⁵ and they are called *Excerpta* in Jerome's list. Consequently it is not certain whether the five fragments that have been preserved in the *Philocalia*¹⁶ belonged to a commentary or to *scholia*.

3 *Leviticus:* the date of composition is uncertain. In Jerome's list they are designated as *Excerpta*; nothing extant.

¹ Eusebius, *Hist. Eccl* VI, 24. 2
² *Idem* ³ Jerome, *Epist.* 33 and 36, 9.
⁴ Pamphilus, *Apologia, Praef.*, Lommatzsch, XXIX, 296 sq , cf VIII, 1-3
⁵ Eusebius Caesar. *Adv. Marcell. Ancyr* I, 4, Lommatzsch, VIII, 4, cf. Pamphilus, *loc cit.* 3; Lommatzsch, XXIV, 328.
⁶ *Philocalia*, 23. ⁸ *Philocalia*, 14
⁷ *Praep Evang.* VI, 11. ⁹ *Hist Eccl* III, 1. 1-3
¹⁰ Cf also Eusebius, *Praep Evang* VII, 20; and Socrates, *Hist Eccl*. VII, 7, on Tome IX, Lommatzsch, VIII, 5-48
¹¹ *Contra Celsum*, VI, 49; cf Jerome, *Epist.* 36. 9, in *Opera*, I, 165 in the edition of Vallarsi.
¹² *Contra Celsum*, VI, 49-51. ¹³ TU, VI, 3, 1890, 119 f.
¹⁴ Cf. *Prol ad Cant. Cantic.*, Lommatzsch, XIV, 314
¹⁵ *Philocalia*, 27, Robinson's edition, 252 ¹⁶ *Philocalia*, 27.

4 *Psalms:* according to Jerome's list there were (1) *Excerpta in Psalmos a* 1 *ad* xv By this was probably meant the commentary on the first twenty-five psalms, mentioned by Eusebius[1] as having been written while Origen was still in Alexandria (2) Forty-six (according to Redepenning, or forty-five according to Pitra) Books of Excerpts on thirty-six (thirty-five) psalms, as far as Psalm ciii (3) *Excerpta in totum Psalterium,* perhaps identical with the *Enchiridion* mentioned by the author of the *Breviarium in Psalterium*[2] Numerous fragments are extant, whose connection with a commentary can only be established in a few cases[8] The date of (2) and (3) is uncertain

5 *Proverbs:* according to Jerome's list, three books Fragments are given (from *Catenae*)[4] in Lommatzsch's edition of Origen's works[5]

6. *Song of Songs:* the first five books were composed in Athens (about 240 A D), and the second five soon afterward in Cæsarea[6] Jerome's list mentions ten books and two "*quos insuper scripsit in adolescentia* "[7] A fragment from this youthful work,[8] and also two others (*Catenae*) from the larger commentary,[9] are contained in the *Philocalia* Extracts are found in the works of Procopius of Gaza[10] Besides, there was a Latin recension in four books by Rufinus[11] Jerome[12] considered that this commentary was Origen's best work

7. *Lamentations:* written in Alexandria[13] Jerome's list gives five books, but, according to Eusebius,[14] there were originally more

---

[1] Eusebius, *Hist. Eccl* VI, 24 2.

[2] Appended to Jerome's seventh volume, Migne, PL, XXVI, 821 ff.

[3] Cf. the fragments in Lommatzsch, XI, 351–379, 384–391, 440–453, XII, 10 sq , 47, 73, 350 sq.

[4] Pamphilus, *Apologia,* 10.

[5] Lommatzsch, XIII, 217–234; XXIV, 410–412. Cf also Mai, NPB. 1–56.

[6] Eusebius, *Hist Eccl.* VI, 32 2.

[7] Cf. also Eusebius, *loc. cit* , Jerome, *Prol. expos. Cant. Cantic sec. Orig* ; Lommatzsch, XIV, 235, *Epist.* 37. 3.

[8] *Philocalia,* 7, Lommatzsch, XIV, 233 sq

[9] Cramer, VIII, 115 f , *Philocalia,* 27

[10] Lommatzsch, XV, 91–108   [11] *Idem,* XIV, 287–437; XV, 1–90.

[12] *Prol. expos Cant. Cantic.,* cf note 7, above.

[13] Eusebius, *Hist Eccl.* VI, 24. 2   [14] *Idem*

Maximus Confessor [1] appears to have been acquainted with a tenth book   Extracts in *Catenae* are given by Lommatzsch [2]

8 *Isaiah:* written about 235 A D [3] Jerome's list makes thirty-six books, though Eusebius [4] was acquainted with only thirty   Two fragments in Latin are preserved in the work of Pamphilus [5]

9. *Ezekiel:* written after 235 A D and completed in Athens about 240 A D [6] According to Eusebius,[6] there were twenty-five books   Jerome's list gives twenty-four (Pitra and Redepenning, twenty-nine)   A fragment from the twentieth book (on Chap xxxiv. 17–19) is contained in the *Philocalia*.[7]

10 *The Minor Prophets:* written after 244 A D   According to Eusebius,[8] Jerome,[9] and Jerome's list, there were twenty-five books, two on Hosea, two on Joel, six on Amos, one on Jonah, two on Micah, two on Nahum, three on Habakkuk, two on Zephaniah, one on Haggai, two on Zechariah, and two on Malachi.   Á fragment from Hosea (Chap. xii) is contained in the *Philocalia* [10]

11 *Matthew:* written after 244 A D , under Philip the Arabian,[11] and after the commentary on Romans [12] It contained twenty-five books, according to Eusebius [13] and Jerome's list   Books X–XVII have been preserved [14] (Chap xiii 36–xxii 33)   Greek fragments from Books I and II are given by Eusebius [15] and in the *Philocalia*,[16] and others in Latin from Books I and VII, by Pamphilus [17]   Besides,

[1] *Opera*, ed Corder. II, 315 D.
[2] Lommatzsch, XIII, 167–216, cf. B Montfaucon, *Bibliotheca Coisliniana*, 42.
[3] Eusebius, *Hist Eccl* VI, 32 1   [4] *Idem*
[5] Pamphilus, *Apologia*, 5 and 7, Lommatzsch, XIII, 235–238 (XXIV, 370 sq., 385–387).
[6] Eusebius, *Hist. Eccl* VI, 32 1 sq
[7] *Philocalia*, 11, Lommatzsch, XIV, 2 sq
[8] Eusebius, *Hist Eccl* VI, 36 2   [9] *De Viris Illust.* 75.
[10] *Philocalia*, 8, Lommatzsch, XIII, 302–304
[11] Eusebius, *Hist Eccl* VI, 26 2.   [12] Cf. XVII, 32.
[13] Eusebius, *Hist. Eccl* VI, 26 2
[14] Lommatzsch, III, 7–IV, 172. Books X–XIV have been translated by John Patrick, ANF, IX, 414–512.
[15] Eusebius, *Hist Eccl* VI, 25. 4 sq
[16] *Philocalia*, 6, Lommatzsch, III, 1–6
[17] Pamphilus, *Apologia*, 5 and 10, Lommatzsch, XXIV, 372, 405 sqq (V, 307–310)

there is a Latin recension in 145 sections (Matt xvi 13–xxvii 63)¹

12 *Mark:* In the *Codex Paris* 939, a commentary on Mark is erroneously ascribed to Origen

13 *Luke:* containing five books, according to Jerome² and Rufinus,³ but fifteen according to Jerome s list⁴

14 *John:* The first five books were written in Alexandria,⁵ probably before 228 A D After the persecution under Maximus, that is, after 238 A D, Origen labored further upon the work⁶, Jerome's list gives thirty-two books, Eusebius⁷ was still acquainted with twenty-two, Jerome⁸ gives the number as thirty-nine, and this may have been correct if Origen carried the commentary beyond Chap xiii 33 Book I, Chap 1 1 *a*, II, 1 1 *b*–7 *a*, VI, 1 19–29, X, 11. 12–25, XIII, iv 13–44, XIX (parts of), viii 19–24, XX, viii 37–52, XXVIII, xi 39–57, XXXII, xiii 2–33⁹ On the (seven) manuscripts, see the remarks of A E Brooke¹⁰ The archetype is a manuscript of the thirteenth century¹¹ Fragments of Books IV and V (literary style of the Apostles, excuses for too great diffuseness) are contained in the *Philocalia*,¹² in *Catenae*, and in Eusebius' *History*¹³ Latin fragments are given by Pamphilus¹⁴ The alleged citation from the second book, made by Pamphilus,¹⁵ is not found in the Greek text [Books I, II, VI, and X, with fragments of IV and

---

¹ Lommatzsch, IV, 173–V, 84 (from Chap xxii 34 on); cf. Cramer, *Ein Prolog* in M Crusius' *Univ Progr*, Gottingen, 1735, also Redepenning, II, 465 f. Lommatzsch, XX, VI–VIII

² Jerome, *Prolog in Hom Orig in Luc.*

³ Rufinus, *Adv Hieronym* II, 19.

⁴ Cf Cramer, *loc cit* (cf. Note 1 above), Redepenning, II, 466–469; Lommatzsch, XX, VIII–XII

⁵ Cf VI, 1   ⁷ *Idem*, VI, 24 1
⁶ Eusebius, *Hist Eccl* VI, 28   ⁸ *Prolog. in Hom Orig in Luc.*
⁹ Lommatzsch, I, 1–160, 173–375, II.
¹⁰ A E Brooke (§ 24 2), TSt, I, 4, 1891, 1–30
¹¹ *Codex Monac Graec.* 191, *saec.* XIII.   ¹² *Philocalia*, 4–5.
¹³ Cf. Bratke (§ 2. 1, above), Lommatzsch, I, 161–172, Eusebius, *Hist Eccl* VI, 25 7–10.
¹⁴ Pamphilus, *Apologia*, 5, Lommatzsch, XXIV, 356 sq (V, 305 sq);
cf. also Eustathius, *De Engastrimytho*, 21 (Jahn, 60).
¹⁵ Pamphilus, *Apologia*, 5, Lommatzsch, XXIV, 361 sq (V, 303 sq.).

V, have been translated by Allan Menzies in ANF, IX, 297-408] On the text of the second book, see J L Jacobi [1]

15 *Romans:* written after 244 A D , but before the commentary on Matthew. According to Jerome's list, it contained fifteen books Two fragments from Books I and IX are contained in the *Philocalia*. [2] a sentence from III, 8,[3] is found in Basil [4]   Besides there is a free Latin recension, in ten books, made by Rufinus, in whose time the text was already corrupt [5]   This recension was not based on the text of the Epistle used by Origen, but on an Itala text [6]

The following commentaries were written during the later years of Origen's life —

16 *Galatians:* according to Jerome's list, fifteen books, but, according to Jerome's introduction to his commentary on the Galatians,[7] there were five   Three Latin fragments from Book I are given by Pamphilus [8]

17 *Ephesians* · Jerome's list gives three books   It was translated by Jerome himself,[9] and a Latin fragment from Book III is found in his book against Rufinus [10]   He also copied from Origen [11] in his commentary on the Epistle to the Ephesians (see the preface)

18 *Colossians:* two books, according to Jerome's list   A Latin fragment from the third (*sic*) book is given by Pamphilus in his *Apology*.[12]

19. *Philippians:* one book, according to Jerome's list. Nothing extant.

20 *Thessalonians:* three books, according to Jerome's list, which possibly covered only the first Epistle   A Latin fragment from the

---

[1] J L. Jacobi, Hallé, 1878, Crusius, etc. (see p. 193, note 1), Redepenning, *Origenes*. II, 469-472; Lommatzsch, XX, pp. XII-XVI.

[2] *Philocalia*, 9 and 25, Lommatzsch, V, 247-260.

[3] Lommatzsch, VI, 211   [4] Basil, *De Spiritu sanc.* 73, cf. also Cramer.

[5] Cf. Jerome, *Adv Rufin.* I, 11, 20, II, 16, 18. Praedestinatus, I, 22, 43; Rufinus, *De Adulteratione librorum Origenis*, Lommatzsch, XXV, 382-400

[6] Westcott, DCB, IV, 116-117 a

[7] *Prooem Comm in Epist. ad Gal* VII, 369, edition of Vallarsi.

[8] Pamphilus, *Apologia*, 5; Lommatzsch, XXIV, 362-370 (V, 261-270).

[9] *Adv Rufin* I, 16, 21; cf. III, 10   [10] *Idem*, I, 28, cf. Cramer

[11] Cf Theo Zahn, GNK, II, 2, 427 N 2.

[12] Pamphilus, *Apologia*, 5; Lommatzsch, XXIV, 372 sq. (V, 273 sq)

third book (on 1 Thes iv. 15-17) is given by Jerome in his Epistle to Minervius and Alexander [1]

21 *Titus*. one book, according to Jerome's list. Five Latin fragments are given by Pamphilus [2]

22 *Philemon* one book, according to Jerome's list, from which a Latin fragment is given by Pamphilus [3]

23 *Hebrews*: not given in Jerome's list But four fragments of a commentary are found in Pamphilus' *Apology* [4]

24 Whether Origen commented on the *Catholic Epistles* and the *Apocalypse* [5] is uncertain

Editions. The commentary on the Epistle to the Romans, in a Latin translation (erroneously ascribed to Jerome), Venice, 1506 and 1512 The commentary on the Gospel of John, in a Latin translation, published by A Ferrarius, Venice, 1551, and by J Perionius about 1554. The first edition of extant original texts (without the fragments in *Catenae*), by P D Huetius, *Origenis in sacras Scripturas Commentaria quaecunque graece reperiri potuerunt*, 2 vols, Rothomagi, 1668 (Paris, 1679; Cologne, 1685) A good summary of the contents of the commentaries on Matthew, John, and the Epistle to the Romans, with special notice of remarkable passages, is given by Westcott On the relation of Procopius of Gaza to Origen, and of Origen to Philo's *Quaestiones*, see P. Wendland, *Neuentdeckte Fragmente Philos*, Berlin, 1891, 109-126

7 (*a*) Of Origen's **apologetical works**, only the eight books κατὰ Κέλσου (**contra Celsum**) are extant [6] The archetype of all the manuscripts that are known is a Vatican codex from the thirteenth century,[7] which contains a comparatively early and complete text. Considerable portions also have been preserved in the

[1] Jerome, *Epist. ad Min. et Alex*. 119. 9, *Opera*, I, 809-814, edit of Vallarsi, Lommatzsch, V, 275-282, cf. Origen, *Contra Celsum*, II, 65
[2] Pamphilus, *Idem*, 1 and 9, Lommatzsch, XXIV, 313-319, 398 sq (V, 283-292).
[3] Pamphilus, *Apol* 6; Lommatzsch, XXIV, 376 sqq. (V, 292-296).
[4] *Idem*, 3 and 5, *Idem*, XXIV, 328, 357 sqq. (V, 297-300).
[5] Cf. *Comm. Ser in Matt* 49.   [6] Lommatzsch, XVIII-XX, 226.
[7] *Codex Vaticanus*, 386, *saec* XIII.

Philocalia. The book was written during the reign of Philip the Arabian, that is, after 244 A D.,[1] and very probably in 248 A.D. It was occasioned by the request of Ambrosius [2] that Origen should refute the charges and objections brought against Christianity [3] by the heathen philosopher Celsus in his 'Αληθής Λόγος (between 177 and 180 A D) The apology takes up the opponent's propositions one by one. After an introduction, in which the main points are briefly cited and reviewed (I, 1–27), the remainder of the work falls into four parts: (1) Refutation of Jewish objections (I, 28–II, 79); (2) of the objections made by Celsus himself against the foundations of Christian doctrine (III–IV); (3) and of those made against particular doctrines (VI–VII, 61), (4) refutation of Celsus' defence of the heathen state-religion (VII, 62–VIII, 71). This work is plainly distinguished from the apologetic pamphlets of the second century by the fact that it was not constructed simply to meet the needs of the passing moment, but that it embodied a scientific discussion with an experienced opponent; was undertaken with all the aids furnished by criticism, history, and philosophy; and that it was, though full of assumptions and prejudices, the most perfect apologetic performance from the standpoint of the Christianity of the early church.[4]

Editions: A Latin translation of *Christi persona*, Rom 1481. D. Hoeschelius, Aug Vind. 1605 Guil. Spencerus, Cantab 1658 W. Selwyn, Cambr 1876 (only first four books) cf F. Overbeck, in ThLZ, 1876, 477 — **Translations**: J L Mosheim, Hamb 1745. J. Rohm, 2 vols. in BKV, 1876–77. Fred Crombie, in ANF, IV, 395–669.

[1] Eusebius, *Hist. Eccl* VI, 36. 2
[2] See § 61. 2, above.
[3] See the Prologue.
[4] Cf Eusebius, *Adv. Hierocl.* 1.

Literature P Koetschau, *Die Textuberlieferung der Bucher des Origenes gegen Celsus*, in TU, VI, 1, 1889 Cf J A Robinson, On the Text of Origen against Celsus, in the Journal of Philology, XVIII, 1890, 288–296 F. Wallis, MSS of Origen against Celsus, in the Classical Review, 1889, 392–398 P Koetschau, *Die Gliederung des ἀληθὴς λόγος des Celsus*, in JprTh, XVIII, 1892, 604–632 K J Neumann, *Der romische Staat und die allgem Kirche*, I, Lpz 1889, 265–273 The literature on Celsus, especially Theo Keim, *Celsus' Wahres Wort*, Zurich, 1873 B Aubé, *La polémique paienne à la fin du deuxième siècle*, Paris, 1878 E Pélagaud, *Étude sur Celse*, Lyon, 1878

The accounts of disputations with heretics have been lost, as follows : —

(*b*) Ζητήσεις(καὶ διαλέξεις)πρὸς Βήρυλλον (of Bostra),[1]

(*c*) *Disputatio cum haeretico quodam*[2] The disputation apparently took place in Athens;

(*d*) *Dialogus adv Candidum Valentinianum,*[3]

(*e*) Διάλογος πρὸς τὸν 'Α[ὰ?]γνώμονα Βάσσον;[4]

(*f*) *Anti-heretical Writings*, without further description of their contents, are mentioned by Pamphilus,[5] Epiphanius,[6] Theodoret,[7] and Nicephorus[8] On the *Philosophumena* and the *Dialogus de recta fide*, see below.[9]

8. The **dogmatic writings** of Origen have suffered most of all from the prejudices of narrow theological opponents, some have perished, and none has escaped unscathed

[1] Cf Eusebius, *Hist. Eccl.* VI, 33 3. Jerome, *De Viris Illust* 60
[2] Cf Origen, *Epist ad quosdam caros suos Alexandriam*, in Rufinus' *De Adulteratione librorum Orig* Lommatzsch, XXV, 389
[3] Cf Jerome's list and Jerome, *Adv. Rufin* II, 9
[4] Cf Julius Afric. *Epist ad Orig. de Susanna* Origen, *Ep ad Afric.* 2
[5] Pamphilus, *Apologia pro Orig.* Pref and 1
[6] Epiphanius, *Haer* LXIV, 5 (Cf LXVI, 21)
[7] *Haer Fab* I, 2, 4, 19, 21, 25, II, 2, 7, III, 1
[8] *Hist Eccl* X, 10. [9] § 91 and § 80 respectively.

(a) Περὶ ἀρχῶν, *De Principiis*, the principal dogmatic work of Origen, is known to posterity only in a mutilated form¹ A number of fragments of the original have been preserved in the *Philocalia*,² also by Marcellus of Ancyra,³ and in Justinian's letter to Mennas, patriarch of Constantinople, anno 543⁴ The whole work is contained in a Latin translation by Rufinus of Aquileia, made in 397 A D, which, according to the translator's own confession (see the Prologue), is often only an arbitrary recasting of the original It is to be regretted that the translation which Jerome made as an offset to that of Rufinus,⁵ and for which he claimed literal fidelity,⁶ has been lost with the exception of a considerable number of fragments contained in the Epistle to Avitus⁷ The work was composed in Alexandria, probably not long before 230 A D,⁸ and treated of the fundamental doctrines of Christian theology,⁹ which were briefly summarized in the preface in accordance with the rule of faith Although its execution, at least in the first three books, is dominated by the author's philosophical and theological views (I, the doctrine of pre-mundane existence, II, of the world in its present condition, III, of the freedom of the will), nevertheless the contents of each book, and more especially of the fourth (IV, Exposition of Scripture), show adherence to an original plan This first systematic compendium of Christian doctrine remained the only dogmatic theology with any independent character belonging to the ancient church.

¹ Lommatzsch, XXI
² *Philocalia*, Chaps 1 and 21
³ Eusebius, *Adv Marc Ancyr* I, 4
⁴ Mansi, *Coll Conc* IX, 523-534
⁵ Cf *Epist* 83-85
⁶ *Epist* 84, 12
⁷ *Epist* 124
⁸ Eusebius, *Hist* VI, 24. 3.
⁹ Schnitzer, XXI sq.

Editions: E. R Redepenning, Lips 1836 An attempt at a reconstruction in German was made by K F Schnitzer, Stuttg. 1835. — **Translation:** Frederick Crombie, in ANF, IV, 239-382.

(*b*) Στρωματεῖς [*Stromata*], containing ten books according to Eusebius[1] and Jerome's list. Besides a Greek fragment,[2] three Latin fragments are preserved in Jerome's work against Rufinus,[3] and in his commentaries on Daniel[4] and Galatians[5] Compare Origen's Commentary on John,[6] and Jerome's reference in his Commentary on Daniel,[7] to Origen's expositions in the tenth book (on Susanna and Bel)[8] According to Jerome,[9] in this work Origen tried (in imitation of Clement) to show the agreement of Christian with philosophic doctrines. Possibly the extracts from philosophical writings mentioned by Eusebius[10] were related to the *Stromata* written while Origen was yet in Alexandria. An extract from this work, made by the presbyter Beatus, is said to exist in the library of the Escurial.[11]

(*c*) Περὶ ἀναστάσεως: two books, according to Eusebius[12] and Jerome's list, Jerome, as quoted by Rufinus,[13] speaks of two books and two dialogues; and afterward

---

[1] Eusebius, *Hist* VI, 24. 3   [2] Cramer, *Catenae in Act Apost.* 10, on 1 12
[3] Jerome, *Adv Rufin.* I, 18
[4] *Idem, Comm. in Dan.* ix 14. (*Opera*, V, 691.)
[5] *Idem, Comm. in Epist ad Galatas*, III, on Gal. v. 13. (*Opera*, VII, 494 sq. Lommatzsch, XVII, 69 sq 75-78.
[6] Origen, *Comm. in Joh* XIII, 45
[7] Jerome, *Comm. in Dan* xiii. 1. (*Opera*, V, 730-736.) Lommatzsch, XVII, 70-75.
[8] Also see Jerome, *Comm. in Jerem.* IV. on Jer. xxii. 24 ff. (*Opera*, IV, 994) *Comm. in Dan.* iv. 5. (*Opera*, V, 646.) *Epist.* 84. 3. *Adv. Rufin.* II, 1.
[9] Jerome, *Epist.* 70, 4   [10] Eusebius, *Hist Eccl* VI, 18. 3.
[11] Cf. Redepenning, *Origenes*, I, p XIII, and II, p IV.
[12] Eusebius, *Hist Eccl.* VI, 24. 2.   [13] Rufinus, *Adv. Hier* II, 47.

in his book against John of Jerusalem,[1] Jerome mentions four books. Two Greek fragments are preserved by Methodius (as quoted by Photius [2]) and by Epiphanius [3] (following the excerpt of Methodius); and four Latin fragments are preserved by Pamphilus.[4] Compare also the excerpt made by Jerome in his book against John of Jerusalem.[5] The work was written at Alexandria before the περὶ ἀρχῶν [6] and the Commentary on Lamentations;[7] that is, before 230 A.D. The contents of this book drew forth a reply from Methodius of Olympus, which embodied much of Origen's material.

(*d*) A little book, *De libero arbitrio*, is mentioned by Origen himself,[8] but we may assume that he had in mind merely the first section of the third book of his Περὶ ἀρχῶν.

(*e*) We can no longer determine the facts as to the writing Περὶ φύσεων, a fragment of which has been preserved by Victor of Capua [9]

(*f*) The existence of a special Συγγραμμάτιον on the "Sin against the Holy Ghost," may possibly be inferred from Athanasius' Four Epistles to Serapion.[10]

9. The fate of the **works** written for purposes of **edification** has been more fortunate, since the nature

---

[1] Jerome, *contra Joh. Hierosolym.* 25.
[2] Photius, *Codex*, 234 (Bekker, 300 ff.)
[3] Epiphanius, *Panarion*, LXIV, 12-16.
[4] Pamphilus, *Apologia*, 7. Lommatzsch, XVII, 55-58 (XXIV, 379-385).
[5] Jerome, *contra Joh. Hierosolym.* 25, 26. (*Opera*, II, 431-434. Lommatzsch, XVII, 60-64.)
[6] Cf II, 10. Redepenning, 223. Lommatzsch, XXI, 229.
[7] Eusebius, *Hist Eccl.* VI, 24. 2.
[8] *Comm. in Epist ad Rom.* VII, 16; Lommatzsch, VII, 167.
[9] *Scholia veterum patrum* (Pitra, SpS, 268)
[10] Athanasius, *Epist. 4 ad Serapion.*, 11, p 709, Montfaucon.

of the subject scarcely furnished occasion for theological heresy, but gave full play to the development of the rhetorical powers of a Christian personality

(a) Εἰς μαρτύριον προτρεπτικὸς λόγος, *Exhortatio ad martyrium*, has been preserved in several manuscripts [1] This treatise was intended to exhort his friends Ambrosius and Protoctetus, a presbyter at Cæsarea, to steadfastness in the approaching persecution (under Maximinus, *i.e.* 235 A.D.).[2] It is an enthusiastic hymn in praise of martyrdom, the pains of which purchase an exceeding reward, while martyrdom itself becomes, like baptism, a means for the forgiveness of one's own sins, and perhaps for those of others also.

Editions · J R. Wetstenius, Basil. 1674 New edition, in preparation, by P. Koetschau. — **Translations** J. Kohlhofer, in BKV, 1874

(b) Περὶ εὐχῆς, *De Oratione*, is preserved in a manuscript at Trinity College, Cambridge;[3] the conclusion, addressed to Ambrosius and the sister Tatiana, is found also in a codex at Paris.[4] It was written before the commentary on Exodus,[5] perhaps in 235 A D., or possibly considerably earlier.[6] In two parts, the author treats of prayer in general (Chaps. 3–17), and of the Lord's Prayer in particular (Chaps 18–30) The conclusion (Chaps 31–32) returns again to the subjects discussed

---

[1] *Codex Venet.* 45, *saec* XIV (lacks caption), *Codex Paris Suppl. Graec* 616, *anno* 1339, and *Cod Basil* A III, 9, *saec* XVI (used in printed text) Fragments are found in *Codex Reg. Paris. Gr.* 945, *saec.* XIV, Lommatzsch, XX, 227 (237)–316.
[2] Neumann, *Der romische Staat*, etc., 228, N. 3.
[3] *Codex Cantab Coll S Trinit*
[4] *Codex Reg. Paris.* (formerly Colbert 3607).
[5] Cf. Chap. 3, Lommatzsch, XVII, 97.
[6] Lommatzsch, XVII, 79 (82)–297

in the first part, which it treats yet further In spite of the fact that the book is unnecessarily burdened with exegetical profundity and philosophical subtlety, it is full of truly edifying thoughts in original setting, and is pervaded with a spirit of genuine piety It is the pearl among all the writings of the Alexandrians. The scholia by an unknown writer, which are added in the editions, stand in no relation to Origen's tractate.

Editions Oxon 1686 J R Wetstenius, Basil 1694 Guil. Reading, Lugd 1728 — Translation J Kohlhofer, in BKV, 1874.

10 Only two of the numerous **Letters** of Origen, mentioned by Eusebius,[1] and in Jerome's list, are extant in their integrity.

(*a*) Ἐπιστολὴ πρὸς Ἀφρικανόν, preserved in numerous manuscripts,[2] was occasioned by the critical doubts touching the history of Susanna,[3] which Julius Africanus[4] had set forth in a letter to Origen during his stay in Nicomedia. This extended reply to a terse letter is no very noteworthy witness to the author's critical acumen. It was written in Nicomedia,[5] during the journey to Athens; that is, probably about 240 A D.

Editions D Hoeschelius, Aug Vind. 1602 (contains only the beginning) J R Wetstenius, Basil 1674. Translated by F Crombie, ANF, IV, 386-392

(*b*) Πρὸς Γρηγόριον ἐπιστολή (preserved in the *Philocalia*),[6] was, possibly,[7] written soon after 238 A.D, with

---

[1] Eusebius, *Hist Eccl* VI, 36. 3. Cf. also VI, 28 and 39; and § 61. 1, above.
[2] Lommatzsch, XVII, 20-48.   [4] Cf § 82 3, *c*.
[3] Dan xiii LXX.   [5] Cf. Chap 15
[6] *Philocalia*, 13. Lommatzsch, XVII, 49-52, XXV, 66-69.
[7] Draeseke differs as to date.

:he fatherly purpose of turning Gregorius Thaumaturgus,[1] his former pupil, from the pursuit of worldly science, and of directing him towards labor in the service of Christianity

Editions See editions of the *Philocalia*, at § 61, 4, above P Koetschau, in SQu, IX, 1894, 40–44 Cf J Draeseke, in JprTh, VII, 1881, 102–126 (the epistle is printed on pp 108–112) Translated by F Crombie, in ANF, IV, 393–394, and by Allan Menzies, ANF, IX, 393–394

(c) Fragments of the following letters are extant: —
1. Πρὸς τινα περὶ 'Αμβροσίου, written from Athens.[2]
2. Πρὸς τινας μεμψαμένους αὐτῷ διὰ τὴν περὶ ἐκεῖνα (scil. τὰ Ἑλλήνων μαθήματα) σπουδήν.[3]
3 *Ad quosdam caros suos Alexandriam Epistola.*[4] According to Jerome, the letter contained an expostulation with Bishop Demetrius on account of his excommunication, and complaints of the perversion of his writings [5]
4. Πρὸς Φώτιον καὶ 'Ανδρέαν πρεσβυτέρους ἐπιστολή.[6]
5 *Epistola ad Gobarum, de undecima.*[7]
6 *Epistola ad Firmilianum de his qui fugiant quaestionem* [8]

(d) The following letters are also mentioned : To the

[1] § 75, below.
[2] Cf. Suidas, *Lexicon*, under "Origen" (Bernh II, 1, 1279. Jerome's *Epist*. 43 1, Lommatzsch, XVII, 5).
[3] Cf Eusebius, *Hist*. VI, 12–14, Lommatzsch XVII, 6.
[4] Cf Jerome, *Adv Rufin*. II, 18, Lommatzsch, XVII, 6 sq. Rufinus, *De Adulterat libror*. Orig , Idem, XVII, 8 sqq., XXV, 388–392.
[5] Cf also the fragment from *Cod. Vindob lat.* 4512, *saec*. XV, fol. 286–287 in *Tabulae Codicorum mss. Vindob*. III 294. Denis, *Codd Theol. Lat. Vindob*. I, 2. Cod. CCCCXLII.
[6] Cf Gallandi, XIV, App p. 10.
[7] Cf. Victor Capuanus, *Scholia ex vet. Patr.*, Pitra, SpS, I, 267.
[8] Cf. *idem*, Pitra, SpS, I, 268.

emperor, Philip the Arabian,[1] and to his wife Severa,[2] to Fabian of Rome,[3] to various bishops,[4] to Beryllus of Bostra,[5] and to Trypho[6] (or from Trypho to Origen?). On the foregoing, see the remarks of Preuschen.[7]

11 With regard to the following, the tradition is uncertain or obscure.

(*a*) *De Pascha*   According to Victor of Capua[8] and Anatolius Alexandrinus,[9] Origen wrote a book with this title, in which were given the data necessary for calculating the date of Easter. The two fragments[10] given by the authors just named are not necessarily spurious

(*b*) *De Nominibus Hebraicis*. According to Jerome,[11] this was an etymological list of Old Testament names, which Origen regarded as a work of Philo, and which "he completed by the addition of Hebrew names occurring in the New Testament, or those that apparently could be derived from the Hebrew" (Zahn) What Jerome gives as his own work probably only supplemented Origen's material with insignificant additions It is possible that the book on "Hebrew measures and weights,"[12] mentioned by Pseudo-Justin,[13] was identical with this work of Origen.

[1] Cf. Eusebius, *Hist.* VI, 36. 3.
[2] *Idem*
[3] *Idem*, cf Jerome, *Epist.* 84 10.
[4] *Idem*
[5] Jerome, *De Viris Illust* 60
[6] *Idem*, 57
[7] In Harnack, LG, 387–389
[8] Cf Victor Capuanus, *Scholia ex vet. Patr.* Pitra, SpS, I, 267.
[9] *De ratione Paschali* , *De pace*, in Jerome's list.
[10] Pitra, SpS, I, 268 B. Krusch, *Studien zur mittalterlichen Chronologie*, Lpz. 1880, 317.
[11] *Praef ad libr. interpret hebraicor. nominum* (*Opera*, III, 1 sqq. Vallarsi, P de Lagarde, *Onomastica sacra*, 1887, p 1, 2d edit p. 26.
[12] Cf Theo. Zahn, GNK, II, 2, 948–953
[13] *Quaestiones ad Orthodoxos*, 86, Otto, III, 3d edit. 112

(c) The tractate, *De Phe litera*,¹ was, possibly, only a part of the exposition of Ps cxviii. (cxix.).

(d) In Jerome's list the titles of the following treatises are also mentioned: *De proverbiorum quibusdam quaestionibus; de Pace (pascha ?); Exhortatoria (epistola ?) ad Pioniam; de Jejunio; de Monogamis et Trigamis homm.* II; *In Tarso homm.* II.²

§ 62. Trypho

Fabricius, BG, 289 sq   Harnack, LG, 405.

Jerome[3] says of **Trypho**, a pupil of Origen, that he was well acquainted with the Holy Scriptures The proof of this statement is said to have been derived from his disquisitions, particularly his book *De Vacca rufa* (Num. xix., which Jerome gives erroneously as Deuteronomy), and his *De Dichotomematibus* (on Genesis xv. 9 ff.). No part of either writing is extant.

§ 63. Dionysius

Editions: S de Magistris, Rom 1796   Routh, RS, III, 221–259; IV, 393–454   Migne, PG, X, 1233–1344, 1575–1602   **Translation**: S D F Salmond, in ANF, VI, 81–120   Literature: Frz. Dittrich, *Dionysius der Grosse von Alexandrien*, Freib 1/B 1867   Th. Forster, in ZhTh, XLI, 1871, 42–77   Fabricius, BG, 278–283. Richardson, BS, 66–68   Harnack, LG, 409–427.

Dionysius, the great bishop of Alexandria[4] and teacher of the Catholic church,[5] was born of heathen parents, probably before the close of the second century.[6] Though already possessing a position of worldly

---

[1] Jerome, *Epist.* 43 1; Cf Rufinus, *Adv. Hieron.* II, 18.
[2] Cf Preuschen, in Harnack's LG, 386.
[3] Jerome, *De Viris Illust* 57.   [5] Athanasius, *Sentent Diony.* 6.
[4] Eusebius, *Hist.* VII, preface.   [6] Cf. Eusebius, *Hist.* VII, 27. 2.

honor, he renounced the prospect of a brilliant career for the sake of the Christian faith.¹ He became a zealous pupil of Origen, and even after the death of his master,² he remained devoted to him in faithful gratitude, though without any servile adherence to his words ³ As the successor of Heraclas he stood at the head of the Catechetical School⁴ from 232 A.D. onward. According to Jerome (69) he was a presbyter. Apparently he did not abandon the School⁵ when he was called in 247/248 to the episcopate.⁶ In the conviction that he could serve the church better by his life than by his death,⁷ he escaped the Decian persecution by flight (250/251 A.D.), but was banished by Valerian (after 257 A.D), first to Libya, and afterward to Mareotis, though without severing his relation with his congregation ⁸ Apparently it was early in 262 A.D. that the edict of toleration, issued by Gallienus, permitted his return,⁹ but want and danger, both to himself and to his congregation,¹⁰ made the last years of his life a period of laborious discipline and trial.¹¹ Age and infirmity prevented him from taking part in the synod assembled at Antioch against Paul of Samosata,¹² 264/265, and he died soon afterward, in 265 A.D.¹³

2. The **writings** of Dionysius are a true reflex of a character at once clever, thoughtful, and averse to all extremes. Almost without exception ¹⁴ his writings were

---

¹ Eusebius, *Hist* VII, 11. 18.
² Cf. § 63, 4 f. 6 below.
⁴ Eusebius, *Hist*. VI, 29. 5; Jerome, *De Viris Illust.* 69.
⁵ Guerike, 71–74.
⁶ Eusebius, *Hist*. VI, 48.
⁷ *Idem*, VI, 40. 3.
⁸ *Idem*, VII, 11.
⁹ *Idem*, VII, 13, 21. 1.
³ Cf. § 63, 3 *b*, below.
¹⁰ *Idem*, VII, 21–22.
¹¹ *Idem*, VII, 22 6.
¹² *Idem*, VII, 27. 2.
¹³ *Idem*, VII, 28. 3.
¹⁴ See § 63, 3 *a–b*.

called forth by some particular occasion, for the most part they were in the form of letters They were not products of learned leisure, but of practical needs, and were directed against religious enthusiasts (Nepos), ecclesiastical hotspurs (Germanus, Novatian), theological (Dionysius of Rome), or ecclesiastical opponents (baptism by heretics). Only fragments of these writings have been preserved Eusebius incorporated in the sixth and seventh books of his *Church History*, with praiseworthy minuteness, whatever seemed to him suitable for the characterization of a troublous time

2 (*a*) The seven extensive fragments from a work Περὶ φύσεως, preserved by Eusebius,[1] may be considered preeminently as a monument to the learning of Dionysius This treatise, which is in the form of a letter, probably dates from the period before the author became a bishop,[2] and it was intended, possibly, to serve as a guide to his son,[3] Timotheus, who is designated as the recipient It is "the earliest coherent refutation of Atomism, based on a Christian view of the world"[4] The subject of the extant fragment refers particularly to the refutation of the theory of Democritus and Epicurus Both plan and execution give evidence of the author's studies as well as of his literary gifts

G Roch, *Die Schrift des alexandrinischen Bischofs Dionysius des Grossen uber die Natur*, Lpz 1882 (Pp 28-41 contains a

[1] Eusebius, *Praep Evang* XIV, 23-27, cf also the small fragments in the *Sacra Parallela*, Rupefucald, f 55 (*Opera*, Johann Damasc, LeQuien, II, 752) from *Codex Vatic* 1553 (Magistris, 67, Mai, NC, VII, 98, 107, 108), and *Codex Coisl* 276 f 148 (Pitra, AS, II, p. XXXVII).
[2] Roch, 18 f
[3] Eusebius, *Hist* VII, 26 2; cf VI, 40 3 ff, Dittrich, 4 f holds a different view
[4] Roch, 58.

translation of the fragments preserved by Eusebius). English translation by S F D Salmond, in ANF, VI, 84-91.

(b) According to his own statement,[1] Dionysius wrote an exposition on the beginning of Ecclesiastes which was still known even to Procopius of Gaza in the fifth century, and which he used in his *Catena* on Ecclesiastes There are no data for determining the date of its composition, but it also may belong to the period before the author became a bishop. According to Procopius,[2] Dionysius opposed the allegorical interpretation of the garments of skins, and other things in the Garden of Eden, whereas according to a fragment of uncertain origin, found in a Vatican manuscript,[3] he himself employed the same interpretation. In any case the statement of Procopius, and the isolated remark of Anastasius Sinaita,[4] that Dionysius wrote a book Κατὰ Ὠριγένους, do not justify the inference that he was only a half-way admirer of Origen, and that he was therefore also a half-way opponent.[5]

(c) The two books Περὶ ἐπαγγελιῶν were directed against the chiliastic dreamings of Nepos, bishop of Arsinoe, which he committed to paper in an Ἔλεγχος ἀλληγοριστῶν.[6] By the application of a spiritual method of interpretation, Dionysius set forth in the first book his own opinion concerning the promise, in order to treat in the second of the character and origin of the Johannine Apocalypse, to which his opponents princi-

---

[1] Cf Eusebius, *Hist* VII, 26. 3   [2] *Comment. in Gen* III, 76
[3] *Codex Vatic* 2022 (Pitra, AS, III, 597).
[4] *Quaestiones*, 23, ed. Gretser, 266.
[5] Otherwise, Harnack, LG, 422 f., cf. 418 f., cf also Pitra, SpS, I, p XVI, 17-19
[6] Fabricius, BG, 290 ff , Harnack, LG, 427 f.

pally appealed¹ Eusebius has preserved five extensive extracts from the second book.² The critical remarks contained therein, particularly those on the differences between the Gospel and the Apocalypse, are not without value even to-day in their clearness and brevity³ The date of composition is uncertain. Dittrich places it between 253 and 257 A D.

(*d*) Ἔλεγχος καὶ ἀπολογία (πρὸς Σαβέλλιον⁴) was the title of a defence in four books, in which Dionysius showed his ability to clear himself from the suspicion of heterodox teachings brought against him by his Roman colleague who bore the same name⁵ The fact that, notwithstanding this book, the Arians appealed to Dionysius, led Athanasius to write a book *De sententia Dionysii* in justification of his predecessor, in various passages of which he interwove extracts from the treatise of Dionysius.⁶ Other fragments are found in Eusebius⁷ and Basil.⁸ The date of composition was 260/261 A D.

4. Numerous **Epistles** and **Deliverances** bear witness to the active interest which the bishop took in ecclesiastical questions, to the skill which he exhibited in dealing with them, to the liveliness and graphic power of his treatment, and not least of all, to the esteem which he enjoyed even far outside of Alexandria and Egypt

---

[1] Eusebius, *Hist.* VII, 24. 3
[2] *Idem*, VII, 24, 25, cf III, 28 3-5.
[3] See also the insignificant fragments from *Codex Vaticanus* 1553, (Mai, NC, VII, 99, 108).
[4] Cf Eusebius, *Praep Evang* VII, 18. 13
[5] Basil of Cæsarea, *Epist* 9
[6] See also the characterization in Chap. 14; and *De decret Nic* 25, *De Syn.* 44.
[7] Eusebius, *Praep Evang* VII, 19
[8] Basil, *De Spiritu Sancto*, 29, 72, cf Mai, NC, VII, 96.

Our information as to the following writings comes principally from Eusebius

(a) One group of epistles deals with the question of the treatment of **the Lapsed** (*Lapsi*)[1] In part they are headed περὶ μετανοίας,[2] and it may be assumed that they all originated at about the same time (251–252 A.D.) and had nearly the same contents

(1) To the Brethren in Egypt:[3] none extant.

(2) To Conon, bishop of Hermopolis;[4] a fragment is given by Pitra[5]

(3) To the church in Alexandria;[6] designated as an ἐπιστολὴ ἐπιστρεπτικὴ

(4) To the Brethren in Laodicea, whose bishop was Thelymidres[7]

(5) To the Brethren in Armenia, whose bishop was Merozanes

(6) To the Romans[8]

Nothing from those marked 3–6 is extant.

(b) The following writings had special reference to **the schism of Novatian.**

(1) To Novatian in Rome; most probably written in answer to his announcement of his entrance upon the Roman see (251 A.D), with an entreaty to preserve the church from schism It is possible that Eusebius has preserved the whole of it[9]

(2) To the Roman Confessors, who adhered to Novatian.[10] It is not extant.

(3) To Fabius (Fabian), bishop of Antioch; probably

---

[1] Eusebius, *Hist.* VI, 46. 1.
[2] Nos. 1, 2, 5, and 6.
[3] Eusebius, *Hist* VI, 46. 1.
[4] *Idem*, VI, 46 2
[5] SpS, I, 15 f   Cf 17, XIV sq
[6] Eusebius, *Hist* VI, 46. 2.
[7] *Idem*, VI, 46 2.
[8] *Idem*, VI, 46 5.
[9] *Idem*, VI, 45
[10] *Idem*, VI, 46 5.

written in 252 A.D , with the intention of dissuading his colleague from siding with Novatian. The fragments preserved by Eusebius[1] relate the suffering and apostasy, the conflict and victory, of the Alexandrian Christians at the time of the Decian persecution.

(4) To Cornelius, bishop of Rome, in reply to his letter concerning Novatian.[2] It was written after the death of Fabian of Antioch; that is, probably in 253 A.D. Nothing besides the sentence on Alexander of Jerusalem[3] is extant.

(5) To the Romans περὶ εἰρήνης.[4]

(6) To the Romans ἐπιστολὴ διακονικὴ διὰ Ἱππολύτου[5] The meaning of the adjective is uncertain: Rufinus gives it as "*de ministriis*"; Valesius, "*de officio diaconi*", Gieseler, "a writing in the service of the church" Lightfoot[6] conjectures that its contents were connected with the regulations made by Fabian of Rome, which are mentioned in the *Liber Pontificalis*.

(7) and (8) To the Roman Confessors,[7] after their return to the church.[8]

No portion of the writings numbered 5–8 is extant. It is possible that the fragment found in a Vatican codex,[9] originally occurred in one of these letters

(c) The question of the **validity of heretical baptism** is discussed in the following letters (254, 257 A.D.)

(1) To Stephanus, bishop of Rome[10] One of the fragments preserved by Eusebius[11] does not appear to touch this question.

---

[1] Eusebius, *Hist.* VI, 41, 42, 44.
[2] *Idem*, VI, 46. 3 sq.
[3] *Idem*, VI, 46. 4
[4] *Idem*, VI, 46 5.
[5] *Idem*, VI, 46. 5.
[6] Apost. Fathers . Clement, II, 372
[7] See No. 3, above.
[8] Eusebius, *Hist* VI, 46. 5.
[9] *Codex Vatican* 2022 (see 3 *b* above).
[10] Eusebius, *Hist* VII, 2, 4, 5 1, 2.
[11] *Idem*, VI, 5 1, 2.

(2) To Sixtus, bishop of Rome. Three fragments have been preserved by Eusebius.[1]

(3) To Philemon, presbyter at Rome. Three fragments have been preserved by Eusebius.[2]

(4) To Dionysius, presbyter at Rome. A fragment is given by Eusebius.[3]

(5) To Sixtus, bishop of Rome. A fragment is given by Eusebius[4]

(6) To Sixtus and the Roman congregation.[5] The church at Alexandria is mentioned as joining in this letter.

(7) and (8) Two short missives to Philemon and Dionysius, mentioned by Eusebius.[6] Though not mentioned in his enumeration of writings on heretical baptism, they may still have referred to this subject.

(d) In the **Sabellian controversy**, Dionysius wrote the following letters: —

(1) To Ammon, bishop of Berenice;[7]

(2) and (3) To Telesphorus and to Euphranor;[8]

(4) To Ammon and Euporus[9] It cannot be determined whether these letters were among those that Eusebius mentions elsewhere[10] At all events they were written before the Apology to Dionysius [of Rome], *i e* likely in 257 A.D.,[11] and according to Athanasius[12] they gave the occasion for the suspicions against the author.[13]

---

[1] Eusebius, *Hist.* VII, 5. 4-6; 6.
[2] *Idem*, VII, 7 1-5.
[3] *Idem*, VII, 8. Cf. 7. 6.
[4] *Idem*, VII, 9. 1-5.
[5] *Idem*, VII, 9. 6.
[6] *Idem*, VII, 5 6.
[7] *Idem*, VII, 26. 1.
[8] *Idem*, VII, 26 1.
[9] *Idem*, VII, 26. 1.
[10] *Idem*, VII, 6
[11] Cf *Idem*.
[12] *Sentent Dionys* 10, 13 Cf *Syn* 43.
[13] Cf *Idem*, 4 18

(e) Ἑορταστικαί, **Easter-Epistles** ·—

(1) To Domitius and Didymus: erroneously referred by Eusebius[1] to the time of the Valerian persecution. It was written before Easter, 251 A.D., from Dionysius' hiding-place in Libya The extant fragments[2] relate the capture, release, and flight of the bishop. According to Eusebius,[3] in this writing Dionysius established an Easter canon for eight years, maintaining that the festival should not be celebrated before the vernal equinox;

(2) To Flavius;[4]

(3) To the Presbyters in Alexandria;[5]

(4) To various persons unnamed According to Eusebius these letters fall in the years 258 to 261 A.D.,

(5) To the Alexandrians, at the time of the civil war and after his return from exile, that is, before Easter, 262 A D ,[6]

(6) To the Egyptian bishop Hierax (see unknown), during the civil war, but later than the preceding.[7] The extensive extract given by Eusebius[8] describes the situation in Alexandria;

(7) To Hermammon and the Brethren in Egypt; toward the end of the ninth year of Gallienus, i e. probably before Easter, 262 A D[9] Eusebius has preserved fragments on Gallus,[10] on Valerian and Gallienus,[11] and on Gallienus;[12]

(8) To the Brethren (in Egypt?) at the time of the

---

[1] Eusebius, *Hist.* VII, 20.
[2] *Idem*, VII, 11 20-23, 24 sq.
[3] *Idem*, VII, 20
[4] *Idem*, VII, 20
[5] *Idem*, VII, 20.
[6] *Idem*, VII, 21. 1.
[7] *Idem*, VII, 21 2
[8] *Idem*, VII, 21 2-10.
[9] *Idem*, VII, 23. 4
[10] *Idem*, VII, 1
[11] *Idem*, VII, 10 2-4, 5 sq. 7-9.
[12] *Idem*, VII, 23 1-3, 4.

plague, apparently before Easter, 263 A.D. Two fragments are given by Eusebius,[1]

(9) To the Brethren in Egypt, after the plague[2] This was probably the regular Festal Epistle of the year;

(10) Some fragments of uncertain origin.[3]

(f) Accounts are given also of the following:—

(1) To Origen (imprisoned at Tyre), περὶ μαρτυρίου (written, 250–251 A D)[4] Perhaps the two fragments from a *catena* by Nicetas of Serra, on the Gospel of Luke,[5] are to be referred to this Epistle The words πρὸς 'Ωριγένη are added by way of marginal gloss to the first of these fragments Their subject is Gethsemane (so Harnack,[6] Dittrich[7] holds a different view, contending that the fragments were derived from a commentary on Matthew, or even on the four Gospels);

(2) Letters to Basilides, bishop of the churches in Pentapolis[8] One of these letters, of uncertain date, gives information in reply to certain questions of Basilides touching the Easter celebration, and more especially the beginning of the Easter fast, together with an extended exposition of the Gospel narrative as to the time of the resurrection. The letter is included in the collections of canonical letters, and hence has been often printed; first by Fronto Ducaeus in 1620 (1622 A D.), but the best editions are those by Routh[9] and A. P. de Lagarde;[10]

(3) To the Bishop Germanus (see unknown). It was

---

[1] Eusebius, *Hist* VII, 22. 2–6, 7–10.   [2] *Idem*, VII, 22 11.
[3] Cf PG, X, 1342. Pitra, AS, II, XXXVII, and Harnack, LG, 419.
[4] Eusebius, *Hist* VI, 46 2.
[5] *Codex Vatican*. 1611, PG, X, 1597–1602.
[6] Harnack, LG, 421.   [8] Eusebius, *Hist*. VII, 22. 3.
[7] Dittrich, *Dionys*. 40.   [9] RS, III, 224–232
[10] *Reliquiae juris Eccl ant*. Lips. 1856, 55–59

written in exile, during the Valerian persecution, as a vindication from the charge of cowardice. The letter was probably intended for a wider circle of readers. Fragments have been preserved by Eusebius,[1]

(4) To Antioch, in the matter of Paul of Samosata, 264 A D[2] Although this letter was appended to the synodical epistle of the bishops assembled at Antioch, addressed to all catholic bishops,[3] it has not been preserved, and the letter of Dionysius to Paul, which is printed by Mansi,[4] is not genuine;

(5) To Aphrodisius; five fragments are contained in a Vatican codex;[5]

(6) To Theotecnus, bishop of Cæsarea, written after the death of Origen, as a eulogy. It is mentioned by Stephanus Gobarus[6]

(g) It is no longer possible to ascertain the facts in regard to the following writings, which were in the form of letters: Περὶ σαββάτου,[7] Περὶ γυμνασίου,[8] Περὶ πειρασμῶν,[9] and Περὶ γάμων[10]

5 On uncertain or spurious writings, and especially on the relation of Dionysius to the Areopagitic literature, see Harnack[11]

---

[1] Eusebius, *Hist.* VI, 40, VII, 11.
[2] *Idem*, VII, 22 2
[3] *Idem*, VII, 30 3   [4] *Concil Collect.* I, 1039-1047.
[5] *Codex Vatican* 1553   (Mai, NC, VII, 96, 98, 99, 102, 107.)
[6] See Photius, *Codex*, 232   (Bekker, 291.)
[7] Eusebius, *Hist* VII, 22, 11.
[8] *Idem*, and for a fragment, see *Codex Vatican.* 1553 (Mai, NC, VII, 98).
[9] *Idem*, VII, 26. 2.
[10] A fragment is found in *Codex Vatican.* 1553 (Mai, NC, VII, 102).
[11] LG, 419 (No. 5), 420 (10), 424-427 (12-14).

§ 64. Anatolius

Fabricius, BG, III, 461-464, VII, 299 sq.   Harnack, LG, 436 f.

Anatolius, a native of Alexandria, left the city after the siege of Brucheium (262 A D) in which he had distinguished himself; was for a time the coadjutor of Theotecnus, bishop of Cæsarea, and from 268 (269 A D) on, was bishop of Laodicea[1]   According to Eusebius,[2] he was an accomplished scholar in philosophy and natural science, and his few **works** are remarkable for the wealth of knowledge which they display.[3]

Eusebius mentions the following : —

(*a*) Περὶ τοῦ πάσχα, from which he preserved a considerable extract.[4]   A *Liber Anatoli de ratione paschali*, in which the portion quoted by Eusebius occurs, also exists in Latin.   Krusch considers the book to be spurious, and refers it to the sixth century, but Zahn defends its genuineness (against which no decisive proofs can be brought).

The *Liber Anatoli* was printed in A Bucher's *De Doctrina temporum Commentarius*, etc , Antwerp, 1634, 433-449   Migne, PG, X, 207-222   Br Krusch, *Studien zur mittelalterlichen Chronologie*, Lpz 1880, 311-327, cf Zahn, FGK, III, 177-196   [Translated by S D Salmond, in ANF, VI, 146-151]   A Anscombe, in *Engl Hist Rev* Jl 1895, X, 515-535, and C. H. Turner, in *Idem*, October, 1895, pp 699-710.

(*b*) 'Αριθμητικαὶ εἰσαγωγαί, in ten books.[5]   Some fragments are contained in the *Theologumena Arithmeticae*.[6]

[1] Eusebius, *Hist* VII, 32. 6-12. [4] *Idem*, VII, 32. 14-19.
[2] *Idem*, VII, 32. 6. [5] *Idem*, VII, 32. 20.
[3] *Idem*, VII, 32. 13.
[6] Paris, 1543, 9, 16, 24, 34, 56, 64.   [For a translation of the fragments given by Fabricius, III, 462, see S D. Salmond, in ANF, VI, 152-153.]

§ 65 *Theognostus*

Routh, RS, III, 407-422 Migne, PG, X, 235-242 — Translation: S D Salmond, in ANF, VI, 155-156 Fabricius, BG, 298 sq Richardson, BS, 70. Harnack, LG, 437-439.

Theognostus, principal of the Catechetical School of Alexandria,[1] in which post he possibly succeeded Dionysius and probably preceded Pierius,[2] wrote a work, under the title Ὑποτυπώσεις, in seven books. According to Photius,[1] these treated the *Loci* of dogmatic theology in the following order: 1. God the Father. 2. Son. 3. Holy Ghost. 4. Angels and demons. 5 and 6. Incarnation of the Redeemer. 7. God's government of the world (περὶ θεοῦ δημιουργίας). Photius gives a summary of the contents. Athanasius[3] and Gregory of Nyssa[4] cited two sentences; the former with the avowed intention of defending the theologian, who was a follower of Origen, against the charge of holding subordinationist views. There is no reason for regarding the passage cited by Athanasius as a disquisition on the sin against the Holy Ghost.[5] Theognostus is not mentioned by Eusebius (or Jerome).

§ 66. *Pierius*

Routh, RS, III, 425-435 Migne, PG, X, 231-246 C. de Boor, in TU, V, 2, 1888, 169 ff.; cf 179 ff — Translation S D Salmond in ANF, VI, 157. Fabricius, BG, 301. Richardson, BS, 70 f Harnack, LG, 439-441

[1] Cf the title ἐξηγητής, Photius, *Codex*, 106
[2] Otherwise, Philip of Side, cf. Dodwell, *Dissertat. in Irenaeum*, 1689. App 488.
[3] *Epist. 4 ad Serap.* c. 11; *Decr. Syn. Nic* 25.
[4] *Contra Eunomium*, III; *Orat.* 3.
[5] So Harnack, LG, 437.

According to Eusebius,[1] **Pierius** was a presbyter at Alexandria, distinguished as an ascetic and scholar, under the episcopate of Theonas (282–300 A.D.). According to Philip of Side, he was the predecessor of Theognostus as principal of the Catechetical School;[2] and according to Jerome,[3] he lived in Rome after the Diocletian persecution. In a poem by the Alexandrian advocate, Theodorus,[4] it is stated that Pierius, together with his brother Isidorus, fell martyr in the persecution. This may be so far true that he was made to suffer for his faith[5] Regarding his **writings**, the following particulars are known : —

(*a*) According to Photius,[6] Pierius wrote a book comprising twelve Λόγοι.[7] Among them were at least two Λόγοι εἰς τὸ πάσχα,[8] a (Λόγος) εἰς τὴν ἀρχὴν τοῦ Ὡσηέ,[9] a (Λόγος) περὶ τῆς θεοτόκου,[10] and another, εἰς τὸ κατὰ Λουκᾶν[11] Philip also cites two short sentences from an unnamed writing of Pierius,[12] which have reference to Mark vi. 17 (Matt. xiv 3). These works earned for their author the title of the "young Origen."[13]

(*b*) Philip of Side had read a Βίος τοῦ ἁγίου Παμφίλου by Pierius By this Pamphilus the friend of Eusebius is meant, who, according to Photius,[14] had been the pupil of Pierius.

[1] Eusebius, *Hist* VII, 32. 26; cf. ch. 30.
[2] Cf Photius, *Codex*, 118–119.
[3] *De Viris Illust* 76.
[4] See Philip of Side (de Boor, 170).
[5] Cf Photius, *Codex*, 119.
[6] Cf. Photius, *Codex*, 118–119.
[7] Jerome, *loc cit.*, "*diversi tractatus,*" Philip of Side, "σπουδάσματα"
[8] Philip of Side a small fragment in de Boor, 170
[9] Philip of Side, cf. Jerome, *Praef in Comm ad Osea* The sentence on 1 Cor 1 7, quoted by Jerome (*Epist* 49, 3), probably belongs here
[10] Philip of Side
[11] Photius, *loc. cit*
[12] de Boor, 16. 9
[13] Jerome, *De Viris Illust* 76.
[14] Photius, *Codex*, 118

§ 67 *Philcas, Hesychius, Pachomius, Theodorus*

Routh, RS, IV, 85-111   Migne, PG, X, 1559-1567 — Fabricius, BG, 305 sq   Richardson, BS, 71   Harnack, LG, 441-443

Phileas, bishop of Thmuis in Egypt, and martyr under Diocletian, wrote a Letter to his congregations on the sufferings of the martyrs at Alexandria, from which Eusebius quoted a long section [1] A letter written in prison by the four bishops, Hesychius, Pachomius, Theodorus, and Phileas, in reference to the Meletian schism, exists in a Latin translation [2] The author of a textual recension of the Septuagint and of the Gospels (of the New Testament?) which attained considerable reputation in Egypt,[3] may possibly be identified with this Hesychius.

§ 68 *Petrus*

Fragments: Routh, RS, IV, 21-82   Migne, PG, XVIII, 467-522   Lagarde, *Reliqu gr* 63-73 — Translations by J B H. Hawkins, in ANF, VI, 261-283 — Fabricius, BG, IX, 316 sq   Richardson, BS, 74.   Harnack, LG, 443-449

Petrus, bishop of Alexandria from 300 till the beginning of 312 A D ,[4] was, according to Eusebius, a model bishop in his virtuous life and in his familiarity with Holy Scripture. He became a martyr, after having escaped the persecution of 306, whereby he had alien-

---

[1] Eusebius, VIII, 16 2-10, cf VIII, 9 7, 13 7, and Jerome's *De Viris Illust* 78   [Translated by S D Salmond, ANF, VI, 162-163]

[2] [Translated by S D Salmond, in ANF, VI, 163-164]

[3] Jerome, *Praef in Libr Paralipom* , *Adv. Rufin* II, 27   *In Isai* lviii. 11, cf *Decr Gelas* VI, 13

[4] Eusebius, *Hist* VII, 32 31, VIII, 13 7, IX, 6. 2, Jerome, *Chronicon ad annum 2320 Abrahami, 19 Dioclet.*

ated a part of the congregation (Meletian schism) Except for a few **fragments** his writings have been lost —

(*a*) Περὶ μετανοίας, written at the commencement of the year 306 [1] Fourteen "Canons" are extant, setting forth the conditions under which the lapsed might be received again into the communion of the church. The writing is an eloquent witness to the wise toleration of the author. The section transmitted in some manuscripts as the fifteenth Canon, belonged to a treatise ;

(*b*) Εἰς τὸ πάσχα or περὶ τοῦ πάσχα, which was dedicated to a certain Tricentius, [2]

(*c*) Περὶ θεότητος, three Greek fragments are preserved in the Acts of the Synod of Ephesus of 431 A D., and four in Syriac are given by Pitra, [3]

(*d*) Περὶ ἀναστάσεως Eight Syriac fragments are given by Pitra, [4] the first of which is identical with one of the Greek fragments mentioned under (*c*),

(*e*) Περὶ τῆς σωτῆρος ἡμῶν ἐπιδημίας. A fragment is given by Leontius of Byzantium, [5]

(*f*) Περὶ ψυχῆς (in at least two books) is mentioned by Procopius of Gaza [6] Two fragments (given by Leontius in his work against the Monophysites[7]), which bear the superscription, ἐκ τοῦ πρώτου λόγου περὶ τοῦ μηδὲ προυπάρχειν τὴν ψυχὴν μηδὲ ἁμαρτήσασαν τοῦτο εἰς σῶμα βληθῆναι, were probably taken from this work [8]

---

[1] See the beginning [Translated by J B. H Hawkins, in ANF, VI, 269–279]

[2] Mai, NC, I, 2, p. 222.   [4] *Idem*, IV, 189–193, 426–429.

[3] AS, IV, 187 sq , 425 sq.

[5] *Liber I contra Nestorian. et Eutychian* , cf. *contra Monophysitas*, in Mai, NC, VII, 134, and *Epist. Justiniani contra Monophysitas* in Mai, NC, VII, 307

[6] *Comm in Gen* III, 76   [7] Mai, NC, VII, 85

[8] Cf also *Epist Justiniani ad Mennam* (Mansi, *Concil. Collec* IX,

The extant fragments mentioned in *c–f* make it apparent that Petrus approached the questions he treated with independence. He differed in a characteristic way from the *Theologumena* of Origen, particularly in the writings marked *d* and *f* (against the preexistence of the soul, fall before the creation of the world, a different conception of the resurrection), but his mode of expression shows plainly enough that he, like Dionysius, was throughout influenced by the theology of Origen;

(*g*) A Letter of Petrus to the Alexandrians has been preserved in a Latin translation.[1] It was written during the persecution of 306 A D on hearing of the machinations of Meletius, against which he gives warning.

(*h*) On doubtful and forged writings, see Harnack.[2]

§ 69 *Alexander*

Migne, PG, XVIII, 523–608 — **Translation:** J. B. H. Hawkins, in ANF, 291–302 — G. Kruger, *Melito von Sardes oder Alexander von Alexandrien?*, in ZwTh, XXXI, 1888, 434–448 — Fabricius, BG, IX, 257–259. Richardson, BS, 74 f Preuschen, LG, 449–451

Of the writings of **Alexander** (bishop of Alexandria from 313 to 326 A D, involved in the Arian controversy at its inception) nothing has come down to us except a **sermon** and part of his correspondence

(*a*) Λόγος περὶ ψυχῆς καὶ σώματος καὶ εἰς τὸ πάθος, has been preserved[3] in a Syriac translation[4] A fragment of it has also been preserved in Arabic[5] The sermon is composed of two parts, the first of which con-

---

503 sq), and Pitra, AS, III, 599. On a Syriac fragment, see Harnack, LG, 447

[1] Cf Sc Maffei, *Osservazioni Letterari*, III, Verona, 1738, 17 (Routh, RS, 51).
[2] LG, 447–449.
[3] Mai, NPB, II, 529–540.
[4] *Codex Vatican Syr* 386.
[5] Mai, SpR, III, 699.

tains lengthy observations on the relation of soul and body which might equally well occur in a psychological tractate, while the second undertakes to prove why it was necessary that the Lord should suffer, and what results His death had for mankind. The complicated manner in which the writing has been transmitted,[1] makes it probable that Alexander modelled this sermon on a writing of Melito [2]

(b) It is possible that four of the fragments of homilies [3] in Syriac, published by Pitra,[4] are spurious

(c) Out of the more than seventy letters which Alexander is said [5] to have written in connection with Arian affairs, the following are extant —

1 A circular letter to all catholic bishops,[6]

2 A letter to Alexander, bishop of Byzantium, given by Theodoret [7] A Syriac fragment also is extant [8] This likewise was probably a circular letter,

3. Καθαίρεσις Ἀρείου,[9] *Depositio Arii*, addressed to the presbyters and deacons of Alexandria and Mareotis,

4 Portions of a letter to Æglon, given by Maximus Confessor, [10]

5 Other letters are also mentioned, viz : to Philogonius, bishop of Antioch,[11] to Eustathius, bishop of Beroea,[12] to the Emperor Constantine,[13] to Silvester, bishop of Rome,[14] and to Arius [15]

---

[1] Kruger (see above), 434–437   [2] Cf. § 40 6
[3] Fragments marked IV, VI, VII, VIII
[4] AS, IV, 199 sq , 433 sq   [5] Epiphanius, *Panarion*, LXIX, 4
[6] Socrates, *Hist Eccl* I, 6, cf Gelasius of Cyzicus, *Hist Conc Nic* II, 3 (Mansi, *Concil Collec* II, 793–802)
[7] *Hist Eccl* I, 4   [12] *Loc cit*
[8] AS, IV, 200, 434, No IX   [13] Epiphanius, *Panarion*, LXIX, 9.
[9] *Codex Paris* 474 al   [14] Liberius, *Epist* 4, 4.
[10] *Opera*, II, 152, 155 (Corder) [15] Socrates, *Hist Eccl*. I, 26
[11] Theodoret, *Hist. Eccl* I, 3 (end)

§ 70 Hierax

Harnack, LG, 467 f.

According to Epiphanius,[1] **Hierax** lived at Leontopolis and was a man of great learning, experienced in medicine and other sciences, versed alike in Greek and Coptic literature, and eminent, finally, in the exposition of Holy Scripture His Commentaries in the Greek and Coptic languages are said to have borne witness to his importance in the last-mentioned field[2] Some **fragments** of his writings (?) against marriage are extant in Epiphanius' *Panarion*[3] It cannot be determined from Epiphanius[4] whether he wrote a book of his own on the Holy Ghost, as Harnack thinks. Epiphanius mentions still another treatise on the Six Days' Work and Psalms.[5]

SUPPLEMENTARY

§ 71 Judas

A. Schlatter, *Der Chronograph aus dem zehnten Jahre Antonins*, in TU, XII, 1, 1894 Fabricius, BG, 176 Harnack, LG, 327, cf 755 f

According to Eusebius,[6] a certain **Judas**, of whom nothing further is known, arranged in a writing, Εἰς τὰς παρὰ τῷ Δανιὴλ ἑβδομήκοντα ἑβδομάδας, some chronological calculations based on the prophecies in the book of Daniel. They extended as far as the tenth year of Severus (202 A D), and prophesied the Parousia of the Lord in the near future Schlatter assumes a mistake

---

[1] Epiphanius, *Panarion*, LXVII, 1.
[2] *Idem*, LXVII, 3, LV, 5.
[3] *Idem*, LXVII, 1-2
[4] *Idem*, LXVII, 3
[5] *Idem*, LXVII, 3
[6] Eusebius, *Hist.* VI, 7, cf Jerome, *De Viris Illust.* 52

in Eusebius' statement, and identifies Judas with the Chronographer (from the tenth year of Antoninus Pius), whom Clement mentions,[1] and whom he used for his calculations Schlatter also thinks that he can be shown to be mentioned in Theophilus' letter to Autolycus,[2] and by Tertullian,[3] Origen,[4] and Epiphanius.[5] The Judas of Eusebius, however, wrote in a time of persecution.

§ 72. Heraclitus, Maximus, Candidus, Apion, Sextus, Arabianus

Fabricius, BG, 172, 175 sq   Harnack, LG, 758 f, 786

Eusebius[6] tells us that he had before him a large number of writings, some of them bearing the names of their authors some of them anonymous. Passing over the latter, he mentions six of the former, which he is inclined to refer to the close of the reign of Commodus, or the beginning of that of Severus These were the writings of Heraclitus, Εἰς τὸν ἀπόστολον; of Maximus, Περὶ τῆς ὕλης,[7] of Candidus and Apion, Εἰς τὴν ἑξαήμερον; of Sextus, Περὶ ἀναστάσεως; and of Arabianus, the title of whose work is not given.

§ 73 Ammonius

O v Gebhardt, in RE, II, 404   Theo. Zahn, FGK, L, 31–34.— Harnack, LG, 406 f.

Eusebius[8] ascribes a treatise, Περὶ τῆς Μωϋσέως καὶ Ἰησοῦ συμφωνίας and other writings to a Christian writer,

---

[1] *Stromata*, I, 21. 147.
[2] III, 24–28.
[3] *Jud* 8
[4] Vv 11
[5] Epiphanius, *Panarion*, XXIX, 4.
[6] Eusebius, *Hist* V, 27, cf. Jerome, *De Viris Illust* 46–51.
[7] *Idem, Praep evang* VII, 21 5. Cf. also, § 76 3 *b*, below.
[8] Eusebius, *Hist* VI, 19 sq.

Ammonius, whom he and those who followed him[1] confounded with the philosopher, Ammonius Saccas. He was probably identical with the Ammonius whom Eusebius calls an Alexandrian, and who composed a **Synopsis** of the Four Gospels (Τὸ διὰ τεσσάρων εὐαγγέλιον), in which Matthew was used as the basis.[2] [He divided the text into sections which are still known as "Ammonian sections."]

§ 74. *Theonas*

Editions · J L Dacherius, *Spicilegium* (see § 2 9 *b*), XII, 1675, 545 sqq , III, 2d edit. 1723; 297 sqq Routh, RS, III, 439-449. Migne, PG, X, 1569-1574. — **Translation**. S D. F. Salmond, in ANF, VI, 158-161
Literature J Havet, *Les découvertes de Jérôme Vignier in Bibl de l'École des Chartes*, XLVI, 1885, 205-271 P Batiffol, *L'Épître de Théonas à Lucien*, Paris, 1886 (*Bull. Crit* VII, 1886, 155-160) Cf Harnack, in ThLZ, XI, 1886, 319-326 — Fabricius, BG, 306. Richardson, BS, 71 Harnack, LG, 790

The letter of a bishop, Theonas, to Lucian, who was a Christian, and also imperial chamberlain, has been preserved in a Latin translation. In it good advice is given to the recipient, as to how he and other Christians at court should order their behavior so as to incline the emperor favorably towards Christianity The situation corresponds with that described by Eusebius,[3] and only **Theonas of Alexandria** (282-300 A.D.) can be regarded as the author Assuming the authenticity of the document, it forms an exceedingly valuable means for determining the state of affairs shortly before the Dio-

---

[1] Jerome, *De Viris Illust.* 55.
[2] Eusebius, *Epist ad Carpianum* Jerome (*loc. cit*), falsely, or by mistake, translates by "*evangelici canones.*"
[3] Eusebius, *Hist. Eccl.* VIII, 1.

cletian persecution. Batiffol attacked this assumption with the assertion that the letter was forged by Jerome Vignier, priest of the Oratory (died, 1661 A D). Some of the internal reasons for this suspicion (*e g* mistakes in the titles used) can be disproved, and others (Latinity, Biblical citations) are met by the supposition that we have to do, not with an ancient version (thus d'Achery), but with a translation made by a Humanist scholar The absence of any tradition is not unexampled, as is seen in the case of the Epistle to Diognetus Havet's assertion that Vignier also forged other (nine) "Acts" in the *Spicilegium*, makes the case very suspicious, but whether the statement itself is beyond all doubt has not yet been investigated

II. WRITERS OF ASIA MINOR

§ 75 *Gregorius Thaumaturgus*

Editions Fr Zinus, Venet 1574, Rom 1594 (cf. BG, VII, 259). Ger Vossius, Mogunt 1604 (first Greek edition), Paris, 1622, *cura Front. Ducaei* (1621, BG, VII, 260) Gallandi, *Bibliotheca vet pat antiq scriptorum eccl* (§ 2 8 *a*), III, 385-469, cf XIV, App 119 Migne, PG, X, 963-1206 — **Translations** J Margraf, in BKV, 1875 (Panegyric, Declaration of Faith, Epistle) S D F Salmond, in ANF, VI, 7-74 (Declaration of Faith, Ecclesiastes, Canonical Epistle, Panegyric, Trinity, Faith, Soul. Homilies, Saints, and Matthew)

Literature L Allatius, *Diatriba de Theodoris*, in PG, X, 1205-1232 J L Boye, *Dissertatio histor de S Greg Thaum. episc Neocaesariensi*, Jena, 1709 H R Reynolds, in DCB, II, 730-737 V Ryssel, *Greg Thaum* Lpz 1880 (JpiTh, VII. 1881, 565-573), cf F Overbeck, in ThLZ, VI, 1881, 283-286 P Koetschau, Introduction to his edition in SQu, IX, 1894 V Ryssel, *Eine syrische Lebensbeschreibung des Greg Thaum* in *Theol Zeitsch aus der Schweiz*, 1894, 228-254 Fabricius, BG, VII, 249-260 Richardson, BS, 65 f Preuschen, LG, 428-436

1. Besides the account of his own life and development which Gregorius Thaumaturgus gives in his eulogy upon Origen (see below), a few particulars are given by Eusebius,[1] Basil of Cæsarea,[2] and Jerome[3] Later writers[4] derived their knowledge of the bishop of Neocæsarea almost exclusively from the Βίος καὶ ἐγκώμιον ῥηθὲν εἰς τὸν ἅγιον Γρηγόριον τὸν Θαυματουργόν, by Gregory of Nyssa, a panegyric of very slight value as a source[5] An account of his life (preserved in Syriac in a manuscript of the sixth century),[6] possibly was derived from an Ante-Nicene Greek original

2. Theodorus, later called **Gregorius**,[7] received from an admiring posterity the title of the "Wonder-Worker," **Thaumaturgus**[8] He was born about 213 A D of a distinguished family in Neocæsarea (Pontus) Educated as a heathen, though acquainted with Christianity from his fourteenth year, he studied jurisprudence While on his way to Berytus (Beirut), where he intended to complete his study of Roman law, he became acquainted with Origen at Cæsarea in Palestine (233 A D), and received from him an impulse toward philosophical and theological studies He remained five years[9] in his master's school, to whom, upon his departure (238), he reared a beautiful memorial of his gratitude in his

---

[1] *Hist Eccl* VI, 30, VII, 14, 28. 1, 30. 2.
[2] *Spir. Sanct* 29, 74, *Epist* 28, 1 sq , 204, 2; 207, 4, 210, 3, 5
[3] *De Viris Illust* 65, *Comm. in Eccles* 4, *Epist.* 70. 4
[4] Preuschen, LG, 434, 436
[5] Printed by Vossius, 234–427, Gallandi, III, 439–461.
[6] *Cod Mus Brit Syr. Add. 14648 Saec.* VI.
[7] See the salutation in Origen's epistle, and Eusebius' *Hist* VI, 30.
[8] So named for the first in the title (not given by Gregory of Nyssa) to the Βίος
[9] Eusebius, *Hist* VI, 30

Panegyric With the intention of entering upon the practice of the law, he returned to his native city There he was chosen bishop, about 240 A D, and became, with his brother Athenodorus,¹ the founder of the provincial church of Pontus He remained its head for, possibly, three decades, and his influence may have been all the more profound because he did not lose himself in the turmoils of ecclesiastical politics. During the Decian persecution (250–251 A D), he, with a part of his congregation, fled to the mountains At the time of the incursion of the Goths and Boradi into Pontus in 253–254 A D, he proved himself a true shepherd ² He took part in the first synod at Antioch against Paul of Samosata,³ 264–265 A D, but before the second he died, about 270 A D His memory remained sacred in the catholic church

On the chronology of his stay at Cæsarea, see J Draeseke, in JprTh, VII, 1881, 103-107, and an opposing view by P Koetschau, in SQu, IX, 1894

3 A busy churchman, completely occupied with questions of practical life, Gregory scarcely found time for authorship, and only little of undoubted genuineness has been transmitted to us On the contrary, the famous name of the orthodox "wonder-worker" was used as a flag of protection for heretical productions His best-known writing was the (*a*) Εἰς Ὠριγένην προσφωνητικός [καὶ πανηγυρικὸς λόγος : πανηγυρικὸν εὐχαριστίας ⁴], called by Gregory himself ⁵ λόγος χαριστήριος It is preserved only in connection with Origen's work against

---

¹ Eusebius, *Hist* VI, 30, VII, 14   ³ Eusebius, *Hist* VII, 30 2
² See his *Epistola canonica*   ⁴ Cf Jerome, *De Viris Illust* 65
⁵ Koetschau (see below), pp 7, 18, 9, 16

Celsus in a Vatican Codex[1] and five other manuscripts
The speech, delivered upon his departure from Cæsarea
(see above), was no ordinary **panegyric**, but a tribute to
the Alexandrian's method of teaching, which came, to
be sure, from an enthusiastic pupil, but which was just
and also minute in its details. In the introduction
(§§ 1–30) the author excuses himself for being per-
suaded, by gratitude to his teacher, to deliver the address
in spite of his limited experience   There then follows a
thanksgiving to God through Christ, to his guardian
angel, and to Origen (31–92), and after this an exact
description of Origen's mode of instruction (93–183)
His separation from his master draws forth his complaints, but over against them he enumerates his grounds
for consolation (184–202)   At the close he asks for
blessing and intercession (203–207)   Apart from its
importance, as a source of information as to the work
of Origen,[2] the address is a remarkable performance
in itself, and in spite of a not infrequent heaviness of
style, the rhetoric is but seldom artificial, the language
good and flowing.

Editions · D Hoeschelius, Aug Vindel, 1605, as a beginning of an edition of the Books against Celsus   J A Bengel, Stuttg 1722   C V de la Rue, *Opera Origenis*, IV. Paris, 1759, App 55–78   C H E Lommatzsch. *Opera Origenis*, XXV, Berol 1848, 339-381   P. Koetschau, in SQu, IX, 1894

(*b*) Ἔκθεσις πίστεως, a short creed (extant in many manuscripts[3] in Greek, Syriac, and Latin), the genuineness of which need not be impugned in spite of the
fact that its earliest attestation is that of Gregory of

---

[1] *Codex Vaticanus graec.* 386.   [3] Preuschen, LG, 429
[2] Cf § 61 1, above.

Nyssa in his Life of Thaumaturgus   Since the formula is said to have been revealed to the author in a vision, it is also known as Ἀποκάλυψις Γρηγορίου.

C P Caspari, *Alte und neue Quellen zur Geschichte des Taufsymbols und der Glaubensregel*, Christiania, 1879, 1–64. F Kattenbusch, *Das Apostolische Symbol*. I, Lpz. 1894, 338–342   The Syriac text in P de Lagarde, *Analecta Syriaca*, Lips et Lugd 1858, and in Pitra, AS, IV, 81 , cf 345 sq

(c) Ἐπιστολὴ κανονική was a communication to the bishops of Pontus, written after the incursion of the Goths and Boradi (Boranians) into Pontus and Bythynia, apparently in 254 A D   It is extant in numerous manuscripts containing the canons of councils [1]   The letter contains regulations for the treatment of those who had been guilty of transgressions against Christian discipline and morality during the incursion of the barbarians, whether committed under compulsion as prisoners or as voluntary abettors of the plunderers   The letter is important both as a first-hand account of the evil conditions occasioned even among Christians by those days of terror, and as witness to the intelligent benignity of Gregory

Routh, RS, III, 256–264, 265–283   J Draeseke, in JprTh, VII, 1881, 724–756 (Letter, see pp 730–736)

(d) A writing entitled Μετάφρασις εἰς τὸν Ἐκκλησιαστὴν Σολομῶντος is, indeed, ascribed in the manuscripts [2] to Gregory Nazianzen , but, according to the testimony of Jerome [3] and Rufinus,[4] it may equally well have been the work of Gregory the "Wonder-Worker,"

[1] Preuschen, I.G., 429 f   [3] *De Viris Illust* 65 , *Comm. in Eccles.* 4
[2] Preuschen, I G, 430   [4] *Hist Eccl* VII, 25.

particularly as the language resembles that of the Panegyric. It consists simply of a periphrastic reproduction of the original.

(*e*) The writing "To Theopompus on the Impassivity and the Passivity of God," is preserved in Syriac in a manuscript in the British Museum [1] It is "a sort of Platonic dialogue upon the question whether from the physical passivity of God there also follows, as a necessary consequence, moral passivity as to the fate of the human race."[2] Well-grounded doubts concerning its genuineness cannot be substantiated. Nothing is known as to the identity of Theopompus; Draeseke's attempted identification of the Isocrates, mentioned in the writing, with the Gnostic Socrates,[3] is not an improbable conjecture. The date of composition was after 240 A.D.[4]

P. de Lagarde, *Analecta Syriaca*, Lips. et Lond. 1858, 46-64 (Syriac text). V Ryssel, *Greg Thaum* Lpz 1880, 71-99 (in German). 118-124, 137 f, 150-157, cf Draeseke, in JprTh, IX, 1883, 634-640 (and in his *Gesammelte patrist Untersuchungen*, Altona and Lpz. 1889, 162-168). Pitra, AS, IV, 103-120 (Syriac), 363-376 (Latin).

(*f*) The Διάλεξις πρὸς Αἰλιανόν has been lost According to Basil[5] the purpose of Gregory was to lead his correspondent from heathenism to Christianity. The want of precision in the use of dogmatic expressions and formulæ, which, under the circumstances, is quite intelligible, does not justify appeal to Gregory as a supporter of the errors of Sabellianism.

[1] *Codex Mus Britt Syr Addit* 12156   [2] Overbeck.
[3] The anonymous writing, *de Recta Fide* (see § 80), edition of Lommatzsch, XVI, 264.
[4] Ryssel holds a different view.   [5] *Epist* 210, 5.

(*g*) "An Ante-Nicene Homily"; published by J. C. Conybeare.[1]

4 The following writings are either probably or certainly **spurious**; some of them were fraudulently attributed to Gregory.

(*a*) Ἡ κατὰ μέρος πίστις (extant in Greek and Syriac), is a trinitarian-christological confession, which "presupposes the Arian, semi-Arian, and Pneumatomachian controversies, as well as the Apollinarian prelude to the christological conflict."[2] The treatise was written by Apollinaris (the younger) of Laodicea about 375[3] or 390 A.D[4] with the purpose of setting forth his conception of the Trinity and of the incarnation of Christ Between 410 and 425 A.D. Apollinarians attributed it to Thaumaturgus.

First published in Greek by Mai, NC, VII, 170–176. P A de Lagarde, *Titi Bostreni contra Manich. libri* IV. *Syr.* Berol. 1859, App 103–113 J Draeseke, *Apollinarios von Laodicea*, in TU, VII, 1892, 369–380 Syriac text, in Lagarde, *Analecta Syriaca*, 1858, 31–42 Syriac and Latin, Pitra, AS, IV, 82–94, 346–356, cf. C. P. Caspari (3 *b*, above), 65–146.

(*b*) To Philagrius, on Consubstantiality, is extant in Syriac. The Greek original of this trinitarian writing is found in Gregory Nazianzen's two hundred and forty-third epistle,[5] where it is headed Πρὸς Εὐάγριον μόναχον περὶ θεότητος.

Syriac text, in Lagarde, *Analecta Syriaca*, 1858, 43–46 Syriac and Latin, in Pitra, AS, IV, 100–103, 360–363. German, by Ryssel, *Greg Thaum* Lpz 1880, 65–70; cf 100–118, 135 f., 147–150, cf.

[1] *Expositor*, 1896, 3, 161–173.
[2] Caspari, p. 69.
[3] Draeseke.
[4] Caspari
[5] Formerly *Orat.* 45.

J Draeseke, in JprTh. VII, 1881. 379–384; VIII, 1882, 343–384, 553–568 (in his *Gesammelte patrist. Untersuchungen*, 1889, 103–162

(c) The Λόγος κεφαλαιώδης περὶ ψυχῆς πρὸς Τατιανόν, ascribed[1] to Gregory in several manuscripts,[2] is a treatise on the nature of the soul. Its author omitted the Scriptures as a source of proof.

Editions: Didacus Hurtadus, Venet. (cf Ryssel, *Greg. Thaum* p 35) A Syriac fragment is given by Lagarde in his *Analecta Syriaca*, p 31.

(d) The Ἀναθηματισμοὶ ἢ περὶ πίστεως κεφάλαια ιβ´ were twelve statements of belief and excommunication. They related to the incarnation of Christ, and were directed against Nestorian, Eutychian, and Apollinarian doctrines.

First published in Latin by Turrianus, in A. Possevinus, *Apparatus criticus*, and afterward in Greek and Latin, by H. Canisius, *Antiquae lectiones*, III, Ingolst 1603, 1 Syriac fragments, in Lagarde, *Analecta Syriaca*, 1858, 65, 23–66, 18, 66, 27–67, 5. Pitra, AS, IV, 95–100, 357–360; cf. J. Draeseke, in *Gesam. patr. Untersuchungen*, 78–102 (Vitalius).

(e) A number of **Homilies**, to wit: —

(1–3) Εἰς τὸν εὐαγγελισμὸν τῆς ὑπεραγίας (παναγίας) θεοτόκου παρθένου τῆς Μαρίας, and

(4) Εἰς τὰ ἅγια θεοφάνεια, ascribed to Gregory in one codex.[3] In very many manuscripts the third address is ascribed to John Chrysostom. The first exists in Syriac and Armenian;[4] the second in Syriac;[5] and the fourth in Syriac,[6] attributed to Chrysostom Draeseke would assign all three to Apollinaris of Laodicea.

J Draeseke, in JprTh, X, 1884, 657–704.

[1] *Codex Patm.* 202 (σβ´), etc.   [3] *Codex Bibl. Cryptoferr*
[2] Fabricius, BG, VII, 257 *vv*.
[4] Pitra, AS, IV, 122–127 (377–381) and 145–150 (396–400).
[5] *Idem*, IV, 150–156 (400–404).   [6] *Idem*, IV, 127–133 (381–386).

(5) Λόγος εἰς τοὺς ἁγίους πάντας (*Sermo in omnes sanctos*) (ascribed to Gregory in the manuscript used by Mingarelli) is to be assigned to a later period on account of its subject and its dependence on the sermons of Chrysostom.[1]

Edition: J A Mingarelli, Bonon. 1770

(6) *In Nativitatem Christi*, in Armenian,[2] Bardenhewer (169) regards it as genuine.

(7) *De Incarnatione Domini*, in Armenian.[3]

(8) *Laus sanctae Dei parae*, in Armenian.[4]

(9) *Panegyricus sermo in sanctam Dei genetricem et semper virginem Mariam*, in Armenian.[5]

(10) *Sermo panegyricus in honorem sancti Stephani;* in Armenian.[6]

5 Finally there exist numerous **fragments,** partly of genuine and partly of spurious writings, in Greek (*catenae*), Syriac, and Armenian: collected by Lagarde [7] and Pitra [8]

6. Concerning an extant [9] (Exposition) of the Proverbs of Solomon, see the remarks of P. Batiffol.[10]

[1] Cf. P. Koetschau, SQu, IX, 1894.
[2] Pitra, AS, IV, 134–144 (386–395).
[3] *Idem*, IV, 144 sq. (395 sq).
[4] *Idem*, IV, 156–159 (404–406).
[5] *Idem*, IV, 159–162 (406 sq.).
[6] *Idem*, IV, 162–169 (408–412).
[7] Lagarde, *Analecta Syriaca*, vv ll.
[8] Pitra, AS, IV, 93 sq. (356), 120–122 (376 sq.), 133 (386), Pitra, SpR, III, 696–699. Cf. Ryssel, *Greg. Thaum* 43–59, 431 f.
[9] *Cod Vatic* 1802
[10] In *Mélanges d'Archéologie et d'Histoire*, IX, 1889, 46 sq.

§ 76. Methodius

Editions: Franc. Combefisius, *Sanctorum patrum Amphilochii Icon*, *Methodii Patarensis*, *Andreae Cret*, *opera omnia*, Paris, 1644 (the beginning of the *de Antexusio*, fragments of the *de Resurrectione*, fragments in Photius, spurious speeches), and *Auctarium noviss*, I, Paris, 1672   Gallandi, *Bibliotheca veterum patrum*, etc (see § 2 8 *a*), III, 663–832.   Migne, PG, XVIII, 1–408   A Jahn, Hal Sax. 1865   N. Bonwetsch, *Methodius von Olympus*, I, Erlangen and Lpz 1891
Translation: Extracts from Photius   Chr F Rossler, *Bibl der Kirchenvater*, II, Lpz 1776, 296–327   W R Clark, in ANF, VI, 309–402   (Banquet, Free Will, Resurrection, Fragments, Simeon and Anna, Palms, Cross and Passion)
Literature: L Allatius, *Diatriba de Methodiorum scriptis*, Rom. 1656   Reprinted in the *Opera Hippolyti*, edited by J A Fabricius, II, Hamb 1718   A Jahn, *S. Methodius platonizans*. (part two of the edition of the works), Hal Sax 1865   G Salmon, in DCB, III, 909–911. A. Pankau, *Methodius, Bischof von Olympos*, in Kath, LXVII, 1887, 2, 1–28, 113–142, 225–250 (separately printed, Mainz, 1888)   N. Bonwetsch (see above).   Fabricius, BG, VII, 260–272. Richardson, BS, 75 f.   Preuschen, LG, 468–478.

1. Nothing further is known regarding the life of **Methodius** than that he was bishop **of Olympus** in Lycia and became a martyr in 311 A.D., toward the close of the Diocletian persecution [1]   We have only Jerome's testimony for the statement that he held the see of Tyre (Cyprus?) after his Olympian episcopate.[2] The mention of Patara by later writers [3] is founded on a misunderstanding; and the designation of Methodius as bishop of Philippi (Philipus), in the superscription of the *De Lepra*, is due to the error of a scribe.   Eusebius took no notice of this opponent of Origen.[4]

[1] Cf. Jerome, *De Viris Illust.* 83.   Socrates, *Hist. Eccl.* VI, 13.
[2] Jerome, *loc. cit.*   [3] *E g.* Leontius Byz., *de sectis*, III, 1.
[4] Cf. Zahn, in ZKG, VIII, 1886, 15–20.

2 Methodius stood in the foremost rank of those who, in the fourth century, opposed the theology of Origen, and consequently he has been either blamed severely or overwhelmed with praise, according to what happened to be the critic's view of the Alexandrian.[1] It was due to the archaic character of his **writings** that they gradually fell into oblivion in the post-Nicene period, while the name of the author remained renowned and current[2] The **Symposium** alone is extant in the original in complete form, of some of his other writings we have only longer or shorter fragments. But the old Slavic translation of a *Corpus Methodianum*,[3] in spite of its abbreviated form, is an excellent supplement to these, and gives a good idea of Methodius' literary labors. Almost all of his writings are in the form of dialogues, evidently in imitation of Plato, and they are written with more or less diffuseness and prolixity, though not without art and imagination

3 The following writings are **extant in** the original, either wholly or in part:—

(*a*) The Συμπόσιον τῶν δέκα παρθένων ἢ περὶ ἁγνείας, extant in Greek in several manuscripts,[4] is a counterpart to Plato's "Banquet," of which it makes copious use. The virgin Gregorion tells Eubulius[5] of a festival held in the gardens of Arete; where, as they walk about, ten virgins sing the praises of chastity as the most excellent means towards deliverance from sin and the attainment of redemption in Christ. At the close,

---

[1] Cf *e.g* Socrates, *Hist. Eccl.* VI, 13; and Allatius, *l c* 83. Fabricius.
[2] Attestations are given by Preuschen, LG, 473-477.
[3] Cf Pitra, AS, III, 612-617. Bonwetsch, *Prolegomena.*
[4] Cf Preuschen, LG, 469 f.
[5] Eubulius, *i e* Methodius, cf. Epiphanius, *Panarion*, LXIV, 63.

the victorious Thecla sings a hymn in twenty-four verses, to Christ the bridegroom, and to the church, his bride

Editions· L Allatius, Rom 1656 P Possinus, Paris, 1657 On the hymn, see W Meyer, in *Abhandlungen der bair Akad der Wissenschaften*, XVII, 1885, 309-323

(*b*) Περὶ τοῦ αὐτεξουσίου (Syriac· "On God, matter, and free will"), extant, in Syriac complete,[1] and in Greek only in fragments, viz 1) Chap 1, 1-7, 5,[2] in a Florentine codex[3] of the tenth century, 2) 5, 1-12, 8 in Eusebius,[4] 3) 3, 1-9, 6, 10, 2-12, 8, 15, 1-5, 16, 1-7, in the *Dialogus de Recta Fide*,[5] 4) 3, 9-8, 1, 8, 11-13, 5, in the *Sacra Parallela*,[6] and in Photius,[7] 17, 1-2 in Photius,[8] 18, 8 and 22, 3-11 (conclusion) in the *Sacra Parallela*,[9] 5) 16, 2-17, 4 and 18, 8 in Leontius and John[10] It is beyond doubt that the author of the *Dialogus* copied the writing of Methodius It may be asserted almost with certainty that Eusebius is in error when he says that a fragment which he gives, was derived from a writing περὶ τῆς ὕλης by a certain Maximus, whom he refers to the end of the second century [11] With this exception, the tradition that these pieces were written by Methodius is entirely favorable, and a comparison with his other writings, as well as the resemblance to Plato,[12] which can be proved in this case also, renders the correctness of this view almost indubitable [13]

[1] Bonwetsch, 1-62
[2] Bonwetsch
[3] *Codex Laurent plut.* IX, 23, saec X al
[4] *Praep. Evang* VII, 22
[5] Cf § 80 2.
[6] *Codex Coisl* 276
[7] *Codex*, 236 (Bekker, 304 *b*-307 *b*)
[8] *Idem* (307 *b*-308 *a*)
[9] *Codex Coisl* 276
[10] *Rerum Sacrar* Lib. II, Tit 3, Mai, NC, VII, 92 ff.
[11] *Hist Eccl* V, 27.
[12] Jahn, 122-124
[13] Otherwise, Salmon

In the dialogue the anonymous representative of orthodoxy attempts to show, against the objections of the Valentinian Valens and his companions, that nothing, not even eternal (evil) matter, has any independent existence when compared with God, and that man alone, of all beings, can keep God's command in freedom of the will.

Editions: J. Meursius, in *Varia divina*, Lugd. Bat 1619, 91–110 (*Opera*, edit Florent VIII, 1746, 726–738 Only Chaps 1, 1–7, 5

Literature: G Salmon, in DCB, III, 884 sq (Maximus) Theo Zahn, in ZKG, IX, 1888, 221–229 (The sources of Adamantius)

(c) The brief treatise "On Life and Rational Action" (*de Vita*), only extant in Syriac,[1] is closely related in subject and treatment to the tractate on the freedom of the will, though apparently no reasons can be alleged in favor of an original connection of the two writings

(d) Περὶ ἀναστάσεως ([Το?]) Aglaophon, on the Resurrection) is extant in Syriac in three books, the second and third being much abbreviated.[2] Methodius' own words[3] give rise to the conjecture that he did not complete the treatise according to his original plan There are extant in Greek: (1) Book I, 20–II, 8 10, preserved by Epiphanius,[4] (2) A number of fragments, from I, 34 (30) onwards, given by Photius,[5] (3) II, 24. 3–25. 10 in two codices,[6] (4) Separate pieces in the *Dialogus de Recta Fide* (see below), in the letter of the emperor Justinian to Mennas, in Procopius of Gaza; in the

[1] Bonwetsch, 61–69.
[2] Cf. *Idem*, 70–283, Pitra, AS, IV, 201–205, 434–438.
[3] See his *de Cibis*, 1.
[4] *Panarion*, LXIV, 12–62   [5] *Codex*, 234 (Bekker, 293 sq)
[6] *Codex Vatic* 1611 and *Codex Palat* 20 (cf Mai, NC, IX, 680 sq).

Sacra Parallela,[1] in Leontius and John,[2] in a Vatican codex,[3] in Andreas of Crete,[4] and in a Moscow codex[5] The treatise consists of the account of a dialogue held in the house of Theophilus at Patara by Eubulius (Methodius), Memian (and Auxentius) with the physician Aglaophon and Proclus of Miletus, on the question of the resurrection, Theophilus acting as judge Aglaophon and Proclus defend the view of Origen that the body is the prison-house of the soul, and accordingly they deny the resurrection of the flesh, bringing forward many physiological reasons. Thus the whole forms a powerful and subtle controversial treatise against the theology of Origen, from whose works (περὶ ἀναστάσεως) long sections are quoted.[6] Use was probably made of the lost treatise of Justin on the resurrection,[7] and certainly of the *Supplicatio* of Athenagoras.[8]

Theo. Zahn, in ZKG, VIII, 1886, 1-15 (use of Justin by Methodius).

(*e*) " On the distinction of meats and on the heifer mentioned in Leviticus (Numbers), with whose ashes sinners were sprinkled " (*De Cibis*): Only preserved in Syriac[9] It is addressed to Cilonia, and proves by numerous citations from Scripture that the sprinklings

[1] *Codex Coisl* 276 and 294, *Codex Rupef* (1450 *Phill.*).
[2] *Rerum sacrarum*, II (cf. Mai, NC, VII, 92, 102).
[3] *Codex Vatic graec.* 1236. John of Damascus, *Sacr. Parallela*, cf also the *Melissa* of Antonius
[4] *Comm. in Apoc.*
[5] *Codex Mosqu. graec.* 385, cf. on these pieces, Bonwetsch, XXV-XXIX.
[6] Cf § 61, 8 *c*.   [7] Cf. II, 18 8-11, Bonwetsch, 231 f
[8] Cf I, 36 6-37 2, Bonwetsch, 129, 12-130, 9
[9] Bonwetsch, 290-307. Cf. also § 62

accomplished through the body of Christ cleanse not only the body but also the soul, more than did the blood of the heifer (Num xix 2-3) and the other purifications contained in the Law: the true heifer is the body of Christ,[1] the laws concerning food are only shadows of good things to come[2] The first five chapters deal at length with the sufferings of the righteous, in recollection of temptations[3] personally experienced.

(*f*) Περὶ λέπρας (on Leprosy, to Sistelius): extant in Syriac in a complete though abbreviated form,[4] in the original, only in a number of fragments[5] It is in the form of a dialogue between Eusebius and Sistelius, and treats of the spiritual sense of the proscriptions in Lev. xiii. 1–6, 47, 49

(*g*) The writings "On the Leech mentioned in Proverbs," and on "The Heavens declare the Glory of God" (*de Sanguisuga*), are only extant in Syriac[6] They consist of expositions of Prov. xxx. 15 ff. (xxiv. 50 ff.), and Ps xix. 2, 5, without any internal connection of the passages, and are addressed to Eustachius.

4. **Fragments** are extant, taken from: —

(*a*) Περὶ τῶν γενητῶν preserved by Photius[7] It contains, in the form of a dialogue, a refutation of Origen's doctrine of the eternity of the world The Origenist herein opposed bears the (allegorical?) name of Centaurus,[8]

(*b*) Κατὰ Πορφυρίου: frequently mentioned by Je-

---

[1] 11, 4.
[2] 8, 1.
[3] Chap 1.
[4] Bonwetsch, 308–329.
[5] *Codex Cotsl* 294 (cf. Bonwetsch, XXXI sq.).
[6] Bonwetsch, 330–339
[7] *Codex*, 235, Bekker, 301–304, Bonwetsch, 340–344
[8] Bonwetsch, 343, 1

rome,[1] and described by him as very voluminous [2] Fragments only are extant [3] Philostorgius [4] considered this writing inferior to that of Apollinaris upon the same subject Use was made of Justin's Apology [5] in the first fragment, [6]

(c) Περὶ μαρτύρων: two small fragments are extant, [7]

(d) Fragments taken from a Commentary on Job are found in a number of manuscripts [8]

5 The following writings are **lost** : —

(a) " On the Body ". mentioned by Methodius himself ; [9]

(b) *De Pythonissa* · mentioned by Jerome [10] and described as written against Origen (witch of Endor ?), [11]

(c) Commentaries on Genesis and the Song of Songs; mentioned by Jerome ; [12]

(d) A dialogue entitled *Xenōn*, mentioned by Socrates,[13] can scarcely be identical with his περὶ τῶν γενητῶν, as Westcott thinks, since in it, according to Socrates' account, he speaks of Origen with admiration.

---

[1] *De Viris*, 83; *Epist.* 48, 13; 70, 3; *Comm. in Dan praef.* and *Cap.* xiii

[2] *Epist* 70, 3

[3] *Codex Monac.* 498, *Saec.* X (*Codex Dresdens.* A. 1, 2, and *Codex Rupef* Bonwetsch, 345-348).

[4] *Hist Eccl* VIII, 14.

[5] *Apologia*, I, 55

[6] Bonwetsch, 346, 17 ff.

[7] Theodoret *Dial* I (*Opera*, IV, 55 f., Schulze), and in *Cod. Coisl* 276 (Bonwetsch, 349)

[8] Pitra, AS, III, 603-610 (Bonwetsch, 349-354).

[9] *De Sanguisuga*, 10, 4 (Bonwetsch, 339, 40).

[10] *De Viris Illust.* 83

[11] Cf reply of Eustathius of Antioch (§ 61 6 *b* 8)

[12] Jerome, *loc cit.*, cf Pitra, AS, III, 617, and Preuschen, LG, 478.

[13] *Hist Eccl.* VI, 13.

6 The following are spurious : —

(*a*) The Oration Εἰς τὸν Συμεῶνα καὶ εἰς τὴν Ἄννην, τῇ ἡμέρᾳ τῆς ἀπαντήσεως, καὶ εἰς τὴν ἁγίαν θεοτόκον, cannot have originated as early as Methodius, because the festival of *Hypapante* (Purification or Candlemas) was not yet celebrated in 300 A D , also because the work "has throughout at its command a theology with the strongly marked terminology of the later Greek church ",[1]

Edition· P P. Tiletanus, Paris, 1598.

(*b*) The oration Εἰς τὰ βαία (*in Ramos Palmarum*) likewise plainly bears the stamp of a later period,

(*c*) The fragments of a *Sermo in Ascensionem Domini nostri Jesu Christi*, preserved in Armenian,[2] are spurious.

§ 77. *Firmilianus*

Firmilianus was bishop of Cæsarea in Cappadocia as early as 232 A D ,[3] and next to Dionysius of Alexandria was the most esteemed Oriental bishop of his time.[4] He is known as a writer only through the **letter** which he sent to Cyprian of Carthage in the matter of heretical baptism The letter was a reply to a lost writing of Cyprian, in which Cyprian's several arguments were considered It is preserved in a Latin version which probably was not by Cyprian, and which, according to Ritschl, was interpolated with the intention of "lending Cyprian's thoughts to his Oriental colleague " Ernst, on the other hand, maintains the genuineness of the whole letter. Basil of Cæsarea[5] speaks of Λόγοι by

---

[1] Bonwetsch, XXXVII   [2] Pitra, AS, IV, 207-209 (439-441)
[3] Eusebius, *Hist Eccl* VI, 26, 27; cf VII, 14
[4] *Idem*, VII, 5 1, 28 1, 30 3 sqq
[5] *Liber de Spiritu Sancto*, 29, 74

Firmilianus, and according to Moses of Chorene[1] he wrote a book *de Ecclesiae Persecutionibus*

The letter to Cyprian is included among the works of Cyprian as *Epist* 75 (edit Hartel, II, 1868, 810-827) Cf O Ritschl, *Cyprian von Karthago*, Gott 1885, 126-134 J Ernst, in ZkTh, XVIII, 1894, 209-259

III WRITERS OF SYRIA AND PALESTINE

§ 78 Paul of Samosata

Mai, NC, VII, 68 sq , 299 Routh, RS, III, 287-367 A Harnack, in RE, X, 193 f — Fabricius, BG, 307 sq Harnack, LG, 520-525

Paul of Samosata, viceroy (*ducenarius*) in the Palmyrene kingdom, was bishop of **Antioch** from about 260 to 268 A.D He attempted to set forth and defend his theological and Christological views in his Ὑπομνήματα,[2] some sections of which have been preserved by Leontius.[3] Five fragments taken from the Λόγοι πρὸς Σαβῖνον, against the authenticity of which there is no internal evidence, are also to be found in a collection of *Doctrinae patrum de verbi incarnatione*, ascribed to the presbyter Anastasius Finally, there are extant a number of fragments taken from the *Disputation* which took place at the (third) Synod of Antioch, 268 A D , between Paul and Malchion, the principal of the rhetorical school at Antioch[4] They were derived from the short-hand report of the Acts of the Synod, and are found in Justinian,[5] in the *Contestatio ad clerum Constantinopoli-*

---

[1] *Historia Armen* (saec V ? VII, VIII ?)
[2] Eusebius, *Hist Eccl* VII, 30 11   [3] *Adversus Nestor et Eutych* III
[4] Eusebius, *Hist Eccl* VII, 29 2 (Jerome, *De Viris Illust* 71), translated by S D. F Salmond, in ANF, VI, 169-171
[5] *Contra Monophys* (Mai, NC, VII, 299)

tanum,¹ in the works of Leontius,² and in Petrus Diaconus³

§ 79. Lucian

Routh, RS, IV, 3-10, 11-17   C P Caspari, *Ungedruckte Quellen zur Geschichte des Taufsymbols und der Glaubensregel*, I, Christiania, 1866 (Preface)   A Harnack, in RE, VII, 767-772   P de Lagarde, *Librorum Vet Test canonicorum pars prior graece*, Gotting 1883   J Wellhausen, 6th edit of F Bleek's *Einleitung in das Alte Testament*, Berl 1893, § 255   F Kattenbusch, *Das Apos Symbol* I, Lpz 1894, 252-273, 392-395 — Fabricius, BG, V, 361 sq , VII, 303-305   Harnack, LG, 526-531

Lucian, born at Samosata⁴ and presbyter of Antioch, separated himself from the communion of the catholic church probably after the deposition of Paul of Samosata (268 A D ?), but he continued to be the most influential leader of a great theological school. On January 7, 312, he became a martyr in Nicomedia,⁵ and his martyrdom atoned in the eyes of posterity for his extra-ecclesiastical position   Jerome⁶ praises his zealous labors upon the text of Holy Scripture; and the **recension of the Septuagint,** which he made, was recognized as the standard in the churches from Antioch to Constantinople   Jerome records further that Lucian wrote *Libelli de fide* and several Letters   No part of the former is

---

¹ *Act. Syn Eph* , Mansi, VI, 1109   ² Leontius, *loc cit.*

³ *De Incarnat et grat Dom Chr ad Fulgent* III, 78 (Latin)   RS, III, 300-302.   Cf also fragments given by Pitra, AS, IV, 183 sq , 423 sq (Syriac and Latin)

⁴ See Suidas, *Lexicon*, under "Lucian."

⁵ Eusebius, *Hist Eccl* VIII, 13. 2, IX, 6. 3, cf the Nicomedian calendar

⁶ *De Viris Illust* 77 (cf *ad Damasum*, *Praef in Evangelia* , *ad Chromat*, *Praef. in Paralipom* , (*Adversus Rufinum*, II, 27), *Epist* 106. 2.

extant unless a formula in the Apostolic Constitutions¹ may be referred to him, as Kattenbusch contends. A sentence from a Letter written from Nicomedia, and addressed to the Antiochians, is found in the *Chronicon Paschale*² In his translation of Eusebius' *Church History*, Rufinus³ has preserved a defence made by Lucian before the judge, which may very well be genuine. It was taken from Eusebius' *Acts of the Martyrs*. An exposition of Job ii 9 f, attributed to Lucian, is found in an anonymous pseudo-Origenistic Arian *Expositio libri Jobi* (about 400 A.D.).

§ 80. *Anonymous: Dialogus de Recta in Deum Fide*

Editions: (1) Of the Greek text, J R Wetstein, Basil, 1674. De la Rue (see § 61), I, 1733, 803-872, cf *praefatio*, XII, and p 800 Migne, PG, XI, 1711-1884 Lommatzsch, *Origenis opera omnia*, XVI, 1844, 246-418 (2) Translation by Rufinus, C P Caspari, *Kirchenhistorische Anekdota*, I, Christiania, 1883, 1-129; cf. preface, pp. III-V.—Literature: F J A Hort in DCB, I, 39-41 Theo. Zahn, in ZKG, IX, 1888, 193-239, and GNK, II, 2, 409-426.

1. The Διάλεξις Ἀδαμαντίου, τοῦ καὶ Ὠριγένους, περὶ τῆς εἰς Θεὸν ὀρθῆς πίστεως, in **five books**, has been preserved in Greek, in seven manuscripts, derived from a single archetype; and in Latin, in the translation by Rufinus This translation is a faithful reproduction of its original, whereas the Greek text represents an "extensive and, toward the close, a more and more complete revision,"⁴ which must have been undertaken between 330 and 337 A.D Origen was regarded as its author even as early as the time of Basil and Gregory,⁵ and

¹ *Apost. Const.* VII, 41.
² Dindorf's edit. I, 516.
³ IX, 6 (on Eusebius, IX, 9).
⁴ Zahn, ZKG, IX, 207.
⁵ *Philocalia*, 24.

also by Rufinus, the authorship being inferred from the introduction of Adamantius as interlocutor. On internal grounds, however, this is impossible, and, besides, the dialogue nowhere indicates that the author meant to pass himself off as Origen. The fact that use was made of Methodius[1] does not, however, prevent the assumption that the author really proposed to make the great Alexandrian the vehicle of his own thoughts. There are no clues to the personality of the author. The work must have been written after about 300 A.D. (Methodius), and probably before the edict of Milan, 313 A D The place of composition was, perhaps, Antioch or its neighborhood

2. The dialogue is composed of a **disputation** between Adamantius, an orthodox believer, and Megethius and Marcus, Marcionites, Marinus, a Bardesanite, and Droserius and Valens, Valentinians Eutropius, a heathen who at the end is converted, acts as judge In the first two books Megethius and Marcus defend their theory of three (or two) principles, on the ground of the opposition between law and gospel, which they attempt to prove by passages taken from their (Marcionite) Testament. In the third, fourth, and fifth books Marinus defends his own theses in opposition to the catholic doctrines of the creation of the devil by God, the birth of Christ through the Virgin, and the resurrection of the flesh The disputation with the Valentinians on the origin of evil, which is foisted into the fourth book, is a digression made purposely by the author, but one which falls outside of the scope of the book as a whole. In it the writings of Methodius on the freedom of the will and on the resurrection[2] are copied In the first dia-

---

[1] Cf No 2, below [2] See § 76. 3 *b* and *d.*

logue use was made of an anti-Marcionite writing which appears to have been known as early as the time of Irenæus and Tertullian, and in which may be found, possibly, the writing of Theophilus of Antioch against Marcion.[1] The dialogue is not a work of art, but it is remarkable for its comparative terseness.

§ 81. *Alexander of Jerusalem*

Routh, RS, II, 161–179. Migne, PG, X, 203–206 — Translation· S D F. Salmond, ANF, VI, 154 (Fragm Epist) — Fabricius, BG, 287. Richardson, BS, 69 f. Harnack, LG, 505–507.

Alexander, a pupil of Pantænus and Clement at the same time with Origen,[2] and bishop of an unknown see in Cappadocia,[3] was called to Jerusalem as the coadjutor of Narcissus,[4] and stood at the head of the congregation, at all events, in 216 A D.[5] He became a martyr in the Decian persecution [6] In the library which he founded at Jerusalem [7] there existed a collection of his **Letters,** from which Eusebius has preserved the following fragments: (1) The beginning and close of a congratulatory epistle written from prison in Cappadocia,[8] to the Antiochians on the occasion of the accession of Asclepiades [9] to the bishopric; (2) A fragment of a letter to the Antinoites in Egypt, written while Narcissus was still alive;[10] (3) A fragment of a letter to Origen;[11]

---

[1] Zahn, 229–236.
[2] Eusebius, *Hist Eccl.* VI, 14. 8.   [3] *Idem.* VI, 11. 1 sq.
[4] Eusebius, *Chronic ad ann. Abrahami* 2231, fourth year of Caracalla; Jerome, 2228, second of Caracalla
[5] Cf. § 61 2.
[6] Jerome, 2268 I, cf Syncellus, 684, 6   [7] Cf. § 58. 3
[8] Cf. Eusebius, *Chronic.* 2219, tenth year of Severus, Jerome, 2220, twelfth year of Severus.
[9] Eusebius, *Hist. Eccl.* XI, 11. 5 sq
[10] *Idem*, VI, 11. 3.   [11] *Idem*, VI, 14. 8.

(4) Fragment of a letter from Alexander and Theoctistus of Cæsarea to Demetrius of Alexandria in regard to lay preaching.[1]

§ 82. *Julius Africanus*

Editions: Gallandi, *Biblioth vet pat.* (see § 2, 8 *a*), II, 337–376. Routh, RS, II, 219–509 Migne, PG, X, 51–108, XI, 41–48. — Translation: S D. F Salmond, in ANF, VI, 125–140 (extant writings) — Literature: G Salmon, in DCB, I, 53–57. A. Harnack, in RE, VII, 296–298. H. Gelzer, *Sextus Julius Afrikanus und die byzantinische Chronographie*, 2 vols. Lpz. 1880–1885 H. Kihn, in KLex, VI, 2005–2009 — Fabricius, BG, IV, 240–246. Richardson, BS, 68 f. Preuschen, LG, 507–513

1. Sextus Julius **Africanus**,[2] was born, according to Suidas, in Libya; apparently he was an officer,[3] and settled at Emmaus[4] (Nicopolis) in Palestine, probably after his return from the expedition of Septimius Severus against the Osrhoenians (in Mesopotamia) in 195 A.D.[5] As envoy to Alexander Severus[6] he rendered service in connection with the constitution of Emmaus as a municipium (or free town) There he lived till after 240 A.D ,[7] holding a prominent position, but not as a bishop,[8] and perhaps not even as a presbyter. He undertook many and extended journeys in Palestine and Syria, to Alexandria (about 211–215 A.D.),[9] and to Asia Minor, and he

---

[1] Eusebius, *Hist. Eccl.* VI, 19. 17 sq ; cf Jerome, *De Viris Illust.* 62.
[2] On the name, see Eusebius, *Chronic. ann Abrahami* 2237, cf. Suidas, *Lexicon*, under Ἀφρικανός.
[3] Gelzer   [4] Not identical with the Emmaus of Luke.
[5] Cf. Syncellus, *Chron.* 669, 20 (Bonn edition).
[6] Thus Syncellus, 676, 6–13. According to Eusebius, *loc. cit.*, to Heliogabalus.
[7] Cf. No. 3 *c*, below.
[8] In spite of statements by Dionysius Bar-Salibi, and Ebed-Jesu.
[9] Eusebius, *Idem*, VI, 31. 2.

stood in intimate relations with the royal house of Edessa, with Abgar VIII Bar Manu and his son.

2. So far as the **literary remains** of Julius Africanus allow an estimate, he appears as a man of sober judgment, independent knowledge, and considerable power of delineation. The absurdities of the *Cesti*, to be sure, are scarcely superior to the nonsense which other writers produced in the same field. But his exegetical works, when compared with the learned elaborations of Origen, are models of scholarly sober-mindedness, and his chronography, which became the basis of all ecclesiastical and civil historiographic writings even down to the Middle Ages, must be regarded, in spite of its shortcomings, as one of the most preeminent productions of early Christian literature.

3. The following **writings** of Africanus, placed in their chronological order, are known : — ¯

(*a*) The Χρονογραφίαι,[1] in five books,[2] was completed in 221 A.D. The fragments extant in Eusebius,[3] Syncellus, and other writers, and the use made of it by the Byzantine historians, afford a sufficient idea of the character and arrangement of this earliest Christian history of the world. The author's purpose was to give a comprehensive and exhaustive compilation of the data of sacred and profane history. In so doing, he presupposed the absolute trustworthiness of the statements of the Bible; but, while keeping ever in view the apologetic aim pursued by Tatian, Theophilus, and Clement, of proving by chronological means the superior antiq-

---

[1] Eusebius, *Hist.* VI, 21. 2. Concerning other unauthentic titles used by later writers, see Gelzer, 26

[2] Eusebius, *Idem*, and *Chronicon*, I, edit of Schoene, 97, 98.

[3] *Praeparat.* and *Demonstrat. evangelica,*

uity of Jewish history, he so widened this purpose that the "presentation and exact fixation of all chronological details became an end in itself."[1] The material of the five books appears to have been divided as follows:[2] (1) From the creation to the partition of the world (years 1–2661); (2) Down to Moses (2662–3707); (3) To the first Olympiad (3708–4727); (4) To the fall of the Persian Empire (4728–5172); (5) To the fourth year of Heliogabalus (5173–5723, 221 A.D.). From the third book onward the presentation is synchronistic, with parallel accounts of Biblical and secular events Besides the works of Christian apologists he made use of chronological handbooks as sources, more especially the chronography of Justus of Tiberias[3] The work does not appear to have contained originally a *canon*, that is, a tabulated summary of events in addition to the chronography Eusebius owed much to Africanus in connection with his chronographical labors, but the Eusebian *Chronicon*, in the translation of Jerome, displaced the work of his predecessor in the West, while Byzantine historiography remained directly dependent upon the influence of Africanus.

Gelzer is engaged upon a compilation of the fragments of the *Chronicon* See, however, RS, 238–309 A v Gutschmid (see § 36 3 *b*) E Schwartz, *Die Königlichsten des Eratosthenes und Kastor mit Exkursen uber die Interpolationen bei Africanus und Eusebius*, in *Abhandlungen der konigl. Gesellschaft der Wissenschaften zu Gottingen*, XI, 2, 1894

(*b*) The Κεστοὶ ἢ παράδοξα[4] was contained in fourteen

[1] Gelzer, p 23.
[2] *Idem*, p. 29   [3] von Gutschmid.
[4] On the first title (embroidered girdles), cf Στρωματεῖς, and the remark at § 60 3 *c*, and on the second, *Geoponica*, I, 1, p 7.

books (according to Photius),[1] or more probably in twenty-four (according to Suidas),[2] and not in nine (according to Syncellus)[3] The work was dedicated to the emperor Alexander Severus, and consisted of an encyclopædia upon questions of natural (agrarian) history and medicine, as well as of military and other matters It was full of senseless and, in part, immoral superstitions. The following portions are extant: (1) An extract (apparently from the sixth and seventh books), bearing on military tactics,[4] is included in the collection of the Tacticians. It contains forty-five chapters in chaotic order (for which a redactor is responsible), and is augmented by thirty-two chapters of foreign origin (2) Thirty-nine fragments probably borrowed only indirectly, which are contained in the Γεωπονικά, i e the collection of matter relating to agriculture, made by Constantinus Porphyrogenneta[5] This collection contains also many sections by Africanus, which are not marked as such (3) A small fragment from the thirteenth book relating to purgatives, contained in two manuscripts of the fourteenth and fifteenth centuries.[6] (4) Sections that were used without mention of the author in the collection of the Ἱππιατρικά, analogous to the Geoponica (5) The section Περὶ σταθμῶν contained in three Paris manuscripts[7] (6) An excerpt, consisting mainly of secret aphrodisiac prescriptions, preserved by M. Psellus, of the thirteenth century That Julius Africanus was

---
[1] Photius, Codex, 34.
[2] Suidas, loc. cit.
[3] Cf No 3, below
[4] στρατηγητικά
[5] Gemoll, 278
[6] Codex Laur. LXXIV, 23, saec XIV, and Codex Barocc 224, saec XV (Muller).
[7] Lagarde

the author is sufficiently attested by the witness of Eusebius,[1] and by internal evidence [2]

Veterum mathematicorum opera, ed M Thevenot, Paris, 1693, 274-316, with the notes of J Boivin, 339-360 — Γεωπονικά, edit J N Niclas, Lips 1781 W Gemoll, *Untersuchungen uber die Quellen, den Verfasser und die Verfassungszeit der Geoponika*, in the *Berliner Studien fur klass Philol und Archaol*, by F Ascherson, I, 1883 — K Mullei, *Zu Julius Africanus*, in JpiTh, VII, 1881, 759 f — Τῶν ἱππιατρικῶν βιβλία δύο, edit S Grynaeus, Basil 1537, 268 — P de Lagarde, *Symmicta*, I, 1877, 167-173 — P Lambecius, *Comment de Aug Bibl Caes Vindob* VII, 222 sqq — J Klein, *Zu den* Κεστοί *des Julius Africanus*, in RhM, XXV, 1870, 447 f

(*c*) The Περὶ τῆς κατὰ Σωσάνναν ἱστορίας ἐπιστολὴ πρὸς Ὠριγένην,[3] transmitted in manuscript along with the reply of Origen,[4] was called forth by an assertion of the genuineness of the history of Susanna made by Origen in a religious discussion The entirely pertinent criticism employed by Africanus, and its terse expression, is the more plainly set off by the reply of the Alexandrian, with its wealth of words and poverty of thought.

(*d*) The **Letter to** (an unknown) **Aristides**, which is preserved in a fragmentary form by Eusebius,[5] in the Epitome of the Eusebian *Quaestiones de differentia Evangeliorum*, and in the *Catenae*, was intended to reconcile, on the basis of information given by relatives of Jesus, the discrepancies between the genealogies of Matthew and Luke by an appeal to the Levitical law of marriage. The author's exegetical sobriety and love of truth is here also very obvious in spite of the mistaken outcome,

---

[1] Eusebius, *Hist* IV, 31 1 [2] Cf especially *Geoponica*, VII, 14

[3] Eusebius, *Hist*, *loc cit*, Jerome, *De Viris Illust* 63. Translation by F. Crombie, in ANF, IV, 385.

[4] Cf. 61. 10 *a*. [5] Eusebius, *Hist*. I, 7 2-15

which, however, was quite acceptable to those who came after.

F Spitta, *Der Brief des Julius Africanus an Aristides* Halle, 1877 (attempt at reconstruction)

4. The statement that Africanus wrote Commentaries on the Gospels,[1] or on other Scriptures of the New Testament,[2] is not confirmed by any trustworthy testimony Africanus was neither the translator of the Legends of the Apostles which pass under the name of Abdias, nor was he the author of the *Acta Symphorosae* in spite of manuscript attestation. Harnack regards it as possible that he translated Tertullian's *Apologeticus*.[3]

§ 83. *Pamphilus*

Routh, RS, III, 487–499, 500–513, IV, 339–392 Migne, PG, X, 1529–1558, XVII, 521–616 (among the works of Origen, cf also Lommatzsch, XXIV, 268–412) L A Zacagnius, *Collectanea* (see § 2 8 *b*), 428–441 J A Fabricius, *Opera Hippolyti*, II, Hamb 1718, 205–217 B Montfaucon, *Biblioth Coisliniana*, Paris, 1715, 78–82 — Fabricius, BG, 301–303. Richardson, BS, 72 Preuschen, LG, 543–550

The biography of **Pamphilus**, written by Eusebius,[4] has been lost Born in Phœnicia (Berytus ?),[5] of a prominent family, Pamphilus studied theology under Pierius in Alexandria,[6] became a presbyter at **Cæsarea**, and fell martyr, in the persecution under Maximinus[7]

---

[1] Dionysius Bar-Salibi. [2] Cf. Ebed-Jesu
[3] Cf § 85 5 *a*.
[4] Eusebius, *Hist*. VI, 32 3, VII, 32, VIII, 13 6, *Martyr Palestin* 11, 3
[5] Simeon Metaphrast   [6] Photius, *Codex*, 118, cf 119.
[7] Jerome, *De Viris Illust* 75 (309 A D)

The principal service rendered by Pamphilus was, perhaps, the founding, or at any rate the organization, of the library at Cæsarea,[1] which he enriched with many manuscripts, among which were some works of Origen copied by himself While in prison, 307–309 A D, he wrote, with the support of his pupil and friend Eusebius, an Ἀπολογία ὑπὲρ Ὠριγένους (πρὸς τοὺς ἐν μετάλλοις διὰ Χριστόν ταλαιπωρουμένους), in five books. After the death of the martyr, Eusebius added a sixth book The work was intended to refute objections to the theology of Origen, by means of the citation of passages from his writings It also contained a large amount of material for the biography of the Alexandrian Only the first book is extant in the untrustworthy translation of Rufinus, a short survey of the whole is given by Photius[2] The assertation of Jerome that Eusebius was the real author of the whole work[3] contradicts not only the statements of Eusebius[4] and Photius, but also Jerome's own earlier statement[5] Jerome[6] mentions **Letters** to friends, and in so doing refers to Eusebius as his authority The statement of Gennadius[7] that Rufinus translated a writing by Pamphilus *Adversus Mathematicos*, probably is due to his confusing it with the Apology The Ἔκθεσις κεφαλαίων τῶν Πράξεων contains a brief statement of the contents of the Acts of the Apostles in forty sections; it was first printed without the author's name, preceding the Commentary of Œcumenius on the Acts, and afterward by Zacagni and

---

[1] Cf. § 58 3.
[2] Photius, *Codex*, 118, cf 117
[3] *Contra Rufin* vv. ll, cf *Epist* 84, 11
[4] *Eccl Hist* VI, 33 4
[5] *De Viris Illust* 75.
[6] *Contra Rufin* I, 9, II, 23
[7] Jerome, *De Viris Illust* 17.

Fabricius as a work of Euthalius of Sulce. It has been claimed by Montfaucon[1] for Pamphilus.[2]

§ 84. *Beryllus of Bostra in Arabia*

Fabricius, BG, 290   Harnack, LG, 514.

Beryllus, bishop of Bostra in Arabia, whose heterodox Monarchian views were refuted by Origen in a disputation,[3] wrote **Letters** and **Treatises**, which, according to Eusebius,[4] were preserved in the library at Jerusalem.[5]

[1] Following *Codex Coisl* 202
[2] Cf. Gallandi, *Biblioth vet patr* (§ 2. 8 *a*), IV, p. III. Translated by S. D F Salmond, in ANF, VI, 166–168.
[3] Cf Eusebius, *Hist.* VI, 33. 1–3.
[4] *Idem*, VI, 20 1
[5] Cf Jerome, *De Viris Illust* 60, *Chronic. ad ann. Abrahami*, 2244; *Alex. Sever.* 6.

CHAPTER II

THE OCCIDENTALS

I. AFRICAN WRITERS

§ 85 *Tertullian*

Editions · B Rhenanus, Basil 1521, 1528, 1536 (Schoenemann, BPL, 17), 1539, cf A Horawitz, in SAW, LXXI, 1872, 662-674   M Mesnartius (J Gangneius), Paris, 1545   S Gelenius, Basil 1550   J Pamelius, Antv 1579 and after   Frc Junius, Franeckerae, 1597   N Rigaltius, Lutet Paris (1628[9?]), 1634, and after   J S Semler, 6 tomi, Hal et Magdeb 1769-1776   Migne, PL, I, II   Frc Oehler, 3 tomi, Lips 1853, 1854, 1851 edit minor, Lips 1854, cf E Klussmann in ZwTh, III, 1860, 82-100, 363-393, and Oehler's reply, *Idem*, IV, 1861, 204-211   A Reifferscheid and G Wissowa, Part I, of CSE, Vol XX, Vindob 1890, cf W v Hartel, *Patristische Studien*, four parts (from SAW), Wien, 1890

Translations   K A H Kellner, 2 vols Koln, 1882   Selected writings in BKV, 1869, 72   S Thelwall, P Holmes, A Roberts, and R E Wallis, in ANF, III-IV, 1-166   C Dodgson, in LFC, X, Oxf 1842 (Apologetic and Practical Treatises)

Literature   A collection of valuable earlier dissertations by J Pamelius, P Allix, N le Nourry, J L Mosheim, G Centnerus, J A Noesselt, J S. Semler, and J Kaye, printed by Oehler in his third volume (see above)   J A W Neander, *Antignostikus Geist des Tertullian und Einleitung in dessen Schriften*, Berl 1825, 2d edit 1849   C Hesselberg, *Tertullian's Lehre* Part 1, *Leben und Schriften*, Dorpat, 1848   H Grotemeyer, *Ueber Tertullian's Leben und Schriften*, Kempen, 1863-1865   A Hauck, *Tertullian's Leben und Schriften*, Erlangen, 1877   J M Fuller, in DCB, IV, 818-864   A Harnack, in *Encyclopædia Britannica*, XXIII, 1888, 196-198   A Ebert. *Allgem Gesch der Litteratur* (see § 2 5), 32-56   E Noeldechen, *Tertullian*, Gotha, 1890 (the numerous essays of this author, scattered in various periodicals, are used in the foregoing work, and also in that mentioned below under 3) Schoenemann, BPL, 2-58 Richardson, BS, 42-47 Preuschen, LG, 669-687

1. Quintus Septimius Florens **Tertullianus**[1] was born at Carthage, not long before 160 A D., as the son of a proconsular centurion,[2] was probably an advocate (it is doubtful whether he was identical with the jurist of the same name), and embraced Christianity, possibly at Rome,[3] previous to 197 A D He became a presbyter of the Carthaginian church, but between 202 and 207 A D,[4] he broke with the catholic communion in order to ally himself with the sect of the Montanists, as a member of which he died probably after 220 A.D.

On the relation of Tertullian to the jurist of the same name (author of *de Castrensi peculio* [Dig XXIX, 1, lex 23, 33, XLIX, 17. 4], and *Quaestiones* [Dig I, 3 37, XLVIII, 2 28]) see P Kruger, *Geschichte und Litteratur der Quellen des romischen Rechts* Lpz 1888, 203 99 (O Lenel, *Palingenesia*, II, 341) What P. Kruger says against the identification of the two has little weight.

2. That radicalism in which every step forward signifies a break with the past distinguished Tertullian also as a **writer** Possessing comprehensive culture and extraordinary knowledge in the domain of history, philosophy, and jurisprudence, he became, after his conversion to Christianity, a despiser of all æsthetic culture, and he gave frequent expression to his hatred toward secular science as folly in the sight of God Nevertheless he became the most original, the most

---

[1] Cf. *De Baptismo*, 20, *De Virginibus velandis*, 17 (*Exhort. castitat.* 13) Lactantius, *Div. institut* V, 1. 23
[2] Optatus, *Schism Donatist* I, 9, Jerome, *De Viris Illust* 53
[3] Eusebius, *Hist* II, 2   [4] Cf *Adv. Marcion*. I, 15.

individual, and, next to Clement of Alexandria, the most important writer of the ante-Nicene period. The most original, since the freedom with which he adopted foreign ideas was only exceeded by the independence with which he made them serve his way of looking at things, the most individual, since scarcely any other Christian writer has succeeded in impressing the stamp of his own individuality so indelibly upon his works. He became the founder of a Christian pamphlet-literature which at a later date became trivial. And as Latin Christian theology paid homage to the genius who coined so many ideas that even to-day have not suffered by abrasion, so in the history of Latin Christian literature he stands as the first, who, renouncing classical culture, created in new forms "a specifically Christian style".[1] He was an orator of the foremost rank, whose ruthless scorn of all compromise did not fit him to be an attorney of actual life, whose more than powerful logic often threw contempt on all sound reason, whose despotic dialectic always blinded, but seldom stood the test of calm reflection. He was a master of language in whom an impetuous disposition, a passion for brevity and terseness, a sensuous fancy and a wealth of plastic thought, a biting wit and a satirical humor, a supreme contempt for the commonplace, and an inexhaustible delight in novel forms of speech, all combined to produce a style, the breathless passion of which might carry the reader away, but at the same time was just as likely to bewilder him with its weight of exaggeration, and tire him by its wealth of grotesqueness. Cyprian recognized in him a master,[2]

---

[1] Ebert, 33 [2] Jerome, *De Viris Illust* 53

but even in his day Lactantius¹ complained that his lack of form and obscurity of style prevented him from receiving the recognition that was his due. Jerome well knew what he said when he advised a lady, his friend, not to compare the rill of his discourse with the river of Tertullian's². Indeed, one half of the famous verdict of Vincent of Lerins is true: *quot paene verba, tot sententiae,* but not the other: *quot sensus, tot victoriae.* Even Isidore of Seville³ copied the African copiously, but in the Middle Ages his writings were scarcely read at all, it was the renaissance that first recalled him from the dead⁴

J G V Engelhardt, *Ueber Tertullians schriftstellerischen Charakter*, in ZhTh, XXII, 1852, 316–319. Jos Schmidt, *De latinitate Tertulliani*, Erlangen, 1870. P Langen, *De usu praepositionum Tertullianeo*, I–III, Monast 1868–1870. H Roensch, *Das neue Testament Tertullians*, Lpz 1871. G R Hauschild, *Die Grundsatze und Mittel der Sprachbildung bei Tertullian*, Lpz 1876 and 1881 — Tertullian's relations to more ancient writers have not yet been sufficiently investigated, see, however, A Harnack, in TU, I, 1, 2, 1882, 220-222 (Tatian), 249–251 (Melito). E Noeldechen, in JprTh, XII, 1886, 279–301 (Clement), and, *per contra*, P Wendland, *Quaestiones Musonianae*, 1886, 49–53. Compare also P. de Lagarde, *Septuagintastudien* (§ 54), 74. Erdm Schwarz, in JclPh, XVI, Suppl, 1888, 405–437, and F Wilhelm (cf § 45) (Varro). For the literature on his relation to Minucius Felix, see § 45. J Jung, *Zu Tertullians auswartigen Beziehungen* in *Wiener Studien*, XIII, 1891, 231–244. — M Klussmann, *Excerpta Tertullianea in Isidori Hispalensis Etymologus*, Hamb 1892. Attestations are given by Preuschen, LG, 679–687, cf 668

3 The **transmission** of Tertullian's writings, with the exception of the *Apologeticus*, which is extant in numer-

¹ *Div Instit* V, 1. 23.   ² *Epist.* 64, 23, *ad Fabiolam.*
³ *Origines*, vv. ll.
⁴ Cf. *Epist Politiani* (Preuschen, LG, 668). ·

ous manuscripts,[1] is in evil case   Besides three older manuscripts,[2] there are a number extant, dating from the fifteenth century, which appear, however, to rest upon the same archetype   The writings *ad Nationes, Scorpiace, de Testimonio Animae, de Spectaculis, de Idololatria, de Anima,* and *dc Oratione,* have been preserved in the *Codex Agobardinus* only, while for the text of *de Baptismo, de Pudicitia,* and *de Jejunio* we are compelled to rely solely upon the editions of Mesnart (Gangneius), or Gelenius, and Pamelius   Finally, a large number of his writings has been lost (see below, No 9)   The condition of the **text**, which is frequently corrupt and which is full of *lacunæ* in the case of the *ad Nationes,* when taken together with the peculiar obscurity of Tertullian's mode of expression, has afforded a wide and much cultivated field for learned conjecture   The **chronology** of the separate writings is involved in considerable difficulty, since unequivocal clues are seldom found   Hence in most cases we can only work on the basis of a pre-Montanistic (till 202/203, or 207/208 A D) and a Montanistic period, though even in this we do not possess an absolutely sure rule

On the subject of textual criticism, see, besides the works already cited, the following —

M Haupt, *Opuscula,* III, 2, 1870, vv ll   Paul de Lagarde, *Symmicta,* I, Gottingen, 1877, 99 ff , II, 1880, 2 ff , *Mittheilungen,* IV, 4 ff   M Klussmann, *Curarum Tertullianearum particulae tres,* Gotha, 1887 (*Codex Agobard ad Nationes*)   J van der Vliet, *Studia ecclesiastica   Tertullianus,* I, Lugd Bat 1891 , and in *Mnemosyne,* XX, 1892, 273–285 (*de Pudicit , de Paenit*)   E

[1] *Codex Paris* 1623, *saec* X, 1656, *saec.* XII, 1689, *saec* XII, etc   See Preuschen, LG, 676 f

[2] *Codex Agobardinus, Paris* 1622, *saec* IX , *Codex Montepessulan.* 54, *saec* XI , *Codex Seletstadiens* 88, *saec* XI

Klussmann, in WclPh, 1893, 145-149, 182-186   Aem Kroymann, *Quaestiones Tertullianeae criticae*, Oenipont 1894 — On the subject of Chronology, see G Uhlhorn, *Fundamenta Chronologiae Tertullianeae*, Gottingen, 1852   H Kellner, in ThQu, LII, 1870. 547-566, LIII, 1871, 585-609   Kath LIX, 1879, 2, 561-589, and *Chronologiae Tertullianeae supplementa Program* Bonn, 1890   G N Bonwetsch, *Die Schriften Tertullians nach der Zeit ihrer Abfassung*, Bonn, 1878   A Harnack, in ZKG, II, 1878, 572-583   E Noeldechen, *Die Abfassungszeit der Schriften Tertullians*, in TU, V, 2, 1888   K J Neumann, *Der romische Staat*, etc (see § 45), *passim*   J Schmidt, in RhM, XLVI, 1891, 77-98 (*de Corona, ad Scapulam, de Fuga, Scorpiace*)   E Rolffs, *Urkunden aus dem ultimontanistischen Kampf des Abendlandes*, in TU, XII, 4, 1895, *passim*

4. In describing the separate **works** of Tertullian, precedence may be given to his *de Pallio* (composed in 208 or 209 A D),[1] because this little work, which related to a personal affair of the author, cannot be classified with the other products of his literary activity. It consists of a defence against the attacks made upon him by his fellow-citizens on account of his rejection of the toga for the pallium when he embraced Montanism This writing, which Moehler[2] calls a "sample of his genius showing how much he could say about that which was most insignificant," gave Tertullian opportunity to allow full play to his sarcastic humor, and exhibits him as a writer, on his most interesting, but at the same time, indeed, his darkest side.

Editions · Frc Junius, Lugd Bat 1595   E Richerius, Paris, 1600   Th Marcilius, Paris, 1614   Cl Salmasius, Lut Paris, 1622, Lugd 1656, Lugd 1626 (with the commentary of J L de a Cerda, BPL, I, 37)

Literature · G Boissier, in *Rev des Deux Mondes*, XCIV, 1889,

---

[1] Cf. Chap. 2, Oehler, I, 925.   [2] Moehler, 734.

Juil 50-78, reprinted in his *La fin du paganisme*, 2d edit, Paris, 1894, I, 259-304.

5 Among the **Apologetic Treatises** of Tertullian, the one that ranks highest and is probably the oldest, is

(a) The *Apologeticus* or the *Apologeticum*,[1] a defence of Christianity composed in the autumn of 197 A D, at Carthage,[2] and addressed to the *praesides* (*antistites*) of the provinces.[3] It was the author's intention that it should replace the forbidden public oral defence,[4] and it bears throughout the stamp of the advocate. The introduction (1-6) attempts to prove that the proceedings against the Christians, resting as they do upon ignorance of Christianity, cast reproach upon all principles of law, and that if the laws of the State appear to justify such proceedings, they themselves will have to be abrogated. The Apology proper is divided into two principal parts. After a concise refutation of calumnies relating to Christian morality (7-9), the charge of atheism is refuted (10-27), and later, that of treason and enmity to the state (28-45). The positive purpose of the author appears plainly, viz the presentation of the Christian faith, and the proof that the Christian man is a useful member of society. The conclusion (46-50) praises the absolute loftiness of Christianity as the religion of revelation in contrast to all human philosophy. A Greek translation, made probably about the beginning of the third century (whether by Julius Africanus is uncertain), was known as late as Eusebius' time,[5] but it

---

[1] On the title, see Oehler, I, 111   [2] Cf Chap 9, Oehler, I, 145
[3] Chap 1, Oehler, 111, Chap 2, Oehler, 117, 120, etc
[4] Chap. 1, Oehler, 113.
[5] Eusebius, *Hist Eccl* II, 2. 5 sq, 25 4, III, 20. 9, 33 3 sq, V, 5 6 sq

appears to have perished early   On the relation of the *Apologeticus* to the *Octavius* of Minucius Felix, see § 45. It is not impossible that a second redaction of the *Apologeticus* is extant.[1]

Among the editions are to be mentioned those of B Benalius (printer), without place or date (Venet 1483)   U Soinzinzeler, Mediol. 1493.   B. Locatellus, Venet. 1494   B Egnatius, Venet. 1515.   S. Haverkampius, Lugd. Bat. 1718.   Frc Oehler, Lpz 1849 Kayser. Paderb 1865   F. Leonard, Namur, 1881   T H Bindley, Lond 1889   Cf A Harnack, *Die griechische Uebersetzung des Apologeticus Tertullians*, in TU, VIII, 4, 1892   P. de Lagarde, *Septuagintastudien* (§ 54), 75–85

(*b*) The two books *ad Nationes*[2] form a polemic which was probably begun before the *Apologeticus*,[3] but which was scarcely published before it as a whole. It is a passionate controversial writing, filled with great bitterness, addressed to a heathen people. The first book contains a refutation of complaints against the morality and worship of Christians, which presents a recension in some respects parallel to the first sixteen (omitting the tenth and eleventh), and the last chapters of the *Apologeticus*, though it is conceived from a different point of view, and differs frequently in details, style, and mode of expression   The second book is a criticism of the heathen belief concerning the gods,[4] its chief underlying source being the *Libri rerum divinarum* of M. Terentius Varro[5]   On the text, see above at No. 3.

Editions: J. Gothofredus, Aureliopoli, 1625. An edition printed at Geneva in 1624 (cf Schoenemann, BPL, 37) does not exist (cf

---

[1] Cf at Chap. 19 the peculiar tradition of the *Codex Fuldensis*.
[2] Jerome, *Epist.* 70, 5, *Contra Gentes*
[3] I, 10, Reifferscheid and Wissowa, in CSE, XX, 74 12.
[4] Cf. *Apologeticus*, 10–11.   [5] Cf. Augustine, *De Civitate Dei*, VII, 1

W v Hartel, *Patristische Studien* (see above), Heft 2, p. 3). Frc. Oehler (with the *Apologeticus*). Lips. 1849.

(*c*) The little writing, *De Testimonio Animae*, is an expansion of an idea only hinted at in the seventeenth chapter of the *Apologeticus*, which is most spiritual, suggestive, and full of poetical beauty. The simple human soul, not yet over-refined by intellectual training, is summoned as a witness for Christianity, whose witness, like that of nature, is the voice of God.

(*d*) The brief epistle, *Ad Scapulam*, addressed to the proconsul of the province of Africa, was written some time after the 14th of August, 212 A.D.,[1] and was intended to warn the governor, who had inaugurated an active persecution of the Christians, of the divine judgment which had hitherto overtaken all persecutors of Christians, and which will inevitably overtake him also. In the second chapter excerpts are made from the *Apologeticus*

Edition: T H. Bindley (with the *De Praescriptione* and *Ad Martyres*), Oxf. 1894.

6. A disputation between a Christian and a Jewish proselyte gave Tertullian occasion to join issue with the claims of the chosen people in his *Adversus Judaeos*. The second part of this writing (Chaps. 9–13), which is by an unknown hand, is only a clumsy compilation of the material relating to the person of Christ founded on Old Testament prophecy, which is presented in the *Adversus Marcionem*.[2] The first part (Chaps. 1–8), on the other hand, is a work of Tertullian, attested by Jerome[3] and by its own peculiar characteristics. It is

---

[1] So Schmidt
[2] III, 13, 18, 20, 23.
[3] *Comm. Dan.* 9 (*Opera*, V, 691).

o be assigned to his pre-Montanistic period, and, perhaps, to an early date.¹ The author proves that the heathen are admitted to participation in the grace of God, which the Jews had forfeited by their own fault: the old covenant, the old law, the old circumcision, have given place to a new, which had been proclaimed by the Messiah of the Christians. The Dialogue between Jason and Papiscus, by Aristo of Pella, was probably utilized in this work, even if it did not altogether give the occasion for its composition.²

¹ J. S. Semler, *Opera Tertulliani*, V, 262–299. J. A. W. Neander, *Antignosticus*, Appendix. A. Harnack, TU, I, 3 (cf. § 35) P. Corssen (§ 35). On the chronological statements of Chapter 8, see A. Schlatter, TU, XII, 1 (cf. § 71), 15–19. Quite lately E. Noeldechen (*Tertullians Gegen die Juden auf Einheit, Echtheit, Entstehung gepruft*, in TU, XII, 2, 1894), has undertaken the task of rescuing the second part also

7. Among the **Anti-Heretical Writings**, the oldest was, (*a*) *De Praescriptione (praescriptionibus) Haereticorum (Adversus Haereticos)*. The expression in the title, borrowed from the Roman law and referring strictly to the defendant's exception based on limitation or possession, is used by Tertullian in the general sense of the demurrer, by virtue of which the complainant is non-suited.³ The work was written in the author's pre-Montanistic period, and originated about 200 A.D. It is an exposition of the catholic conception of authority and tradition, and is a classic of its kind. The principal portion of the book (Chaps. 15–40) discusses the demurrer (or demurrers) by reason of which heretics

¹ Noeldechen, 195. ² Cf. § 35.
³ Chaps. 21, 22, 35, 45 Cf. *Adv. Marcion.* I, 1; Oehler, II, 49; *Adv. Hermogenem*, 1, *Adv. Praxean*, 2, etc.

are non-suited *a limine* Preceding this is an introduction (8–14), dealing with the general idea and distinguishing characteristics of heresy; the conclusion (41–44) contains certain deductions drawn from the lack of morality and of ecclesiastical and religious zeal on the part of the heretics.

Editions: J. Quintinus, Paris, 1561. Chr. Lupus, Bruxell. 1675 (with extensive commentary) E Preuschen, in SQu, III, 1892. T. H Bindley (with the *Ad Martyres*, and *Ad Scapulam*), Oxf 1894.

(*b*) For many years Tertullian was engaged upon an exhaustive refutation of the greatest opponent of early catholic Christianity The final redaction of his work is known as the five books *Adversus Marcionem*. The first form (apparently in one book[1]) was hastily written, and the author himself replaced it with a second, more complete edition, which was stolen from him by a "brother."[2] The first book of the third edition was written in the fifteenth year of Septimius Severus, *i e*. 207–208 A.D.,[3] and the other four were separated from it by an interval which, however, cannot have covered many years.[4] Against Marcion's doctrine of two Gods, Tertullian, in his first book, urges that a good God who is not at the same time a Creator, cannot exist; in the second, that the Creator is the true God; the object of the third is to prove the identity of the Christ who appeared upon earth with the Christ foretold in the Old Testament. After this refutation of Marcion's theology and Christology, there follows in the fourth and fifth books an examination of Marcion's New Testament and also a critical exposition of his *Antitheses*.

[1] Cf. II, 1.
[2] I, 1.
[3] I, 15.
[4] Cf. Hauck, 338 f Noeldechen differs in his view.

(c) The writing, *Adversus Hermogenem*, which was composed not long after the *De Praescriptione*,[1] was directed against the doctrine of the eternity of matter maintained by the Carthaginian artists and philosophers. In the first portion (1–18), Tertullian unfolds the philosophical and religious reasons which weigh against this assertion, he then exposes (19–34) the lack of convincing force of the arguments adduced by his opponent from Scripture, and finally, with little wit and huge enjoyment, he reduces him *ad absurdum* (35–45). It is possible that the controversial treatise of Theophilus of Antioch[2] was employed in this writing.[3]

(d) The writing *Adversus Valentinianos*, which was written after the preceding,[4] and which belongs to the author's Montanistic period,[5] is an unedifying and vulgar repetition of the account given by Irenæus in his *Adversus Haereses*. It nowhere gives any evidence of any attempt to understand the trend of his opponent's thought

(e) The *Scorpiace* (*adversus gnosticos scorpiacum*) professes to be a remedy for the bites of the scorpions of the church, that is, of the Gnostics, who, by their poison, seek to seduce Christians, particularly in the matter of steadfastness in persecution. Tertullian proves that such steadfastness is a Christian duty, commanded by God. The situation presupposed in the work may correspond with the period of persecution under Scapula, and it may therefore have been composed in the year 213 A D This would agree with the fact that the second book against Marcion seems to be presupposed in Chapter 5.

---

[1] Cf. Chap 1 (beginning)
[2] § 42. 3 b.
[3] Cf Harnack, LG, 200 (Hermogenes).
[4] Chap. 16, Oehler, II, 404.
[5] Cf. the expression *"Proclus noster"* in Chap. 5.

(*f*) The work *De Carne Christi*, probably written not long after the *De Anima*,[1] was directed against the docetism of Marcion, Apelles, and the Valentinians whose low estimate of the material compared with the spiritual made it impossible for them to accept an actual incarnation of the heavenly Christ After a refutation of the heretics (2–16), there follows a positive proof from Scripture of Tertullian's materialistic line of thought (17–24). Closely connected with this work was

(*g*) The *De Resurrectione Carnis*.[2] This subject, which had often been discussed by the Apologists,[3] Tertullian handled with great energy and reckless logic. The presentation of the Scriptural doctrine (18–62), which in the introduction was set forth as the only normative one, is preceded by the proof from reason (3–17) The conclusion contains a description of the resurrection body and its identity with the earthly body. This Tertullian attempted to base upon the words of Paul. It is possible that Justin's work on the resurrection furnished the author with his material.[4]

(*h*) *Adversus Praxean* was the last anti-heretical work which Tertullian wrote It was composed certainly long after his defection from the church.[5] It combated a phase of Patripassian Monarchianism which probably appeared for the first time under Callixtus; *i.e* after 217 A D In opposition to heretical error, the author developed his doctrine of the subordinational (economic) Trinity.

[1] See No 8, below.
[2] Cf. *De Carne Christi*, 1, 25, and *De Resurrec. Carnis*, 2 (Oehler, II, 469) *De Anima* is mentioned in Chaps 2 (Oehler, II, 470) and 17 (*Idem*, 488), and touched on in 42 (*Idem*, 521) and 45 (*Idem*, 524)
[3] Cf Justin, Tatian, Athenagoras, Theophilus, and Irenæus
[4] Cf. § 36. 3 *a*.   [5] Chap. 2.

Edition E Welchman, Cantabr 1731
Literature R A Lipsius, in JdTh, XIII, 1878, 701–724   On the possibility that the Dialogue of Jason and Papiscus was used in the *Adversus Praxean*, see P Corssen (cf § 35), 31–44

8 The necessity of a thorough explanation of his ideas as to rational psychology led Tertullian to the composition of one of his most renowned treatises, one which is distinguished by knowledge of the subject and by excellence of treatment, while it is also, it must be admitted, remarkable for many absurd and narrow assertions   The **De Anima** was written later than the second book against Marcion,[1] and at all events in the Montanistic period,[2] and was directed not only against the idealistic and materialistic philosophers and the Gnostics (who were under the influence of the former), but more especially against all physicians and students of the natural sciences, who are often mentioned.   For their refutation a four-volumed work of Soranus, a learned member of the sect of the *Methodici* and an earlier contemporary of Galen,[3] may have served as a source   The material is treated in four sections: (1) On the nature of the soul and its powers (Chaps 4–22), (2) On the source and formation of the soul (23–35); (3) On the development of the soul and, more especially, its relation to evil (36–49); and (4) On the fate of the soul after death (50–58)

9 Tertullian addressed his attention as a writer, in a special degree, to questions of Christian **morals and church discipline**   A large number of treatises written in all periods of his life give evidence of this, as

---
[1] Chap 21 (Reifferscheid and Wissowa, CSE, XX, 335, 3).
[2] Chap 9   (*Idem*, 310, 17)
[3] Chap. 6   (*Idem*, 306, 24, 28)

well as of the rigor with which he uniformly answered these questions The first were written in his official ecclesiastical capacity [1] (probably that of a presbyter), the last were inspired by the Montanist's raging hatred toward the alleged laxity of the catholic church in questions of discipline Exact dates of composition are almost everywhere impossible

(a) The first group comprises **four writings**: *De Baptismo, De Poenitentia, De Oratione,* and *De Patientia* The first three were addressed to catechumens,[2] and certainly belonged to the beginning of Tertullian's literary activity The fourth took shape, probably, not very much later [3] Noeldechen holds a different view with regard to it, however, and places it as late as 204 A D The first tractate expounds baptism as the necessary condition of the reception of salvation It was occasioned by the doubts that had arisen in the congregation in consequence of the disturbances caused by a member of the heretical party of Quintilla [4] The final chapters (17–20) were intended to bring to remembrance the rules for the bestowal and reception of baptism [5] The writing on Penance is divided into two parts, the first of which, after a discussion of the nature of repentance, treats of the pre-baptismal penance of the sinner (1–6), while the second expounds the possibility and character of confession, the *poenitentia secunda,* that is, penance after baptism (7–12) The writing on Prayer consists of brief remarks upon the Lord's Prayer as the *breviarium totius evangelii* (1, close; 2–8), and of longer

---

[1] Cf Bonwetsch, 28   [2] Cf *Bapt* 1, *Poenit* 6, *Orat* (whole subject)
[3] Cf *Patientia,* 12, with *Poenit*
[4] *Baptism* 1, according to a more correct reading.
[5] Cf Chap 17 (beginning)

instructions as to the time, place, nature, and method of prayer, closing with a lofty description of its effects (9-29) Especially characteristic of the author, who found solace in speaking of that which was not granted to himself (Chap 1), is the spirited treatise on Patience, with its skilful personification of the Christian virtue whose chaste and pure image as the foster-daughter of God is contrasted, at the close, with the so-called "patience" of the heathen (Chaps 15–16)

Editions *Poenitentia*, by E Preuschen, in SQu, II, 1891 (together with the *De Pudicitia*) *Oratio*, by G Pancirolus, and L A Muratorius, in *Mur Anecdot* II, Patav 1713, 1–56 *Patientia*, Orius, Matrit 1644

Literature E Preuschen, *Tertullians Schriften de Poenitentia und de Pudicitia, mit Rucksicht auf die Bussdisciplin untersucht*, Giessen, 1890

(*b*) While the foregoing writings are couched in quiet and comparatively elevated language, a strident key is struck in the **tractates** *De Spectaculis, De Idololatria,* and *De Cultu Feminarum*, I and II They were written at a time when minds were deeply stirred, a period of confessional friction, if not of bloody persecution of Christians by the heathen They may all have been written before the *Apologeticus* (196–197 A D), and the *De Spectaculis* before the *De Idololatria*[1] and the first part of the *De Cultu*[2] The treatise on Shows (*De Spectaculis*) attempts to prove the assertion that the frequenting of plays is incompatible with true religion and real obedience toward the true God (Chap 1) The reasons given by heathen and Christians in defence of such amusements are refuted by pointing out that all

[1] See Chap 13   [2] See Chap 8.

theatrical plays are associated with the worship of idols (Chaps 2–13), and the deduction is drawn from the character of the plays themselves, that frequenting them stands in direct contradiction to Christian holiness (Chaps. 15–30) In the final chapter a description of the last judgment gives the author opportunity to vent his hatred of art in the most un-Christian manner. The writing on Idolatry transfers what was said of theatrical exhibitions to the whole field of the fine arts and of public life: the reefs and bays, the shallows and straits of idol-worship (Chap 24), are so numerous that even a good Christian can steer his little bark safely through them only by the exercise of the utmost caution. Each of the two books on the Adornment of Women is complete in itself: the first, called *De Habitu Mulierum* in the manuscripts (except the *Codex Agobardinus*), characterizes female adornment as an invention of the devil, and proposes to prove that ornaments and fine clothes lead to ambition and prostitution; but the author broke off before he arrived at this conclusion. The second book is milder and kindlier, though it is not more yielding than the first It does not follow the plan of the first book, but takes up certain isolated thoughts which occur in it, giving warnings against coquetry and fashionable folly in a style that betrays a familiar knowledge of the arts of feminine toilet.

Editions *De Spectaculis*, E Klussmann, Rudolphopol 1877
Literature E Noeldechen, *Die Quellen Tertullians in seinem Buch von den Schauspielen*, in *Philol Suppl.* VI, 2, 1894, 727–766

(c) The brief exhortation, *Ad Martyres* (*martyras*), was, according to Harris and Gifford, intended for Perpetua and her companions¹ It was written either shortly before or after the *Apologeticus*² (197 A D) It comforts those who were imprisoned during the persecution, with the thought that for them entrance into the prison signifies only an exit from a far worse one, and it urges them to suffer, for the sake of God and the truth, that which even a gladiator endures for the sake of empty fame.

Edition T H Bindley (together with the *De Praescriptione* and the *Ad Scapulam*), Oxf 1894

(*d*) The similarity of subject justifies us in classifying together the **three writings**, *Ad Uxorem*, *De Exhortatione Castitatis*, and *De Monogamia*, although the first was written before his break with the church (about 203–207 A.D), and the last, which must have preceded the second by a considerable interval, is to be assigned to a point toward the close of Tertullian's literary activity. In the books To his Wife the author expounds his view (giving the reasons therefor), that the re-marriage of a widow, even if not absolutely forbidden, is nevertheless reprehensible, and conflicts with both the command of God and the idea of marriage (Book I) In any case, re-marriage with a heathen is inadmissible (Book II) He makes no concealment when he exalts the virginal condition above the married state (I, 3), and yet, at the close (II, 9), he is not, on this account, prevented from warmly praising the happiness of true marriage. The Exhortation to Chastity was addressed to a widowed colleague It compares second marriage,

¹ J R Harris and S K Gifford, *The Acts of the Martyrdom of Perpetua and Felicitas* Lond 1890, p. 31 (cf § 105 7)
² Compare the close of the book

as the result of sensual desire, to fornication; and the author does not entirely omit a similar imputation with regard to the first (Chap. 9) Similar views are again presented in the treatise on Monogamy, only they are more pointed, and are augmented by the polemic of a "Pneumatic" against the "Psychics," who were willing to admit even to the episcopal office a man who had been twice married (Chap 12). On the *De Monogamia*, see the views of Rolffs [1]

(*e*) The tractate, *De Corona Militis*, sounds like an echo of the writings treated above (under *b*). It was occasioned by a Christian soldier's refusal to wear the laurel wreath according to custom, and was written in August or September, 211 A.D, at a time when persecution threatened [2] The delicate question as to whether he was justified in this course of action, Tertullian answers with a most decided affirmative; and he intensifies his affirmative to a demand that the Christian shall keep himself entirely aloof from the military profession (Chap. 11)

(*f*) The persecution under Scapula was the occasion of the treatise, *De Fuga in Persecutione*, written toward the close of 212 A.D The duty of the Christian, and especially of the clergy, under no circumstances to avoid persecution, is insisted upon uncompromisingly.

(*g*) Tertullian had already discussed, and answered affirmatively, the question as to the veiling of virgins [3] After he became a Montanist, he again returned to the subject, in his *De Virginibus velandis*, treating it with great minuteness. Contrary to his oft-expressed view,[4]

---

[1] E Rolffs (§ 3, above), TU, XII, 4. 50-109
[2] Schmid, 81-84.
[3] *De Oratione*, 21-22   [4] Cf. *De Praescriptione*, etc

he would not admit the accusation of *praescriptio novitatis*, which his opponents brought against him, but defended the practice which he advocated by pointing out its internal reasonableness, which habit could not offset (Chap 2) The Paraclete, the Scriptures, and the discipline of the church were appealed to as final proofs

(*h*) The **latest** literary **productions** of Tertullian, *De Jejunio adversus Physicos*, and *De Pudicitia*, were replete with bitter, almost morbid, hatred toward the catholic church, which in the *De Pudicitia* was more marked on account of its violent attacks on the Roman church The ascetic spirit which could scent lasciviousness in a second marriage was only able to characterize the Catholics as gluttons when they observed moderation in fasting,[1] and toward the close the polemic becomes indecorous. In spite of its want of moderation, a more sympathetic vein is struck by the treatise on Modesty, which is an interesting companion-piece to that on Penance, with its energetic repudiation of the possibility of a second penance for mortal sins. The point of his polemic is directed against the "edict of the Pontifex Maximus" (that is, probably, of Callixtus, bishop of Rome, 217–222 A D), according to which the sins of adultery and fornication might be forgiven to those who did penance Thereby the virgin bride of Christ must suffer hurt (Chap 1); forgiveness belongs to God, not to the church (Chap 3). The proof from Scripture occupied the principal part of the work (Chaps 6–20), and in this matter the Old Testament had to yield to the New The author recognized only the martyr's baptism of blood as expiation for sin: he

[1] At the beginning of the book.

did not admit the right of the confessor to forgive sins

Editions· of the *De Pudicitia*, E Preuschen, in SQu, II, 1891 (with the *De Poenitentia*)
Literature. E Preuschen (see 9 *a*, above) E Rolffs, TU, XI, 3, 1893 (cf § 95 2), and TU, XII, 4, 1895 (No 3, above), 5–49

10 The following writings have been lost:—

(*a*) All that was written in Greek· viz the recension of *De Spectaculis*[1] and *De Virginibus velandis*,[2] the disquisition, *De Baptismo Haereticorum*,[3] the great work, Περὶ ἐκστάσεως (*De Ecstasi*) in six books, which were very probably written in Greek Connected with these was a seventh book, *Adversus Apollonium*,[4] which, according to Jerome, was directed, in the interest of the Montanists, against the church. Traces of it are found, apparently, in the anti-Montanistic controversial writing[5] used by Epiphanius in his *Panarion*.[6]

C. P Caspari, *Om Tert graeske Skrifter*, in *Forthandlinger i Vedensk Selsk i Christiania*, 1875, bl 403 Th Zahn, in GNK, I, 1, 49 A. Harnack, in TU, VIII, 4, 7 (cf. 5 *a*, above) H G Voigt. *Eine verschollene Urkunde* (cf. § 40 3 *a*, above), 35–47, 108–111

(*b*) *De Spe Fidelium*, which was originally contained in the *Codex Agobardinus*, treats, according to Tertullian[7] himself, of the Christian future hope as contrasted

---

[1] Cf. *De Corona*, 6 (Oehler, I, 430)
[2] Cf. *De Virginibus*, 1 (Oehler, I, 883).
[3] Cf *De Baptismo*, 15 (Reifferscheid and Wissowa, SCE, XX, 214, 1–7)
[4] Jerome, *De Viris Illust.* 24, 40, 53 Cf. also Praedestinatus, 26, 86
[5] § 53 2 *f.*
[6] *Panarion*, XLVIII, 2–13.
[7] *Adv Marcion* III, 24 (Oehler, II, 155 f).

with that of the Jews, which is to be interpreted allegorically¹

(c) *De Paradiso*, originally embraced in the *Codex Agobardinus*, contained² the remark that all souls, except those of martyrs, are to await the day of the Lord in the nether world

(d) *Adversus Apelleiacos (Apelliacos)* Tertullian³ himself attests the fact that he wrote a work under this or a similar title. Harnack⁴ considers it very likely that use was made of it in the *Philosophumena*.

A Harnack, *De Apellis gnosi monarchica*, Lips. 1874 (cf. § 27. 4), *passim*.

(e) *De Censu Animae (adversus Hermogenem)* is mentioned in the *De Anima*⁵ It was directed against Hermogenes' principle of the material origin of the soul According to Harnack,⁶ this work was read even by Philastrius⁷

(f) *De Fato* is mentioned in the *De Anima*⁸ as a work which Tertullian had certainly in view, and a citation is given by Fulgentius Planciades⁹

(g) *De Aaron vestibus* is mentioned by Jerome¹⁰ as contained in the list of Tertullian's writings, but he never saw it.

---

¹ Jerome, *De Viris Illust* 18, *Comm. Ezech.* XI, on xxxvi, 1 sqq. (*Opera*, V, 422), *Comm Isai* XVIII, *Praef* (*Opera*, IV, 767, 768)

² *De Anima*, 55 (Reifferscheid and Wissowa, CSE, XX, 389, 4 sq).

³ *De Carne Christi*, 8 (Oehler, II, 442).   ⁴ *De Apellis*, etc., p 47

⁵ *De Anima*, 1 (SCE, XX, 298). Cf 3 (*Idem*, 303, 17 sqq), 11 (*Idem*, 315, 22 sq), 21 (335, 3), 22 (335, 14 sqq), 24 (*Idem*, 337, 13 sq , 339, 18)

⁶ LG, 200   ⁷ *Haeres* LIV.

⁸ *De Anima*, 20   Reifferscheid and Wissowa, CSE, XX, 333, 11 sq.

⁹ *Expositio sermon antiqu. ad Chalcid.*, after Nonus Marcellus, Mercer's edit. 652

¹⁰ *Epist.* 65, 23.

(*h*) Jerome[1] asserts that Tertullian, in his youth, was engaged on the question, *De Nuptiarum angustiis* (*ad amicum philosophum*) Although this is not in itself impossible,[2] it is at the same time unlikely, since Tertullian would scarcely have omitted to make some reference to it in one of his later writings on the same subject.

(*i*) In the index to the *Codex Agobardinus*, the following writings are also mentioned, which must have been contained in the manuscript originally: *De Carne et Anima, De Animae Summissione,* and *De Superstitione Saeculi.* It is not impossible, however,[3] that the last two were identical with the *De Testimonio Animae* and the *De Idololatria*, while the title of the first recalls a treatise by Melito with the same title [4]

(*k*) On the possibility of a redaction of the *Passio Perpetuae et Felicitatis* having been made by Tertullian, see below [5]

11. The following writings and poems, occasionally **ascribed** to Tertullian, were not by him: —

(*a*) In a Vatican codex of the tenth century [6] there follows after Beda's Chronicle, etc, a fragment of an apologetical writing, *De execrandis gentium diis*, which Juarez held to be undoubtedly by Tertullian, in spite of the variations in style which he noted   The origin of the fragment is, however, altogether uncertain, though in one passage [7] there is a striking resemblance to Aristides.[8]

---

[1] *Ep* 22, 22, cf. *Adv. Jovinian*, I, 13.
[2] Cf. Pamelius, in Oehler, III, 7.
[3] Cf the index as given by M Klussmann, *Curar Tert.* (cf § 85. 3), p 12 sq.
[4] Cf § 40. 3 *i*, above.
[5] Cf § 105 7.
[6] *Codex Vatic.* 3852, *saec.* X.
[7] Oehler, II, 768, 8, to the end.
[8] Aristides, IX, 7. (Seeberg)

Edition J M Suaresius, Rom 1630
Literature Oehler, II, 766-768   A. Reifferscheid, in SAW, LXIII, 1869, 740

(b) In a codex of the eleventh century,[1] and in late manuscripts of the works of Tertullian, a tractate is found as a supplement to the *De Praescriptione Haereticorum*, entitled *Adversus omnes Haereses*,[2] which gives a summary view of all the heresies from Dositheus to Praxeas. The treatise is certainly not by Tertullian, but by some later writer, who possibly remodelled the *Syntagma* of Hippolytus. On the possibility that Victorinus of Pettau may have been the author, see below.[3]

(c) On the works, *De Trinitate* and *De Cibis Judaicis*, by Novatian, see below [4]

(d) The five books, *Adversus Marcionem*, written in bad Latin, and without any claim to be poetry, in spite of the hexameters, are no longer extant in manuscript. They very likely originated in the fourth century (Hilgenfeld says in the third), in Africa (according to Oxé), or in Rome (Huckstadt and Harnack)

Editions G Fabricius, 1562. Oehler, II, 781-798
Literature E Huckstadt, *Ueber das pseudo-tertullianische Gedicht adversus Marcionem*, Lpz 1875, cf A Hilgenfeld, in ZwTh, XIX, 1876, 154-159, and A Harnack, in ThLZ, I, 1876, 265 f A Oxé, *Prolegomena de carmine adversus Marcionitas*, Lpz 1888, cf A. Harnack, in ThLZ, XIII, 1888, 520 f

(e) Two poems, *De Sodoma* and *De Jona*, poetical compositions based on Gen. xix and the Book of Jonah,[5] are ascribed to Tertullian in various manuscripts [6] Ac-

---

[1] *Cod Seletstadtiens.* 88, *saec* XI.
[2] Oehler, II, 751-765. Cf. also *Corpus Haereseolog.* ed. Oehler, I, 1856, 269-279.
[3] Cf § 93. 2.
[4] Cf. § 92. 3 *a*, *b*
[5] Fragments only, in Müller, 330 f.
[6] Peiper, XVIII sq

cording to Peiper,[1] they belonged to a writer of the sixth century; according to Ebert, they originated in the fourth.[2]

Editions: Guil Morellius, *Opera Cypriani* (cf. § 86), 1561 (*De Sodoma*). Fr Juretus, *Bibl. Patr.* VIII (Jonah) Chr. Daumer, Lips 1681   Oehler, II, 769-773   Guil. Hartel, in *Opera Cypriani* (cf. § 86), III, 1871, 289-301.   R Peiper, in CSE, XXII (*Cypriani Galli poetae Heptateuchos*, etc.), Vindob. 1891, 212-226.
Literature L Muller, in RhM (new series), XXII, 1867, 329-344, XXVII, 1872, 486-488   A. Ebert, *Allgem. Gesch. der Litteratur* (cf § 2. 5), 122-124   M. Manitius, *Geschichte der christlich-lateinischen Poesie*, Stuttg 1891, 51-54.

(*f*) The poem, *De Genesi*, which has also been ascribed to Tertullian (or Cyprian), according to Peiper, formed the beginning of a large work entitled *Heptateuchos*, written by a certain Cyprian who lived in Gaul, in the sixth century; according to Ebert, it belonged to the fourth century

Editions. Guil Morellius, 1561.   Oehler, II, 774-776.   Guil. Hartel, *loc. cit.* 283-288   R Peiper, *loc cit* 1-7.   Cf. A Ebert, *loc. cit.* 119.

(*g*) The poem, *De Judicio Domini*, published by G Fabricius as a work of Tertullian, is of uncertain origin.[3]

§ 86. *Cyprian*

Editions: J. Andreas, Rom. 1471. reprinted, Venet. 1471, 1483; Memmingae, 1477; Daventriae, 1477; Paris, 1500; Paris, 1512. D. Erasmus, Basil. 1520, 1530; Colon, 1544 (H. Gravius). L. Latinius (P Manutius), Rom. 1563. Guil. Morellius, Paris, 1564. J. Pamelius, Antv. 1568 and after.   N. Rigaltius Lutet. Paris. 1648.   J. Fell, Oxon. 1682 and after.   St. Baluzius and Pr. Maraus, Paris, 1726.   Migne, PL, IV, 193-1312.   Guil. Hartel, in CSE, III, Pars I-III, Vindob.

[1] XXVII sq.   [2] Cf. § 86. 6 *h*.   [3] Oehler, II, 776-781.

1868-71; cf Lagarde, in GGA, 1871, 14, 521-543 (*Symmicta*, I. 1887, 65-78) — Translations U Uhl, Jos. Niglutsch, A Egger, in BKV, 2 vols. 1869-79 E. Wallis, in ANF, V, 267-596 (Life and Passion, Epistles, Treatises, Seventh Council of Carthage, Doubtful Writings) H Carey, in LFC, XVII, Oxf 1844 (Epist.). C. Thornton, *Idem*, III, Oxf 1839 (Treatises)

Literature J Pearson, *Annales Cyprianici*, Oxon 1682 (reprinted in Fell's edition of the *Opera*, Oxf. 1700) F W Rettberg, *Thasc. Caec. Cyprianus*, Gott 1831. E W Benson, in DCB, I, 739-755. J Peters, Regensburg, 1877. B. Fechtrup, *Der heilige Cyprian*, I, *Cyprians Leben*, Munster, 1878. O Ritschl, *Cyprian von Karthago*, Gott. 1885 Schoenemann, BPL, 77-134 Richardson, BS, 59-63, Harnack, LG, 688-723.

1. For a knowledge of Cyprian's life after his conversion to Christianity, we have, besides his own works, an almost direct source in the *Vita Caecilii Cypriani*, ascribed to a deacon named Pontius.[1] There is no reason to doubt that it was written soon after the bishop's death. **Thascius Caecilius Cyprianus**[2] was born, possibly, at Carthage, about 200 A.D., of a wealthy and prominent family; he was a teacher of rhetoric at Carthage,[3] and was won over to Christianity by a presbyter named Caecilius (Caecilianus),[4] was promoted rapidly (248-249 A.D) to the episcopate, and presided over the Carthaginian church for a decade during a very troublous time, being very much involved in questions of ecclesiastical law and discipline (penance and heretical baptism). He escaped the Decian persecution by flight, but fell a victim to that under Valerian, on Sept. 14, 258.[5]

[1] Cf. Jerome, *De Viris Illust* 68.
[2] Cf *Epist*. LXVI, inscr., *Ep* 4, Hartel, 729, 15, and Benson, 739.
[3] Lactantius, *Div Inst* V, 1. 24, Jerome, *Comm. Jon* 3.
[4] Pontius' *Vita*, 4 Cf. Jerome, *De Viris Illust* 67.
[5] *Act. procons* Hartel, CXIV, 1 sq , Prudent. *Peristeph* 13.

2. All of Cyprian's literary **works** were written in connection with his episcopal office; almost all of his treatises and many of his letters have the character of pastoral epistles, and their form occasionally betrays the fact that they were intended as addresses. These writings are pervaded by a moderate, clear-sighted, and gentle spirit. Cyprian possessed none of that character which makes the reading of Tertullian so interesting and piquant, but he had other qualities instead, which the latter did not, more especially the art of presenting his thoughts in simple, smooth, and clear language, with a certain completeness of form, a style which was not wanting, on this account, in warmth and persuasive power The strong attraction which his master's writings had for him [1] is reflected in the freedom with which he reproduced in his treatises whatever he had read; but he was not, by reason of this, merely a copyist, for even where his dependence is greatest he shows an unmistakable individuality His writings were collected at an early date, and were much read Pontius' *Vita* already presupposes a collection of his tractates in chronological order.[2] A list of writings which goes back to a copy made in 359 A.D., contains, after the Scriptures of the Old and New Testament, twelve tractates of Cyprian and thirty-four letters to or by him [3] Even to-day his treatises and letters (for the most part separate) are preserved in numerous manuscripts, the earliest of which go back as far as the sixth century [4] Even Commodianus made frequent use of Cyprian's writings,[5] though without mentioning his

[1] Jerome, *De Viris Illust.* 53
[2] Goetz, 41 f., Harnack, LG, 695 f
[3] Mommsen.
[4] Cf. Hartel, *Praef*, and Harnack, LG, 697-701.
[5] Dombart.

name, and Lactantius celebrated him as the true herald of wisdom and truth[1] The plagiarist, Lucifer of Calaris, copied from him.[2] Letters by Cyprian were preserved in the library at Cæsarea.[3] Though Eusebius himself shows but slight knowledge of Cyprian,[4] numerous testimonies as to his person and writings are to be found in the works of Jerome and Augustine[5] At an early date his name was woven into the legend about the magician, Cyprian of Antioch.

K. Goetz, *Geschichte der Cyprianischen Litteratur bis zu der Zeit der ersten erhaltenen Handschriften*, Basel, 1891 Th Mommsen, *Zur lateinischen Stichometrie*, in *Hermes*, XXI, 1886, 142-156, XXV, 1890, 636 ff. W Sanday and C H Turner, *The Cheltenham List of the Canonical Books of the Old and New Testament and of the Writings of Cyprian*, in *Studia Biblica et Ecclesiastica*, III, Oxf. 1891, 217-325 Cf. also Zahn, GNK, II, 1, 388 f Th Zahn, *Cyprian von Antiochien und die deutsche Faustsage*, Erlangen, 1882 (especially page 84 ff)

3. Like Tertullian, and often in imitation of him, Cyprian took certain apologetic, dogmatic, and practico-ecclesiastical themes as subjects of his **treatises** The following, arranged in the order indicated by the *Vita Pontii*,[6] are undoubtedly genuine. —

(a) *Ad Donatum (de gratia dei)* This composition, whose addressee is not otherwise known, may have been penned before the Decian persecution, and it must have been written, as the introduction and conclusion show, in a period of quiet and peace Its purpose was to set forth in a pure and clear light the new life after regeneration with its moral effects, as contrasted with the

---

[1] *Div. Inst* V, 1. 24
[2] Hartel, Harnack, and Goetz
[3] Eusebius, *Hist* VI, 43 3
[4] Harnack, LG, 702
[5] *Idem*, 704-713.
[b] Chap. 7.

night of heathenism and its moral degradation which were known to the author from personal experience The form is poetic and pleasing, but the style, adorned with many showy phrases that recall the rhetorician, aroused the displeasure of Augustine.[1]

Edition · J. G Krabinger, Tubingen, 1859 (contains also Orat, Mortal, Demetr, Oper et Eleem, Bon pat, Zel et liv.).
Translation E Wallis, in ANF, V, 275-280

(b) *De Habitu Virginum*,[2] apparently, was written before the persecution, and reminds one of the expressions of Tertullian both in word and thought. It contains exhortations to females, but particularly[3] to virgins vowed to chastity, to refrain from all luxurious and worldly living, in order that it may not happen to them as to the daughters of Zion,[4] and in order that, finally, in heaven they may become intercessors for the saints.[5]

Edition. J G Krabinger, see *d*, below, cf. J. Haussleiter, *Die Composition des Hirtenbriefs "ad virgines,"* in *Comment Woelfflt.* Lpz 1891, 382-386

(c) *De Lapsis*[6] was written in 251 A.D., after the Decian persecution, and after Cyprian's return to his congregation[7] In powerful and energetic language, which was deeply affected by the moral indignation of the author, he treats of a matter which events at Carthage had made a burning question: the restoration of the

[1] Cf *Doct Christ.* IV, 16.
[2] Cf Jerome, *Epist* 22, 22; 130, 19, Augustine, *Doct Christ.* IV, 21. 47.
[3] Cf Chap 3
[4] Isa. iii. 16, 24   [5] Cf the conclusion.
[6] Cf *Epist* 54, 3, Hartel. 623, 18 f., Pacian, *Ep* 3, Augustine, *Epist* 98, 3, *De fide et op* 19, 35, *De bapt* IV, 9. 12, Fulgent, *Ad Trasimund.* II, 17
[7] See the Introduction.

lapsed to ecclesiastical fellowship. This, Cyprian would make dependent upon penitent confession and the practice of severe penance.

Edition J. G. Krabinger, see *d*, below.

(*d*) *De Catholicae Ecclesiae Unitate*[1] was called forth in 251 A.D., by the schisms in Carthage, but particularly by the Novatian schism at Rome. It became the best known writing of Cyprian because in it the dogma that the church alone can confer salvation[2] was set forth, though without any admixture of papal conceptions[3].

Editions J. Stephanus, Lond. 1632. G. Calixtus, Helmst. 1657. J. G. Krabinger, Tubingen, 1853 (together with *De lapsis* and *De habitu virginum*).

(*e*) *De Dominica Oratione*[4] was written, possibly, in 252 A.D., and contains an extended exposition of the Lord's Prayer,[5] prefaced by some general remarks and concluded with directions concerning the spirit of prayer, the connection of prayer with good works, and the times of prayer. The course of thought is similar to that in Tertullian's treatise, but the treatment is generally independent.

Edition Brixiæ, 1483. Sine loco, 1528. J. G. Krabinger, cf *a*, above.

(*f*) *Ad Demetrianum*,[6] defended, in elevated diction,

---

[1] Cf *Epist* 54, 3, Hartel, 623, 19-22, Fulgent, *Remissio peccatorum*, I, 21 [*de simplicitate praelatorum*]

[2] Cf especially Chap 6, Hartel, 214, 23 f

[3] Cf Hartel, III, p XLIII f and the remarks on text-criticism, I, 212 ff. on the interpolations in Chap 4

[4] Cf Hilarius, *Comm Matth* 5, 1, Augustine, *c. Julian* II, 3 6, *contra duas epist Pelagii*, IV, 9. 25, 10, 27, etc

[5] §§ 7–27

[6] Cf Lactantius, *Divinae Inst*, V, 4 3, Jerome, *Epist.* 70, 3.

the Christians against current heathen slanders, but particularly against the accusation that the atheism of Christians was chargeable with the hard times, famine, and pestilence, an accusation that the addressee must have spread Cyprian retorts, adding the remark that this old world itself must perish, and that the misery of the times is but the precursor of divine judgment, which is imminent The conditions presupposed in the book make it possible that it was written in the year 253

Edition J G Krabinger, cf *a*, above.

(*g*) *De Mortalitate*[1] was written under similar conditions, in 253 or 254 A D, and forms an excellent companion to the address to Demetrian Cyprian combated the faithlessness of those members of the congregation who could not understand why the faithful were not spared from pestilence, urging triumphant assurance, demanding trustful subjection to God and his natural laws, and pointing to the imminent end of this world, and the promise of a better

Edition J G Krabinger, cf *a*, above J Tamiettius, August Taui 1887

(*h*) *De Opere et Eleemosynis*[2] was apparently written at about the same time, and had the purpose of urging prosperous members of the congregation to aid their fellow-believers who were suffering by reason of the prevailing want His noble exhortations came to a

---

[1] Cf. Augustine, *contra duas Epist Pelagii*, IV, 8 22, 10 27, *contra Julian* II, 8 25, *Praed Sanct* 14, 26, *Epist* 217, 22

[2] Cf Jerome, *Epist* 66, 5, Augustine, *contra duas Epist. Pelagii*, IV, 8. 21, 10 27, *contra Julian*, II, 8 25

climax in a striking introduction of Satan, and in an ironical presentation of his transitory benefits.¹

Edition: J G Krabinger, cf *a*, above

(*i*) *De Bono Patientiae* ² was written at the time of the third council, or shortly before, that is, in the summer of 256 A.D, in reference to heretical baptism It was intended to show the writer's peaceable intention, and to quiet the minds that had been excited by the controversy, without, however, making mention of the burning question. In spite of any dependence, this composition cannot be designated as a "copy bordering on plagiarism," on Tertullian's *Pudicitia*, ³ on the contrary, Cyprian's style manifests itself plainly in its form, as well as in some peculiar arrangements of thought

Edition· J Stephanus, Oxon 1633   J G Krabinger, cf *a*.

(*k*) *De Zelo et Livore* ⁴ sprang possibly from the same period. It portrays envy and jealousy, those poisonous plants propagated by the devil, with their destructive consequences, and exhorts to their suppression by means of contemplation of the heavenly kingdom

Edition J G Krabinger, cf *a*, above

(*l*) *Ad Fortunatum de Exhortatione Martyrii* ⁵   This little work, regarded by the author as simply an outline,⁶ was prepared at the request of Fortunatus, and contained

---

¹ Chap 22.
² Cf *Epist* 73, 26, Hartel, 798, 27–799, 2, Augustine, *contra duas Epist Pelagii*, IV, 8 22
³ Ebert, 58
⁴ Cf. Jerome, *Comm Gal* III, 5, Augustine, *Bapt* IV, 8 11
⁵ Cf Jerome, *Epist* 48, 19   ⁶ *Praef* 3, Hartel, 318, 11 ff.

a collection of Biblical citations arranged according to a plan of Cyprian's own, warning Christians against idolatry,[1] and the things of this world,[2] exhorting them to endurance,[3] and comforting them with the hope of eternal reward [4] Since there is no reason in the case of this particular work for deviating from the chronological order given in the *Vita Pontii*, the period of prosecution presupposed in the *Ad Fortunatum* is to be understood to be that under Valerian, and the composition may, therefore, be assigned to the year 257.

Associated with the foregoing were two other compositions which, apparently, did not exist in the collection of Pontius, the first of them is mentioned earliest in the list of 359 A D., and the second by Jerome.[5]

(*m*) *Ad Quirinum testimoniorum (adversus Judaeos) libri III*[6] was undertaken at the wish of Quirinus, a spiritual son of Cyprian [7] The work sets forth the doctrine of divine salvation on the basis of passages from Holy Scripture, with a special arrangement of the same Thus the first book treats of the displacement of Judaism and its institutions by Christianity, the second was intended to furnish proof of the Messiahship of Christ,[8] the third, which probably was added later,[9] contains the principles of Christian ethics that are derivable from Scripture

B Dombart, *Ueber die Bedeutung Commodians für die Textkritik der Testim Cypr*, in ZwTh, XXII, 1879, 374–389 J Hauss-

[1] § 1–5.
[2] § 6–7
[3] § 8–10
[4] § 11–12
Epist 70, 5
[6] Cf Jerome, *Dialog adv Pelag* I, 32, Augustine, *contra duas Epist. Pelagu* IV, 8 21, 9 25, etc
[7] Cf, perhaps, *Epist* 77, 3, Hartel, 835, 19
[8] Cf *Praefatio*, Hartel, 35 f   [9] *Praef* Hartel, 101.

eiter, *Die Echtheit des dritten Buches der Testim*, in *Comm Woelffl Lips* 1891, 379-382

(*n*) The Tractate *Quod Idola Dii non sunt* (*de idolorum vanitate*) is not mentioned in the *Vita Pontii*, it is missing from the list of 359, and the manuscripts speak against, rather than in favor of, its genuineness [1] Not much were lost should it prove to be spurious, since the first nine chapters present a compilation from the Octavius of Minucius Felix,[2] and the concluding chapters were abridged from Tertullian's *Apologeticus* [3]

Editions Together with Minucius Felix, Lutet Paris, 1643 (folowing Rigaltius) J Haussleiter, in ThLB, XV. 1894, 482-486, considers the *Quod idola dii non sunt* to be of Roman origin, and, in all probability, a work of Novatian

4 The **Letters** of Cyprian are not only an important source for the history of church life and of ecclesiastical law on account of their rich and manifold contents, but in large part they are important monuments to the literary activity of their author, since, not infrequently, they are in the form of treatises upon the topic in question Of the eighty-one letters in the present collection, sixty-six were written by Cyprian, and fifteen were addressed to him In far the majority of cases, the chronology of their composition, as far as the year is concerned, presents no difficulties, more precise assignments are mainly conjectural, and consequently their sequence cannot be absolutely fixed. Against the assignments made by Pearson, on which the following summary is based,[4] objections have been raised by

---

[1] Goetz, 129, cf. besides Jerome as cited above, Augustine, *De unic bapt contra Petil.* 4, 6, and *De bapt* VI, 44 87

[2] Cf. Minucius Felix, 20-27, 18, 32   [3] Chaps 21-23

[4] Cf. also Hartel, Vol II   [The numeration of Pearson (1682) is fol-

Fechtrup, and particularly by Ritschl,[1] which, in part, are worthy of notice.

(*a*) References to contemporary conditions are wanting in the case of the first four letters, they may fall previous to the Decian persecution.

1 (R II, W [2] 65) *Cyprianus presbyteris et diaconibus et plebi Furnis consistentibus salutem* This letter has reference to a testamentary appointment of a priest as guardian, contrary to the decree of an ancient African Synod

2 (R LXIV, W 60) *Cypr Eucratio salutem* Negative decision of the question of a bishop, whether an actor who had become a Christian might give instruction in his art. It is referred by Ritschl to the period after the establishment of the new conception of the church, about 254 A D, and it is placed by Wölfflin and Weyman in connection with the work *De Spectaculis* (see 5 *a*, below)

3 (R LXVI, W 64) *Cypr Rogatiano salut* Answer to the query of a bishop as to how he should proceed against a refractory deacon Assigned by Ritschl to the period after the adjustment of the controversy with schismatics, about 254

4 (R LXV, W 61) *Cyprianus, Caecilius, Victor, Sedatus, Tertullus, cum presbyteris qui praesentes aderant Pomponio fratri salut* Synodical reply to the query of a bishop as to what treatment is to be accorded to young women who practise unchastity It may belong with *De habitu virginum* (cf 3 *b*, above) Ritschl puts it about 254 A D

(*b*) A large number of the letters belong in the period of the Decian persecution and of Cyprian's absence from Carthage (250–251 A D)

5 (R IV, W 4) *Cypr presbyteris et diaconibus fratribus*

lowed in the Oxford translation of the Fathers (H Carey, LFC, 1844) For the convenience of the English reader the translator has added the numeration followed by E Wallis, in ANF, V, noting the same by " W " The letters number eighty-two, No 1 being the *Ad Donatum*. This numeration corresponds with that of Migne as far as Epistle 24, after that there is a difference of one on account of a misprint in the case of Epistle 25, which was perpetuated in the subsequent numeration — TRANS]

[1] Cited as R in the following pages   [2] See note 4, p 289

CYPRIAN

carissimis salut Exhortation to discretion and to the maintenance of discipline and order 250 A D

6 (R V, W 80) *Cypr Sergio et Rogatiano et ceteris confessoribus in deo perpetuam sal* Encouragement of confessors to resolute steadfastness 250 A D

7 (R III, W 35) *Cypr presbyteris et diaconibus fratribus carissimis sal* Reasons for his absence, and request for care for the poor 250 A D

8 (R VI. W 2) [Address not preserved Letter of the Roman Clergy to the Carthaginian 250 A D]

9 (R VII, W 3) *Cypr presbyteris et diaconibus Romae consistentibus fratribus sal* Felicitation upon the glorious death of bishop Fabian 250 A D

10 (R XII, W 8) *Cypr martyribus et confessoribus Jesu Christi domini nostri in Deo patre perpetuam sal* Praises the martyrs and confessors, and exhorts to resolute steadfastness. 250 A D

11 (R XI, W 7) *Cypr presbyteris et diaconibus fratribus sal* Persecution a divine punishment for disobedience and laxity, against which prayer is recommended as the best remedy 250 A D

12 (R X, W 36) *Cypr presbyteris et diaconibus fratribus sal* Exhortation to care for confessors and to sedulous manifestation of the respect that belongs to martyrs 250 A D

13 (R VIII, W 6) *Cypr Rogatiano presbytero et ceteris confessoribus fratribus sal* Exhortation to confessors to practise humility and good morals, and denunciation of past faults 250 A D.

14 (R IX, W 5) *Cypr presbyteris et diaconibus fratribus sal* Denunciation of the immorality of certain clergy, and exhortation to the rest to care for the poor and the confessors during his necessary temporary absence 250 A D

15 (R XV, W 10) *Cypr martyribus et confessoribus carissimis fratribus sal* First discussion of the question of the treatment of the lapsed, rejection of the claims of confessors, demand for a rigid enforcement of penance 250 A D

16 (R XVI, W 9) *Cypr. presbyteris et diaconibus fratribus sal* Prohibition of the reception of the lapsed into the congregation simply upon the intercession of confessors 250 A D

17 (R XVII, W 11) *Cypr fratribus in plebe consistentibus sal* Application to the laity of the exhortations of letters 15 and 16. 250 A D

18 (R XVIII, W 12) *Cypr presbyteris et diaconibus fratribus sal* Prescriptions applicable to the lapsed when *in casu mortis* 250 A D

19 (R XIX, W 13) *Cypr presbyteris et diaconibus fratribus sal* Repetition of the prescriptions given in 18, occasioned by a query 250 A D

20 (R XX, W 14) *Cypr presbyteris et diaconibus Romae consistentibus fratribus sal* Justification of his flight, and account of proceedings in cases of the lapsed 250 A D

21 (R XIII, W 20) [*Celerinus Luciano*] The Roman confessor entreats the Carthaginian to prepare *libellos pacis* in the case of two lapsed females 250 A D]

22 (R XIV, W 21) [*Lucianus Celerino domino si dignus puero vocari collega in Christo sal*] Answer to 21 250 A D]

23 (R XXIII, W 16) [*Universi confessores Cypriano papati sal*] Announcement that they have prepared *libellos pacis* in favor of all lapsed persons, and are waiting Cyprian's assent 250 A D]

24 (R XXI, W 18) [*Cypriano et compresbyteris Carthagine consistentibus Caldonius sal*] Declaration of a bishop upon the question of the lapsed 250 A D]

25 (R XXII, W 19) *Cypr Caldonio fratri sal* Answer, agreeing to 24 250 A D

26 (R XXIV, W 17) *Cypr presbyteris et diaconibus fratribus sal* Answer to 23, with a reference to the necessity of a postponement of a decision 250 A D

27 (R XXV, W 22) *Cypr presbyteris et diaconibus Romae consistentibus fratribus sal* Continuation of the account given in 20, in reply to a communication received from the Roman clergy (see Chap 4) 250 A D

28 (R XXVI, W 24) *Cypr Moysi et Maximo presbyteris et ceteris confessoribus delectissimis fratribus sal* Praise of the addressees and of other confessors (cf 27, 4) on account of their steadfastness and of their maintenance of discipline 250 A D

29 (R XXVII, W 23) *Cypr presbyteris et diaconibus fratribus sal* Notice of the ordination of a lector and of a sub-deacon 250 A D

30 (R XXVIII, W 30) [*Cypriano papae presbyteri et diaconi Romae consistentes sal*] Reply to 27, with assurance of continued observance of the practice of penance which had never been relaxed in the Roman congregations 250 A D] Cf § 92 5

CYPRIAN 293

31 (R XXIX, W. 25.) [*Cypriano papae Moyses et Maximus presbyteri et Nicostratus et Rufinus et ceteri qui cum eis confessores sal* Reply to 28 250 A D]

32 (R XXX, W 31) *Cypr presbyteris et diaconibus fratribus sal* Transmitting letters 27, 30, and 31 with a request for their further circulation 250 A D

33 (R XXXI, W. 26) *Adversus lapsos* The address is lost; written by Cyprian to the lapsed in reply to an improper petition, and intended to admonish them and to urge them to patience and humility 250 A D

34 (R. XXXII, W. 27) *Cypr. presbyteris et diaconibus sal.* Approbation of the exclusion of a presbyter and a deacon from the communion 250 A D

35. (R. XXXIII, W. 28) *Cypr presbyteris et diaconibus Romae consistentibus fratribus sal* Letter to accompany 33, and the communication from the lapsed presupposed therein, together with a communication made to the clergy of Carthage upon the same matter 250 A D

36. (R XXXIV, W. 29) [*Cypriano papati presbyteri et diacones Romae consistentes sal* Answer to 35 250 A D] Cf § 92 5

37. (R XXXV, W 15) *Cypr. Moysi et Maximo presbyteris et ceteris confessoribus fratribus sal* Praise for their steadfastness. 250 A D

38 (R. XXXVI, W. 32.) *Cypr presbyteris et diaconibus item plebi universae sal* Notice of the ordination of Aurelius, a confessor, as lector 250 A D

39 (R XXXVII, W 33) *Cypr presbyteris et diaconibus et plebi universae fratribus sal* Notice of the ordination of Celerinus, a confessor, as lector. 250 A D.

40. (R XXXVIII, W 34) *Cypr. presbyteris et diaconibus et plebi universae carissimis ac desideratissimis fratribus sal* Notice of the ordination of Numicidus, a confessor, as presbyter. 250 A D

41 (R XXXIX, W. 37) *Cypr Caldonio et Herculano collegis item Rogatiano et Numidico compresbyteris sal* First mention of the schism of Felicissimus and of the expulsion of the schismatic and his adherents from church communion 251 A D

42. (R XL, W 38.) [*Caldonius cum Herculano et Victore collegis item Rogatiano cum Numidico presbyteris* Notification that the commands of Cyprian had been executed 251 A D]

43 (R XLI, W. 39) *Cypr plebi universae sal* Warning

against Felicissimus, with mention of the fact that his machinations would prevent the bishop's return to Carthage before Easter 251 A D

(c) Another group is composed of letters in which the Novatian schism has prominent place 251–254 A D

44 (R XLIII, W 40) *Cypr. Cornelio fratri sal.* Recognition of the election of Cornelius, repudiation of Novatian 251 A D

45 (R XLII, W 41) *Cypr Cornelio fratri sal* Excuses for the delay in recognizing Cornelius Apparently written before 44 251 A D

46 (R XLV, W 43) *Cypr Maximo et Nicostrato et ceteris confessoribus sal* Exhortation to those who had seceded to Novatian to return 251 A D

47 (R XLVI, W 42) *Cypr. Cornelio fratri sal.* Letter sent along with 46 251 A D

48 (R XLIV, W. 44) *Cypr Cornelio fratri sal* Answer to the complaint of Cornelius that Cyprian had caused the congregation of Hadrumetum to write to the Roman clergy instead of Cornelius 251 A D

49 (R XLVIII, W 45) [*Cornelius Cypriano fratri sal.* Account of occurrences at Rome expulsion of those who had seceded to Novatian, and reception of repentant confessors 251 A D] Cf § 95

50 (R XLVII, W 47) [*Cornelius Cypriano fratri sal* Notice that several adherents of Novatian had gone to Carthage 251 A D] Cf § 95

51 (R L, W 46) *Cypr Cornelio fratri sal* Reply to 49 251 A D

52 (R LI, W 48) *Cypr Cornelio fratri sal* Reply to 50 251 A D

53 (R XLIX, W 49) [*Cypriano fratri Maximus, Urbanus, Sidonius, Macarius, sal* Announcement of their return to the church (cf 49) 251 A D]

54 (R LII, W 50) *Cypr Maximo presbytero item Urbano et Sidonio et Macario fratribus sal* Reply to 53 251 A D

55 (R LIII, W 51) *Cypr Antoniano fratri sal.* An extended communication to the Numidian bishop Antonianus, who, having first recognized Cornelius, afterward inclined to Novatian justification of his own course in relation to the lapsed (Chaps 1–7), justification of Cornelius (8–23), warning against Novatian (24–30) Written before the synod of 252 A D

(d) During the years 252-254 A D, Cyprian dealt with many subjects in a number of letters

56. (R LVII, W 52) *Cypr Fortunato, Ahymno, Optato, Privatiano, Donatulo, et Felici fratribus sal* Reply to a query in regard to the lapsed. Apparently written before Easter, 253 (or 252).

57. (R LVIII, W. 53) *Cypr Liberalis Caldonius* (39 names follow) *Cornelio fratri sal* Synodical communication of a determination to receive into the communion all truly penitent lapsed persons, in view of the impending renewal of persecution 253 or 252 A.D.

58. (R. LIX, W 55.) *Cypr plebi Thibari consistenti sal.* Letter of salutation, with reasons for declining an invitation. Reference to impending persecution 253 or 252

59 (R. LV, W. 54) *Cypr Cornelio fratri sal.* Extended refutation of the suspicions aroused by Felicissimus, who had gone to Rome, and had succeeded in impressing Cornelius. 252 A D.

60 (R LX, W 56) *Cypr Cornelio fratri sal.* Congratulations upon his exile 253 or 252 A D

61. (R LXII, W. 57) *Cypr. cum collegis Lucio fratri sal.* Congratulations upon his return from exile 253 A D

62. (R LXI, W 59) *Cypr Januario, Maximo, Proculo, Victori, Modiano, Nemesiano, Nampulo, et Honorato fratribus sal.* Letter to accompany a considerable contribution in aid of the congregations of the above-named Numidian bishops, which had suffered from depredations by robbers. 253 A D

63 (R I, W 62) *Cypr. Caecilio fratri sal. (de sacramento calicis [dominici])* Letter occasioned by the mistaken practice that had sprung up in certain congregations, of employing water instead of wine in the sacrament References to contemporary events are lacking It is referred by Ritschl, on account of Chap 13 (Hartel's edit 711, 18-22), and of the way in which the duties of bishop are spoken of, to the period before the Decian persecution(?)

64 (R LIV, W 58) *Cypr et ceteri collegae qui in concilio adfuerunt numero LXVI Fido fratri sal* Synodal letter on the premature restoration of a lapsed presbyter, and on the question of the baptism of children 252 or 253 A.D Cf § 96

65 (R LVI, W 63) *Cypr Epicteto fratri et plebi Assuras consistenti sal* Demand to the bishop of Assuras, who had done sacrifice in the persecution, to demit his office, and a warning against the lapsed who are impenitent 253 A D

66 (R. LXIII, W 68) *Cypr qui et Thascius Florentio cui et*

Puppiano fratri sal. Reply to calumnies, apparently those of a layman   254 A D

(*e*) The following letters originated in the period of the controversy with Stephen of Rome concerning heretical baptism

67 (R LXXII, W. 67) *Cypr Caecilius, Primus* (34 names follow) *Felici presbytero et plebibus consistentibus ad Legionem et Asturicae item Aelio diacono et plebi Emeritae consistentibus fratribus in domino sal*   Synodical communication in reference to the deposition of the bishops Basilides and Martialis, and their restoration by Stephen of Rome, which Cyprian declares to be unjustifiable. Referred by Ritschl (p 225) to the council held in the spring of 256. Cf § 96

68. (R LXVII, W. 66) *Cypr. Stephano fratri sal.* Exhortation to use every endeavor to fill again the see of Arles, which had been rendered vacant by the secession of Bishop Marcian to Novatianism   254 A D, and apparently before No 67

69. (R LXVIII. W 75.) *Cypr Magno filio sal.* First letter in reference to heretical baptism denial of its validity, but accompanied with assent to the validity of clinical baptism   254 A D.

70 (R LXIX, W. 69) *Cypr. Liberalis Caldonius* (28 names follow) *Januario* (17 names follow) *fratribus sal*   Synodical writing on the subject of heretical baptism   255 A D   Cf § 96.

71. (R LXX, W. 70) *Cypr Quinto fratri sal*   Letter written to accompany 70, with a refutation of certain objections to Cyprian's notion of heretical baptism.   255 A D

72 (R LXXIII, W 71) *Cypr et ceteri Stephano fratri sal.* Announcement of the decision regarding heretical baptism, accompanied by copies of the letters 70 and 71   Attributed by Ritschl to the council of September, 256   Cf. § 96

73 (R LXXI, W 72.) *Cypr. Jubaiano fratri sal.*   The most extended treatment of heretical baptism ; with a refutation of a letter sent to Cyprian by Jubaianus (was it written by Stephen? Ritschl, p 116), and with sharp attacks upon the Roman bishop.   256 A D

74 (R. LXXIV, W. 73) *Cypr. Pompeio fratri sal*   Treatment of the same subject with still sharper polemic   256.

75 (R LXXV, W. 74.) [*Firmilianus Cypriano fratri in domino sal*]   Cf. § 77.

(*f*) The remaining letters belong to the period of Valerian's persecution (257-258 A D).

76 (R. LXXVI, W 76) *Cyprianus Nemesiano* (10 names follow) *coepiscopis, item compresbyteris et diaconibus et ceteris fratribus in metallo constitutis martyribus Dei patris omnipotentis et Iesu Christi domini nostri et Dei conservatoris nostri aeternam sal* Encouragement and consolation in view of the impossibility of then celebrating the divine sacrifice. 257 A D

77. (R. LXXVII, W. 77) [*Cypriano fratri Nemesianus Dativus Felix et Victor in domino aeternam sal*. Reply to 76. 257]

78. (R. LXXVIII, W. 78.) [*Cypriano fratri et collegae Lucius t qui cum eo sunt fratres omnes in deo sal*. Reply to 76 257 A D]

79. (R. LXXIX, W. 79) [*Cypriano carissimo et dilectissimo Felix, Jader, Polianus una cum presbyteris et omnibus nobiscum ommorantibus apud metallum Siguensem aeternam in Deo sal.* Reply to 76. 257 A D.]

80. (R. LXXX, W. 81.) *Cypr. Successo fratri sal* Informing him concerning Valerian's second edict and the death of Sixtus, bishop of Rome (died Aug. 6, 258).

81. (R. LXXXI, W. 82) *Cypr. presbyteris et diaconibus et plebi universae sal*. Written while fleeing from the officers of the Proconsul. At the close, a benediction upon the churches.

A. Harnack, *Die Briefe des römischen Klerus aus der Zeit der Sedisvacanz im Jahre 250*, in *Theologische Abhandlungen Carl von Weizsacker gewidmet*. Freib. 1892, pp 1–36

5 The **three treatises** that follow are enumerated among the spurious writings of Cyprian, though hitherto the impossibility of their genuineness has not been demonstrated.

(a) *De Spectaculis;* a summons to renounce heathen theatrical exhibitions, and to fix the eye upon the glorious spectacle which awaits the Christian in the future. The work has been preserved, apparently, in only three manuscripts, the oldest of which[1] dates from the fourteenth century, though it presupposes a source considerably earlier. The list of 359 A.D. does not

[1] *Codex Paris.* 1658,

mention it, and it is attested by no ancient writer. It is impossible to maintain the reasons alleged against its composition about the middle of the third century, apparently by a bishop who was separated from his congregation, and it cannot be denied that it is closely allied to Cyprian's genuine writings, or that use was made in it of Tertullian's work bearing the same title. Wolfflin, consequently, decides in favor of its composition by Cyprian,[1] while Weyman defends the authorship of Novatian, principally on the ground of considerable stylistic similarity. Demmler has sought to exploit these indications by an exact comparison of the usage of language.

E Wolfflin, in the *Archiv fur Lat. Lexikographie und Grammatik*, VIII, 1893, 1–22. C Weyman, in HJG, XIII, 1892, 737–748, XIV, 1893, 330 f   J. Haussleiter, in ThLBl. XIII, 1892, 431–436, XV, 1894, 481 f. A Demmler, in ThQu, LXXVI, 1894, 223–271, also printed separately, Tubingen, 1894. On this, cf. C. Weyman, in WklPh, 1894, 1027–1032.

(*b*) The tractate, *De Bono Pudicitiae*, must not be separated from the foregoing   It has been preserved in only three manuscripts,[2] and it lacks ancient attestation   Matzinger has attempted to prove that it was written by Cyprian, basing his argument upon resemblances of style, and so striking is its dependence upon Tertullian that the theory thereby gains much force. With this view Hausleiter disagrees.   Upon similar premises, Weyman has sought to establish Novatian's claim to be author of this tractate also.   At all events, the author was a bishop[3] who was separated from his congregation at the time of composition.

[1] Against this view, see Haussleiter.   [3] Chap. 1, Hartel, 7 f.
[2] Among others, the *Codex Paris.* 1656, xiv cent.

S Matzinger. *Des heiligen Cyprian Traktat: De bono pudicitiae*, Nurnberg, 1892 C Weyman, J Haussleiter, A Demmler (see above)

(*c*) In contrast with the two foregoing treatises is a third, *De Laude Martyrii*, a sermon on the nature, significance, and value of martyrdom.[1] This seems certain of recognition as a composition of Cyprian on the basis of its excellent attestation: Lucifer used it extensively, it is mentioned in the list of 359 A D.; Augustine[2] was acquainted with it, and it is preserved in all the manuscripts. If it could be proved[3] that it was included among Cyprian's writings as early as the collection in the *Vita Pontii*, he might certainly be regarded as its author This, however, has been disputed by Matzinger, and more recently Harnack has advocated Novatian's authorship.[4]

6 The following works, though ascribed to Cyprian, are certainly **spurious** : —

(*a*) The tractate, *Ad Novatianum*, or more correctly, the treatise (sermon ?) on Novatian, addressed to the brethren. It has been preserved in only one manuscript[5] It must have been composed immediately after the persecution[6] under Gallus and Volusianus According to Harnack,[7] Sixtus II, of Rome, was the author. Its conclusion is lost.

(*b*) The treatise, *De Rebaptismate*, which is no longer

---

[1] Chap. 4, Hartel, 28, 16.   [2] *Contra Gaudent.* I, 30, 34
[3] So Goetz (39), and Harnack (LG, 718).
[4] Matzinger, 2 and 9. A. Harnack, in TU, XIII, 4, 1895. Cf. C. Weyman, in *Litt. Rundschau f d kathol Deutschl* 1895, 329–333.
[5] *Codex Vossian. Lat 40, X Cent* The *editio princeps*, Daventria, 1477, was based upon another manuscript
[6] Cf Chap 5, Hartel, 56, 20, Chap 6, Hartel, 57, 27 f.
[7] A. Harnack, in TU, XIII, 1, 1895.

extant in manuscript form, waged polemic from the standpoint of Roman practice, against Cyprian and other episcopal representatives of heretical baptism [1] Although it must be assigned to the third century at latest, it presupposes a considerable literature [2] upon the subject The author was a bishop With regard to the remark of Labbé that the tractate is ascribed by three Vatican manuscripts to the monk Ursinus, mentioned by Gennadius,[3] see Harnack [4] In Chap. 17, the *Paulli Praedicatio* [5] is cited

 Editions N Rigaltius, in *Observationes ad s. Cypriani epistolas*, Paris, 1648. Routh, RS, V, 283–328

(*c*) Under the title, *De Aleatoribus* (*Adv. aleatores*), there has been preserved in several manuscripts,[6] a sermon against dice-playing, as being an invention of the Devil, and therefore idolatry It is couched in awkward, but powerful and spirited language, and it is inspired by holy, moral earnestness The author was a bishop who was deeply impressed by the consciousness of the demands of his position and calling To think, with Langen, of Cyprian in this connection, is impossible by reason of variations of style On account of the relation of the writing to the canon of the Old and New Testaments, but particularly to the *Shepherd* of Hermas (and the *Teaching of the Apostles*), and also because of its position in regard to penance, Harnack favors a pre-Cyprianic date of composition; and in view of the first chapter, he, following the lead of Pamelius

---

[1] Cf. *eg* Chap. 1. Hartel, 70, 16 ff., 27 ff.
[2] Cf. Hartel, 70, 3 ff.   [4] LG, 718 f.
[3] *De Viris Illust* 27   [5] Hartel, 90, 20. Cf § 19.
[6] *Codex Monac.* 208, *saec* IX. *Trecens* 581, *saec* VIII–IX. *Reginens.* 118, *saec.* X *Paris.* 13047, and others of later date.

and others, thinks of a Roman bishop, proposing Victor [1] as its author (189–199 A D) Others,[2] on the other hand, contend that its obvious relationship to Cyprian is explicable only on the supposition of frequent perusal and of an absolute familiarity with the writings of the Carthaginian bishop, though they are not willing to deny absolutely a connection with a Roman bishop [3] Nevertheless, the hypothesis of Harnack cannot be completely superseded except upon full investigation, which shall assume an African, non-Roman, origin for the writing.

Editions: Cf the *texts* given by Harnack in *Texte und Untersuchungen*, V, 1, pp 11–30 A Miodonski, pp 57–111 (contains German translation) — A Hilgenfeld, pp 12–26 *Étude*, etc (see below), 15–22 — Literature · A Harnack, *Der pseudocyprianische Traktat de aleatoribus*, in TU, V, 1, 1888 (list of numerous recensions in *Étude*, etc , 12 f) E Wolfflin, in ALG, V, 1888, 487–499, and reply by A Harnack, in ThLZ, XIV, 1889, 1–5 J. Haussleiter, in ThLB, IX, 1889, 41 f , 49 f (proof of dependence upon the third book of Cyprian's *Testimonia* . theory that Celerinus revised the writing to express the collective judgment of the Roman clergy) A C McGiffert, in *The Presbyterian Review*, Jan 1889 (proposes Callixtus as author) J Langen, in HZ, LXI, 1889, 479 ff (review of Harnack , cf. also *Deutscher Merkur*, XX, No. 5). F X. Funk, in HJG, X, 1889, 1–22. A. Miodonski, *Anonymus adv aleatores, und die Briefe an Cyprian, Lucian, Celerinus, und an den Karthaginiensischen Klerus* (Cypr *Epist* 8, 21–24), Erlangen and Lpz 1889 (preface by E Wolfflin) A Hilgenfeld, *Libellum de aleatoribus*, Freiburg, 1/B, 1890 (holds the author to have been a Novatianist, in the time of Constantine) *Étude critique sur l'opuscule de aleatoribus*, par les membres du séminaire d'histoire ecclésiastique établi à l'université catholique de Louvain, Louvain, 1891 J Haussleiter, *Beruhrungen zwischen der Schrift Cyprians "ad virgines" und*

---

[1] Cf Jerome, *De Viris Illust.* 34.
[2] Wolfflin and Miodonski, cf. particularly the *Étude*, etc. (see Literature), pp. 61–101.
[3] Miodonski proposes Melchiades as the author.

dem Anonymus "adv aleatores," in Comm Wölfflin, Lp7 1891, 386-389 A Miodonski, Kritik der ältesten lateinischen Predigt: "adv aleatores" (same, pp 371-376) C Callewaert, Une lettre perdue de S Paul et le "De aleatoribus," Louvain, 1893

(*d*) *De Pascha computus*, which is preserved in one manuscript, was written before Easter, 243 A.D, in the fifth year of Gordianus,[1] and contains computations of Easter, beginning with the Exodus, analogous to those in Hippolytus' $\dot{a}\pi\acute{o}\delta\epsilon\iota\xi\iota\varsigma$ $\chi\rho\acute{o}\nu\omega\nu$ $\tau o\hat{v}$ $\pi\acute{a}\sigma\chi a$.[2] The author does not mention Hippolytus, and, though he works upon the same basis, any direct influence by Hippolytus is made improbable by the existence of important variations in details   The Scripture citations appear to point to an African origin, though Harnack regards its identity with Novatians' *De Pascha* as possible

G. Salmon, *Chronicon Cyprianicum*, in DCB, I, 508 f.

(*e*) **Three anti-Jewish writings**, which have been attributed to Cyprian, are of quite different origin   The treatise *De duobus montibus (de monte Sina et Sion adv. Judaeos*) is an attempt to prove by means of all sorts of allegorical absurdity, that Sinai and Zion are types of the Old and New Covenants. It contains antique features, and is preserved in the first three manuscripts mentioned above [3]   Harnack [4] regards it as possible that it was a translation from the Greek   The letter *Ad Vigilium episcopum de judaica incredulitate*,[5] on the other hand, probably dates from the fifth century at the earliest, since it was addressed to Bishop Vigilius of Tapsus, and was sent to accompany a translation of the *Dialogue of Jason and Papiscus*,[6] which had been

[1] Cf. Chap 22.   [4] *Lit Gesch* 719
[2] Cf. § 91. 7 a   [5] *Codex Reginens* 118 al
[3] See note 6 on p 300.   [6] Cf. § 35 and the literature cited there.

made by a certain Celsus[1] The third writing, *Adversus Judaos*, is mentioned as early as the list of 359 A.D, and it may be older than the time of Cyprian The oldest manuscripts containing it are the same as those mentioned above[2] Harnack connects it with the name of Hippolytus,[3] as a translation from the Greek, while Draeseke denies that it was written by Hippolytus

J Diaeseke, *Zu Hippolytos' Demonstratio adversus Judaos*, in JprTh, XII, 1886, 456-461.

(*f*) The following writings, cited only by title, are post-Constantinian They have not been minutely investigated as to their place of origin. (1) *Oratio* I and *Oratio* II. (2) *De duodecim abusivis saeculi* (3) *De singularitate clericorum*

(*g*) The tractate *De duplici Martyrio* appears to be a bald forgery, which Lezius regards as a fabrication by Erasmus.

Fr. Lezius, *Der Verfasser des pseudocyprianischen Tractates de duplici martyris Ein Beitrag zur Characteristik des Erasmus*, in NJdTh, IV, 1895, pp 95-110, and 184-243

(*h*) **Poems**: (1) *Genesis;* (2) *Sodoma;* (3) *De Jona*, (4) *Ad senatorem ex christiana religione ad idolorum servitutem conversum*, (5) *De pascha (de cruce)*, (6) *Ad Flavium Felicem de resurrectione mortuorum* These have no connection with the bishop of Carthage On those, numbered 1-3, which have also been attributed to Tertullian, see above.[4]

(*i*) The *Exhortatio de Paenitentia*, which was first published in 1751, and which Hartel has not incorporated

---

[1] Chap. 10, Hartel, 132 16.
[2] See note 6 on p 300
[3] *Lit Gesch* 719, cf § 91 5 *b*
[4] See § 85 11 *e, f.*

in his edition, was directed against the Novatianists, and is composed of Biblical citations arranged after the plan of the work *Ad Fortunatum* A comparison of the Biblical text with passages found in Hilary and Lucifer, leads to the conclusion that the work belongs to the close of the fourth century.

Editions. Trombellius, in *Anecdota Canon. Regular. S. Salvatoris evulg* tom II, 1, Bonn, 1751, 1-32   C Wunderer, *Bruchstucke einer africanischen Bibelubersetzung in der pseudocyprianischen Schrift Exhortatio de paenitentia*, Erlangen, 1889 (text on pp. 11-29)

(*k*) On other forgeries under the name of Cyprian, see Harnack's *History of Literature*.[1]

§ 87. Arnobius

Editions · Faustus Sabaeus Brixianus, Rom 1543(?). S Gelenius, Basil 1546   D Erasmus (S Gelenius), Basil 1560. Balduinus, Lugd Bat 1569 (the first time without Minucius Felix). D Heraldus, Paris, 1605   Cl Salmasius (A Thysius), Ludg Bat 1651   J C Orelli, 3 vols Lips 1816-17   Migne, *Patrol Lat* IV, 349-1372   Frc Oehler, in *Bibl patr eccl*, edid   E G Gersdorf, XII, Lips 1846   A Reifferscheid, in CSE, IV, Vindob 1875

Translations   F A v Besnard, Landshut, 1842 (contains a comprehensive commentary)   A H Bryce and H Campbell, in ANF, VI, 413-540

Literature   P. K. Meyer, *De ratione et argumento Apologetici Arnobii*, Hafniae, 1815   E Klussmann, in *Philologus*, XXVI, 1867, 362-366   J. Jessen, *Ueber Lucrez und sein Verhaltniss zu Catull und Spateren*, Kiel, 1872, p. 18   Frc Wassenberg, *Quaestiones Arnob criticae*, Monast, 1877 (text criticism)   H C G. Moule, in DCB, I, 167   G Kettner, *Cornelius Labeo*, Naumb'g, 1877. A Reifferscheid, *Analecta critica et grammatica*. Ind Scholar. Viatisl 1877-78   *Idem, Coniectanea*, Ind Scholar Vratisl 1879-80, pp 8-10   W Kahl, in *Philol Suppl* V, 1889, 717-807 (distinguishes between two C Labeos).   J Mulleneisen, *De C. Labeo fragmentis*,

[1] *Lit Gesch* 722 f

studiis, adsectatoribus Marb Chatt 1889, pp 34-40 A Rohricht, cf § 60 2 Also *Die Seelenlehre des Arnobius*, Hamb 1893 Schoenemann, BPL, 147-172. Richardson, BS, 76 f Harnack, LG, 735 f.

(1) **Arnobius**[1] was a teacher of rhetoric at Sicca in proconsular Africa during the reign of Diocletian, and after he embraced Christianity, in order to show that he was Christian,[2] he wrote seven books **Adversus Nationes**,[3] or *adversus gentes* according to Jerome They have been preserved in a Paris codex[4] The accusation that was current[5] among his contemporaries, to the effect that Christianity was chargeable with all the misery of the world, formed a starting point for an apology for Christianity (Books I-II), with this was combined a justification of belief in the eternal, uncreated, "first" God, and in Christ, who himself is God in human form, the instructor and benefactor of mankind, the miraculous being who had destroyed idolatry, and had set proper bounds to human conceit Mention of philosophers gave occasion for a long excursus on the origination, nature, and destination of the soul[6] Since this topic was not germane to the plan of the book, its discussion evidently sprang from the necessity which the author felt, to give expression to his views in regard to these questions Books III-VII contain a violent polemic against heathenism, in Books III-V, attack is made on the polytheistic doctrine of God on account of its senselessness and immorality, and in Books VI-VII,

[1] For the name, see Reifferscheid, 1879-80, p. 9
[2] Cf Jerome, 79, and *Chron. ann. Abr* 2343.
[3] Thus the manuscript caption, cf Jerome, 79
[4] *Codex Paris 1661, saec IX (Codex Dij 6851*, possibly of the sixteenth century, is simply a copy of the foregoing).
[5] See above, § 86 3 *f*. [6] II, 14-62

on the pagan services of temple and sacrifice. The
confused character of the final chapter is explicable,
perhaps, on the supposition that the author, under the
pressure of external circumstances,[1] broke off abruptly
with some remarks hastily thrown together.[2] The date
of composition cannot be fixed exactly, but the year
303 [3] is to be preferred to 296 A.D.[4]

(2) As a **writer**, Arnobius was only little better than the
reputation given him by Jerome.[5] He neither possessed
a clear mind, nor did he wield a facile pen. He wrote
hastily, tumultuously, and with little intelligence. Nevertheless one cannot deny a certain amount of sympathy
to his declamatory pathos, and it is possible to find many
a pleasing passage in the midst of his long-winded
tirades. Where the rhetorician assumed the rôle of the
philosopher, as particularly in the second book, he does
not give evidence of profound study. The didactic
poem of Lucretius exercised great influence over him
both in respect to form and matter, and from it he drew
material for his opposition to the Platonic (Neoplatonic)
philosophy. He had, nevertheless, read Plato also.
The words of Holy Scripture are very seldom employed,[6] and his conceptions at important points stand
in contradiction thereto.[7] Arnobius made use of the
Protrepticus of Clement of Alexandria as source for his
statements concerning Greek mythology, and for that of
Rome he plundered the writings of Cornelius Labeo,
who lived apparently after 250 A.D., and who was inter-

---

[1] See above
[2] Reifferscheid's edit XIV. Different view, Kettner, 34-40
[3] Book IV, 36
[4] Cf II, 71
[5] *Epist* 58, 10, but see Orelli
[6] Cf Oehler, XIV-XVIII.
[7] Cf especially II, 36

ested not only in antiquarian, but also in religious and theological questions Arnobius' polemic seems to have been directed frequently against the attempts of Labeo and his associates to restore the Neoplatonic philosophy Among later writers, Jerome alone shows definite knowledge of Arnobius' work[1] Gelasius ranked it among the Apocrypha. Tritemius'[2] additions to Jerome's account, including a statement concerning a composition *De rhetorica institutione*, is beyond our control

§ 88. Lactantius

Editions Sublaci, 1465 (Conr Sweynheim and Arn Pannartz), Romae, 1468 (same printers) J Andreas, Romae, 1470 Venet 1471 (Ad de Ambeiga) Venet 1472 (Vindelinus de Spira) Venet. 1493 (Vinc Benolius) J Parrhasius, Venet 1509. J B Egnatius, Venet 1515 H Fasitelius, Venet 1535 Colon 1544 (P Quentel) J L Buenemann, Lips 1739 (2 Tom , Hal Sax 1764, Bipont 1786) O F Fritzsche in *Bibl patr eccl*, ed E G Geisdorf, X, XI, 2 Tom , Lips 1842–1844 Migne, *Patrol Lat* VI, VII S Brandt and G. Laubmann, in CSE, XIX, XXVII, Vindob 1890–1893 (not yet complete)

Translations Wm Fletcher, ANF, VII, 3–328 (Div Inst , Epit , Anger of God, Workmanship of God, Persecutors, Fragm , Phoenix, and Passion of the Lord)

Literature The older works of Le Nourry (Appar II) St Baluzius (Paris, 1679) P Bauldri (Utr 1692), in PL P Bertold, *Prolegomena zu Lactantius*, Metten, 1861 E Ebert, in RE, VIII, 364 ff E S F Foulkes, in *Dict Chr Biogr* III, 613–617 O Bardenhewer, in *KLex* VII, 1310–1316 A Mancini, *Quaestiones Lactantianae*, in *Studi storici*, II, 1893, 444–464, and in reply, S Brandt, *Adnotatiunculae Lact*, *Idem*, 1894, 65–70 — Schoenemann, BPL, 177–264 Richardson, BS, 77–81 Preuschen, LG, 736–744

1. L Caelius[3] Firmianus **Lactantius** was born of heathen[4] parents, about 260 A D, in Africa (not Pice-

---

[1] Cf also *Epist* 60, 10, and 70, 5
[2] Cf *Script Eccl* (§ 2 2), 53.
[3] Not Caecilius
[4] *Divinae Inst* I, 1. 8.

num) He was a rhetorician, a pupil of Arnobius, and was called by Diocletian, probably soon after 290, to the position of professor of rhetoric in Nicomedia, where, probably, he first embraced Christianity After the beginning of the persecution he was compelled to relinquish his office, Jerome says, on account of lack of pupils He was certainly still in Nicomedia up to 305 A D,[1] and in 307[2] he apparently already had removed to Gaul (Treves), where, when an old man according to the unsupported statement of Jerome, he became the instructor of Crispus the emperor. He died about 340[3]

S Brandt, *Ueber das Leben des Lact* (SAW, CXX), separately printed, Wien, 1890.

2 Lactantius was **distinguished** among all early Latin Christian writers by the elegance and superiority of his style, which won for him the title of the Christian Cicero[4] He was possessed of taste, fine feeling, and facility, but, like the Roman rhetorician, he was lacking in originality Moreover, he was possessed of lovable modesty, and he was perfectly clear in regard to the limitations of his ability[5] With the exception of Jerome and Augustine, no ancient ecclesiastical writer surpassed him in knowledge of the classics, and he has preserved for us many a passage from writings that have otherwise perished. He appears to have had less familiarity with the Holy Scriptures · the numerous quotations, particularly in the fourth book of the *Divinae Institutiones*, were borrowed from Cyprian's *Testimonia*

[1] Cf particularly, *Idem*, V, 11. 15.   [2] See, however, 4 *b*, and 6, below
[3] Cf Jerome, 80, and *Chron. ad ann Abr* 2333.
[4] Pico da Mirandula   [5] *De opificio dei*, toward the close

As to Christian writers, he was acquainted with and used Theophilus of Antioch, Minucius Felix, Tertullian, and Cyprian Points of contact with the works of his teacher Arnobius, from whom he differed in regard to his hostile attitude to Lucretius, are uncertain. The writings of Lactantius have been much read from the earliest times, and even Lucifer of Calaris extracted largely from him Jerome quoted from him frequently. Even now he is extant in two hundred and twenty manuscripts, the oldest of which[1] belong to the sixth and seventh centuries, and the first periods of the art of printing vied in various editions.

Prolegomena and Indices of the edition of Brandt and Laubmann H Roensch, *Beitrage zur patristischen Textgestalt und Latinitat.* II, *Aus Lactantius*, in ZhTh, XLI, 1871, 531-629 S Brandt, *Der St. Galler Palimpsest der Divinae Institutiones des Lact* (SAW, CVIII), Wien, 1885 *Idem, Lactantius und Lucretius*, in *Jahrbucher f Philol* CXLIII, 1891, 225-259 *Idem, De Lact. apud Prudentium vestigus* (*Festschrift*), Heidelb 1894

3. Jerome[2] knew of **three works** which Lactantius wrote while still a pagan, but they have been lost.

(*a*) The *Symposium* was a youthful composition, written in Africa, in which "learned, perhaps grammatical questions, or possibly only a single one, were treated"[3] in the manner beloved by Greeks and Romans. In spite of the view of Heumann, Symphosius' collection of enigmas had nothing to do with this work.

(*b*) The *Hodoeporicum* was a description of the journey from Africa to Nicomedia couched in hexameters.

---

[1] *Codex Bononiens.* 701, and *Codex Sangallens. rescript.* 213, both of the sixth and seventh centuries.
[2] *De Viris Illust.* 80.   [3] Brandt, p. 130.

(c) The *Grammaticus*, which "took its rise from his special studies in grammar and rhetoric, was written possibly in Africa, otherwise in Nicomedia."[1]

For the above and for what follows, compare S Brandt, *Ueber die Entstehungsverhaltnisse der Prosaschriften des Lact und des Buches De mortibus persecutorum* (SAW, CXXV), Wien, 1891, and the *Prolegomena* to the second volume of Lactantius' Works (CSE, XXVII, p XXXVIII f and LXXXII) — *L. Caeli Firmiani Lactantii Symposium, sive Centum epigrammata tristicha aenigmatica* [first published by Pithou, 1500] . . Chr Aug Heumannus, Hanov. 1772

4. The first product of the **literary activity** of Lactantius after embracing Christianity was

(a) The little treatise *De Opificio Dei* (*vel formatione hominis*, as it is called by Jerome), which was written after the commencement of the persecution[2] and before the *Divinae Institutiones*,[3] that is, probably in 304 A.D. It was addressed to a former pupil, Demetrianus, and was intended to exhort him not to forget his highest good in the midst of the temporal goods that had been richly showered upon him. Its principal subject is a demonstration of divine providence based upon the adaptability and beauty of the human body[4] Following are some psychological discussions,[5] and preceding is a reference to the importance of human reason[6] Only a couple of side references indicate that the author was a Christian, and in the course of the argument use is not made of Christian conceptions. His claim to independence in the continuation of the discussion of the problem which had been inadequately handled by

[1] Brandt, p. 124.
[2] Cf. I. 1, 7, 20, 1.
[3] Cf *Div. Inst.* II, 10, 15.
[4] §§ 5-13.
[5] §§ 16-19.
[6] §§ 2-4

Cicero,¹ is ill founded in so far as it is susceptible of proof that Lactantius derived his philosophical material from others, and particularly from a hermetic writing that is no longer extant. In regard to an addition made to Chapter 19, see the following paragraph.²

S. Brandt, *Ueber die Quellen von Lact.'s Schrift De opificio dei*, in the *Wiener Studien*, XIII, 1891, pp. 255-292.

(*b*) The *Divinae Institutiones* (not *Institutiones divinae*) formed Lactantius' principal work. It was an apology for the Christian religion, and was called forth by heathen pamphlets.³ Its purpose was not limited to a defence, but, after the manner of *Institutes* of Roman law,⁴ it was to serve as a positive introduction to the substance of Christian teaching.⁵ It was begun in Nicomedia, probably in 304, and it was completed in Gaul,⁶ possibly as early as 307 or 308, at all events before 311 A.D. In the first book (*de falsa religione*) the popular polytheistic belief was controverted and monotheism asserted, the existence of divine providence being meantime assumed to have been proved. In the second book (*de origine erroris*) the source and cause of human corruption were shown to be the demons and their chief, the Devil, and in this connection use was made of very unchurchly mythological speculations The third book (*de falsa sapientia*) denied that heathen philosophy contained wisdom or can lead to wisdom; true wisdom consists in knowledge and adoration of God. The fourth book (*de vera sapientia et religione*)

¹ See Chap. 1.
² Toward the close of *b*.
³ Cf. V, 2-4.
⁴ Cf. I, 1. 12.
⁵ V, 4. 3.
⁶ V, 2 2; II. 15

pushed this train of thought further on its positive side, by showing that a correct knowledge of God was to be obtained through Christ, the Logos of God and the teacher of men, to whom mankind owed, as the fifth book (*de justitia*) showed, its restoration to righteousness, which had disappeared from this world since the golden age of Saturn. True adoration of God, as the author proceeded to show in the sixth book (*de vero cultu*), consisted in the practice of this righteousness; binding men to reverence toward God (*religio*) and to love for their fellowmen (*humanitas*), the duties of which can only be correctly determined by Christian, not by philosophical ethics. The seventh book (*de vita beata*) formed the crown of the whole, painting the divine reward for human virtuous action, eternal blessedness, in strong colors which recall the ancient chiliastic hopes. Examination of this work shows certainly that Lactantius made use of other men's material more than appears on the surface, and in view of the imposing array of heathen and Christian authors from whom he persistently borrowed, there is not over much of his own constructive thought remaining. Considered as to their form, however, his *Institutiones* constitute the most complete of all Christian apologies. The text was augmented apparently as early as the fourth century by a Christian admirer, who added some dualistic passages [1] which carry out certain tendencies of Lactantius in this direction. There were added also two longer addresses in praise of Constantine the Great.[2]

[1] II, 8, elaborating § 7, and VII, 5; cf. also *de opificio dei*, 19, elaborating § 8.
[2] I, 1. 12, and VII, 26. 10; cf. also the frequently inserted brief apostrophes to the Emperor.

J. G. Th. Mullerus, *Quaestiones Lactantianae*, Gottingen, 1875
P. Meyer, *Quaestionum Lactantianarum particula prima*, Julich,
1878, 1-4. S. Brandt, *Ueber die dualistischen Zusatze und die Kai-
seranreden bei Lactantius*, I, II (SAW, CXVIII, CXIX), Wien,
1889.

(c) The *Epitome Divinarum Institutionum* has been preserved complete only in a Turin codex of the seventh century,[1] from which it first became known in 1711.[2] It is not a mere mechanical abridgment of the larger work, but is a brief re-elaboration of the subject in one book, made at the request of "brother Pentadius" and dedicated to him. To be sure, it is closely allied to the principal work, but it contains many additions, alterations, and transpositions. There are no sufficient grounds for doubting its authenticity.[3]

Editions: Chr. M. Pfaff, Paris, 1712. J. Davisius, Cantabr. 1718.
Translations· P. H. Jansen, in BKV, 1875 At the close, the Sibylline Books are introduced by way of proof. Wm. Fletcher, ANF, VII, 224 f.

(d) The treatise, *De Ira Dei*,[4] dedicated to a certain Donatus, is the fulfilment of an intention announced in the *Institutiones*,[5] of showing, in opposition to the philosophical assertion of the passionlessness of God, the necessity of divine wrath, without which penal justice is unthinkable. The date of composition is uncertain, but reference is twice made to the *Divinae Institutiones*[6]

Translation· R. Storf, in BKV, 1875. Wm. Fletcher, ANF, VII, 359 ff.

[1] *Codex Taurin. Reg. Tabul.* I b, VI, 28, saec. VII.   [2] Maffei, Pfaff.
[3] See Brandt, *Entstehungsverhaltnisse*, etc , pp. 2-10.
[4] Cf. Jerome, *Comm. in Ephes.* II, 4.   [5] II, 17. 5.
[6] Chap. 2, 5-6, and 11, 2,

5. The following named writings, which Lactantius wrote after he became a Christian, and probably after the *Divinae Institutiones*, have been lost, probably owing to the predominance of secular contents.

(*a*) *Ad Asclepiadem*[1] *libri duo.*[2] Subject unknown.

(*b*) *Ad Probum epistularum libri quattuor.*[3] This work is assigned by Teuffel and Schwabe[4] to the pre-Christian period. It treated of metrical and geographical subjects, and apparently, also, of philosophical and theological questions[5] Fragments have been preserved by Jerome,[6] and Rufinus the grammarian.[7]

(*c*) *Ad Severum epistularum libri duo;*[8] written in Gaul

(*d*) *Ad Demetrianum*[9] *epistularum libri duo.*[10] According to Jerome,[11] Lactantius expressed himself, in these letters, in regard to the Holy Spirit in an offensively dogmatic manner

(*e*) A fragment with a superscription, *De Motibus Animae*, and ascribed in a marginal gloss to Lactantius, exists in a manuscript in the Ambrosian Library, at Milan[12] Its contents (doctrine of the emotions) do not stand in contradiction to genuine expressions of the

---

[1] Cf. *Divin. Instit.* VII, 4. 17.   [2] Jerome, *De Viris Illust* 80
[3] Jerome, *Idem*, 80.
[4] Cf § 2 5, above.
[5] Cf Damasus, *Epist. ad Hieron.*, and Jerome, *Epist.* 35, 1.
[6] *Comm Galat* II, *Praef.* (*Opera*, VII, 425).
[7] *Gramm Lat* edit. Putsche, VI, 564 7–565. 2. Cf *Opera*, edit. Brandt, 155 f ; 158 (Victorinus), 163, and also his *Entstehungsverhältnisse*, etc., 125 f
[8] Jerome, 80 and 111.
[9] Cf. *De opif. Dei*, 1, 1, and *Divin. Inst.* II, 10. 15.
[10] Jerome, 80.
[11] *Comm. Galat.* II, 4 (*Opera*, VII, 450), and *Epist.* 84, 7
[12] Codex F. 60 Sup , VIII–IX Century.

author,[1] and hence may quite readily have originated in one of his writings now lost.

L A Muratorius, *Antiqu Ital* III, 1740, 849   S Brandt, *Ueber das in dem patristischen Excerptencodex F.* 60 *Sup der Ambrosiana enthaltene Fragment des Lactantius de motibus animae* (*Gymn Progr*) Heidelb 1891, *idem, Entstehungsverhaltnisse*, etc , p. 127

6 The book, *De Mortibus Persecutorum*, is preserved in only one manuscript,[2] where it is ascribed to one L. Cæcilius   It is an incendiary composition of most unpleasant character, full of fanaticism, exaggerations, and frightful descriptions of repulsive occurrences. After a brief description of previous persecutions of Christians, and of the fate of the persecutors, the author turns to contemporary events in the period of Diocletian, concerning whose horrors he speaks from the position of an eyewitness, not as a historian, but as a controversialist   The work was composed, probably, in 314 to 315 A D. in Nicomedia   Seeck places it in Gaul, in 320–321. Lactantius' authorship of it has recently been attacked by Brandt, in opposition to Ebert, on weighty grounds; and it would be excluded entirely if it could be established beyond all doubt, that Lactantius was in Gaul as early as 307–308 A D   Then only would Brandt's arguments, based on grammar, style, and difference of temper between the indubitably genuine writings of Lactantius and the *De Mortibus*, be unassailable   The circumstance which especially favors its genuineness is that Jerome[3] was acquainted with a work of Lactantius entitled *De Persecutione*, and the consequent difficulty of supposing that soon after the

---

[1] Cf. *Div Inst* VI, 14–17, and *De Ira Dei*, 15–20
[2] *Codex Paris. Lat* 2627   [3] *De Viris Illust* 80.

author's death an anonymous writing should have been attributed to him by one who had good knowledge of his other writings

Editions   St. Baluzius, *Miscellanea*, II, Paris, 1679, 1–46, 345–363, also separately   M   Fr   Dübner, Paris, 1863 — **Translations**   P H Jansen, in BKV, 1875   Wm Fletcher, in ANF, VII, 301 ff — A Ebert, *Ueber den Verfasser des Buches de mortibus persecutorum*, in ASGW, V, 1870, 115–138   P Meyer, *Quaest Lact* (cf 4 *b*, above), 4–8   S Brandt, *Entstehungsverhaltnisse*, etc , 22–123, and JclPh, 1893, 121–138, 203–223   (J) Belser, in ThQu, LXXIV, 1892, 246–293, 439–464   O Seeck, *Geschichte des Untergangs der antiken Welt*, Vol I, Supplement, Berl 1895, 426–430.

7. Several **Poems** are ascribed to Lactantius.

(*a*) *De Ave Phoenice*[1]   The myth of the phœnix is related (in 85 distiches), in its later form, according to which the bird burns itself in order to rise again from its own ashes (a worm or chrysalis). An introduction describes the sojourn of the bird as a priest in the grove of Phœbus   The poem is well attested by tradition as belonging to Lactantius,[2] but an unfinished controversy exists in regard to its genuineness. Earlier scholars were inclined to deny the poem to Lactantius, on account of the antique character of its fundamental conceptions, while later scholars, such as Riese, Dechent, Manitius, and Loebe, claim that its harmony with Christian conceptions are proof of its genuineness   Brandt maintains that Lactantius was its author, but he assigns the poem to his heathen period   The last supposition would be excluded if, as Harnack holds, the first epistle of Clement[3] were employed in the poem.

[1] *Codex Paris.* 13048, saec VIII–IX.
[2] Gregory of Tours, *De cursibus ecclesiasticis*.
[3] Chap 25.

A Riese, in RhM, XXXI, 1876, 446-452. H Dechent, in RhM, XXXV, 1880, 39-55 A Ebert (cf § 2 5, above), 97-101 M. Manitius (§ 2. 5), 44-49. R Loebe, *In scriptorem carminis de Phoenice observationes*, in JprTh, XVIII, 1892, 34-65 (many references to the literature) S Brandt, in RhM, XLVII, 1892, 390-403. A Harnack, *Neue Studien*, etc. (cf § 7, above), p 8 f.

(*b*) *De Passione Domini*, no longer extant in manuscript, was written in hexameters, and, according to Brandt, was a humanistic production that originated between 1495 and 1500 A.D. In it Christ relates the story of his own life, suffering, and death, urging others to follow him by referring to the everlasting reward.

S Brandt, *Ueber das Lact zugeschriebene Gedicht de passione domini*, in *Comm Wolfflin*, Lpz 1891, 77-84 *Opera Lact* II, pp XXII-XXXIII, where a fuller account of the earliest editions is given The first publisher was probably the author M Manitius (cf § 2 5), p 49 f

(*c*) *De Resurrectione* (*Domini*), extant in numerous late manuscripts, and ascribed to Lactantius, was a work of Venantius Fortunatus, of the sixth century.

Opera Lact II, pp XXXIII-XXXVIII The latest edition of the poem, which has not been included by Brandt, is found in *Opera Venantii Fortunati*, edit. F. Leo, Berol. 1881 (*Monument. Germ. hist. Auct antiquiss.* IV, I).

SUPPLEMENTARY

§ 89. *Commodianus*

Editions: E Ludwig, 2 fascic Lips. 1877-1878. B. Dombart, in CSE, XV, Vindob. 1887. — Translation R. E. Wallis, in ANF, IV, 203-218 (*Instructions*).
Literature B. Dombart (cf § 86. 3 *m*, above). Fr Hanssen, *De arte metrica Commodiani*, in *Dissertat. philol.* V, Argentor. 1881, W Meyer (cf § 76 3 *a*), 288-307. G. Boissier, Paris, 1886.

A Ebert (§ 2 5, above), 88-95 M Manitius (§ 2. 5, 85 11 *e*, above), 28-42 Harnack, LG, 731

1 The poems of **Commodianus** are our only source of information concerning him. Even Gennadius[1] knew nothing further, though his characterization of the poet, and Gelasius' condemnation, form the only ancient testimonials. Commodianus, born and educated as a heathen, was possibly a Jewish proselyte before he embraced Christianity He appears to have labored as a bishop about the middle of the third century.[2] The inference drawn from the superscription to the last of the *Instructions*, that he lived at Gaza, in Palestinian Syria, is probably incorrect

2. Commodianus was the first Christian Latin **poet**, though not exactly by the grace of God. But it is to be borne in mind as over against the fact that he poetized in barbarous Latin and in halting hexameters, that he employed the language of the people, in order to be able to reach them, and that originality cannot be denied to his poetical forms (acrostics, strophes, rimes, and line-formations), as long as prototypes for the same cannot be found[3] The wretched state of preservation of the text of both poems renders their interpretation difficult, and besides it is obvious that clearness of thought must suffer, to say the least, by reason of a forced and unnatural style, in the absurd attempt to write poetry in acrostic hexameters (as in the *Instructions*) Traces are apparent in both poems, showing that he had read classical writers, particularly Virgil;[4] the Biblical citations were taken from Cyprian's *Testi-*

---

[1] *De Viris Illust.* 15.
[2] Cf the subscription in the codex of the *Instructiones*.
[3] Meyer, p 306 f. Cf., however, pp. 369-379.   [4] Dombart, III-VII.

monia,¹ and use was made of Hermas,² Minucius, Tertullian, and Cyprian

3 (*a*) The **Instructiones** *per litteras versuum primas* have been preserved in a manuscript of the ninth century,³ and in two others dependent⁴ upon it. The work consists of eighty acrostics of various length, composed in rhythmic hexameters, and is divided into two books which, apparently, are not correctly marked off in the manuscript.⁵ The first book begins by satirizing the heathen gods, and then continues by attacking the superstition, the sensuality, and the worldly pleasures of the heathen It proceeds thence to consider the Jews and their associates, closing with a view of Antichrist and the end of time. The second book contains exhortations and reproofs for Christians of every age and station Their form may have recommended them for memoriter commitment. Since all three books of Cyprian's *Testimonia* were employed in both books⁶ of the *Instructiones*, the earliest date that can be fixed for their composition is in the sixth decade of the third century (250–260 A D).

Editions: N Rigaltius, *Tulli Leuc* 1649 (following a copy made by J. Sirmond). Migne, *Patrol. Lat.* V

(*b*) The **Carmen Apologeticum** (*adversus Judaeos et Gentes*), preserved in a manuscript of the eighth century,⁷ contains 1060 verses (mutilated toward the close of the manuscript), which treat of the following subjects⁸ in six sections: (1) Introduction, stating the

---
¹ Dombart. ² Harnack, in ThLZ, IV, 1879, 52 f.
³ *Codex (Cheltenham) Berol.* 1825, *saec.* IX
⁴ So Rose.
⁵ So Ebert. ⁷ *Codex Cheltenham*, 12261, *saec* VIII.
⁶ Dombart ⁸ Roensch, 169 f.

poet's past life and his purpose in writing, together with an exhortation,[1] (2) Doctrine of God, man, and Redeemer,[2] (3) Meaning of the names "Son" and "Father",[3] (4) Hindrances that prevent the Gospel from forcing its way in the world,[4] (5) Admonition to the Jews, and warning to heathen against entrance into Judaism, as well as against remaining in idolatry;[5] (6) Description of the last things[6] The last subject was handled by the poet with special liking. In the treatment he borrowed from the Apocalypse, the Sibylline Books, the Fourth Book of Ezra, and Jewish myths. The date of composition of the poem appears to be definitely fixed in the year 249 A.D by a reference to impending (Decian) persecution, and to the passage of the Goths over the Danube.[7] In favor of this conclusion is the fact that only the first two books of Cyprian's *Testimonia* are used.

Editions: J B Pitra, in SpS, I, 1852, XVI–XXV, 21–49 and 537–543 H Roensch, in ZhTh, XLII, 1872, 163–302 (with annotations) A Ebert, in ASGW, V, 1870, 387–420 C Leimbach, *Ueber Commod.'s Carmen apol. adv. gentes et Judaeos* Schmalkald, 1871.

II. ROMAN WRITERS

§ 90. Caius

Routh, RS, II, 125–158 S. D F Salmond, in ANF, V, 601–604 (Fragm) G Salmon, in DCB, I, 384–386 A. Harnack, in RE, III, 63 f J Gwynn, *Hippolytus and his "Heads against Caius,"* in *Hermathena*, VI, 1888, 397–418 A. Harnack, *Die Gwynn'schen*

[1] L. 1–88
[2] 89–276
[3] 277–578.
[4] 579–616.
[5] 617–790.
[6] 791–1060.
[7] Vers. 808 ff.

Cajus- und Hippolytusfragmente, in TU, VI, 3, 1890, 121-128
Th Zahn, *Hippolytus gegen Cajus*, in GNK, II, 2, 973-991 (cf I, 24, N. 3). — Fabricius, BG, 284-286 Harnack, LG, 601-603.

In the library at Jerusalem,[1] Eusebius[2] read a work in the form of a dialogue written at Rome under Zephyrinus, by an ecclesiastical and highly educated man named **Caius**, against Proclus the Montanist, and he preserved a couple of sentences therefrom. The conjecture based upon these extracts that Caius attacked the Johannine Apocalypse as a work of Cerinthus, has been confirmed by the five brief **fragments** found in the recently discovered excerpts from Hippolytus' refutation of Caius. One may infer from Eusebius[3] that Dionysius of Alexandria was acquainted with the dialogue. The statements concerning Caius, made by Photius[4] on the basis of scholia, are either false or unreliable.[5]

§ 91. *Hippolytus*

Editions J A. Fabricius, 2 Tom Hamb 1716-1718. Gallandius (cf § 2 8 *a*), II, 409-530 Migne, *Patrol Graec* X, 261 (583)-962 P A de Lagarde, Lips Lond 1858 Cf *Analecta Syriaca* (§ 75 3 *e*), pp 79-91 G. N Bonwetsch and H. Achelis, *Hippolytus Werke*, I, *Exegetische und homiletische Schriften*, Lpz 1897, in *Die griechischen christlichen Schriftsteller der ersten drei Jahrhunderte*, I, Lpz 1897.

Translations J H Macmahon, in ANF, V, 9-258 (Haer, Exeg Dogm and Hist. Fragm Spurious Pieces).

Literature The earlier literature has become antiquated for the most part, since the discovery of the *Philosophumena* K W Haenell, *Commentatio historico-critica de episcopo* Gotting 1838 E J. Kimmel, *De Hippol vita et scriptis*, I, Jenae, 1839.

[1] Cf. § 58 3, above
[2] Cf. *Hist. Eccl* VI, 20. 1-3, cf. II, 25. 6, III, 28. 1 f., 31. 4.
[3] *Hist. Eccl.* VII, 25. 1-3   [5] Cf. § 91. 5 *a, g, h*, and *i*.
[4] *Codex*, 48, Bekker, 11, 40-12, 17.

Chr C J Bunsen, *Hippolyt und seine Zeit*, 2 vols Lpz 1852, 1853. J Dollinger, *Hippolyt und Kallistus*, Regensb 1853 (Engl transl, by A Plummer, Edinb 1876) C P Caspari, *Ungedruckte Quellen* (cf § 18), III, Christiania, 1875, 377-409 J Jacobi, in RE, VI, 139-149 G Salmon, in DCB, III, 85-105 J B. Lightfoot, *Hippolytus of Portus*, in *S Clement of Rome* (cf § 7), II, 317-477 K J Neumann (§ 45), *Der romische Staat*, etc, pp 257-264 G Ficker, *Studien zur Hippolytfrage*, Lpz 1893 — Fabricius, BG, 183-197. Richardson, BS, 55-58. Harnack, LG, 605-646

1 The darkness which has shrouded the life of Hippolytus has been dissipated to some degree by the discovery of his *Philosophumena* The data preserved by tradition may be combined with his own statements in this work as follows : **Hippolytus** was born of Greek-speaking parents, possibly at Rome, in theology he was a pupil of Irenæus,[1] as a presbyter of the Roman church under Zephyrinus (199–217) he was distinguished for his learning. Presumably, questions of theology and church discipline brought him into sharp conflict with this bishop, or, at all events, with his successor, Callixtus, and in consequence Hippolytus stood for a time as bishop at the head of a separate congregation In 235 A D he, together with the Roman bishop Pontianus, was exiled to Sardinia,[2] and there, very probably, he died (Erbes holds a different view). The Roman church commemorates him as a saint on the thirteenth of August, the anniversary of his burial (236, 237) on the Via Tiburtina[3] His canonization either presupposes a reconciliation before his death,[4] or

---

[1] Photius, *Codex*, 121   [2] *Catalogus Liberianus a* 354
[3] Cf. *Depositio Martyrum*, *Catal. Liberian.*, and *Martyrol. Roman.* under this day.
[4] *Inscript. Damas.*, Harnack, LG, 612.

is connected with the fact that his name gave occasion to continue the heathen festival of Virbius (the son of Theseus, who was transported to Aricia), under cover of a festival in honor of a Christian martyr[1] In view of the recognized importance of Hippolytus it is strange that even Eusebius, so soon afterward, knew nothing further in regard to his person than that he was bishop of an unknown see,[2] and it is also strange that almost every trace of knowledge of the Roman schism became lost[3] There are extant, nevertheless, numerous attestations of his Roman episcopate,[4] and the statement that he was bishop of Portus, repeated even by Lightfoot, did not make its appearance till the seventh century.[5] His namesake, Hippolytus of Thebes, whose period is quite uncertain,[6] has been frequently confounded with him.

Lists of attestations are given by Lightfoot, II, 318-365, and by Harnack, LG, 605-613   E. Erbes, *Die Lebenszeit des Hippolytus*, etc, in JprTh, XIV, 1888, 611-646   C Weyman, *Seneca und Prudentius*, in *Comment. Wölfflin*, Lpz. 1891, 281-287.

2   The most notable witness to the **literary activity** of Hippolytus is the list of his writings on the statue erected to him at Rome, perhaps immediately after his death,[7] and discovered again in 1551.[8] The fact that this list is not complete is shown by the independent lists of

[1] Cf. Prudentius, *Peristephanon*, XI, *De Passione S. Hippolyti.*
[2] *Hist. Eccl.* VI, 20 2, cf Jerome, *De Viris Illust.* 61.
[3] Cf, however, Ficker, pp. 109-115.
[4] Apollinaris of Laodicea   Greek manuscripts
[5] *Chronicon Paschale*, cf., however, Gelzer (§ 82), II, 1. N. 1.
[6] Cf Fabricius, VII, 198-200, Ficker, p. 1 f   [7] So Ficker
[8] In the following pages this list is designated as V. or as the "Statue List."

Eusebius[1] and Jerome.[2] To judge by these data the literary productivity of Hippolytus was very varied and comprehensive, extending into exegetical, homiletical, apologetico-polemical, didactic, chronographical, and ecclesiastico-legal domains. Unfortunately his writings have been preserved in so fragmentary a condition that it is scarcely possible to draw conclusions from them touching his intellectual and literary significance. His principal polemical work[3] lacks independence, and the weakness of his chronographical works is obvious,[4] yet it was not without reason that his cycle was engraved upon his statue As an exegete he trod paths of his own, and in spite of his lack of taste in the use of typology, he was distinguished by comparative sobriety. Photius[5] was probably correct in praising the clearness and perspicacity of his style, though he was not willing to accord him the title of "Attic." Quite properly he was an object of admiration in the Roman congregation of the third century in which scientific studies were not cherished, and he was the first and only occidental of this period whose many-sided erudition recalls that of the Alexandrians

Editions of the Statue List J Ficker, *Die altchristlichen Bildwerke im christlichen Museum des Laterans*, Lpz 1890, pp 166-175 (where. p 174 f, exact data are given regarding older editions and literature), and A Harnack, LG, 605-610 N Bonwetsch, *Die christliche vornicanische Litteratur in altslavischen Handschriften*, in LG, 893-897.

3 **Exegetical Works:** With a single exception,[6] only

[1] *Eccl Hist.* VI, 22, denoted in following by E or Eusebius.
[2] *De Viris Illust* 61, denoted in following by J or Jerome.
[3] See No. 5 g, below.
[4] See the possibly too severe criticism of Gelzer [cf § 82], II, 23
[5] *Codex*, 121, 202   [6] Under *p* below.

fragments of the exegetical writings of Hippolytus have been preserved, while some of them are only known by title.

(a) Εἰς τὴν ἑξαήμερον ([V: κοσμογονία] E J) To this writing belonged, apparently, a fragment on the location of the Garden of Eden, which is preserved in the *Sacra Parallela*.[1] Use was made of the commentary of Ambrose [2]

(b) Εἰς τὰ μετὰ τὴν ἑξαήμερον (E), apparently identical with

(c) Εἰς τὴν Γένεσιν (J. and Leontius) A considerable fragment, preserved by Jerome,[3] employs Isaac, Rebecca, Esau, and Jacob respectively as types of God the Father, of the Holy Spirit, of the Jews and the Devil, and of the church or Christ. It was used by Leontius and John [4] On the numerous *Catena*-fragments, see the remarks of H Achelis [5]

(d) *In Exodum:* (J) The existence of this commentary is not beyond all peradventure [6]

(e) Εἰς τὰς εὐλογίας τοῦ Βαλαάμ. A fragment, treating of Christ as the God-man, is preserved in Leontius' work against Nestorius and Eutyches [7]

(f) Εἰς τὸν Ἑλκανᾶν καὶ εἰς τὴν Ἄννην. Four fragments, possibly belonging to a homily, have been preserved by Theodoret.[8]

(g) Εἰς τὴν ἐγγαστρίμυθον.[9] In a fragment edited by

---

[1] Lagarde, § 20   [3] Cf. Jerome, *Epist.* 36, 19
[2] Cf. Jerome, *Epist.* 84, 7, 48, 19.
[4] *Rerum Sacrarum*, II, Lagarde, § 19 (on Gen 11 7)
[5] In Harnack's LG, 628-633.   [6] Cf LG, 633, No. 25.
[7] *Contra Nest et Eutych.*, Lagarde, 51.
[8] *Dialog contra Haeret* I, II (Lagarde, 53, 54).
[9] So the Statue List. Jerome gives *De Saul et Pythonissa*, Nicephorus, in *Hist. Eccl*, gives Περὶ Σαοὺλ καὶ Πύθωνος.

S de Magistris,[1] as belonging to Hippolytus,[2] there is given an interpretation of the apparition (a demon as Samuel) which differs from that of Origen [3]

(*h*) Εἰς τοὺς ψαλμούς [4] Theodoret [5] cited passages from this exposition on the ii, xiii, xxiv, and quite likely on the cxix Psalms These quotations, however, may have originated in homilies quite as well A large fragment in the *Codex Casanatensis*,[6] which treats of the superscription, author, division, and order of the Psalms, is in whole, or in large part, not by Hippolytus,[7] as is apparent from its disagreements with a fragment preserved in Syriac [8]

(*i*) Περὶ παροιμιῶν [9] On the numerous *Catena* fragments, see the remarks of H Achelis [10]

(*k*) *De Ecclesiaste* [11] Nothing extant, the fragment [12] ascribed to Hippolytus by Magistris, is simply the *Responsio* to *Quaestio XLIII* of Anastasius Sinaita.

(*l*) Εἰς τὸ ᾆσμα [13] A fragment has been preserved by Anastasius Sinaita.[14] A Syriac commentary, edited en-

---

[1] *Acta Mart Ostiens* 1795, 19
[2] Migne, PG, X, 605-608
[3] Cf § 61 6 *b* 8, above
[4] So the Statue List and Jerome, though Jerome does not mention Hippolytus among the expositors of the Psalms in his *Epist.* 112, 20 Nicephorus, in his *Hist Eccl*, mentions Περὶ Ψαλμῶν.
[5] *Loc cit* Lagarde, 126-129.
[6] *Codex Casanat* O I 10 (Lagarde, 125)
[7] Overbeck (cf 6 *a* below), p. 6 f
[8] Lagarde, *Anal Syriaca*, 83-87 Pitra, AS, IV, 51-54, 320-323, cf also Migne, PG, X, 721-726, and Pitra, AS, III, 528.
[9] So Jerome and Nicephorus [11] So Jerome.
[10] In Harnack, LG, 634-637 [12] Lagarde, 135.
[13] Eusebius Jerome, *In canticum canticorum*. Nicephorus, εἰς τὸ ᾆσμα τῶν ᾀσμάτων
[14] Anast. Sinaita, *Quaest* 41 (Lagarde, 145)

tire by Moesinger,[1] and in part by Martin,[2] did not come from Hippolytus in its present shape.[3]

(*m*) *In Esaiam*[4] A citation[5] from this is given by Theodoret,[6] and two are in a Coislin Codex.[7]

(*n*) *In Jeremiam* The existence of such a commentary[8] is doubtful.[9]

(*o*) Εἰς μέρη τοῦ ’Ιεζεκιήλ.[10] The large fragment published by Martin[11] is of uncertain origin.[12]

(*p*) Εἰς τὸν Δανιήλ.[13] This commentary has been preserved entire, or at least nearly so, in two Greek,[14] and one Slavonic[15] manuscripts, but only the fourth book has been published as yet. Besides these, there are numerous Greek, Latin, Syriac, Armenian, and Slavonic fragments[16] The attestations are given by Bardenhewer.[17] The commentary is divided into four books: I. The Story of Susanna. II The Song of the Three Children III–IV. Daniel, Chap. i–vi, and vii–xii. The exposition of the first mentioned is a masterpiece of typology. The interpretation of the fourth monarchy of Daniel[18] is animated by intense hatred toward the

[1] *Monum Syriaca*, II, 9–32.
[2] Pitra, AS, IV, 36–40, 306–310.
[3] Cf. LG, 638, No. 32.
[4] So Jerome.
[5] Εἰς τὴν ἀρχὴν τοῦ ῾Ησαίου. Homily ?
[6] *Dialog* II (Lagarde, 55).
[7] *Codex Coisl* 193 (Lagarde, 56; cf. *Addenda*, p. 216).
[8] Assemani, *Bibl orient.* I, 607.
[9] Cf LG, 639, No. 34, and Ficker, 98.
[10] So Eusebius Cf. Assemani, *loc. cit.*
[11] Pitra, AS, IV, 41–47, 311–317, cf. also Lagarde, *Anal.* 90 f.
[12] LG, 639, 35.
[13] So Apollinaris of Laodicea, Jerome, and Nicephorus.
[14] *Codex Chalc.* and *Codex Vatopadi*, 260.
[15] *Codex Monast Tschudow*
[16] Lagarde, 57–124, cf. also Bardenhewer, 36–66. Harnack, LG, 640 f., Nos 5–12, and Ficker, 107 f
[17] Bardenhewer, pp 9–35.
[18] Cf. particularly on chap. 7.

Roman empire The chronological explanations were intended to support the belief that Antichrist was not to be expected then, either during or after the horrors of the persecution by Severus The commentary was written after the book *De Antichristo*, to which the author makes reference,[1] and before the *Chronicon;* that is, apparently, about 202 A.D., or a little later.[2] A controversy which promises to end in discrediting the genuineness of the work has arisen concerning the exact date of the birth of Christ[3] contained in the commentary.

O Bardenhewer, *Des heiligen Hippolytus von Rom Commentar zum Buche Daniel,* Freiburg, 1877. B Γεωργιάδης, Περὶ τοῦ ὑπομνήματος τοῦ ἁγίου Ἱππολύτου ἐπισκόπου Ῥώμης εἰς τὸν Προφήτην Δανιήλ (Ἐκκλησιαστικὴ Ἀλήθεια, 1885, May–Oct pp. 10–21). *Idem,* Τοῦ ἁγίου Ἱππολύτου ἐπ. κ. μάρτ περὶ ὁράσεως τοῦ προφήτου Δανιὴλ λόγος δ'. (*Idem,* 21–24, 49–64, 1886, May–Oct. 225–247, 273–287); cf J B Lightfoot, *Clement,* II, 391–394. A Harnack, in ThLZ, XVI, 1891, 33–38. J. H Kennedy, *Part of the Commentary of S. Hippolytus on Daniel,* Dublin, 1888. E. Bratke, *Das neu entdeckte vierte Buch des Danielkommentars von Hippolytus,* Bonn, 1891. Ph. Meyer, *Eine neue Handschrift zum Danielkommentar des Hippolytus,* in ThLZ, XVI, 1891, 443 f. G. Salmon, *The Commentary of Hippolytus on Daniel,* in *Hermathena,* XVIII, 1892, 161–190. E Bratke, *Die Lebenszeit Christi im Daniel-Commentar des Hippolytus,* in ZwTh, XXXV, 1892, 120–176 A. Hilgenfeld, *Die Zeiten der Geburt, des Lebens, und des Leidens Jesu nach Hippolytus, Idem,* 257–281 *Idem, Die Lebenszeit Jesu bei Hippolytus, Idem,* XXXVII, 1893, 106–117. F. X. Funk, *Der Danielkommentar Hippolyts,* in ThQu, LXXV, 1893, 115–123. See also the literature cited at 6 *a,* below.

(*q*) *In Zachariam.*[4] Nothing extant.

(*r*) *In Matthaeum.*[5] Apparently some fragments of

[1] Bratke, 6, 27.   [3] Bratke, 19, 1–7.
[2] Salmon holds differently.
[4] So Jerome, cf. also his *Comm. Zachar praef.* (Opera, VI, 777–778).
[5] So Jerome, in *Comm. Matth praef.* (Opera, VII, 7–8).

this commentary have been preserved. It is possible that the fragment (homily?),[1] cited by Theodoret as ἐκ τοῦ λόγου τοῦ εἰς τὴν τῶν ταλάντων διανομήν, belonged to it.

Harnack, LG, 641, No. 38   J. Gwynn, *Hippolytus on S. Matth* xxiv. 15–22. (*Extract from an unpublished Commentary of Dionysius Barsalibi* [Rich, 7185, fol. 5, v°, line 10]), in *Hermathena*, XV, 1889, 137–150.

(*s*) It is doubtful whether Hippolytus wrote a commentary on Luke. Two fragments on Luke ii. 7 and 22 are given by Lagarde.[2] The three little pieces which Theodoret extracted from a λόγος εἰς τοὺς δύο λῃστάς,[3] probably belonged to a homily.

(*t*) *De Apocalypsi*.[4] A commentary on the Apocalypse which the Palatine Elector, Ott-Heinrich, appears to have owned, as late as his day in manuscript form, is certainly to be distinguished from the Apology for the Apocalypse, and from the work against Caius   The fragments of a commentary bearing the name of Hippolytus, and preserved in Arabic, which Lagarde[5] has recently published, have not yet been investigated sufficiently as to their genuineness.   The fragment published by Bonwetsch from an ancient Slavonic translation (Rev. xx. 1–3), is regarded by Bratke as spurious.

C P Caspari, *Hippolytea*, in *Theol. Tidsschr f. d evang luth. Kirke i Norge*, III   Raekke, vol. 3, Part 4. 1891, 567–572 , cf O v Gebhardt, in DLZ, XIII, 1892, 651 f   N Bonwetsch, *Zu Hippolyts Datierung der Geburt Christi*, in ThLB, XIII, 1892, 257 f   E Bratke, *Das angebliche Fragment aus Hippolyts Kommentar zur Offenbarung Johannes, Idem*, 503–506, 519–522.   J Friedrich, *Ueber die*

---

[1] Lagarde, 14l.
[2] *Idem*, 139–140.
[3] *Idem*, 142.
[4] So Jerome, Syncellus, and Jacob of Edessa.
[5] *Analecta Syriaca*, app 24–28.

Schrift auf der Statue Hippolyts von Rom: υπερ τον κατα Ιωανην ε[υαγγ]ελιου και αποκαλυψεως, in *Rev Intern de Théol.* (*Internat. Theol. Zeitschr.*), II, 1894, 123–128.

4. One might form a safe opinion in regard to Hippolytus' performances as a preacher,[1] if the very spirited and powerful address Εἰς τὰ ἅγια θεοφάνεια[2] were of undisputed genuineness. The Προσομιλία *de laude domini salvatoris* (called by Nicephorus, περὶ ἐπαίνων τοῦ κυρίου ἡμῶν Ἰησοῦ Χριστοῦ), which was delivered in the presence of Origen, has been lost. Many of the fragments already cited[3] apparently originated in homilies, since "undoubtedly the exegetical and homiletical writings of Hippolytus are in part not to be sharply distinguished from each other."[4] The second of the writings mentioned by Eusebius, Περὶ τοῦ πάσχα,[5] was a homily, provided the fragment ἐκ τῆς εἰς τὸ πάσχα ἐξηγήσεως[6] and two Syriac fragments[7] were related thereto. The Syriac fragments seem to betray acquaintance with Melito[8] Achelis thinks that he recognizes extracts from Hippolytus' homilies on Matt. iv. and xxv. in the fragment of homilies preserved in the *Canones Hippolyti*, xxx.

A translation of the speech εἰς τὰ ἅγια θεοφάνεια, by F J Winter, in *Predigt der Kirche*, XXII, Lpz 1893, 13–19 S. D. F Salmond, in ANF, V, 234–237 — H Achelis, *Zwei Fragmente hippolytischer Predigten*, in *Die ältesten Quellen*, etc. (see No 8, below), Anhang, II.

[1] Photius, *Codex*, 121.
[2] Lagarde, p. 2.
[3] Cf. No 3 *g*, *h*, *m*, *r*, *s*, above.
[4] Caspari, 382 *h*, 194.
[5] Cf. Jerome, see No. 7 *a–b*, below.
[6] *Conc. Lateran ann 649*, Lagarde, 143.
[7] *Hippolyti sermonis de pascha*, AS, IV, 55 f., 323 f. [Lagarde, *Anal. Syriaca*, 88 f.].
[8] Cf. § 40. 6.

5 Hippolytus directed his **polemical** writings against heathen, Jews, and heretics

(a) In his *Philosophumena*,[1] Hippolytus cites as his own a treatise Περὶ τῆς τοῦ παντὸς οὐσίας, which must be identical with the book mentioned in the Statue List as Πρὸς Ἕλληνας καὶ πρὸς Πλάτωνα ἢ καὶ περὶ τοῦ παντός, and out of which a considerable fragment[2] has been preserved, bearing the caption Ἰωσήπου ἐκ τοῦ (πρὸς Ἕλληνας) λόγου τοῦ ἐπιγεγραμμένου κατὰ Πλάτωνος (Πλάτωνα) περὶ τῆς τοῦ πάντος αἰτίας. Even in his time, Photius[3] had read the work under this title, and ascribed it to Caius, since to him he also attributed the *Philosophumena* In this work, which is composed of two short books, Hippolytus, according to Photius' statement, proved that Plato contradicted himself, refuted the false assertions of the Platonist, Alcinous, concerning the soul, matter, and the resurrection, meantime stating his own view, and, finally, demonstrated the antiquity of the Jews as compared with the Greeks. The extant fragment contains some foreign elements.[4] It describes the place of the demons, and in connection therewith treats of Hades, the joy of the righteous, and the pains of sinners In one passage[5] there is a reference to earlier writings treating of Christ as judge. Jerome[6] appears to have read the book.

(b) A considerable fragment[7] of the Ἀποδεικτικὴ πρὸς Ἰουδαίους has been preserved. It is possible that the first line of the Statue List refers to this work; other-

---

[1] X, 32, edit of Duncker and Schneidewin, 536, 19.
[2] Lagarde, 6; cf also 17, and Pitra, AS, II, 269 f.
[3] Photius, *Codex*, 48.
[4] Overbeck (cf. 6 a, below), p 4 f. [6] *Epist.* 70, 4.
[5] Lagarde, 71, 1. [7] Lagarde, 5.

wise it is not mentioned. In it proof is brought from Scripture passages that "the Jews boast without reason of having condemned Jesus of Nazareth to death, and of having given him vinegar and gall to drink, since this had drawn upon them frightful threatenings and awful sufferings"[1] Magistris[2] was incorrect in appending the Pseudo-Cyprianic treatise *Adversus Judaeos* to it as a continuation[3]

(*c*) Photius[4] had read a Σύνταγμα πρὸς ἁπάσας τὰς αἱρέσεις, which is not contained in the Statue List, but is mentioned by Eusebius, Jerome, and Nicephorus, as well as by the *Chronicon Paschale*,[5] etc. Hippolytus himself also refers to it[6] According to Photius, who possibly was acquainted only with an extract from it,[7] it was a brief treatise, compiled from the addresses of Irenæus, clear and simple, but not exactly in Attic style It embraced thirty-two heresies from Dositheus to Noetus The outline of this lost composition can be reconstructed from the works of the plagiarists, Pseudo-Tertullian, Philastrius, and Epiphanius, who treated of the same theme[8] It was probably composed about 200 A.D.

(*d*) A composition which is preserved in a Vatican Codex[9] of the thirteenth century, and elsewhere, and which bears the title Ὁμιλία Ἱππολύτου εἰς τὴν αἵρεσιν Νοήτου τινός,[10] was not a homily, but the conclusion of an anti-heretical work. It remains uncertain, however,

---

[1] Caspari, 395. [2] *Acta Martyr Ostiens*
[3] Cf. § 86 6 *e*, above. Text-critical material, in Ficker, 105.
[4] *Codex*, 121.
[5] P 12 f, edit Dinsdorf, contains a citation, Lagarde, 12
[6] *Philosophumena, Prooem*, edit. Duncker and Schneidewin, 3, 19 f.
[7] So Lipsius.
[8] So Lipsius Cf § 22 and the literature cited there
[9] *Codex Vatic.* 1431, *saec* XIII   [10] Lagarde, 3.

rhether we are to suppose this composition to have
een an otherwise unmentioned, large work against all
Monarchians,¹ or the *Syntagma*² The latter supposi-
on would be the more probable if it could be shown that
'hotius had read merely an extract from the *Syntagma*
t is held by Lipsius and Voigt that Epiphanius³ copied
he first eight chapters without acknowledgment; Kat-
enbusch doubts this, considering it probable that Hip-
iolytus made use of his own *Syntagma* in his "Homily,"
nd that Epiphanius was dependent only on the former.⁴

Cf the literature cited at § 22   Also, H Voigt, *Eine verschollene
Irkunde*, Lpz 1891, pp 135-138   P. Batiffol, *L'abbaye de Rossano*,
'aris, 1891   Ficker, 100-105, 106 f.   F Kattenbusch, *Das apost.
ymbol*, pp 354-358   E Rolffs, *Urkunden*, etc (§ 85 3).

(*e*) A work, Πρὸς Μαρκίωνα, is mentioned by Eusebius,
erome, Syncellus, and Nicephorus   Nothing is known
n regard to it, and there is therefore no ground on which
o base the alluring identification of it with the *Chronicon*.⁵

(*f*) The writing, Κατὰ μάγων,⁶ appears to have treated
if deceptions similar to those practised by Marcus, who
vas characterized by Irenæus⁷ and Hippolytus⁸

(*g*) In 1842 A D Books IV-X of a work, Κατὰ πασῶν
αἱρέσεων ἔλεγχος (Λαβύρινθος πασῶν αἱρέσεων?), were discovered by Minoides Mynas in an Athos manuscript of
he fourteenth century. The first book had been long
known in several manuscripts under the separate title

¹ So Volkmar and Harnack   ³ *Haeres*, LVII.
² So Fabricius and Lipsius
⁴ Cf also Gelasius, *Testimon de duabus naturis in Christo. (Max. Bibl.
atr.* [§ 2 8 *a*] VIII, 704)
⁵ Cf No 6 *c*, below
⁶ *Philosophumena*, VI, 39, edit. Duncker and Schneidewin, 298, 47.
⁷ *Adv Haeres*. I   ⁸ Cf. note 6, above.

Φιλοσοφούμενα, but it had been incorrectly attributed to Origen and printed among his writings That Hippolytus was the writer of this work, though it is not mentioned in the Statue List nor by Eusebius or Jerome, appears to be rendered certain by internal evidence, particularly by its references to the *Syntagma*, to the work περὶ τῆς τοῦ παντὸς οὐσίας,[1] and to the *Chronicon*,[2] by its undeniable relationship to writings that are recognized to be genuine, such as the *Noetus* and *Antichrist*, and by the impossibility of making any other authorship even probable Theodoret and Photius[3] were acquainted with it, or perhaps with the tenth book only, under the title Λαβύρινθος,[4] and erroneously supposed it to be a work of Caius The author's purpose, expressed in the *Prooemium*, was to refute all heresies by proving that they had drawn all their wisdom from heathen philosophy For this purpose he presents, in the first book, the views of the Greek philosophers, using, however, scanty excerpts[5] as his sources and betraying very meagre special knowledge. Nothing can be made of the contents of the second and third books (mysteries, Babylonian, Chaldean ?), for in the recapitulation in the tenth book just these missing books (and the fourth also) are passed over in silence[6] The fourth book, which lacks its beginning, treats of astrology and its alleged arts, use being made of Sextus Empiricus Not till the fifth book does the presentation of heretical theories begin, continuing thence to the close of the ninth book The first twenty-nine chapters of the tenth book contain a recapitulation of what has preceded, followed, after a

---

[1] Cf 5 *a*, above.
[2] X, 39.
[3] Codex, 48
[4] Cf X, 5
[5] Cf Diels, 145–154.
[6] Cf, however, X, 6, at beginning.

lacuna in the manuscript, by a chronological sketch occupying Chapters 30 and 31. Chapters 32 to 34 contain Hippolytus' confession of faith. An investigation of the sources used for the delineation of the Gnostic system[1] has shown that those sections in which Hippolytus copied from (Justin), Irenæus, and Tertullian, together with some brief notices which the author wrote independently and upon personal knowledge, are beyond suspicion, but that on the other hand a whole array of other statements rests upon the accounts which Hippolytus must have taken from a forger. The sections of the ninth book which treat of the dissensions inside the Roman congregation, are of particular interest[2]. The date of composition is to be placed in the later years of the author's life, if the passage in X, 30, really has reference to the *Chronicon*. On the last point Salmon holds a different view.

Editio princeps of the *Philosophumena*, by Jac Gronovius, in *Thesaurus graec antiq*. X, 1701, 257-291. Cf the editions of Origen by De la Rue, I, 872-909, and Lommatzsch, XXV, 279-338. G. Roeper, *Emendationsversuche zu Hippolyts Philosophumena*, in *Philologus*, VII, 1852, 511-553, 606-637, 667. The latest edition by H Diels, *Doxographi graeci*, Berol 1879, 551-576, cf 144-156. *Editio princeps* of the complete work, by E Miller, Oxon 1851. L Duncker and F G. Schneidewin, Gottingen, 1859. P Cruice, Paris, 1860.

Literature : Cf G Volkmar, *Hippolytus und die romischen Zeitgenossen*, Zurich, 1855. P de Smedt, *De auctore Philosophoumenon*, in *Dissert sell*, Ghent, 1876. G Salmon, *The Cross-References in the Philosophumena* in *Hermathena*, XI, 1885, 389-402. cf A Harnack, in ThLZ, X, 1885, 506 f. Th Zahn, in GNK, I, 1, 24, N 2 cf also II, 2, 987. H Stahelin, *Die gnostischen Quellen Hippolyts in seiner Hauptschrift gegen die Haretiker*, in TU, VI, 3, 1890.

---

[1] So Salmon and Stahelin   [2] Cf No. 1, above.

(*h*) Eusebius[1] has preserved considerable portions of a Σπούδασμα μετὰ τῆς 'Αρτέμωνος αἱρέσεως, which was called ὁ σμικρὸς λαβύρινθος by Theodoret[2] and by him ascribed to Origen Photius[3] alleged that a Λόγος κατὰ τῆς 'Αρτέμωνος αἱρέσεως was written by Caius. Very probably this composition is to be attributed to Hippolytus

(*i*) Among his polemical writings are to be enumerated also the two treatises in which Hippolytus defended the genuineness of the Gospel and Apocalypse of John, viz: (1) Ὑπὲρ τοῦ κατὰ Ἰωάννην εὐαγγελίου καὶ ἀποκαλύψεως,[4] which apparently was directed against the Alogi and was copied by Epiphanius.[5] and (2) Κεφάλαια κατὰ Γαίου,[6] for the defence of the Apocalypse, certain fragments of which (taken from Dionysius Bar-Salibi) have been preserved in the commentary on the Apocalypse[7]

6 Only one of the **dogmatic** writings of Hippolytus has been preserved entire

(*a*) Περὶ Χριστοῦ καὶ 'Αντιχρίστου: so called by Photius,[8] Jerome calls it *De Antichristo*, Nicephorus, Περὶ τῆς παρουσίας τοῦ ἀντιχρίστου; the Codex, Περὶ τοῦ σωτῆρος ἡμῶν Ἰησοῦ Χριστοῦ καὶ περὶ τοῦ ἀντιχρίστου. It is preserved (whether it is complete is doubtful) in a manuscript of the tenth century,[9] not yet published, and in two late Greek and two old Bulgarian manuscripts Hippolytus mentions it in his commentary on Daniel.[10] Further attestations are given by Overbeck

---

[1] V, 28.
[2] *Haer. fab* II, 5.
[3] *Codex*, 48.
[4] Statue List and Ebed-Jesu.
[5] *Haeres*. LI.
[6] So Ebed-Jesu.
[7] Cf. § 90, the article on Caius, and the literature cited there.
[8] *Codex*, 202.
[9] *Codex Hieros saec* X (Achelis)
[10] Bratke, 6, 27; 11, 20.

and Lagarde¹ The author proposes to reveal, to a certain Theophilus, under the seal of silence toward unbelievers, the secrets of the final age contained in the prophetical writings² He begins with a characterization of Antichrist, who in all respects is the antithesis of Christ,³ quotes the prophetic witnesses,⁴ and shows that, as the predictions of Daniel have been fulfilled in regard to the first three kingdoms, so that with regard to the fourth, the Roman empire,⁵ typified by ancient Babylon,⁶ must also be accomplished Following is a description of the events that are to precede the end of the world, particularly the appearance and domination of Antichrist after the manner of Augustus,⁷ coupled with persecution of the faithful, until, finally, Christ shall make an end of all terrors, and shall conduct the pious into glory⁸ The book shows the influence of Irenæus (for instance, in the exposition of Rev xiii 18), and was apparently written at the time of the persecution by Severus, about 202 A.D.

Editio princeps, M Gudius, Paris, 1661 Fr Combefisius, in *Auctar biblioth graec patr noviss* I, Paris, 1672, 26–50 — Translations V Grone, in BKV, 1873 S D F Salmond, ANF, V, 204–219

Literature Frz C Overbeck, *Quaestionum Hippolytearum specimen*, Jena, 1864 Newostrujew, *The Tractate of St Hippolytus on Antichrist in an Ancient Slavonic Translation according to a Manuscript of the Twelfth Century*, Moscow, 1868 (in Russian), cf A Harnack, in ThLZ, XLV, 1875, 38–61 E Bratke, *Ein arabisches Bruchstuck aus Hippolyts Schrift uber den Antichrist*, in ZwTh, XXXVI, 1893, 282–290

¹ Overbeck, 12–42 (cf. also Harnack, LG, 620). Lagarde, 1.
² §§ 1–4.
³ §§ 5–14.
⁴ §§ 15–26.
⁵ §§ 27–35.
⁶ §§ 36–41.
⁷ § 49.
⁸ §§ 42–67.

(b) From a Λόγος περὶ ἀναστάσεως καὶ ἀφθαρσίας, which Jerome calls *De resurrectione*, Anastasius Sinaita[1] made a quotation in regard to the angelic state of men after the resurrection.[2] Theodoret[3] has preserved two fragments on the same subject, taken from an 'Επιστολὴ πρὸς Βασιλίδα τινά[4] Some fragments which apparently belong to the same writing are found in four Syriac manuscripts,[5] though they are marked as belonging to a *Sermo de resurrectione ad Mammaeam imperatricem* Very probably the name of the addressee was obtained by conjecture, and the writing itself was identical with one cited in the Statue List as Προτρεπτικὸς πρὸς Σεβηρεῖναν (probably Julia Aquilia Severa). If the notice in the Statue List is not a later addition to the original, Hippolytus must also have written[6] Περὶ θεοῦ καὶ σαρκὸς ἀναστάσεως.

(c) Concerning a Λόγος περὶ θεολογίας, we are only informed by means of a citation in the Acts of the Lateran Synod of 649 A D.;[7] and a writing, mentioned in the Statue List (a later addition?) as Περὶ τἀγαθοῦ καὶ πόθεν τὸ κακόν, may have had anti-Marcionite contents, and have been identical with the treatise, Πρὸς Μαρκίωνα[8] Ebed-Jesu mentions a work, Περὶ οἰκονομίας[9]

7 The following were the **chronographical** writings of Hippolytus: —

(a) The 'Απόδειξις χρόνων τοῦ πάσχα καὶ τὰ (καθὰ, κατὰ, κατὰ τὰ) ἐν τῷ πίνακι, as it is given in the Statue

---

[1] *Hodeg* 23
[2] Chap. 9
[3] *Eranist dial.* II and III, *Opera*, IV, 131, 232 sq
[4] Lagarde, 10
[5] Pitra, AS, IV, 61–64, 330 sq. [Lagarde, *Anal Syr.* 87 sq]
[6] Achelis, in LG, 606.
[8] Cf 5 *e*, above
[7] Lagarde, 8.
[9] Assemani (§ 2 8 *b*), III, 15.

List, was very probably identical with the first of the writings, Περὶ τοῦ πάσχα, mentioned by Eusebius [1] According to Eusebius, it contained chronological notices and an Easter canon of sixteen years, which was reckoned from the first year of Alexander Severus It is to be assumed, consequently, that the reckoning of the Easter festival according to a cycle of sixteen years for the period from 222 to 233 A D, which is engraved on the statue, belongs to this work (perhaps as a second book) The fragment concerning the character and time of the passover observed by Christ, which has been preserved in the *Chronicon Paschale*,[2] was taken from the first book of a work, Περὶ τοῦ ἁγίου πάσχα. Compare also the epicrisis in the *Chronicon* of Elias of Nisibis (eleventh century)[3] Salmon has made it probable that the canon was put forth in 224 A D. Compare also the pseudo-Cyprianic writing, *De Pascha computus* [4]

(b) On the second of the writings mentioned by Eusebius, Περὶ τοῦ πάσχα, see above [5]

(c) The work mentioned in the Statue List as Χρονικῶν (βίβλος ?) is lost in the original, and only fragments remain, which have to be picked out from the later Byzantine chroniclers [6] It can be reconstructed, however, to a certain degree, on the basis of Latin translations or redactions: (1) from the *Liber generationis* (*mundi*), which has been handed down in two forms (a) separately, in a number of manuscripts,[7] (b) in the 15th section of the Chronographer of 354 A D., who

[1] Cf. Jerome and Syncellus [2] I, 12 sq. edit Dindorf.
[3] Lagarde, *Anal. Syr.* 89 sq Pitra, AS, IV, 56 sq, 324 sq.
[4] § 86. 6 d [5] Cf No 4, above
[6] Mommsen, 86 sq, cf Pitra, AS, II, 274-282. A list is given by Gutschmid, 378 (242).
[7] Mommsen, 78-81, Frick, CCX–CCXV.

goes back to a *Chronicon* of 334,[1] and (2) from the statements in so-called *Barbarus Scaligeri*[2]. Two recensions of the original must have been used as the basis of these compilations, the longer of which, the *Chronicon Alexandrinum*, was probably the older[3]. Hippolytus' Chronicle closed with the last year of Alexander Severus, and, perhaps, was his last work[4]. On insufficient grounds, Frick has contended that Hippolytus' Chronicle did not form the basis of the *Liber generationis*, but on the other hand, he has shown[5] that Hippolytus borrowed from Clement[6]. Gutschmid, Mommsen,[7] and Frick[8] assert that Hippolytus made use of the Chronography of Africanus. This conclusion is doubted by Salmon,[9] not without reason. The list of bishops contained in Hippolytus' chronicle may be extracted from the Chronographer of 354 A D (13th section)

Cf the Editions of the *Liber generationis* and of *Barbarus Scaligeri*, by Th Mommsen in *Chronica minora saec* IV, V, VI, VII (*Monum Germ Auct antiq* IX), I, Berl 1892, 78-140, and C. Frick, in *Chronica minora*, I, Lips 1893, 1-111 (184-264). First edit by Canisius, in *Lect antiqu* II, 1601, 154 sqq

Literature A v Gutschmid, *Zur Kritik des* διαμερισμὸς τῆς γῆς, in RhM, XIII, 1858, 377-408 (in his *Kleine Schriften*, V, 1894, 240-273), *Idem*, *Untersuchungen uber den* Δ τ γ, etc, in his *Kleine Schriften*, 585-717, *passim*. G Salmon, in DCB, I, 506-508 (*Chronicon Canisianum*), *Idem*, in *Hermathena*, X, 1891, 161 sqq (?) H Gelzer (cf § 82), II, 1-23 J J Hoeveler, *Die Excerpta latina Barb* (*Festschrift*), Bonn, 1895, 193-214

[1] Manuscripts given by Mommsen, 17-33
[2] *Chronicon Alexandrinum*, cf besides Mommsen and Frick, Eusebius' *Chron libr. duo*, edit A Schoene, I, 1875, App 175-207
[3] So Mommsen
[4] Cf also, 5 g, above
[5] pp VI-XXV
[6] *Stromat* I, 21 109-136
[7] p 86
[8] pp XXXV-XL
[9] DCB, I, 507

8 Finally, the works of Hippolytus on **ecclesiastical law** are to be mentioned.¹

(*a*) In the Διδασκαλία τῶν ἁγίων ἀποστόλων περὶ χαρισμάτων,² with which the eighth book of the Apostolic Constitutions³ opens, there may be recognized with probability a more or less thorough redaction of a work of Hippolytus which appears in the Statue List as Περὶ χαρισμάτων ἀποστολικὴ παράδοσις The discussions contained therein concerning the significance of gifts of grace reach their climax in the statement that even the possession of a charism does not constitute a man pious, and that consequently an ignorant or immoral bishop is no true bishop According to Achelis, Hippolytus wrote this dissertation while still a member of the larger communion, aiming it against Zephyrinus, *i.e.* before 217 A.D.

Cf the Editions of the Apostolic Constitutions (Lagarde, 230-236) H Achelis (see *b*, below), Anhang I, 269-280

(*b*) In the eighth book of the Apostolic Constitutions⁴ there is a section⁵ entitled Διατάξεις τῶν αὐτῶν ἁγίων ἀποστόλων περὶ χειροτονιῶν διὰ Ἱππολύτου, which also represents a redaction of an older writing. Achelis, with good reason, assumes that the source was the (38) *Canones Hippolyti* which have been preserved in Arabic, though in a much revised form. He is probably incorrect, however, in identifying it with the ἀποστολικὴ παράδοσις⁶ of the Statue List, and in supposing that it had been worked into the Egyptian Canons⁷ before

¹ Cf Jerome, *Epist* 71, 6.
² Manuscripts noted by Harnack, LG, 643.
⁵ Manuscripts noted by Harnack, LG, 643.
⁶ See *a*, preceding.
³ Chaps 1 and 2
⁴ Chaps. 4 sqq.
⁷ § 98. 4.

its contents passed into the Constitutions. Funk, on the other hand, considers that the Canons were a late compilation based upon the Constitutions If Achelis is right, it is possible, with him, to regard the Canons as the document that was intended to constitute the platform of the opposition-church in the conflict with Callixtus The Canons,[1] after an introduction,[2] deal with the ordination of the clergy,[3] rules concerning catechumens, women, baptism,[4] fasting,[5] oblations, and the love-feast (*agape*),[6] Paschal fasts,[7] the healing of the sick,[8] eucharistic service,[9] daily morning worship,[10] and finally, the observances of daily life [11] On the fragments of sermons contained in Canon XXX, see above.[12]

Editions D B de Haneberg, *Canones S Hippolyti arabice e codicibus romanis cum versione latina, annot et proleg* Monach. 1870 Latin version, H Vielhaber's improved form of Haneberg's translation, given by H Achelis, pp 38-137 (see below) —**Translation** V Grone, in BKV, 1874

Literature H Achelis, *Die ältesten Quellen des orientalischen Kirchenrechts Erstes Buch. Die Canones Hippolyti*, in TU, VI, 4 1891 — *Idem*, in ZKG, XV, 1894, 1-43 — F X Funk, *Die apostolischen Konstitutionen*, Rottenb 1891, 254-280 *Idem*, in ThQu, LXXV, 1893, 594-666, and separately, Tubingen, 1893 A. Harnack (review of Funk, 1891), in StKr, LXVI, 1893, 403-420

9 **Poetical works** of Hippolytus would be attested if anything could be made out of the entry in the Statue List, as follows : ᾿Ω[ι]δαὶ [ε]ἰς πάσας τὰς γρ[α]φάς (Harnack : ᾠδαὶ διακόσιαι. πάσας τὰς γραφάς).

[1] Arrangement given by Achelis, 140-142.
[2] Canon I.
[3] Canons II-IX.
[4] X-XIX.
[5] XX, XXXII.
[6] XXXII-XXXVI
[7] XXII
[8] XXIV.
[9] XXXVII, XXVIII, XXX.
[10] XXX.
[11] XXV-XXVII, XXIX, XXIII, XXXVIII.
[12] See No. 4, above.

See H Achelis, *Ueber Hippolyt's Oden und seine Schrift "Zur grossen Ode,"* in *Gotting Nachrichten, Phil Hist. Klasse*, 1896, pp 272-276 Also P Battiffol, *Les prétendues "Odae in Scripturas" de St Hippolyte,* in *Rev bibl internat* V, 1896, 268-271

10. The following, ascribed to Hippolytus, are probably or certainly **spurious**.

(*a*) The eight fragments of Κατὰ Βήρωνος καὶ Ἥλικος περὶ θεολογίας καὶ σαρκώσεως [1] κατὰ στοιχεῖον λόγος [2] preserved by Anastasius Apocrisiarius, in which, perhaps, the remains of the *Theological Outlines* of the Areopagite are to be found.

Cf J Dräseke, *Beron und Pseudo-Hippolytus,* in ZwTh, XXIX, 1886, 291-318 *Idem, Gesammelte patristische Untersuchungen,* Altona and Lpz 1889, 56-77 Opposite view, J Langen, in *Rev. Intern. de Théol.* II, 1894, 34.

(*b*) Διήγησις This relates to an attempt to violate a Christian virgin at Corinth, and to her rescue by a brave youth.[3] Palladius[4] had read it as the work of a γνώριμος τῶν ἀποστόλων, named Hippolytus. It calls to mind the legends of the Diocletian period.

(*c*) The Λόγος περὶ τῆς συντελείας τοῦ κόσμου καὶ περὶ τοῦ ἀντιχρίστου καὶ εἰς τὴν δευτέραν παρουσίαν τοῦ κυρίου ἡμῶν Ἰησοῦ Χριστοῦ,[5] is a long composition which circulated in many manuscripts and versions. "At the earliest, it belongs to the ninth century," and was first published by J. Picus in 1556.[6]

(*d*) Four (five) fragments with dogmatic contents, preserved in Armenian, and published by Pitra.[7]

[1] Cf. No 6 *b, c,* above. [4] *Historia Laus.* 148.
[2] Lagarde, 4 [5] Lagarde, 14.
[3] *Idem,* 144
[6] J Picus, Paris, 1556; cf Newostrujew (cf. 6 *a,* above).
[7] Pitra, AS, IV, 70 sq. (336 sq).

(e) Material which originated with Hippolytus may possibly be found in the fragments ascribed to an Hippolytus, in an anonymous Arabic *Catena* on the Pentateuch The *Catena*, however, dates from the tenth century at the earliest.

O Bardenhewer (cf 3 *p*, above), 30-40. P. de Lagarde, *Materialien zur Kritik und Geschichte des Pentateuchs*, Heft 2, Lpz 1867. The commentary on Genesis, Migne, *Patrol. Graec.* X, 701-712 ("Fragmenta dubia in Pentateuchum") belongs here.

(*f*) Nothing certain can be said about the sentence with psychological contents, printed by Lagarde,[1] nor concerning the fragment περὶ τῶν ιβ΄. ἀποστόλων, ποῖ ἕκαστος αὐτῶν ἐκήρυξεν καὶ ποῦ ἐτελειώθη given by Migne.[2]

Cf *Constitutiones Apost.* edit. P de Lagarde, 282–284, and N. Bonwetsch, in LG, 896 sq.

§ 92. Novatian

Editions : M Mesnartus (J Gangneius), Paris, 1545 (among the works of Tertullian) E Welchmanus, Oxon 1724 J Jackson, Lond 1728. Migne, *Patrol Lat* III, 911–1000
Translation : R E Wallis, in ANF, V, 603–650 (Trinity, Meats).
Literature · A Harnack, in Herzog and Plitt, *Realencyclop* XI, 652–667 G T Stokes, in DCB, IV, 58–60 — Schoenemann, BPL. 135–143 Richardson, BS, 63 sq Preuschen, LG, 652–656

1. Concerning the life and works of Novatian, there are extant only the testimonials of his opponents, which give wholly *ex parte* statements, or distorted accounts of the facts.[3] **Novatianus**[4] was of unknown extraction,

---

[1] Lagarde, 145.   [2] Migne, *Patrol. Graec.* X, 951–954.

[3] Cf Cyprian, *Epist* 44, 45, 49, 52–55, 59, 60, 68, 69, 73. *Epist. Cornelii* in Eusebius, VI, 43. *Ep. Dionys. Alex.* 1 c VI, 45. Pseudo Cyprianus, *ad Novatianum*.

[4] So Cyprian and the Latin tradition. Eusebius, VI, 43, gives Νοουάτος; later writers, Ναυάτος.

ossibly an African, not a Phrygian, in spite of the
tatement of Philostorgius.¹ He was baptized during a
evere illness, and was ordained presbyter by the Roman
ishop, it is alleged, against the protest of the entire
lergy, and of many of the laity. In March, 251, he
ras consecrated as bishop in opposition to Cornelius,
nd, at the head of a rigorous party, he became the
riginator of a great schism in which for a time the
rhole church was involved, and whose traces can be
ollowed in the Orient even into the Middle Ages. The
tatement that he was a martyr under Valerian, rests
olely upon the testimony of Socrates ²

2. Very little has been preserved from the numerous
treatises **and letters** of Novatian,³ among the rest being
is principal work in (now lost) manuscripts of Ter-
illian. That which is extant confirms the assertion of
erome⁴ that Novatian possessed an original literary
tyle, and also the judgment of his opponent, Cyprian,⁵
rho ascribed to him philosophical training and rhetori-
al ability.⁶ A comprehensive and thorough investiga-
.on of Novatian's literary activity is still wanting

3 There have been **preserved** : —

(*a*) The composition *De Trinitate* (*de regula fidei*),
rhich was early ascribed to Tertullian or Cyprian,⁷ may
afely be claimed for Novatian on the testimony of
erome⁸ This work, which was written at all events

---

¹ *Hist Eccl* VIII, 15   ² *Hist Eccl.* IV, 28
³ Cf their enumeration by Jerome, *De Viris Illust.* 70, cf. *Epist.* 10, 3,
id 36, 1.
⁴ *Contra Rufinum*, II, 19.   ⁵ *Epist* 55, 24.
⁶ Cf. also the spiteful remarks of Cornelius, *loc cit*
⁷ Cf. the controversy between Rufinus (*de adult. librr. Orig.* Lom-
atzsch, XXV, 395) and Jerome (*Contra Rufin* II, 19)
⁸ *De Viris Illust.* 70.

before the schism, treats first of God and his attributes;[1] second (coupled with a rejection of the theological theories of Sabellius), of Christ as the true God-man;[2] and closes, after a brief exposition of the doctrine of the Holy Ghost,[3] with a defence of the doctrine of the Trinity against Monarchian objections [4] Theologically, the author was under the influence of Irenæus and Tertullian;[5] his book, both in form and contents, was an important contribution, being the sole presentation of the doctrine of the Trinity in the Western church before Augustine.

Edition: Whiston, in Sermons and Essays, 1709.
Translation: Chr. Fr. Rossler, in Bibl d KVv III, Lpz. 1777, 278-307 (Extract). R. E Wallis, in ANF, V, 611-644.

(*b*) The small treatise in epistolary form, *De cibis Judaicis* (*Novatianus plebi in evangelio stanti salutem*) was written in a time of persecution,[6] that is, probably, in 250 A.D., and does not presuppose the existence of the schism Preceding it there had been two other writings which are also mentioned by Jerome, viz. *De Circumcisione* and *De Sabbato*. These Jewish questions appear, consequently, to have been burning. Novatian treated the question of distinctions touching food, by showing that the divine prohibition held good for Jews, but that for Christians only one prohibition existed, that they should eat no meat offered to idols.

4. Nothing is known touching the circumstances under which the remaining **works** mentioned by Jerome were written: *De Pascha, De Sacerdote, De Oratione*

---

[1] 1-8
[2] 9-28
[3] 29
[4] 30-31.
[5] Jerome, *loc cit.* ἐπιτομὴν operis Tertulliani faciens.
[6] Chap 1.

(the older manuscripts, except the Vatican, read thus, the Vatican has *ordinationi*), *De Instantia* (περὶ τῶν ἐνεστώτων), and *De Attalo* (*multaque alia*) Harnack conjectures that the first mentioned was identical with the Pseudo-Cyprianic writing *De pascha computus*[1]

5 (*a*) In the collection of Cyprian's letters, two writings have been included, the first of which[2] certainly,[3] the second[4] very probably, was written by Novatian as correspondent for the Roman congregation during the vacancy of the see after the martyr death of Fabian[5]

(*b*) Weyman and Demmler[6] have sought to show that the Pseudo-Cyprianic writings *De Spectaculis* and *De bono pudicitiae* proceeded from Novatian. According to Harnack, the work *De laude martyrii*[7] also was written by Novatian.

III. THE REMAINING OCCIDENTAL WRITERS

§ 93   *Victorinus of Pettau*

Editions. *Theophylacti Ennarrationes in Pauli epp* edit J Lonicerus, Paris, 1543 (Apoc)   M. de la Bigne (cf § 2 8 *a*), VI, 713-730 (edit Colon 1618, III, 136-142) (Apoc)   A Rivinus, Gotha, 1652 (Apocryphal writings)   *Max Bibl Patr* (cf § 2 8 *a*), III, 1677   Cave (cf § 2 4 *b*), I, 1688, 102-104   Gallandi (cf § 2 8 *a*), IV, 49-64   Migne, *Patrol Lat* V, 281-344   Routh, RS, III, 453-473 (*de fabrica mundi*)

Translation R E Wallis, ANF, VII, 341-368 (Creation, Apoc)

Literature J Launoius, *De Victorino episcopo et martyre dissertatio*, Paris, 1653, 2d edit 1664   J Haussleiter, *Die Kommentare des Victorinus, Tichonius und Hieronymus zur Apokalypse*, in

---

[1] Cf. § 86. 6 *d*.
[2] *Epist.* 30.
[3] Cf. *Epist.* 55, 5
[4] *Epist* 36
[5] Cf Harnack (§ 86 4, close).
[6] Cf § 86 5 *a–b*.
[7] § 86 5 *c*

ZkWL, VII, 1886, 239–257   H A Wilson, in DCB, IV, 1128 sq
J Haussleiter, *Der chiliastische Schlussabschnitt im echten Apokalypsekommentar des Bischofs Vict von Pettau*, in ThLB, XVI, 1895, 193–199 — Schoenemann, BPL, 144–147   Preuschen, LG, 731–735

1. **Victorinus**, bishop of Petavio (Pettau, in Styria), fell a martyr in the Diocletian persecution [1]   The statement of Cassiodorus [2] that in his earlier years he had been a rhetorician, probably arose from confounding him with Victorinus Afer, of the fourth century   Jerome [3] names him as author of commentaries on Genesis,[4] Exodus, Leviticus, Isaiah, Ezekiel, Habakkuk, Ecclesiastes,[5] the Song, Matthew,[6] and, finally, on the Apocalypse   In these, Victorinus had copied Origen,[7] and Jerome [8] has more to say regarding the good intention, than concerning the execution of these works, whose Latin betrays the born Greek.   A single **fragment**, published by Cave from a Lambeth manuscript, is extant : *De fabrica mundi*   It may be genuine, and, in that case, it must be referred to the commentary on Genesis   There is also a commentary on the Apocalypse, in a shorter [9] and a longer [10] recension, by means of which perhaps the original work may be reconstructed after the removal of the portions that Jerome wove into it from the work of Tichonius   Attention is due to the remarks of Kattenbusch,[11] who

---

[1] Cf Jerome, *De Viris Illust*. 74, *Martyr. Roman.* 2d November.
[2] *Inst. div lit.* 5 and 7
[3] Cf. Jerome, *De Viris Illust* 74.   [4] Cf *Epist.* 36, 16.
[5] Cf. *Comm Ezech.* on iv, 13   *Opera*, V, 425.
[6] Cf. *Comm Matth praef*, and Cassiodorus, *loc. cit.*
[7] Jerome, *Epist.* 84, 7, 61, 2
[8] *De Viris Illust* 74, cf *Epist* 58, 10, 70, 5 ; *Contra Rufin.* I, 2.
[9] Published by Lonicerus and De la Bigne.
[10] Published by Gallandi and Migne
[11] F Kattenbusch (cf. § 18), p 213 f.

reckons with the possibility that even Tichonius himself remodelled the commentary Recently Haussleiter has discovered the genuine conclusion of the commentary¹ 2. In the last place, Jerome² names among the works of Victorinus a treatise *Adversus omnes haereses* It may be that it is contained in the Pseudo-Tertullian supplement to *De praescriptione haereticorum*, since Victorinus, according to Jerome,³ copied Hippolytus, whose *Syntagma* presumably was used in that tractate.⁴ A striking relationship exists between the genuine portions of the commentary on the Apocalypse and the Pseudo-Tertullian poem *Adversus Marcionem*.⁵ The other things printed (by Rivinus) under the name of Victorinus do not belong to him.

§ 94. *Reticius of Autun*

Harnack, LG, 751 f.

Reticius, bishop of Autun, took part as representative of the Emperor Constantine, in the Anti-donatist synod held at Rome in 313 A.D. He wrote a *Commentary* on the *Song of Songs*, in which, according to the statements of Jerome,⁶ a most curious sort of exegesis was practised. A sentence from a writing by him against *Novatian*⁷ has been preserved by Augustine.⁸ Harnack⁹ supposes that Reticius was the author of the Pseudo-Cyprianic writing *Ad Novatianum*.

[1] In the *Codex Ottobon Lat 3288 A*. [2] *De Viris Illust* 74.
[3] *Epist.* 36, 16
[4] So Harnack, cf § 85. 11 *b*, above
[5] Haussleiter, p. 254 ff.; cf also § 85. 11 *d*.
[6] *Epist* 37, 1; cf 5. 2, and *De Viris Illust*. 82.
[7] Jerome, *De Viris Illust* 82.
[8] *Contra Julian Pelag*. I, 3, 7, and *Op. imp. cont. Jul.* I, 55.
[9] LG, 718, 752.

CHAPTER III

EPISCOPAL AND SYNODAL WRITINGS

§§ 63. 4, 68, g, 69 c, 74, 75. 2 c; 77; 81; 84; 86 4

§ 95. Roman Bishops

1 Nothing worthy of credence is known with regard to the literary activity of **Zephyrinus** (*circa* 199–217 A.D.). Optatus of Mileve [1] alleges that he wrote against the heretics [2]

2. **Callixtus** (217–222 A D) in an edict, which possibly was prefaced with full reasons,[3] declared fleshly sins to be venial, and the episcopal power of the keys to be indisputable. Tertullian's writing, *De Pudicitia*, in which Callixtus was attacked, furnishes material for the reconstruction of this edict, which possibly was written in Greek.[4]

J B De Rossi, in *Bull Archeol Christ* 1866, 26. A Harnack, in ZKG, II, 1878, 582   Herzog und Plitt, *Realencykl* VIII, 420; X, 562   E Preuschen (cf § 85 9 a), 48 f   E Rolffs, *Das Indulgenz-Edikt des romischen Bischofs Callist* in TU, XI, 3, 1893 (reconstruction) — Harnack, LG, 603-605.

3 **Pontianus** (230–235 A.D) appears to have put forth a writing in the matter of the condemnation of Origen [5]

---

[1] *Schism. Donat* I, 9
[2] Cf Hippolytus, *Philosophumena*, IX, 21, Harnack, LG, 597
[3] So Rolffs.   [4] Cf. § 85 9 h
[5] Cf Jerome, *Epist* 33, 4, (84, 10; Eusebius, VI, 36. 3); Harnack, LG, 648

4 Eusebius[1] mentions three[2] letters of **Cornelius** (251-253), written in Greek to Fabius of Antioch, which he had read at the library in Cæsarea Eusebius[3] has preserved seven fragments (some of them extensive) of the third letter which was written in connection with Novatianist affairs Besides, Cornelius wrote at least seven letters to Cyprian, two of which have been preserved,[4] while the existence of the other five can be inferred from Cyprian's letters.[5]

Fabricius, BG, 191-293. Routh, RS, III, 19-89. Harnack, LG, 650-652.

5 **Stephanus**[6] (254-257 A.D) wrote to the Syrian and Arabian congregations,[7] and also to the Oriental bishops,[8] as well as to Cyprian,[9] in the controversy in regard to heretical baptism

6 **Sixtus II** (257-258 A D), according to Harnack,[10] wrote the treatise *ad Novatianum* which stands under the name of Cyprian

7. Athanasius[11] has preserved a considerable fragment taken from a writing of **Dionysius** (259-268 A D.) against the Sabellians In it the question of the generation of the Son by the Father is discussed Besides, Dionysius wrote to his namesake, Dionysius of Alexan-

---

[1] *Hist. Eccl* VI, 43.
[2] Jerome (*De Viris Illust.* 69) incorrectly says, four
[3] §§ 5-20   [5] *Epist.* 45, 1, 48, 1; 50, 59, 1-2.
[4] Cyprian, *Epist.* 49 and 50   [6] Harnack, LG, 656-658.
[7] Dionys. Alex. in Eusebius, *Eccl. Hist* VII, 5. 2.
[8] *Idem*, VII, 5. 4
[9] *Epist* 74, 1 (a sentence is there given).
[10] Cf. § 86 6 *a*.
[11] *Decreta Synod. Nic* 26, cf *Sentent Dionys.* 13.

dria, in the same matter,¹ and he addressed a letter of consolation to the congregation at Cæsarea in Cappadocia ²

Fabricius, BG, 293 f   Routh, RS, III, 371–403   Harnack, LG, 659

8 A fragment (containing a confession of faith) belonging to a letter forged by the Apollinarists and ascribed to **Felix** (269–274) was read at the Synod of Ephesus, 449 A D ³

§ 96   Acts of Synods

1 Only meagre remains of the documents, connected with the **acts** of the numerous synods of the third century, have come down to us   The following have been **lost**: The acts of the synods convened by Bishop Demetrius at Alexandria in 231 or 232 A D with a view to the condemnation of Origen,⁴ the acts of the synod held at Bostra (about 244 A D), in reference to Beryllus,⁵ in which Origen took part⁶ (these Eusebius⁷ had seen⁸); the acts of an Arabian synod held about the same time, in reference to the Thnetopsychitae, in which also Origen took part,⁹ the acts of the synods in reference to Novatianist affairs, held at Rome in 251¹⁰ and 252 A.D¹¹ and at Carthage in 251,¹² and also various

---

¹ Athanasius, *Sentent Dionys* 13   ² Basil, *Epist* 70
³ Cf C P Caspari (cf § 75 3 *b*), 111–123, — Harnack, LG, 659 f
⁴ § 61 2
⁵ § 84   ⁶ § 61. 7 *b*.
⁷ *Hist Eccl* VI, 33 3, cf Jerome, *De Viris*, 60, and Socrates, *Hist Eccl*. III, 7
⁸ Harnack, LG, 514 f
⁹ Eusebius, *Hist Eccl* VI, 37, August *Haer* LXXXIII; LG, 515.
¹⁰ Eusebius, *Hist Eccl* VI, 43 2, cf Cyprian, *Epist* 55, 6
¹¹ Cyprian, *Epist*. 52.   ¹² Cyprian, *Epist* 55, 6, 59, 13.

African synods held in reference to the controversy on heretical baptism, and finally the Acts of the first two synods directed against Paul of Samosata.

2. The following have been **preserved**:—

(*a*) A writing in reference to the question of penance, directed to Cornelius of Rome in the year 253,[1] by forty-two African bishops gathered under the presidency of Cyprian;

(*b*) A writing in reference to infant baptism, composed by Cyprian and fifty-six bishops, and directed to Fidus in the year 253 (252 ?),[2]

(*c*) A writing by Cyprian and thirty-six bishops to Legio and Emerita in Spain, in the year 256,[3] in reference to the reinstatement of Bishops Basilides and Martialis;

(*d*) Two writings of the first and third (second) synods assembled at Carthage in connection with the controversy concerning heretical baptism, which were issued in the years 255–256,[4]

(*e*) The protocol of the third Carthaginian synod, in connection with the baptismal controversy of the year 256, under the title *Sententiae episcoporum num LXXXVII de haereticis baptizandis*,[5]

On the Carthaginian synods, see Routh, RS, III, 93–217

(*f*) A writing of Bishops Hymenæus (of Jerusalem), Theophilus, Theotecnus (of Cæsarea), Maximus, Proclus, and Bolarius, to Paul of Samosata, composed before 268, in which they explain to him their belief, which

---

[1] Cyprian, *Epist* 57; cf § 86. 4.   [3] Cyprian, *Epist.* 67; cf 86 4
[2] Cyprian, *Epist* 64, cf § 86 4   [4] Cyprian, *Epist* 70–72, cf § 86 4
[5] Cyprian, *Opera*, ed. Hartel, I, 433–461, Harnack, LG, 728 f

they allege to have been derived from the Apostles.[1] No manuscript is known.[2]

(*g*) A number of fragments from the writing in which the bishops assembled at Antioch (probably in 268), acquainted Dionysius of Rome and Maximus of Alexandria with the excommunication pronounced on Paul According to Jerome's[3] statement (which is probably worthless), the writing was composed by Malchion, the opponent of Paul[4] The fragments are given, part by Eusebius,[5] part by Leontius,[6]

(*h*) With regard to the fragments of the disputation between Paul of Samosata and the presbyter Malchion, following the shorthand reports of the Acts of the Synod of Antioch, see above [7]

[1] On the names, cf Eusebius, *Hist Eccl*. VII, 30. 2.
[2] Routh, RS, 289–299, LG, 525 f.
[3] Jerome, *De Viris Illust* 71
[4] Cf § 78, translated by S D. F. Salmond, in ANF, VI, 169–171.
[5] Eusebius, *Hist Eccl* VII, 30
[6] *Adversus Nestor et Eutych* III, Routh, RS, 303–313, Harnack, LG, 520 f
[7] Cf § 78

THIRD SECTION

ECCLESIASTICAL LITERATURE IN THE SECOND AND THIRD CENTURIES

§ 97. *Symbols and Creeds*

Literature: See § 18. A. Harnack, *Dogmengeschichte*, 3d edit. (§ 2. 7. *e*), I, 320–337 C P Caspari, *Hat die alexandrinische Kirche zur Zeit des Clemens ein Taufbekenntniss besessen, oder nicht?* in ZkWL, VII, 1886, 352–375 — Harnack, LG, 235, 262, 291, 551, 667.

The African **baptismal symbol**, which can be reconstructed from Tertullian's writings principally,[1] is to be traced back to the Roman[2] On the other hand, the confession whose existence in Irenæus'[3] works can be proved, may have been an inheritance from Asia Minor. The question whether a fixed and formulated baptismal confession existed at Alexandria as early as the time of Clement[4] may be answered in the affirmative with Caspari, rather than in the negative with Harnack. But still, the question as to the extent to which the Oriental national churches possessed baptismal confessions in the third century, is, at the present state of investigation, as little ready for decisive answer as is the other question, whether the single demonstrable case[5] of relationship between the Cæsarean baptismal con-

---

[1] Harnack, *Patr Apost.* 118–123.　[3] Harnack, *Idem*, 123–127.
[2] Cf. Tertullian, *Praescript.* 36.　[4] *Stromata*, VII, 15, 90
[5] See the Cæsarean baptismal symbol; Hahn, § 116

fession and the Roman symbol, justifies the conclusion that the Oriental type of symbol was dependent upon the Roman, or is to be urged as showing that the Roman symbol originated in the East (Asia Minor). The symbol of Gregory Thaumaturgus exhibits no kinship to the Roman.[1] On the symbol of Lucian the martyr, see above.[2]

§ 98 Church-Orders

Harnack, LG, 28, 451-466, 515-518

The great law-book of the Greek (Oriental) church, the **Apostolic Constitutions,** and the collections of church-orders of the Copts, Ethiopians, and Arabians, were first compiled as such during and after the fourth century Scholarship is busy in ascertaining the sources that were employed in their construction; some of them reaching back into the second and third centuries. So far as these efforts have met with success, their results must here receive attention

1. Under the title **Didascalia,** *i e.* catholic doctrine of the twelve Apostles and of the holy disciples of our Redeemer, there has been preserved in the Syriac language[3] a church-order which, as is generally recognized, lies at the basis of the treatment of the same subjects in the first six books of the *Apostolic Constitutions*. After some exhortations to Christians in general,[4] it treats of the qualifications, duties, and rights of bishops,[5] of matters in dispute between Christians,[6] of gatherings for worship,[7] of widows, deacons, deaconesses, and

---

[1] Hahn, § 114, cf. § 75. 3 *b*, above.
[2] § 79, above
[3] *Codex Sangerm. Syr.* 38.
[4] Chaps. 1-3
[5] Chaps. 4-9.
[6] Chaps. 10-11
[7] Chaps 12-13

orphans,[1] of martyrs and the influence of martyrdom,[2] of fasts,[3] of the training of children,[4] and of heresies,[5] closing with a recapitulation of the principles of the Apostles in the composition of the *Didascalia*,[6] and warnings against Jewish tendencies[7] This *Didascalia* originated in Syria or Palestine, but views vary in regard to the date of its composition Funk sees in the Syriac *Didascalia* an exact reproduction of the original Greek text, and considers it " approximately certain that the work originated before the middle of the third century," and as " quite probable that it belonged even to the first quarter of the century " Harnack feels compelled to "recognize, in the copy translated by the Syrians, a slight modification of the original *Didascalia*,"[8] and ascribes "the latter to the first half of the third century, the former to the second half " Kattenbusch suggests the query whether the *Didascalia* may not have been made by Lucian[9] for his congregation The author was acquainted with the *Didache* (in what form is doubtful), the Epistles of Ignatius,[10] and the fourth book of the Sibylline Oracles,[11] according to Funk, he had also read Justin and Hegesippus (?) The Arabian and Ethiopian *Didascalia* are of later origin and are not treated here[12]

Editions (P de Lagarde), 1854 (Syriac). *Idem* (P Botticher), in C C J Bunsen, *Analecta Ante-Nicaena*, II, Lond 1854 (Retranslation into Greek, with use of the text of the Constitutions)

[1] Chaps. 14–18
[2] Chaps 19–20
[3] Chap 21.
[4] Chap 22.
[5] Chap 23
[6] Chaps 24–25
[7] Chap 26
[8] Cf the Antinovatianist (?) sections in Chaps. 6–7
[9] Cf. § 79, above
[10] Cf Zahn's edit , 336 f.
[11] Funk, 74
[12] Funk, 207–242.

Exact indication of contents (according to information furnished by Socin) in Funk, *Die Apost Konstit* (§ 81 8 *b*), pp 28-40 A Harnack, StKr, 1893, 404 f (cf § 91 8 *b*). F Kattenbusch, *Das Apost Symbol* I, Lpz 1894, p 394

2. The foremost place among the ecclesiastical writings which were highly esteemed by the Southern and Northern Egyptians, by the Ethiopians and by the Egyptian Arabians, from the period of the ancient church, was occupied by the Κανόνες ἐκκλησιαστικοὶ τῶν ἁγίων ἀποστόλων, i e. **Ecclesiastical Canons**[1] (Apostolische Kirchenordnungen) The name given in the *Codex Vindobonensis* is Αἱ διαταγαὶ αἱ διὰ Κλήμεντος καὶ κανόνες ἐκκλ. τ. ἁ. ἀ., and in the Ethiopian edition, *Canones patrum apostolorum sanctorum quos constituerunt ad ordinandam ecclesiam sanctam;* a title which also applies to the Egyptian Church-Order (No 4, below) Its thirty[2] canons contain ethical[3] and ecclesiastical[4] prescriptions They have been handed down (*a*) in Greek,[5] (*b*) in Coptic, both in a Southern Egyptian (Sahidic or Theban) and in a Northern Egyptian (Memphitic) edition, the latter being dependent upon the former, (*c*) in Ethiopic, in a form also dependent upon the Theban,[6] and (*d*) in Arabic, still unpublished. The moral regulations have been handed down sepa-

---

[1] Known in Germany generally (though not uniformly) as *Apostolische Kirchenordnungen* (Apostolical Church-Orders, or Canons) The term, "Ecclesiastical Canons," approves itself as being nearest to the Greek, but English usage varies These Canons are to be distinguished from the "Apostolical Canons" (erroneously called "Ecclesiastical Canons" in ANF, VII, 500-505), which are usually appended to the Apostolic Constitutions

[2] So Lagarde, following the Theban edit

[3] 4-14

[4] (1-3) 15-20.

[5] *Codex Vindob hist graec.* 45

[6] Cf. however, Funk, 247.

rately: (*a*) in Greek,[1] in two manuscripts of the tenth and fourteenth centuries, and (*b*) in Syriac [2] It is susceptible of proof [3] that in this form they do not represent the original of, but fragments from, the longer recensions. According to Harnack's investigations, this church-order was a clumsy compilation from earlier writings, made in Egypt about 300 A.D., use having been made of the *Didache* [4] and the Epistle of Barnabas for the moral regulations, and of two disquisitions dating from the second century, for the canonical regulations. The latter two are designated by Harnack as Κατάστασις τοῦ κλήρου,[5] and Κατάστασις τῆς ἐκκλησίας.[6] In these portions the Pastoral Epistles were much used

Editions H Ludolf, *Comment. in hist Aethiop.* Francof 1681, 314 sqq (Ethiopic and Latin), cf W Fell, *Canones Apostolorum aethiopice*, Lips 1881 J W Bickell, *Geschichte des Kirchenrechts*, I, Giessen, 1843, 107–132 (Greek). H Tattam, *The Apostolic Constitutions or Canons of the Apostles, in Coptic, with an English Translation*, Lond 1848 (Memphitic version) A P. de Lagarde, *Reliquiae juris eccles antiquissimae*, Lips 1856 (Greek, according to *Codex Vindob*, and with retranslation into Greek from *Codex Sangerm Syr* 38, cf remarks on the Theban edition in *Codex Muss Britt* 440, Sup IX–XX) *Idem, Aegyptiaca*, Gottingen, 1883 (Theban text, following the *Codex Mus Britt Orient* 1320, Ann 1006) J. B Pitra, *Juris ecclesiastici graecorum historia et monumenta*, I, Rom. 1864, 75–88 (*Codex Vindob* and *Codex Ottob*) A. Hilgenfeld, in *Nov Test*, etc (§ 3), IV, 1866, 93–106, 2d edit 1884, 110–121 O de Gebhardt, in *Patr. Apost* (§ 3), I, 2 (2d edit), 1878, XXVIII–XXXI (*Codex Mosqu*). F. X Funk, in his edition of the *Doct*

---

[1] *Codex Mosqu. graec. CXXV, saec X* (Canons 4–14), and *Codex Ottob. graec.* 408, *saec. XIV* (4–13), where a fragment of the *Didache* is found, not contained in other recensions.

[2] *Codex Sangerm Syr* 38 (3–14)

[3] So Harnack.

[4] The earliest *Didache*, cf § 21 3.

[5] Canons 16–21.

[6] Canons 22–28.

apost. (§ 21), 50–74 A Harnack, in TU, II, 1–2, 1884, 225–237 (Greek), and TU, II, 5, 1886, 7–31 (Canons 16–28, Greek and German)

Literature See the prolegomena and commentaries of the various editions, especially Bickell, pp 87–97, 178 sqq *passim* (gives the older literature [Vansleb Ludolf]), and Harnack, *loc cit.* II, 1, 2, 193–241 (on the Διδαχή and the so-called Ecclesiastical Canons), II, 5 (on the sources of the so-called Ecclesiastical Canons). A. Krawutzcky, *Ueber das altkirchliche Unterrichtsbuch: "Die zwei Wege oder die Entscheidung des Petrus,"* in ThQu, LXIV, 1882, 359–445. F. X Funk (§ 81. 8 *b*), pp 243 sq.

3. The facts cannot be determined with certainty in regard to the **Duae Viae** *vel Judicium secundum Petrum* (*Petri*), which Rufinus substituted in his Latin rendering of Athanasius'[1] list of canonical writings, in place of the Διδαχή καλουμένη τῶν ἀποστόλων.[2] The *Didache* cannot be meant, since at another place [3] Rufinus designates it correctly as *Doctrina quae dicitur apostolorum*.[4] Apparently,[5] reference is made to the Ecclesiastical Canons, and the second title is sufficiently explained by the "Judgment" of Peter in the thirtieth canon.

4. The so-called **Egyptian Church-Order**, that is, the thirty-two canons which follow the Ecclesiastical Canons in the Egyptian law-book, forms, according to Achelis,[6] the intermediate step between the canons of Hippolytus and the eighth book of the Apostolic Constitutions, and therefore must have originated, at the latest, in the first half of the fourth century. Funk [7] differs from this view, holding that the Church-Order was an extract from the Constitutions.

[1] *Festal Epistle*, 39.
[2] *Exposit in symb. Apost.* 38: cf Jerome, *De Viris Illust.* I.
[3] Transl. Eusebius, *Hist. Eccl* III, 25.
[4] Cf. the fragment given by v. Gebhardt.
[5] Harnack holds otherwise
[6] Cf § 91. 8 *b*.
[7] Cf. § 91 8 *b*

SUPPLEMENTARY

§ 99. *The Pseudo-Clementine Epistles De Virginitate*

Editions. J J. Wetstenius, Lugd Bat 1752; Migne, PG, I, 379–452 (following Cl Villecourt, Paris, 1853). J. Th Beelen, Lovan 1856, F X. Funk, in *Opera Patr. Apost.* (cf § 3), II, 1–27 (Latin) — Translations. P. Zingerle, Wien, 1827. B P. Pratten, in ANF, VIII, 53–66.

Literature. The prolegomena and commentaries connected with the editions. B F. Westcott, *A General Survey of the History of the Canon of the N. T.*, Cambridge and Lond, 5th edit 1881, pp 186 sq. J. M. Cotterill, *Modern Criticism and Clement's Epistles to Virgins*, Lond. 1884, cf. Harnack, in ThLZ, IX, 1884, 265–268. J. B. Lightfoot, *S. Clement of Rome* (cf § 3), I, 407–414 A Harnack, *Die pseudo-clement. Briefe de virginitate und die Entstehung des Mönchtums*, in SBBA, 1891, 359–385. — Richardson, BS. 91 sq. Harnack, LG, 518 sq.

Epiphanius[1] and Jerome[2] were acquainted with epistles of Clement of Rome, in which he extolled virginity. Thereby are intended the **two epistles,** *De Virginitate*, which have been preserved in a manuscript of the Syriac New Testament.[3] These letters were written by an ascetic to ascetics, male and female, with the purpose of setting forth in brightest light the advantages of celibate life, and of indicating the means and ways for avoiding its incidental dangers. Antiochus of Saba (as late as about 620 A.D.) inserted considerable sections of the Greek original in his *Pandectes*.[4] A fragment[5] is found in a British Museum codex[6] in Syriac, translated out of the *Testimonies of the Fathers*, of Timotheus

---

[1] Epiphanius, *Panarion*, XXX, 15.
[2] Jerome, *Adv. Jovin.* I, 12 Cf. Cotterill.
[3] *Codex Colleg. Remonstr. Amstelod. 184. ann. 1470.*
[4] Cotterill, 115–126.
[5] I, 5 end–6 beginning.   [6] *Codex Mus. Britt. Addit.* 12156.

of Alexandria (457 A.D) The position of the epistles in the Bible-codex shows that they enjoyed the greatest respect in Syria The same is evidenced by the name which Epiphanius applied to them, 'Επιστολαὶ ἐγκύκλιαι, and by the testimony of Bar-Hebræus, Bar-Salibi, and others They were written in Syria (or Palestine) The date of composition is controverted. Clement cannot be seriously claimed to have been their author.[1] But on the other hand, the letters bear signs of great antiquity, so that their composition in the second century, as held by Westcott, or in the third, as held by Harnack, does not seem impossible, though the asceticism which they describe is as easily imaginable at the beginning of the fourth century as during the third. The argument derived from the silence of Eusebius may be met by the possible supposition that it was not till after Eusebius' time that the letters were classed with the works of Clement by a forger, who, imitating the Epistles to the Corinthians, and with the purpose of displacing them, made two out of what was originally one.[2] The suggestion of Cotterill, that the letters may have been forged on the basis of the passages in Epiphanius and Jerome, deserves no serious consideration.

[1] Contrary to the view of Beelen   [2] So Harnack.

FOURTH SECTION·

LEGENDS

§ 100 *In General*

The entire simplicity and purity of the canonical accounts of the life and deeds of Jesus and his Apostles, only become fully evident to one who compares them with the luxuriant **legendary growths** which in later centuries entwined themselves upon the original stem. Their roots have already been considered.[1] These fables, indeed, with which believers, particularly those of the Oriental churches, embellished the life of Jesus, had not gained any fixed and recognizable literary form in the second and third centuries The Abgarus-myth[2] constitutes an unimportant exception Instead, ecclesiastical phantasy had taken possession of the story of the lives of the Apostles in most complete fashion It has already been seen[3] how far the Gnostics appear to have called this literature of romance into existence. In just this field the limits are very obscure where Gnostic and ecclesiastical elements merge together: in catholic recensions of the Acts of Thomas, John, and Andrew,[4] much of Gnostic material has been preserved, and *vice versa*, the catholic Acts of Peter and Paul[5] show many characteristics that remind one of Gnosticism The Pseudo-Clementine writings,[6] the circumstances of

---

[1] § 16 5-6, above. [3] §§ 22 and 30. [5] § 102
[2] § 101 [4] See § 30. [6] § 103.

whose origin are doubtful, form the best example of the sort of literature that was read in the churches.

§ 101 *The Legend of Abgarus*

Editions · of the *Doctrina Addai:* (1) Syriac (and English) W Cureton, *Ancient Syriac Documents relative to the Earliest Establishment of Christianity in Edessa*, Lond 1864 (incomplete). G Phillips, *The Doctrine of Addai, the Apostle*, Lond 1876 (2) Armenian (and French) J R Emin, *Léroubna d'Édesse Histoire d'Abgar*, in Langlois' *Collection des historiens anc et mod de l'Arménie*, I, Paris, 1867 Alishan, *Laboubnia, Lettre d'Abgar*, Venezia, 1868, cf Dashian, in *Wien Zeitsch f d Kunde d Morgenl* IV, Hefte 1–3 (3) Greek C. Tischendorf (§ 30), 261–265, cf Lipsius (below), pp 3–6
Literature R A Lipsius, *Die edessenische Abgarsage*, Braunschw. 1880 Th Zahn, *Ueber die Lehre des Addai*, FGK, I, 350–382. K C A Matthes, *Die edess Abgarsage auf ihre Fortbildung untersucht*, Lpz 1882 L J Tixeront, *Les origines de l'église d'Édesse et la légende d'Abgar*, Paris, 1888 R A Lipsius, in DCB (Thaddeus), IV, 875–880, *Idem, Apokry Apostelgesch* (§ 30), *Ergänzungsheft*, 105–108 S Baumer, in ZkTh, XIII, 1889, 707–711 M Bonet-Maury, in *Rev de l'hist des Relig* 1887, 269–283 E Nestle, *de Sancta Cruce*, Berl 1889 R Duval, *Histoire pol rel et litt. d'Édesse*, Paris, 1892 Richardson, BS, 105 sq Harnack, LG, 533–540

From the imperial archives at Edessa, Eusebius[1] obtained information in regard to a Syriac writing in which the story of the wondrous **healing of Abgarus** the Fifth (Ukkâmâ, *i e* the Black, 13–50 A.D) was told Abgarus by letter besought the personal assistance of Jesus, the miraculous physician, and Jesus, also by letter, denied the request, but promised after his ascension to send one of his disciples. In fact, Thaddeus, being sent by Thomas (Jude) in compliance with a heavenly

---

[1] Eusebius, *Hist Eccl* I, 13

command, went to Edessa, cured the sick prince, and set about the conversion of the people to Christianity Eusebius [1] reproduced this correspondence and the history of Thaddeus in literal translation. Whether that which he relates a little later [2] from ancient accounts,[3] in regard to the christianizing of Edessa, came from the same source or not, is uncertain, but quite probable. The legend probably originated not long subsequent to the historical entry of Christianity into Edessa, that is not long after 200 A.D,[4] but concerning the time when it took definite literary form, nothing certain can be said. An enlarged edition of the story exists in the so-called **Doctrina Addai** (*Acta Thaddaei, Acta Edessena*), in which the story of the miracle-working picture of Christ is combined with the form of the legend as known to Eusebius. Since this story was not yet known in Edessa at about 385 A D,[5] the *Doctrina* could not have originated before ± 400, and this conclusion is rendered probable by internal reasons as well.[6] From the Syrians the story passed on to the Armenians,[7] and it is also extant in a modified form in Greek. In the decretal of Gelasius,[8] the letter of Jesus to Abgarus is rejected as apocryphal

§ 102 *The Acts of Peter and of Paul*

Literature and abbreviations, cf. § 30. Preuschen, LG, 128-131, 134-137.

[1] Eusebius, *Hist Eccl* I, 13. 5.
[2] *Idem*, II, 1 6 sq
[3] *Idem*, II, 1. 8
[4] § 25. 1.
[5] Cf *Peregrinatio ad loca sancta*, edit. Gamurrini, *edit. major*, 65-68, *minor*, 34-37
[6] Zahn holds otherwise
[7] Moses of Chorene
[8] VI, 54.

1. Πράξεις Παύλου[1] are first cited by Origen,[2] and, possibly, may have been known as early as Clement[3] Lactantius seems to have drawn his account of the preaching of Peter and Paul at Rome,[4] from these Acts Eusebius[5] names the Acts, and Nicephorus Callisti[6] owes to them his account of the sojourn of Paul at Ephesus, which is also cited from them by Hippolytus in his commentary on Daniel.[7] In the *Catalogus Claromontanus* and in the *Stichometry* of Nicephorus, the number of stichoi is given as 3560 and 3600 respectively[8] As a whole, the Acts are lost The **martyrdom** of Paul has been preserved in revised form : in (*a*) a shorter recension, (1) in Greek, in codices[9] of the ninth and following centuries, and in Slavonic, Ethiopic, and Coptic (incomplete) translations dependent upon the Greek; and (2) in Latin (incomplete),[10] and in (*b*) a longer form,[11] constituting the so-called Linus text [12] **Contents:** Paul, who had raised a cup-bearer of the king from the dead, testifies before Nero in regard to the king whom he expects to come and to subdue all earthly kings. In consequence, Nero causes many Christians to be seized.[13] Paul gives fuller information in regard

---

[1] Cf. Lipsius, AG, II, 284-366 , Egh, 47-54 , AA, 23-44, 104-117, cf 118-177, 178-222, 223-234 Zahn, GNK, II, 2, 865-891.

[2] *Comm Joh.* XX, 12 , Lommatzsch, II, 222. *Princ* I, 2 3 , Lommatzsch, XXI, 46

[3] *Strom* VII, 11 63. VI, 5. 42?   [5] *Hist. Eccl.* III, 3. 5; 25. 4.

[4] *Divinae Inst* IV, 21 2.   [6] *Hist Eccl.* II, 25.

[7] Preuschen, 129, following Bonwetsch

[8] Cf also the List of the sixty canonical books

[9] *Codex Patm 46, saec* IX, and *Codex Ath Vatop 79, saec* X-XI. On the translations, see Lipsius, LIV sq , Preuschen, 130.

[10] *Codex Monac 4554, saec* VIII-IX, *22020, saec* XII, *19642, saec* XV

[11] Zahn, 872-876, against Lipsius, AG, II, 1, 155-162

[12] AA, 23-44   [13] Chaps 1-3

to that king, to the prefect Longus and the centurion Cestus to whom he is delivered,[1] and is then beheaded.[2] By means of his appearance before the emperor, he effects the release of the Christians.[3] From Luke and Titus, Longus and Cestus received the seal.[4] The writing may have originated in Alexandria, Palestine, or Antioch, between 150 and 180 A.D.[5]

2. Jerome[6] must have had the Catholic **Acts of Peter**[7] in mind when he stated that the περίοδαι *Petri* mentioned Peter's wife and daughter. Another of his remarks[8]. appears to have reference to a form of the Clementines different from that which is now extant. Lipsius[9] has found that the Catholic Acts (which are characteristically distinguished from the Gnostic by the harmonious cooperation of the two great apostles) were used by Cyril of Jerusalem,[10] Sulpicius Severus,[11] and Asterius of Amasea.[12] The remnants that are extant in the so-called Marcellus texts treat of the Μαρτύριον τῶν ἁγίων ἀποστόλων Πέτρου καὶ Παύλου. They exist in two (three) recensions · (*a*) in Greek, in a manuscript of the twelfth century,[13] and in Latin in numerous manuscripts,[14] in both cases without the account of Paul's journey,[15] (*b*) in Greek (Latin [old Italian], and Slavonic), in numerous manuscripts,[16] containing the account

[1] Chap 4
[2] Chap 5
[3] Chap 6
[4] Chap. 7.
[5] So Zahn
[6] *Adv Jovin.* I, 26.
[7] Cf Lipsius, AG, II, 1, 284–366, Egh, 47–54, AA, 118–234
[8] *Comm ad Gal* 1 18
[9] pp. 331–333
[10] *Catal* VI
[11] *Hist Eccl* II, 28
[12] *Hom in app prin Petr et Paul* (Combefis, *Auctar noviss* I, Paris, 1648, 168)
[13] *Codex Marcian cl* VII, *37, saec* XII
[14] AA, LXXV-LXXXIII
[15] Chaps 1–21
[16] AA, LXII-LXVII

of the journey, and differing from (*a*) in detail at a number of places. The "Martyrdom" relates first the journey of Paul from the island of Melita to Rome, the murder of his companion Dioscurus, and the punishment visited upon Puteoli on account of this crime, a vision of Paul in Appii Forum, and the announcement of his arrival to Peter[1]. Then the conflicts with the Jews and the effect of the apostolic preaching upon the heathen priests are described[2]. Next Simon Magus appears, and in his presence the emperor, who had been won over by him, examines the apostles as to their preaching[3]. Simon seeks in vain to manifest his power by reading their thoughts[4]. The trial is continued, and Simon repeatedly offers before the emperor, who is becoming impatient, to fly up toward heaven.[5] When he ventures the attempt next day, he plunges down, in answer to the prayer of Peter[6]. In spite of this miracle the apostles are condemned to die, Paul by beheading, and Peter by crucifixion with his head downward, after having told the brethren of his meeting with the Lord.[7] He is interred on the Vatican, but the emperor flees from the enraged people[8]. The deposit of the relics (in a place prepared for them) forms the conclusion[9]. According to Lipsius, a writing of the second century whose apologetical purpose was to reconcile Petrine Jewish Christianity with Pauline heathen Christianity, formed the basis of these recensions, but it is possible to ascribe to them a more innocent origin.

[1] Chaps 1–21
[2] Chaps 22–31.
[3] Chaps 32–43.
[4] Chaps 42–48
[5] Chaps 49–71
[6] Chaps 72–77
[7] Chaps 78–83.
[8] Chaps 84–86
[9] Chaps 87–88.

3 The **Acts of Paul and Thecla**[1] are extant in (*a*) Greek, in a number of manuscripts,[2] (*b*) in Latin, in various translations, (*c*) in Slavonic (still unpublished), (*d*) in Syriac, from the fifth century, (*e*) in Arabic,[3] and (*f*) in Armenian[4]. The work contains a story which is largely invented, but which, nevertheless, exhibits traces of a historical background[5]. It relates the history of a young woman of respectable family in Iconium, who, captivated by the preaching of the apostle, left her father's house and her affianced lover, suffered much torment and persecution, and, finally, after having been wonderfully saved from the jaws of beasts, and commissioned by Paul, successfully preached Christianity, at first at Iconium, and later, in Seleucia. According to Tertullian,[6] the author was a presbyter of Asia Minor, who was deposed on account of his audacity. In telling the story, he had the purpose of making Paul the vehicle of his own conception of Christianity as a message of continence, and its reward — resurrection — based upon belief in one God and his Son, Jesus Christ, and this lesson he sought to make effective through the example of Thecla. A starting-point was furnished to the author by the Acts of the Apostles, but mainly by the Pastoral Epistles, and it would appear that his intention was to contrast his own conception of Paul with the picture of him furnished by these Epistles. We do not possess these "Acts" in their original form, but in abbreviated, though not extensively altered, shape, and freed from

[1] Μαρτύριον τῆς ἁγίας . Θέκλης. Πράξεις Παύλου καὶ Θέκλης. Jerome's name, Περίοδαι *Pauli et Theclae*

[2] Lipsius, AA, XCIX sq [3] Assemani (§ 2. 8 *b*), III, 286

[4] Conybeare, F C , *The Apology and Acts of Apollonius and Other Monuments of Early Christianity* Lond 1894, p 49 sqq.

[5] So von Gutschmid and Ramsay [6] *Bapt* 17.

some, but not all, of the excrescences that are suspicious from an ecclesiastical point of view[1] Consequently, the determination of the circle to which the author belonged is not easy To regard him, with Lipsius, as a Gnostic of ascetic tendencies, is forbidden by the similarity of his Christian conceptions to those which are known to have existed in the church of the second century[2] The date of composition is limited by the use of the Pastoral Epistles on one side, and Tertullian's mention of them on the other, and probably it is to be sought between 160 and 190 A D Zahn places it before 150 A D For references to the legend in the writings of the Fathers, see the works of Lipsius[3] The narrative (appended to some manuscripts) of the deeds of Thecla in a cave at Seleucia in Isauria, and of how she vanished into the mountain away from her pursuers, has nothing to do with the original legend

Editions B Mombritius, *Sanctuarium sive vitae sanctorum* (cf § 104), II, 303-306 (Latin) J E Grabe (§ 2 8 *b*). I, 87 (95)-128 (Greek and Latin) *Bibl Casin* III, Florileg 271-276 (Latin) C Tischendorf (cf § 30), 40-63 W Wright (cf § 30 4), II, 116-145 (English translation from the Syriac) R A Lipsius, AA, 235-272 F C Conybeare (§ 105 6), 49 (61)-88, English translation from Armenian)

Literature The prolegomena to the various editions A Ritschl (cf § 8), 2d edit pp 292-294 A v Gutschmid (§ 30) C Schlau. *Die Acten des Paulus und der Thecla und die altere Thecla-Legende*, Lpz 1877, cf Th Zahn, in GGA, 1877, 1292-1308 J Gwynn, in DCB, IV, 882-896 R A Lipsius (§ 30). AG, II, 1, 424-467, Egh, 61 sq , 104 G Wohlenberg, *Die Bedeutung der Thekla-Akten fur die neutestamentliche Forschung*, in ZkWL. IX, 1888, 343-362

[1] Cf Jerome, *De Viris Illust* 7
[2] See the second Epistle of Clement
[3] Lipsius, 427 sq , cf also *Peregrin ad loc sanct* (edit Gamurrini, *edit major*, 74, *minor*, 43

Th Zahn, GNK, II, 2, 892-910. W M Ramsay, *The Church in the Roman Empire before A.D 170*. Lond 1894, 3d edit. 375-428

§ 103. *The Pseudo-Clementine Recognitions and Homilies*

Editions: (1) *The Homilies* · J B Cotelerius (cf § 3. init) A Schwegler, Stuttg. 1847 A R M Dressel, Gottingen, 1853 Migne, *Patrol Graec* I, 19-468 (text of Dressel) P de Lagarde, *Clementina* Lpz 1865 (The introduction was reprinted in *Mittheilungen*, I, Gottingen, 1884, 26-54) (2) *The Recognitions* · J Sichardus, Basil 1504 (according to Richardson), 1526, 1536 J B Cotelerius (cf § 3). E O Gersdorf, in *Bibl Patr Eccl Lat* I, Lips 1838 Migne, *Patrol. Graec* I, 1201-1454 (3) *The Epitome:* A Turnebus, Paris, 1555 A R M Dressel, Lips 1859 The Syriac version of Recognitions I–III, and Homilies X–XII (not complete), XIII-XIV, was edited by P de Lagarde, Lips 1861 E C Richardson is engaged upon a critical edition of the Recognitions (LG, 229 sq)

Translation. Thomas Smith, in ANF, VIII, 73-346 (Recog Hom).

Literature J L Moshemius, *De turbata per recentiores Platonicos ecclesia comm* §§ XXXIV-XL, in the appendix to his translation of Ralph Cudworth's *Systema intellectuale*, Jenae, 1733 F C Baur, *Die christliche Gnosis*, Tubingen, 1835 A Schliemann, *Die Clementinen nebst den verwandten Schriften*, Hamb 1844. A. Schwegler (§ 27 2), I, 364-406, 481-490 A Hilgenfeld, *Die clement. Recog und Hom.* Jena, 1848 G Uhlhorn, *Die Homilieen und Recognit des Clemens Rom* , Gotting 1854 cf A Hilgenfeld, in ThJ, XIII, 1854, 483-535 J Lehmann, *Die clementin Schriften mit besonderer Rucksicht auf ihr litterar Verhaltniss*, Gotha, 1869 , cf Th Zahn, in GGA, 1869, 905-917. and R A Lipsius, in PKZ, XIX, 1869, 477-482 R A Lipsius, *Die Quellen der romischen Petrussage*, Kiel, 1872 A Hausrath, *Neutestamentl Zeitgeschichte*, IV, 2d edit. Heidelb 1877, 133-153 G Salmon, in DCB, I, 567-578 G Uhlhorn, in RE, III, 277-286 E Renan, *Marc-Aurèle*, Paris, 1882, 74-101 A Harnack (§ 2 7 c), 3d edit. 293-300 Ch Bigg, *The Clementine Homilies*, in *Studia Bibl et Eccl* II, Oxf, 1890, 157-193 J Langen, *Die Clemensromane*, Gotha, 1890.— Richardson, BS, 92-95 Preuschen, LG, 212-231

1. Under the name of **Pseudo-Clementine writings** in the narrower sense, the following works are included:—

(a) Κλήμεντος τοῦ Πέτρου ἐπιδημιῶν κηρυγμάτων ἐπιτομή, 20 Ὁμιλίαι (Διάλογοι[1]), extant in Greek[2] and in part in a Syriac version.[3] Preceding this are Ἐπιστολὴ Πέτρου πρὸς Ἰάκωβον, Διαμαρτυρία περὶ τῶν τοῦ βιβλίου λαμβανόντων (directions as to use), and Ἐπιστολὴ Κλήμεντος πρὸς Ἰάκωβον,

(b) Ἀναγνώσεις (Ἀναγνωρισμοί, *Recognitiones*), in ten books, the original being lost, but extant in numerous manuscripts[4] containing the Latin translation by Rufinus[5] Books I–III are also extant in Syriac,[6]

(c) Ἐπιτομή (or Κλήμεντος ἐπισκόπου Ῥώμης περὶ τῶν πράξεων, ἐπιδημιῶν τε καὶ κηρυγμάτων Πέτρου ἐπιτομή) in a twofold form

2 In the **Homilies**, Clement, whom Peter had installed as bishop of Rome shortly before his death, tells the story of his own career to James, the principal bishop of the church, as he had been directed by his dying master[7] After having sought for truth in vain in the schools of the philosophers, the intelligence that the Son of God had appeared in Judea impelled him to investigate the correctness of the wonderful report upon the spot[8] In Alexandria he met Barnabas, who introduced him to Peter at Cæsarea Peter immediately won him over to his doctrine and caused him to witness his disputation with Simon Magus[9] The interval, until the beginning of the war of words, Peter spent in initiating his pupil

[1] Eusebius, *Hist Eccl.* III, 38 5.
[2] *Codex Paris. graec* 930, *saec* XII, and *Codex Ottobon.* 443, *saec.* XIV.
[3] *Codex Mus. Brit Syr. Add* 12150, *ann* 411
[4] Preuschen, LG, 229 f
[5] Lagarde, *Clem* 1865, Introd 27.
[6] See above, note 3
[7] Cf the Second Epistle.
[8] I, 1–7.
[9] I, 8–22

more nearly in his teachings¹ In the disputation, which lasted three days (though we have only an account of the first, which related to the statements of scripture concerning God), Peter overcame Simon, who fled, pursued by Peter and Clement² They followed him a long time without overtaking him: in Sidon, Berytus, Biblus, Tripolis — he had already been in all of them³ Finally they caught him up in Laodicea, and there the magician was completely routed in a debate (on knowledge of God by means of visions, and on the doctrine of the supreme God, and of evil) which lasted four days.⁴ Peter was able adroitly to turn a stratagem of the vanquished to his further hurt, and he lost his adherents also in Antioch Peter, who everywhere upon his journey had founded and organized congregations, departed then to Antioch, evidently to continue his labors there after the same manner⁵ Such is the thread of discourse, but it is interrupted by numerous episodes: a disputation between Clement and the Alexandrian grammarian Appion,⁶ a long account by Clement concerning his own earlier life,⁷ the finding of his mother,⁸ of his brothers,⁹ and finally of his father,¹⁰ the conversion of his mother to Christianity, etc The theological doctrines of Peter occupy most space, and the principal purpose of the account appears to have been to propagate these doctrines in the form of a **tale.** In this teaching Christianity appeared to be only an improved edition of the Mosaic religion, and the doctrine was that of Gnostic Jewish Christianity (Elchesaitism). The letter of Peter to James,

[1] II–III, 29.
[2] III, 30–73
[3] VII–XII, 2.
[4] XVI–XIX
[5] XX.
[6] IV, 6–27, VI.
[7] V.
[8] XII.
[9] XIII.
[10] XIV.

which precedes all, adjures the latter to preserve the book thus sent to him inviolate from the non-elect, and with this demand James complies while making it known to his presbyters. The **Recognitions** treat the same materials with considerable deviations, especially in the didactic portions, partly by addition, partly by subtraction. At the close, the founding of the church at Antioch and the baptism of Clement's father by Peter are narrated. The book gained its name from the "Recognitions" in the seventh book. The **Epitome** is a meagre abstract of the Homilies. enriched by foreign elements, such as extracts from the letter of Clement to James, from the Martyrdom of Clement according to Simeon Metaphrastes, and from a writing περὶ τοῦ θαύματος τοῦ γεγονότος εἰς παῖδα ὑπὸ τοῦ ἁγίου ἱερομάρτυρος Κλήμεντος, attributed to Ephraim, bishop of Chersonesus.

3. The riddle in literary history, occasioned by the obvious **relationship** between the Homilies and the Recognitions, cannot be solved by supposing one recension to be dependent upon the other[1]. On the contrary, both give evidence of being elaborations of (one or) more originals, whose basal form may have been called Κήρυγμα(τα) Πέτρου. In the mean time, the question[2] of the sources and unity of content of the two recensions is not answered, and it cannot be advanced, except on the basis of an exact comparison of texts, and particularly of an investigation of the Biblical and extra-canonical citations[3]. For this reason the question of the origin and purpose, the time and place of composi-

---

[1] Hilgenfeld (1848) made the Homilies dependent on the Recognitions, and Uhlman (1854) the Recognitions on the Homilies
[2] Uhlhorn (1878), cf Hilgenfeld, Lehmann, and Lipsius.
[3] Cf particularly Lagarde, 1865, introduction.

tion, of the Pseudo-Clementine literature still awaits a final solution. Presupposing their unity, Baur[1] regarded them as a document of the Judaism, dominant in the primitive Roman congregation. Lipsius[2] assumes that their oldest basis was the strongly anti-Pauline *Acta Petri*, which originated long before the middle of the second century, and that a fragment thereof, the Preaching of Peter, was worked over about 140–145 A.D. in the anti-Gnostic interest. He thinks that the Ἀναγνωρισμοὶ Κλήμεντος proceeded from these Acts, and were worked over again twice independently, even during the second century, in the Homilies (anti-Marcionite) and in the Recognitions (Jewish-Christian, with catholic tendencies). Hilgenfeld has clung to his view,[3] that the Recognitions and Homilies are to be traced back through the Περίοδαι Πέτρου to a Πέτρου κήρυγμα, and that they are "a very fertile and rich mine for the history and development of Roman Jewish Christianity."[4] Over against these and other views, Harnack defends the opinion that the Recognitions and Homilies in their present form did not belong to the second century, but, at the earliest, to the first half of the third;[5] that they were not written by heretical Christians, but, most probably, by catholic Christians (on account of the views as to the canon, polity, theological position, etc.), with the purpose, not of formulating a theological system, but of instructing to edification, and, besides, of

---
[1] Cf. also Schwegler.
[2] Cf also A. Hausrath, *Neutestamentl. Zeitgesch.* 2d edit., IV, 1877, 133–153
[3] Cf *Nov. Test* etc. (§ 3), 2d edit. IV, 51 f.
[4] Hilgenfeld (1854, p 535).
[5] Cf. also Lagarde (1865), and Zahn (GGA, 1876, 1436).

opposing heretical manifestations; and, finally, that even the author of the Recognitions and Homilies apparently was acquainted with their original Jewish-Christian sources only in their catholic form. Bigg regards the Homilies as an Ebionite recension of an older catholic original The Pseudo-Clementine writings originated in Eastern Syria.[1] Where and by whom they were worked over cannot be fixed, but good reasons can be adduced in favor of Rome.[2]

4. The oldest **attestation** of the Pseudo-Clementine writings is Origen, who in his commentary on Matthew[3] cited some sentences similar to passages in both works.[4] Eusebius[5] was acquainted with a voluminous writing which contained Πέτρου καὶ ’Αππίωνος διάλογοι, and which must have stood in close relationship to the Clementines. In the Bardesanite dialogue *De fato*,[6] a passage is copied[7] from the Recognitions,[8] unless, indeed, the dialogue formed the original. Basil and Gregory inserted a passage from the fourteenth (now the tenth) book of the Recognitions into the *Philocalia*.[9] Epiphanius[10] speaks of περιόδοις καλουμέναις ταῖς διὰ Κλήμεντος γραφείσαις, which were in use among the Ebionites Paulinus of Nola[11] appears to have undertaken to translate the Clementines in spite of insufficient knowledge of Greek. Rufinus was governed in his translation[12] by the same prejudices as in his ren-

---

[1] So Uhlhorn.   [2] So Harnack.
[3] *Comm. Matth Ser* 77 (Lommatzsch, IV, 401).
[4] *Recog.* VII, 38, *Homil* XIII, 13.
[5] *Hist. Eccl* III, 38. 5   [6] Cf. § 25. 2.
[7] Cf. Eusebius, *Praep Evang.* VI, 10 11–36
[8] *Recog.* IX, 19–27
[9] Chap 23 (Robinson's edit. 210–212).   [11] *Ep.* XLVI, 2, Hartel, 387.
[10] *Panarion*, XXX, 15.   [12] See No. 1, above.

lering of the *Principia* of Origen;[1] he was unable to make the heresies of the book agree with the recognized orthodoxy of the Roman Clement, and therefore held that they were interpolations.[2] One is unwilling to suppose that Jerome, who copied Eusebius in Chapter 15 of his *De Viris Illustribus*, was unacquainted with the work of Rufinus.[3] Further attestations are given by Preuschen.[4]

[1] Cf. § 61. 4, and 8 a.
[2] Rufinus, *Adult. libror. Orig.* (Lommatzsch, XXV, 386); cf. *Peror. in Orig. Comm Rom.* (Lommatzsch, VII, 460), and the preface of his translation of the *Rec. ad Gaudentium episcopum*.
[3] Cf. *Adv. Jovin.* I, 26, *Comm. ad Gal.* 1. 18; see, however, § 101. 2
[4] In Harnack's LG, 224–229.

FIFTH SECTION

THE MARTYROLOGIES

Editions: B Mombritius, *Sanctuarium sive Vitae sanctorum*, 2 Tomi, no date or place (according to Neumann, p 275, 4, before 1480) L Surius, *De probatis sanctorum vitis*, Colon 1570-1575. *Acta Sanctorum*, etc, edit. J. Bollandus all. (§ 2. 8 c). Th. Ruinart, *Acta*, etc (§ 2 8 c) The *Depositio martyrum*, in Th. Mommsen (§ 91 7 b), p. 71 sq. The *Calendarium antiquissimum ecclesiae Carthaginiensis*, in J Mabillon, *Veter Analect* III, Paris, 1682, 398-401, cf 402-422 The Syrian martyrologies by W. Wright, in the *Journal of Sacred Literature and Biblical Record*, VIII, Lond 1866, 45-56 (Syriac); 423-432 (English), German, by E Egli, in *Altchristliche Studien*, Zurich, 1887, 5-29. The *Martyrium Hieronymianum*, edit by J B de Rossi (†) and L Duchesne, in *Acta Sanctorum*, preceding the second part of the second volume for November, Bruxel 1894

Literature · S Le Nainde Tillemont, *Mémoires*, etc. (§ 2. 3 a), vols. iv, v. L Duchesne, *Les sources du martyrologe Hiéronymien*, in *Mélanges d'Archéol et d'Hist* V, 1885, 120-160 Cf. Harnack, in ThLZ, XIII, 1888, 350-352. K J Neumann (§ 45), *passim*, and 274-331 Cf the *Analecta Bollandiana* (§ 2 8 c), and the catalogues of the *Codices hagiographici* of Brussels, Ghent, Paris, Milan, Chartres, Le Mans, etc, published therein Preuschen, LG, 807-834 The figures used in connection with the abbreviation Boll (= *Acta sanctorum*, edit Bollandus, etc) are those of the original edition as far as the fifth volume for October. Ruin (= Ruinart) is cited in the handy edition of 1859

§ 104. *In General*

The rapt veneration with which the entire church nourished itself upon the deeds and fortunes of her great apostles, has a counterpart in the interest that single congregations or groups of congregations showed in the glorious end of the heroes, who for their faith met death firmly as a sacrifice to the civil power or the rage of the rabble At even an early date,[1] men celebrated the memorial day of such martyrs, and martyr-calendars gradually arose, such as exist to-day in the Roman *Depositio martyrum* in the Chronographer of the year 354, in the old Carthaginian Calendar, dating from the beginning of the sixth century, in the Syrian *Martyrologium*[2] and in the *Martyrologium Hieronymianum*, dating from the period of Sixtus III of Rome (432–440 A D) The last named, which itself was compiled from several originals,[3] became the source of the later martyrologies On such memorial days the history of the martyr in question was read, it might be a copy of the protocol of the judicial process which had been acquired in some way, and about which an edifying framework could be fashioned, or it might be a rehearsal of the facts given by eye-witnesses of the martyrdom according to the best of their knowledge, though without concealing their Christian standpoint. Unfortunately the genuine Acts of the great majority of martyrs who are known by name, so far as such ever existed, have been displaced by later legends[4] Even the Συναγωγὴ τῶν ἀρχαίων μαρτυρίων by Eusebius of Cæsarea, in which that learned historian collected everything that he could ascertain,[5] has been lost and only his work on the Palestinian martyrs[6] during Diocletian's persecution is extant.

---

[1] *Martyr Polycarp* 18.
[2] Manuscript of the year 412.
[3] So Duchesne and Harnack.
[4] E g Simeon Metaphrastes.
[5] Cf. *Hist Eccl* IV, 15 47, V, *proem* ; 2, 4 3, 21. 5
[6] B Violet, *Die palastinischen Martyrer des Eusebius von Casarea*, TU, XIV, 4, Lpz 1896.

§ 105 From Antoninus Pius to Septimius Severus

1. Passio Polycarpi. Eusebius inserted in his *Church History*,[1] literally or in abstract, the larger part of a letter written by the congregation of Smyrna to that of Philomelium (Phrygia), and to all other congregations of the holy catholic church,[2] concerning the martyr-death of their bishop **Polycarp** and his associates, under the proconsulate of the L. Statius Quadratus on the 23d February, 155 A.D[3] The whole letter is extant in Greek in five manuscripts.[4] There exists, besides, a *Passio Polycarpi* in numerous Latin manuscripts which are based in part on Rufinus' translation of Eusebius' account, in part, on an independent but careless version of a Greek original which differed from the recension now extant, and in part on both[5] Eusebius' account is also preserved in a Coptic version. The freshness and directness of the narrative speak for themselves, and neither form nor content gives sufficient occasion for the assumption of forgery or interpolation. The additions to the manuscripts of the *Martyrium*, respecting date, dedication, and transmission,[6] were appended later.

Compare the editions (§ 3) of Zahn (XLVIII-LV, 132-168), and Lightfoot (I, 588-702, II, 935-998, 1005-1014) — Translation: Roberts and Donaldson, in ANF, I, 39-44 — A Harnack, *Die Zeit des Ignatius* (§ 9) E Amélineau, *Les actes coptes du martyre de St Polycarpe* in the *Proceedings of the Soc. of Biblical Archæology*, X, 1888, 391-417 Cf A Harnack, in ThLZ, XIV, 1889, 30 sq. — Bollandus (Jan 13), Jan II, 691-707 Ruinart, 74-99.

---

[1] *Hist. Eccl* IV, 15.
[2] So the manuscripts of the *Martyrium*, Eusebius gives the address as "To the churches in Pontus"
[3] Cf § 8 1.
[4] *Codd. Mosq.* 159, *Hieros S. Sep* 1 *all.*
[5] Harnack, 77-90.
[6] Chaps. 20-22.

2 *Passio Carpi, Papyli et Agathonicae* The Acts of Carpus, Papylus (of Thyatira), and Agathonice (whose martyr-death occurred at Pergamos,[1] and is recorded by Eusebius after that of Polycarp and Pionius[2]), are preserved in a Paris codex[3] It contains no date, but the original record may be assigned with great probability to the time of Marcus Aurelius Certain features, the locality, and not least of all, the fanaticism that appears in the conduct of Agathonice, and which the writer approves, combine to make the conclusion possible that the martyrs did not stand far removed from the radical Montanistic movement even if they were not themselves Montanists. A longer recension, which emanated from Simeon Metaphrastes, and which is extant in numerous manuscripts, incorrectly places the martyrdom in the time of Decius

Editions B Aubé, in *Revue archéol* 1881, 348 sqq *Idem, L'église et l'état dans la seconde moitié du IIIe siècle*, Paris, 1885, 499–506 A Harnack, in TU, III, 3, 4, 1888, 433–466 Cf Th Zahn, FGK, I, 279 J B Lightfoot (see above), I, 625 sq.— Boll (Apl. 13), Apr II, 120–125, 968–973

3 *Acta S Justini philosophi et soc ejus* Under the prefecture of Junius Rusticus, *i e* between 163 and 167 A D., the Christian philosopher Justin[4] and the Christians Charito, Charitus, Euelpistus, Hierax, Paon, and Liberianus were martyrs at Rome The simple and plain[5] account apparently reproduces the steps of the proceedings faithfully. Eusebius appears not to have been acquainted with it.

[1] Eusebius, *Hist. Eccl* IV, 15. 48.
[2] Cf § 106.
[3] *Codex Paris. graec* 1468.
[4] Cf § 36.
[5] MSS. *Codex Vatic.* 655 *Cod Cryptens.*

Editions C Otto, in *Corpus*, etc (cf. § 33), IJI, 3d edit 1879, 266-278 (cf. XLVI-L) — Boll (Apl 13) Apl II, 104-119. Ruinart, 101-107 — Translation M. Dods, in ANF, I, 305-306.

4 *Epistola Ecclesiarum Viennensis et Lugdunensis* In the year 177,[1] the congregations at **Lugdunum** (Lyons) and **Vienne**, in Gaul, were overtaken by severe oppression They sent an account of their afflictions to the congregations of Asia Minor and Phrygia, most of which Eusebius inserted in his History[2] The writing contains a very lively and clear description of the persecution

Boll (June 2) June I, 160-168 Ruinart, 107-117.

5 *Acta proconsularia martyrium Scilitanorum.* On the 17th of July, 180 A D., at Carthage, the Christians, Speratus, Nartzallis, Cittinus, Donata, Secunda, and Hestia [Vestia], of Scili, were sentenced to death by the sword, and executed by the proconsul, P Vigellius Saturninus They are known as the **Scillitan Martyrs**. The Acts, which are distinguished by their brevity of form, are preserved in Latin and Greek. The Latin form[3] seems more closely allied to the original; in connection with it, the Greek form, which exists in a Paris codex,[4] and in several Latin recensions,[5] is to be taken into account.

Editions and Literature · J Mabillon (see § 104). IV, 153 (*Codex Augiens*). C Baronius, *Annales eccl ad ann. 202* (according to lost manuscripts) H Usener, *Acta mart Scilit graec. edita,* Ind Schol ,

[1] Eusebius, *Hist. Eccl.* V, introd., see also the statement of the *Chronicon,* after *Ann Abr 2183*
[2] *Hist Eccl.* V, 1-3 Transl , ANF, VIII, 778-784
[3] *Codex Mus Britt. 11880, saec.* IX (cf. fragment in *Cod Augiens.*).
[4] *Codex Paris graec 1470, Ann 890*
[5] *E g Codex Carnot 190, Bruxell. saec.* XII

Bonn, 1881   B Aubé, *Les Chrétiens dans l'empire Romain*, etc. Paris, 1881, 503–509 (*Cod Paris suppl lat 2179* [Silos])   *Analecta Bollandiana* (§ 2 8 c), VIII. 1889, 5–8 (*Cod Carnot*)   On the *Codex Bruxell* , cf *Catalogus*, etc (§ 104), I, 1, 50, 133   J A Robinson (see No 7, below) in TSt, I, 2 1891, 106–121 (*Codex Mus Britt* , *Codex Paris* 1470, *Baron* , *Cod. Paris* 2179)   In B Aubé's *Étude sur un nouveau texte des martyrs Scillitains*, Paris, 1881, pp 22–39, the then known texts are printed — Translation Neumann, 72–74   J A Robinson, ANF, IX, 285 — Boll (July 17), July IV, 204–216   Ruinart, 129–134 (Cod Colbert).

6 Eusebius relates [1] that a cultivated man, named **Apollonius**, well versed in philosophy, was executed in the time of Commodus, on account of his Christianity, after having defended his faith eloquently before the Senate and before his judge, Perennis (until 185, *Praefectus praetorio*)   The Acts were incorporated by Eusebius in his collection [2]   His statements are verified by the "*Martyrdom of St Apollonius, the Ascetic*," which are extant in Armenian , but the assertions of Jerome,[3] that Apollonius was a senator, and was condemned by the Senate, and also that he wrote an extended defence, are shown to be embellishments of the account of Eusebius   It is even doubted whether Apollonius was a Roman citizen   It is not very clear from the Acts what *rôle* was played by the Senate in the proceedings, their beginning being lost   The defensive speech of Apollonius is of interest on account of its relation to apologetical literature   It is possible that Tertullian was acquainted with it when he wrote his *Apologeticus*   The Bollandists found an interpolated Greek text in the *Codex Paris 1219*

Editions and Literature   F C C(onybeare) in *The Guardian*, 1893, June 18 (English translation), following the Armenian in the

[1] *Hist Eccl* V, 21.   [2] Cf § 104   [3] *De Viris Illust* 42

collection of martyrologies published by the Mechitarists (Venice, 1874), I, 138-143 *Idem, The Apology and Acts of Apollonius, and Other Monuments of Early Christianity*, Lond 1894, 29-48 A Harnack, in SBBA, 1893, 721-746 (German translation by Burchardi). R Seeberg, in NKZ, IV, 1893. 836-872 E G Hardy, *Christianity and the Roman Government*, Lond 1894, 200-208 Th Mommsen, in SBBA, 1894, 497-503 A Hilgenfeld, in ZwTh, XXXVII, 1894, 58-91, 636 sqq Anal Boll XIV, 1895, 284-294.

7. *Passio SS. Perpetuae et Felicitatis.* On the 7th of March, 203 (202) A D , five catechumens, Vibia **Perpetua**, who belonged to a good family, **Felicitas** and Revocatus, both slaves, Saturus and Saturninus, suffered martyrdeath under the governor Hilarianus, apparently at Carthage (not at Tuburbo or Thuburbo) An eyewitness has given with dramatic power a most realistic and striking account of this martyrdom, interweaving therewith the visions of Perpetua and Saturus according to their own accounts. The hypothesis that the author, who was evidently a Montanist, was no less a person than Tertullian,[1] has been defended on good grounds by Robinson. The Revelation of John, and apparently the Shepherd of Hermas (but in no case the Apocalypse of Peter), exerted an influence upon these visions The narrative is preserved in two forms : the older in both Greek[2] and Latin[3] The peculiar relation between the two texts may perhaps be explained by the supposition of publication in both languages (Tertullian!). The later and shorter form has been preserved in Latin in numerous manuscripts. It incorrectly transfers the martyrdom to the period of Valerian

---

[1] Cf. *De Anima*, 55
[2] *Codex Hieros S Sep. 1. saec* X.
[3] *Codd Compendiens.* [*Paris Lat 17626*] *saec* X; *Casin. saec.* XI (*Salisb.*), *Ambrosian. C. 210, infr saec.* XI (still unpublished).

and Gallienus. Augustine was acquainted with the Acts.¹

Editions and Literature L Holstenius, Rom 1633 (Cod Casin) B. Aubé, *Les Chrétiens*, etc (cf 5, above), 509–525 (shorter form) *Catalogus*, etc (cf § 104), I, 1 158–161 (*Idem*) J R Harris and S K Gifford, *The Acts of the Martyrdom of Perpetua and Felicitas*, Lond 1890 (Cod Hieros.), cf Harnack, in ThLZ, XV, 1890, 403–406 O v Gebhardt, in DLZ, XII, 1891, 121–123, L Duchesne, in *Compt rend de l'Acad de l'Inscrip et belles-lettres*, XIX, 1891, 39–54, and L Massebieau, in *Rev de l'Hist des Relig* XXIV, 1891, 97–101 J. A. Robinson, *The Passion of S Perpetua, newly edited from the MSS*, in TSt, I, 2, 1891, cf A Harnack, in ThLZ, XVII, 1892, 68–71, Th Zahn, in ThLB, XIII, 1892, 41–45, Anal Bolland. XI. 1892, 100–102, 369–373 (*Un nouveau manuscript des Actes der Saintes Félicité et Perpétue. Cod Ambros.*) — Translation G Kruger, in *Christliche Welt*, III, 1890, 785–790 (abbreviated) — Boll (Mar. 7) March I, 630–638 Ruinart, 134–167 (Compend Salisb.).

§ 106 *From Decius to Licinius*

In the following list are contained the names, given by Ruinart, Tillemont, the *Dictionary of Christian Biography*, and Preuschen, of those martyrs in connection with whom genuine acts, or acts that appear to possess a genuine basis, are extant In most cases, an exact investigation is lacking For manuscripts, etc , see Preuschen, in Harnack's *Litteraturgeschichte*

1. *Passio Pionii.* After the martyrdom of Polycarp, and before that of Carpus and his companions, Eusebius[2] mentions that of the Marcionite Metrodorus, and that of Pionius, both of whom suffered martyr-death at Smyrna. While Eusebius has in mind the period of Marcus Aurelius, the Latin Acts[3] place the martyrdom of Pionius and his sister(?) Sabina, Asclepiades, the

---

[1] Cf. the passages in Neumann, p. 300.   [3] Two *Codd. Colbert all.*
[2] *Hist. Eccl.* IV, 15. 46–47.

Montanist Macedonia, Lemnus and the (Marcionite) presbyter Metrodorus, under the second consulate of Decius (and Vettius Gratus), *i e.* in the year 250 (March 12) It is possible that the unpublished Greek Acts[1] will show that Eusebius, who incorporated the Acts in his collection,[2] in this case also[3] was right, and that the Latin Acts are only a recension of the genuine text[4]

Literature Th Zahn, *Patr. Apost* (§ 3) D L, 164–165 J B Lightfoot, *Apost Fathers* (§ 3), I, 622–626, 695–702 An edition of the Greek Acts has been announced, by O v Gebhardt. — Boll (Feb 1) Febr I, 37–46 Ruinart, 185–198

2. *Acta disputationis S Achatii episc et mart* Achatius (or Acacius), bishop of Antioch in Phrygia, martyr (confessor) under Decius He has been confounded with Acacius, bishop of Melitene, in Armenia Secunda

Boll (Mar 31) Mart III. 903–905 Ruinart, 199–202

3 *Acta S. Maximi mart* Maximus, martyr in Asia Minor (Ephesus ?) under Decius, proconsulate of Optimus

Boll (Apl 30) Apl III, 732 sq Ruinart, 202–204.

4. *Acta S. Luciani et Marciani* Lucianus, Marcianus, Florius, martyrs in Nicomedia, under Decius, on Oct 26. Compare Prudentius, *Peristeph.* 11.

Boll. (Oct 26) Oct XI, 804–819 Ruinart, 210–214

5. *Acta S. Cypriani* Cyprian, bishop of Carthage, met martyr-death, after a year's imprisonment, on Sept 14, 258, under Valerian, Galerius Maximus being pro-

---

[1] *Cod Venet Marc 359, saec.* XII.
[2] Cf. § 104.
[3] As in the case of Carpus, which see
[4] So Zahn

consul. A number of manuscripts of the *Acta proconsularia*, and an account in Cyprian's life, written by the deacon Pontius, have been preserved.

Boll. (Sep 14) Sept IV, 191-348 (*Vita*, 325-332, *Acta*, 332-335). Ruin 243-264 Hartel (*Opera Cypriani*), III, pp. CX-CXIV (*Acta proconsul.*).

6 *Acta SS Fructuosi, Eulogii et Augurii martyrum.* The oldest Spanish Acts. Fructuosus, bishop of Tarragona, and two of his deacons, Eulogius and Augurius, became martyrs under Valerian and Gallienus (proconsuls, Aemilianus and Bassus), on Jan. 21, in the year 259, according to Augustine, who was acquainted with the Acts. See his *Sermon*, 273, and also Prudentius, *Peristeph.* 6.

Boll. (Jan. 21) Jan II, 339-341. Ruinart, 264-267.

7. *Passio SS. Jacobi, Mariani, etc.* Jacobus, a deacon, and Marianus, a lector, martyrs under Valerian.

Boll. (Apl. 30) Apl. III, 745-749 Ruinart, 267-274

8. *Passio SS. Montani, Lucii et aliorum martyrum Africanorum* Montanus and Lucius, martyrs at Carthage, soon after Cyprian, about 259

Boll. (Feb. 24) Febr III, 454-459. Ruinart, 274-282.

9. *Martyrium S. Nicephori.* Nicephorus, martyr under Valerian and Gallienus, about 260, place unknown.

Boll (Feb 9) Febr. II, 283-288. Addit. 894 sq. Ruinart, 282-288.

10. *Acta SS. MM. Claudii, Asterii et aliorum* Claudius, Asterius, Neo, brothers, martyrs at Ægea, in Cilicia, under the governor (*praeses*) Lycias, probably 303 (not 285).

Boll. (Aug. 23) Aug. IV, 567-572 Ruinart, 308-311.

11 *Passio Genesii mimi* Genesius, a play-actor at Rome, martyr, 303 (285)

Boll (Aug 25) Aug V, 119-123   Ruinart, 311-313

12 *Passio Rogatiani et Donatiani* Rogatianus and Donatianus, of good family, brothers, martyrs at Nantes under Diocletian and Maximian.

Boll (May 24) May V, 279-281.   Ruinart, 321-324

13 *Acta Maximiliani* Maximilianus, martyr at Thebeste, in Numidia, under Diocletian, on March 12, 295, consulate of Tuscus and Anulinus

Ruinart, 339-342

14 *Acta Marcelli* Marcellus, centurion, martyr at Tingis (Tangier), in Mauretania, on Oct 30 (298)

Boll (Oct 30) Oct XIII, 274-284   Ruinart, 342-344

15 *Passio Cassiani* Cassianus, court clerk, martyr at Tingis The Acts form an appendix to those of Marcellus

Ruinart, 344 sq

16 *Passio S Procopii* Procopius, lector and exorcist, born at Jerusalem, residing at Scythopolis, martyr on July 7, 303, at Cæsarea in Palestine (cf Eusebius, *Mart Pal* I, 1)

Boll (July 8) July II, 551-576   Ruinart, 380 sq

17 *Acta S Felicis*. Felix, bishop of Tubzoca (Thibaris, in Numidia?), martyr at Carthage under the proconsulate of Anulinus, on Aug 30, 303

Boll. (Jan 14) Jan II, 233   Ruinart, 388-391. St. Baluzius, *Miscellanea*, II, Paris, 1679, 77-81.

18 *Passio S Savini*. Savinus, martyr at Rome under Maximian

Baluzius, *loc cit* 47-55.

19. *Acta SS Saturnini, Dativi, et aliorum plurimorum martyrum in Africa.* Saturninus, a presbyter, Dativus, a senator, and many other men and women from Abitina, martyrs at Carthage under the proconsulate of Anulinus, on Feb. 11, 304. The acts were produced by the Donatists at the disputation in 411, and were acknowledged by the Catholics (Augustin *Brevic. collat.* III, 32).

Boll (Feb 11) Febr. II, 513-519   Ruinart, 413-422   Baluzius, 56-76

20 *Acta SS Agapes, Chioniae, Irenes, etc.* Agape, Chionia, and Irene, from Thessalonica, martyrs on the first of April (so Ruinart), 304.

Boll (Apl 3) Apl I, 245-250   Ruinart, 422-427.

21 *Acta SS Didymi et Theodorae.* Didymus and Theodora, martyrs at Alexandria (303?), cf. Ambrosius, *Virg* II, 4.

Boll (Apl 28) Apl III, 572-575.   Ruinart, 427-432.

22. *Passio S. Irenaei, Episc. Sirm.* Irenæus, bishop of Sirmium, in Pannonia, martyr under Diocletian and Maximian, on 25th March (6th April) (304)

Boll (Mart 25) Mart III, 555-557.   Ruinart, 432-434

23. *Passio S. Pollionis et aliorum martyrum.* Pollio, lector at Cibalæ in Pannonia, martyr at about the same time with Irenæus, on 28th (27th) April (304).

Boll. (Apl. 28) Apl III, 565-567.   Ruinart, 434-436.

24. *Acta S. Eupli diac. et mart.* Euplius, deacon, martyr at Catania, in Sicily, under Diocletian and Maximian (304).

Ruinart, 436-439.

25 *Passio S Philippi episc* Philippus, bishop of Heraclea, martyr at Adrianopolis (304)

Boll (Oct 22) Oct IX, 537-553 (Palmé). Ruinart, 439-448

.26 *Acta SS Tarachi, Probi, et Andronici* Tarachus of Claudiopolis in Isauria, Roman citizen, previously a soldier, Probus of Side (Perge) in Pamphylia, philosopher, Andronicus of Ephesus, of eminent family, martyrs at Tarsus, under Diocletian and Maximian (304)

Boll. (Oct 11) Oct. V, 560-584   Ruinart, 448-476

27. *Acta S Crispinae mart*   Crispina of Thagara; according to Augustine a member of a prominent and wealthy family, a martyr at Thebeste under the proconsul Anulinus, on Dec 5 (304)   (See Augustine, *in Psalm.* CXX n 13; CXXXVII, n. 3, 14, 17; cf. *Serm.* 286, 354)

Ruinart, 476-479

28 *Passio S Sereni mart*   Serenus, a Greek, gardener, martyr at Sirmium, in Pannonia, under Maximian (307 ?)

Boll (Feb. 23) Febr III, 364-366.   Ruinart, 516-518.

29 *Acta SS Phileae et Philoromi.*   Phileas (bishop of Thmuis, cf § 67) and Philoromus, subordinate officers, martyrs at Alexandria under the prefect Culcianus (306).

Boll (Feb 4) Febr I; 459-464   Ruinart, 518-521

30 *Passio S. Quirini episc et mart.* Quirinus, bishop of Siscia in Upper Pannonia, martyr under Diocletian and Maximian, cf. Eusebius, *Chron. ad. ann. 310.* Prudentius, *Peristeph* 7.

Boll. (June 4) June I, 380-384   Ruinart, 521-525.

31. *Passio S. Petri Balsami*   Petrus Balsamus of

Eleutheropolis, martyr at Aulana, in Samaria, under Galerius (311). Probably identical with Petrus Abselamus, an ascetic, mentioned by Eusebius (*Mart Palest* 10, 2).

Boll. (Jan. 3) Jan. I, 128 sq   Ruinart, 525–527.

32. *Passio S. Quirionis, Candidi, Domni, etc. (quadraginta martyres).* At Sebaste, in Armenia, **forty** Christians (the so-called "Forty Knights") are said to have become **martyrs** under Licinius, about 320 A.D.[1] Ruinart omitted their Acts as spurious, and the Bollandists inserted the Latin translation, not the Greek original Bonwetsch defended the possibility of their genuineness, and published in Greek[2] and old Slavonic[3] a *Testament* of the martyrs, wherein they gave directions concerning their remains   This is declared by Bonwetsch, in agreement with Haussleiter, to be genuine.

Editions of the *Testament:* P Lambecius, *Commentarii de bibliotheca Caes. Vidobonensi,* IV, Vienn 1671 (Greek), 2d edit (by A F Kollarius), IV, Vienn 1778, 225 sqq. (Greek and Latin). M Bonwetsch, in NKZ, III, 1892, 705 (713-721)-726, cf J. Haussleiter, *Idem,* 978–988   Boll (Mar 10) Mar. II, 12–29.

[1] Cf Basilius M *Orat* XIX
[2] *Cod Vienn. Theol* X
[3] *Codices of the Library of the Troitzko-Sergiew. Laura* at Moscow, No 180 (1859) and 755 (1628). *saec.* XV.

INDEX

Abdias, **92**, 95, 253.
Abgar VIII Bar Manu, 249.
Abgarus of Edessa, **75**, 363.
Abgarus, Legend of, **364** f
Acacius of Melitene, 386.
Achatius of Antioch (Phrygia), 386
Acta Agapes, Chioniae, etc 389,
Archelai, 70, Claudii, Asterii, etc
387, Crispinae, 390, Cypriani,
386, Didymi et Theodorae, 389,
disput. Achatii, 386, Edessena,
365, Eupli, 389, Felicis, 388,
Fructuosi, Eulogii, etc 387, Justini, **381**, Luciani et Marciani,
386, Marcelli, 388, Mart Scilitanorum, **382**, Maximi mart. 386,
Maximiliani, 388, Acta Nerei et
Achillei, 90, Phileae et Philoromi,
390, Proconsularia, 387, Saturnini, Dativi, etc. 389, Symphorosae, 253; Tarachi, Probi et
Andronici, 390, Thaddaei, 365
Acts of Andrew, 55, 88, 89, **94**, 363,
of Andrew and Matthew, 95, of
the Apostles, 13, 27, **57** f, 61, 188,
254, 369, Gnostic, **88** ff, of John,
88, 89, **90**, 363; of Justin, 106,
of Lateran Synod (649 A D), 338,
of Martyrs, 379, of Paul, 89, 363,
366, of Paul and Thecla, **369** f,
of Peter, 89, **89**, 363, **367**, 375,
of Peter and Andrew, 95, of Peter
with Simon, 90, of Philip, 89, of
Pilate, **57**, of Synod of Ephesus
(431 A D), 220, of Synods, **352** ff,
of Thomas, 38, 89, 363

Adamantius (see Dialogus de Recta
Fide), 174, 245 f
Adelphius, 85
Aeglon, 222
Aelian, 231.
Aelius, deacon, 296
Aemilianus, proconsul, 387
Aetius, Placita of, 112
African baptismal symbol, 355.
Agape, martyr, 389
Agapius, 94
Agathonice, martyr, 381
Aglaophon, physician, 238, 239
Agrippa Castor, 70, **143**
Ahymnus, 295
Alcinous the Platonist, 331
Aleatores, adv See Pseudo-Cyprian
Alexander, of Alexandria, 124, 128,
221, bishop, 164, of Byzantium,
222, of Jerusalem, 161, 171, 175,
211, **247**, Severus, 248, 251, 339,
340
Alexandria, School of, **160** ff.
Alexandrians, Epistle to, 16
Allegorical interpretation, 208, 277,
302, 325
Allegory, Use of, 182
Ἀλλογενεῖς, 83
Alogi, **154**, 336.
Altercatio Jasonis et Papisci. See
Jason
—— Simonis et Theophili, 105.
Amastris, Epistle to Church in, 156
Ambrose (Ambrosius), 51, 81, 190,
325, 389
Ambrosiaster, 90.

393

394   INDEX

Ambrosius, friend of Origen, 176, 196, 201, 203, a Greek, 113, (Oratio ad Graecos), 113
Ammon of Berenice, 212
Ammonian sections, 225
Ammonius, of Alexandria, **224**, Saccas, 175, 176, 225.
Amos, 173, 192
'Αναβατικὸν 'Ησαίου, 83, Παύλου, 83
Anastasius, Apocrisiarius, 343, presbyter, 243, Sinaita, 124, 127, 162, 172, 208, 326, 338.
Anatolius, Alexandrinus, 204, of Laodicea, **216**.
Andreas, of Crete, 239, Monophysite monk, 101, presbyter, 203
Andrew, 52.
Andronicus, martyr, 390.
Anicetus of Rome, 72, 78, 145.
Anonymus, Arabicus, 82, Eusebianus, 153.
Anti-Donatist Synod (313 A D), 349.
Anti-Gnostic Writings, 121 f, 267
Anti-Heretical Writings, **99**, 134, 148, 121 f, **265**, 267, 268, 279, 332, 333, 334, 349, 350.
Anti-Jewish Writings, 302, 319, 331, 346   See also Judaism
Anti-Marcionite Writings, 111, 134, 143, 144, 247, 266, 269, 279, 333, 338, 349
Anti-Montanistic Writer (Eusebius), 122, 144.
Anti-Montanistic Writings, 122, 125, 127, 144, 153 f, 276, 321.
Anti-Novatianist Writings, 349, 357.
Anti-Valentinian Writings, 267.
Antichrist, 336 f
Antilegomena, 37, 41.
Antinoites of Egypt, 247.
Antiochian school, 115.
Antiochians, Epistles to, 30, 245, 247.
Antiochus of St. Saba, 27, 39, 361
Antiquity, Argument from, **98**, 249.

Antonianus, bishop, 294
Antoninus Pius, 76, 102, 106, 108, 121, 122, 123, 128, 224, 380.
Antonius (Melissa), 114, 239.
Anulinus, proconsul, 388, 389, 390.
Apelleiaci, 277
Apelles, **81** f., 119, 143, 268.
Apelles' Gospel, 82.
Aphraates, 17, 120.
Aphrodisius, 215
Apion, **224**
Apocalypse of Abraham, 83
'Αποκαλύψεις τοῦ 'Αδάμ, 83.
Apocalypse of John, 14, 19, **35**, 37, 39, 42, 195, 208, 209, 320, 321, 329, 336, 337, 348, 384, of Paul, 38, of Peter, **36** f., 42, 65, 93, 171, 384
Apocalypses, 13
Apocrypha (O T.), 103.
Apocryphal Gospels, **50** f
Apollinaris, of Hierapolis, 112, **122** f, 144, 153; of Laodicea, 47 (?), 112, 116, 232, 233, 241, 323, 327
Apollinarian controversy, 232, 233.
Apollinarians, 232, 352
Apollonius, 113, **153**, 154, 155, 276, Acta (martyr), **383**, the Anti-Montanist, 61.
Apologetic literature, **61**, **97** ff., 100 ff, 383.
Apology, of Aristo, 104 f., Arnobius, 305, Aristides (see also Aristides), **102** f., Athenagoras, 131, Clement of Alex., 166, Dionysius, 209, (Epist. to Diognetus), 137, Hermias, 137 f, Irenæus, 151, Justin, **107** ff, Lactantius, 311; Lucian, 245, Melito, 128; Miltiades, 122, Minucius Felix, 139 f, Origen, **195** ff, Quadratus, **100** f; Tatian, 118, Tertullian, **262** f; Theophilus, 134, Victor, 156
'Απόφασις μεγάλη, 83.
Apostles' Creed, **59**

INDEX

Apostolic Constitutions, 25, 31, 67, 68, 245, 341 f., **356**, 360, doctrine, 145, 149, 354, writings, 98.
"Apostolical Canons," **358**.
Apostolici, 88, 92, 94.
Appion, Alexandrian grammarian, 373, 376
Aquila's version, 105, 179
Aquilinus, 85
Arabianus, **224**
Aramaic Gospel, 46
Archontici, 83, 84, 85.
Areopagite literature, 215.
Arian controversy, 221, 222, 232.
Arians, 209
Aristides, 61, 67, **101** ff, Apology of, 103 f, 113, 129, 132, 137, 140, 278, Letter to, 252
Aristo of Pella, **104** f., 265.
Aristotle, 115
Arius, 222.
Arnobius, 138, 165, **304** ff, 308, 309
Artemon, 336
Asceticism, 362, of Origen, 175.
Asclepiades, 314, bishop, 247, martyr, 385
Asterius, of Amasea, 367, martyr, 387, Urbanus, 152–3
Athanasius, 32, 41, 45, 65, 200, 205, **209**, 212, 217, 351, 352, 360
Athenagoras, **130** f, 140, 160, 239
Athenians, Epistle to, 156
Athenodorus, **228**
Atomism, 207.
Atticus, 91.
Augurius, deacon, martyr, 387.
Augustine, 54, 88, 89, 91, 92, 95, 126, 150, 177, 185, 263, 283, 284, 285, 286, 287, 288, 289, 299, 308, 349, 385, 387, 389, 390.
Augustus, 337.
Aurelius, lector, 293.
Autolycus, **133**, 224.
Auxentius, 239
Avitus, Epistle to, 198.

Bacchylides of Pontus, 157
Bacchylus of Corinth, 158.
Baptism, 125, 270
Baptismal creed, Roman, **59**.
Baptismal symbols, **355**
Barbarus Scaligeri, 340
Barcochba, 105, 137
Bardesanes, **75** f, 94, 160
Bardesanite writing (De fato), 76, 376
Bardesanites, 17, 88, 246.
Barhebræus, 75, 362
Barlaam and Joasaph, 102
Barnabas, apostle, 19, Epistle of, 18 ff, 26, 39, 65, 67, 171, 359
Basil of Cæsarea, 178, 194, 209, 227, 231, 242, 245, 352, 376, 391.
Basilides, 55, 69, **70** f, 71, 72, 78, 143, Bishop, 296, 353, of Pentapolis, 214.
Basilidian incantations, 71.
Basilidians, 55, 107.
Bassus, proconsul, 387.
Beatus, presbyter, 199.
Beda, 54.
Beron, 343.
Beryllus of Bostra, 197, 204, **255**, 352.
Bible, 162, 249, 275, 288, 308
Bible, citations from, 304, 306.
Biblical textual criticism, 178, 244.
Bishops, **99**, 356, of Rome, **155**, **350**, writings of, **350**
Blastus, Roman, 150
Boethus the Alexandrian, 130.
Bolanius, bishop, 353
Breviarium in Psalterium, 191.

Cæcilius, 139 f., (Cæcilianus), 281, bishop, 290, 295, 296.
Cæcilius, L., 315.
Cæsarea, Library at, 254; School of, 161, 176.
Cæsarean baptismal symbol, **355**
Cainites, 82, 83, 84
Caius, **320** f., 329, 331, 334, 336.

396　INDEX

Caldonius, bishop, 292, 293, 295, 296
Calendarium ecclesiae Carthag., 379.
Callimachus, 91
Callistio, 143.
Callixtus, 268, 275, 301, 322, 342, **350**.
Candidus, **224**, Valentinian, 197
Canon, 12, 134, 300.
Canones Hippolyti, 330, 341, 360.
Caracalla, 75, 128, 175, 247.
Caricus, an "ecclesiastical man," 157
Carpocrates, 77
Carpocratians, 77.
Carpus, martyr, 381, 385, 386.
Carthaginian Calendar, 379
Cassianus, John, 41, Julius, 54, **86** f, martyr, 388
Cassiodorus, 185, 186, 348.
Catalogus Claromontanus, 20, 37, 366, Liberianus, 42, 44, 322.
Catechetical School of Alexandria, **160** ff., 162, 163, 169, 175, 206, 217, 229.
Catenæ, 2, 124, 128, 151, 178, 181, 186, 191, 192, 193, 234, 252, 325, 326, 344
Catholic Church, 99; Epistles, **18**, 22, 195
Celerinus, 292, 301; lector, 293.
Celestine I, 161.
Celibacy, 361.
Celsus, 103, 104, 140, 178, **195** f., 229, — (Pseudo-Cyprian), De judaica incredulitate, 302.
Centaurus, 240.
Cerdo, 78
Cerinthus, Jewish-Christian, **52**, 68, 321.
Cestus, centurion, 367.
Charito, martyr, 381
Charitus, martyr, 381.
Chastity, 236, 273.
Chionia, martyr, 389.
Χρήσεις, 2.

Christ, 104, 111, 157, 305, 312, 317, 325, and Antichrist, 336, Birthdate, 328
Christian ethics, 283, 288
Christians, accused by heathen, 305, warnings to, 288, 319.
Chronicon Alexandrinum, 340, Edessenum, 75; Paschale, 123, 124, 127, 128, 145, 170, 245, 323, 332, 339
Chronographer (10th year of Ant. Pius), 224, of 354 A.D., 339, 340, 379.
Chrysophora, Epistle to, 156.
Chrysostom, John, 19, 233, 234.
Church orders, 356.
Cicero, 140, 311.
Cilonia, 239
Cittinus, martyr, 382.
Claudius, martyr, 387.
Clement, of Alexandria, 2, 16, 19, 20, 23, 31, 36, 39, 41, 50, 54, 55, 56, 60, 62, 66, 70, 71, 72, 73, 74, 77, 78, 86, 87, 90, 92, 105, 117, 119, 124, 154, 160, **162** ff., 175, 180, 199, 247, 249, 258, 259, 306, 340, 355, 362, 366, of Rome, 44 (?), 62 f., 361, 376; First Epistle, **21** ff, 27, 62, 65, 316, Second Epistle, 25, 54, **62** f., 370.
Cleobius, 68.
Clinical baptism, 296.
Cnossians, Epistle to, 156
Cohortatio ad Gentiles, **112**, 138.
Colossians, **15**, 79, 118, 194
Commodianus, 89, 135, 282, **317** ff.
Commodus, L, 131, 133, 144, 145, 157, 162, 224, 383.
Confessions Felix, 352, Gregory Thaum., 229, 232, 233, 356, Hippolytus, 335, Irenæus, 355. See also Symbols
Conon of Hermopolis, 210.
Constantine, 222, 312, 349.
Constantinus Porphyrogenneta, 251.

INDEX 397

Consubstantiality, 232
Corinthians, 15, 23 f, 79, 118, 119, 188, Apocryphal correspondence, 17
Cornelius, of Rome, 211, 294, 295, 345, 351, 353, Labeo, 306.
Creed, Roman, 59
Creeds and symbols, 355.
Crescens the Cynic, 106.
Crete, Epistle to churches in, 156.
Crispina, martyr, 390
Crispus, emperor, 308.
Cyprian, of Antioch, 283, of Carthage, 104, 105, 140, 242, 258, 280 ff, 308, 309, 318, 319, 320, 344, 345, 347, 351, 352, 353, 386 ff, of Gaul, 280
Cyril of Jerusalem, 148, 186, 367, 390

Damasus, 314.
Daniel, 199, 223, 327, 336, 337, 366.
Dativus, bishop, 297.
——, senator, martyr, 389
De Aleatoribus (see Aleatores), 66, 67, 156, 300
De Fato, Dialogus, 76, 376.
De Recta Fide. See Dialogus
De Virginitate, two epistles, 25, 361 f.
Decian persecution, 206, 211, 228, 247, 281, 283, 284, 290 ff., 295, 320
Decius, 176, 381, 385, 386
Demetrianus, 285, 286-310, 314.
Demetrius, of Alexandria, 175, 203, 248, 352; deacon, 150.
Democritus, 207.
Depositio Martyrum, 322, 379.
Deuteronomy, 184
Dialogus de Recta Fide, 79, 81, 197, 231, 237, 238, 245 f
Diatessaron of Tatian, 120.
Dicta probantia, 2
Didache, 14, 42, 63 f., 65, 103, 109, 300, 357, 359, 360.

Didascalia, 341, 356
Didascalia Petri, 61.
Didymus (various persons), 152, 154, 213, 389
Diocletian, 219, 305, 308, 315, 388, 389, 390
Diocletian persecution, 218, 226, 235, 379.
Diognetus, Epistle to, 103, 113, 117, 135 ff., 226.
Dionysius, of Alexandria, 205, 217, 221, 242, 321, 351-2, the Areopagite, 343, Bar-Salibi, 120, 248, 253, 329, 336, 362; of Corinth, 23, 66, 155, 156 f., Roman presbyter, 212, of Rome, 207, 209, 212, 351, 354.
Dioscurus, 368.
Docetæ, 82, 86
Docetism, 32, 52, 157, 268.
Doctrina Addai, 120, 365.
Doctrine, Compendium of Christian, 198.
Dogmatic system, Marcion's, 80
Dogmatic Writings Hippolytus, 336 f., Origen, 197 f
Domitian, 16, 23, 35, 44, 92, 127.
Domitius, 213.
Domninus, Epistle to, 157.
Donata, martyr, 382
Donatianus, martyr, 388.
Donatists, 389.
Donatulus, 295.
Donatus, 283, 290, 313.
Dositheus, 68, 279, 332.
Droserius, a Valentinian, 246.
Drusiana, 91.
Duae Viae, 21, 66, 360

Easter, canon, 339, controversy, 150, 151; date of, 302, 338, Epistles, 213.
Ebed Jesu, 96, 120, 248, 253, 336, 338.
Ebionites, 51, 88, 376.

Ecclesiastes, 186, 208, 230, 326, 348.
Ecclesiastical canons, **358**, 360.
Edessa, School of, **160**.
Egetes, 95.
Egyptian, canons, 341; Church-Orders, 358, **360**.
Elchesaitism, 373.
Eleutherus of Rome, 145, 147, 148, **155**
Elias of Nisibis, 339.
Elpistus of Pontus, 157.
Emerita of Spain, 353
Encratites, 54, 86, 88, 91, 92, 94, 117, 144
Ephesians, Epistles to, **15**, 30, 33, 42, 79, 118, 194.
Ephraem Syrus, 17, 76, 81, 88, 120.
Ephraim of Chersonesus, 374
Epictetus, 164, Bishop of Assuras, 295.
Epicurus, 207
Epiphanes, **77**.
Epiphanius, xxiii, **2**, 51, 52, 54, 60, 70, 71, 72, 76, 78, 79, 82, 83, 88, 89, 91, 92, 94, 117, 118, 132, 144, 148, 152, 154, 174, 177, 179, 180, 197, 200, 223, 224, 236, 238, 276, 332, 333, 336, 361, 362, 376.
Episcopacy, Monarchical, 33.
Episcopal, order, **32**, 44; writings, **350**.
Epistle to Diognetus, 135 f.; James, (Pseudo-Clementine), **372**.
Epistles, in Easter controversy, 158, (N.T.), 12, of Alexander (Alex.), 222; Alexander (Jerusalem), 247, Aristides, 104; Beryllus, 255, Clement, First, 21 ff, Cyprian, 289, De Virginitate, **361**, Dionysius (Alex.), 209, Dionysius (Corinth), 156, Ignatius, 28 ff., Julius Africanus, 252, Lucian, 244, Melito, 129, Novatian, 345, Origen, 202, Pamphilus, 254, Polycarp, 27, Serapion, 157; Valentinus, 72.
Epistola Eccles. Vien. et Lugdun., 382.
Epitome, Pseudo-Clementine, 372, 374.
Erasmus, 180, 303
Ἐρωτήσεις Μαρίας, **83**, 84.
Esnic the Armenian, 82.
Eubulius, 236, 239.
Eucratius, bishop, 290
Euelpistus, martyr, 381.
Eugenius, 91
Eulogius, deacon, martyr, 387.
Euphranor, 212
Euplius, deacon, martyr, 389
Euporus, 212.
Eusebius, of Cæsarea, xxiii, **2**, 19, 20, 23, 26, 29, 31, 36, 41, 46, 47, 48, 50, 52, 55, 61, 62, 65, 70, 72, 76, 81, 82, 87, 88, 89, 91, 95, 100, 102, 105, 106, 107, 108, 109, 110, 111, 112, 113, 114, 116, 117, 118, 119, 121, 122, 123, 124, 125, 127, 128, 133, 134, 143, 144, 145, 146, 148, 150, 151, 152, 153, 155, 156, 157, 158, 160, 161, 162, 164, 166, 168, 169, 170, 171, 172, 174, 175, 176, 177, 179, 180, 181, 190, 191, 192, 193, 197, 198, 199, 202, 203, 204, 205, 206, 207, 208, 209, 210, 211, 212, 213, 214, 215, 217, 218, 219, 223, 224, 225, 227, 228, 235, 237, 242, 244, 245, 247, 248, 249, 250, 252, 253, 254, 255, 257, 262, 283, 321, 323, 324, 326, 327, 330, 332, 333, 334, 336, 339, 340, 344, 350, 351, 352, 354, 362, 364, 365, 366, 372, 376, 377, **379**, 380, 381, 382, 383, 385, 386, 388, 390, 391, of Emesa, 128, of Thessalonica, 101
Eustachius, 240
Eustathius, of Antioch, 185, 193, 241, of Berœa, 222.

INDEX 399

Euthalius of Sulce, 255
Eutrepius, Epistle to, 129
Eutropius, a heathen, 246.
Eutyches, 325
Eutychians, 116, 233
Evagrius, 105, 232
Evangelium duodecim Apostolorum, 51
Evodius, 95.
Excerpta Theodoti, 54, **74**
Exegetical works Hippolytus, 324 f, Julius Afric, 249, Origen, 181 f
Exodus, 183, 190, 201, 325, 348
Ezekiel, 187, 192, 327, 348
Ezra IV, 320

Fabian, of Antioch (see Fabius), of Rome, 204, 210, 291, 347.
Fabius of Antioch, 210, 211, 351.
Fasting, 275.
Faustus, 88
Felicissimus, 295, schism of, 293, 294
Felicitas, martyr (see Perpetua), 384.
Felix, bishop, 295, 297, presbyter, 296, of Rome, **352**, Tubzoca, 388.
Female adornment, 272
Festal Epistle of Dionysius, 214.
Fides Nicæna, 67
Fidus, bishop, 295, 353
Fihrist, 77
Firmilianus, 203, of Cæsarea, **242** f, **296**
Flavius, 213, Clement, 23; Felix, 303
Flora, 73.
Florentius, 295.
Florinus, 26, Florinus, **74**; Roman presbyter, 150.
Florius, martyr, 386.
Forgeries, 16, 25, 28, 33, 114, 116, 203, 215, 228, 232, 234, 242, 278, 302, 304, 343, 362.
Fortunatus, 287, 288, 295
Forty Martyrs, 391

Fronto, M Cornelius, 140, 141.
Fructuosus of Tarragona, 387.
Fulgentius Planciades, 277, of Ruspe, 284, 285

Galatians, **15**, 79, 188, 194, 199
Galen, 269.
Galerius, 391, Maximus, proconsul, 386
Gallienus, 206, 213, 386, 387
Gallus, 213, 299
Gelasius, 333, decretal of, 41, 54, 89, 152, 177, 307, 318, 365, of Cyzicus, 222.
Generation of the Son, 351
Genesis, 128, 173, 182, 190, 241, 279, 280, 325, 348
Genesius, martyr, 388.
Γέννα Μαρίας, 83.
Gennadius, **3**, 126, 133, 254, 300, 318
Γεωπονικά, 251.
Germanus, bishop, 207, 214
Glaucias, 70
Gnosis, Christian, 21, 167, 168
Gnostic, Acts, **88** f, Ebionism, 51, Gospels, **83** ff, literature, **68** ff
Gnosticism, 16, 44, 49, 146, 160, 335
Gnostics, 55, 82, 83, 117, 154, 159, 167, 169, 173, 267, 269, 363 See also Anti-Gnostic Writings
Gobarus, 203
God, Christian doctrine of, 133, 320, polytheistic theory, 305, 311.
Gordianus, 302
Gortyna, Epistle to church in, 156
Gospel, according to the Egyptians, **54**, 63, according to the Hebrews, **50** f, of Andrew, **54**, Barnabas, **54**, Bartholomew, **54**, Basilides, 70, Eve, 83, Judas, 83, Matthias, **54** f, Peter, 37, **52**, 58, 157, Philip, **54**, 83, Thomas, **55**, 65, 83, the Twelve Apostles, **51**

400   INDEX

Gospel harmony, of Ammonius, 225,
    Post-Hieronymian, 121, of Tatian,
    120
Gospels, 13, 27, 46, 51, 53, 98, 120,
    135, 214, 219, 253.
Gregorion, 236.
Gregory, Nazianzen, 61, 178, 230,
    232, 245, 376, Nyssa, 66, 114,
    180, 217, 227, 229, Thaumaturgus,
    174, 176, 203, **226** ff., 356, of
    Tours, 147, 316
Gundaphorus, Indian king, 93.

Habakkuk, 192, 348.
Hadrian, 70, 100, 102, 106, 109.
Haggai, 192
Harmonius, **76**
Heathen, charges against Christians,
    286, writings against, 111, 112,
    113 ff., 118, 123, 137, 166, 263,
    305, 319, 331.
Hebrew names, 204.
Hebrews, Epistle to, **16**, 25, 33, 79,
    152, 188, 195.
Hegesippus, 23, 50, 107, **145** f, 149,
    357
Heliogabalus, 76, 128, 248, 250
Heraclas of Alexandria, 206
Heracleon the Valentinian, 61, **73**,
    180
Heraclitus, **224**
Heraclius, 73
Herculanus, bishop, 293
Heretical baptism, 207, **211**, 276,
    287, 296, 300, 351, 353.
Heretics, disputations with, 197,
    writings against (see Anti-heretical Writings)
Hermammon of Egypt, 213
Hermas, Shepherd of, 19, **38** ff, 62,
    65, 67, 170, 300, 319, 384
Hermes Trismegistus, 311.
Hermias, **137**.
Hermogenes, 69, 267, 277, 334.
Hestia, martyr, 382.

Hesychius, bishop, **219**
Hexapla, 179.
Hierax, of Egypt, 213, of Leontopolis, **223**, martyr, 381
Hilarianus, governor, 384.
Hilary of Poitiers, 185, 285, 304.
Hippolytus, 2, 44, 54, 55, 72, 73, 75,
    78, 80, 82, 83, 107, 128, 134, 148,
    154, 161, 165, 211, 279, 302, 303,
    321, **321** ff., 349, 350, 366, of
    Thebes, 323.
Homilies, 181, Pseudo-Clementine,
    363, 367,**371** f, of Valentinus, **72**
Homily, of Aristides, 104, Clement(?), 63, Gregory Thaumaturgus, 232, 233, Hippolytus, 330.
Honoratus, bishop, 295
Hosea, 192, 218.
Hyginus of Rome, 72.
Hymenæus of Jerusalem, 353.
Hymns, of Bardasanes, 76, **94**,
    Clement, 168, Coptic, 86, Methodius, 237, the Naassenes, 83.
Hypapante, Festival of, 242.

Iconoclastic controversy, 91.
Idolatry, 272
'Ιερά. See Leontius and John
Ignatius of Antioch, **29** ff., Epistles
    of, 26, 27, **28** ff, 149, 357
Ildefonsus of Toledo, 3
Impassivity of God, 231, 313
Incantations, Basilidian, 71.
Incarnation, 268
Infant baptism, 353.
Innocent I., 54, 89, 91, 95.
Inspiration of Scripture, 173, **190**.
'Ιππιατρικά, 251.
Irenæus, 2, 23, 26, 27, 29, 31, 41, 47,
    51, 55, 58, 70, 71, 72, 73, 77, 78,
    82, 83, 107, 110, 111, 115, 117, 121,
    134, 144, **146** f, 158, 159, 165,
    247, 267, 322, 332, 333, 335, 337,
    346, of Sirmium, martyr, 389.
Irene, martyr, 389

INDEX 401

Isaiah, 186, 192, 327, 348
Isidore (Basilidian), 55, **71**, of Pelusium, 90, of Seville, 3, 259.
Isidorus, 218
Isocrates, 231.
Itala, 194.

Jacob of Edessa, 329
Jacobus, deacon, martyr, 387.
Jader, 297.
James, bishop, 372, Epistle of, **18**, 25, 33, 42, two Epistles to, 25
Januarius, bishop, 295, 296
Jason and Papiscus, dialogue, **104**, 265, 269, 302
Jeremiah, 182, 186, 327.
Jerome, 3, 17, 20, 23, 27, 32, 41, 51, 54, 62, 75, 76, 82, 102, 105, 116, 117, 125, 126, 131, 133, 134, 135, 141, 143, 144, 146, 148, 151, 153, 155, 157, 162, 171, 175, 176, 177, 179, 180, 181, 185, 186, 187, 190, 191, 192, 193, 194, 195, 197, 198, 199, 200, 203, 204, 205, 206, 217, 219, 224, 225, 227, 228, 230, 235, 241, 244, 247, 248, 250, 252, 253, 254, 255, 257, 258, 259, 263, 264, 276, 277, 278, 281, 282, 283, 284, 285, 286, 287, 288, 289, 306, 307, 308, 309, 310, 314, 315, 323, 324, 325, 326, 327, 328, 329, 330, 331, 332, 333, 334, 336, 338, 339, 341, 345, 346, 348, 349, 350, 351, 352, 354, 360, 361, 367, 370, 377, 383
Jerome's list, **178**, 184, 185, 186, 187, 188, 190, 191, 192, 193, 194, 195, 197, 199, 202, 204, 205
Jesus, 104, 332, 363, 364; discourses of, 149
Jeū, Books of, **84 f**
Jewish material in Apocalypse, 35.
Jews. See Anti-Jewish Writings.
Job, 185, 241, 245
Joel, 192.
Johannine theology, 137.

John, Gospel of, 33, 48, **49** f, 53, 73, 103, 118, 120, 180, 187, 199, 209, 336, Epistles of, 18, 27, Apocalypse of, **35**, 37, apostle, 49, 147, 170, of Damascus, **2**, 61, 239, of Jerusalem, 200, Malalas, 134; the Presbyter, 26, 35.
Jonah, 192, 279
Joshua, 182, 184
Jubianus, bishop, 296.
Judaism, 21, 32, 79, 320, at Rome, 375, literature of, 13, writings against, **98** f, 104, 110, 137, 264, 277, 288, 302, 319, 331, 346
Judas (chronographer), **223**.
Jude, Epistle of, 18, 364
Judges, 185
Judicium secundum Petrum. See Duae Viae
Judith, 65.
Julia Aquilia Severa, 338.
Julian, 112.
Julius, Africanus, 75, 112, 117–8, 133, 161, 197, 202, **248** f, 262, 340; Cassianus, 54, **86** f., of Rome, 60.
Junius Rusticus, prefect, 381.
Justin, 53, 55, 56, 57, 59, 78, 98, **105** f, 118, 121, 127, 129, 132, 134, 136, 140, 149, 239, 241, 268, 335, 357, **381**, the Gnostic, 82, of the seventh century, 115
Justinian, 177, 198, 238, 243.
Justus of Tiberias, 119, 250.

Κατάστασις τῆς ἐκκλησίας, 359.
Κατάστασις τοῦ κλήρου, 359.
Κηρύγματα Πέτρου, 42, 62, 374.
Kings, Books of, 185.
Kosru, Armenian king, 76.

Lacedæmonians, Epistle to, 156
Lactantius, 62, 133, 134, 141, 259, 281, 283, 285, **307** f., 366
Lamentations, 191, 200.

INDEX

Lapsed, the, **210**, **220**, 230, 254, **284** f., 291, 292, 293, 294, 295.
Laodiceans, Epistle to, 16, 79.
Laus Heronis. 30
Legio of Spain, 353.
Lemnus, martyr, 386.
Leo I, 89, 91.
Leonidas, 95.
Leonides, 175
Leontius and John, **2**, 170, 237, 239, 325
Leontius of Byzantium, 114, 116, 220, 235, 243, 244, 325, 354
Leucius Charinus, 89, 91, 92.
Levi, 52
Leviticus, 183, 190, 239, 240, 348.
Libelli pacis, 292
Libei Generationis, 339, 340.
Liber Pontificalis, 211.
Liberalis, bishop, 295, 296.
Liberianus, martyr, 381
Liberius of Rome, 222
Licinius, 385, 391
Linus, 90, Linus-text, 366.
List of Sixty Canonical Books, **20**, 65, 366
Logia of Papias, **46**
Λόγια τοῦ κυρίου, 46
Logos, 166, 167, 312.
Longus, prefect, 367.
Lord's Prayer, 201, 285.
Lucian, 225, presbyter of Antioch, **244**, 356, 357, 386
Lucianus, 292.
Lucifer of Calaris, 283, 299, 304, 309.
Lucius, bishop, 295, 297, martyr, 387.
Lucretius, 306, 309.
Luke, companion of Paul, 58, 105, 367, Gospel of, 48, 49, 56, 73. 78, 79, 181, 187, 188, 193, 214, 218, 329
Lycias, governor, 387
Lyons and Vienne, 147, 382

Macarius, bishop, 294, Magnes, 36, presbyter in Edessa, 160–1.
Macedonia, Montanist, 386
Magnesians, Ignatius to, 30.
Magnus, 296.
Malachi, 192.
Malchion, 243, 354.
Mammæa, empress, 338.
Manichæans, 88, 89, 91, 92, 94
Manichæism, 77
Marcellus, of Ancyra, 60, 190, 198, centurion, martyr, 388
Marcellus texts, 367.
Marcian, 151, bishop, 296.
Marcianus, martyr, 386
Marcion, 16, 76, **77** f, 107, 143, 144, 149, 152, 247, 266, 268, 269, 279, 333, 349
Marcion's Gospel, 79, 81, 82
Marcionite controversy, 124, Scriptures, 79, 246, 266, writings (see also Anti-Marcionite Writings), 16
Marcionites, 78, 126, 143, 167, 246.
Marcosians, 55
Marcus, 333, Aurelius, 108, 121, 122, 127, 130, 131, 133, 137, 141, 144, 381, 385, a Marcionite, 246
Marianus, lector, martyr, 387
Marinus, a Bardesanite, 246
Mark, Gospel of, 46, 48, 170, 193, 218
Marriage, 168, 223, 273
Martialis, bishop, 296, 253
Martyrdom, 168, 201, 214, 241, 272, 275, 287, 299, 303, 347, Apollonius, 383, Paul, 366, Peter, 90, Peter and Paul, 367, Polycarp, 147
Martyrium Ignatii, 30, **34**, Nicephori, 387; Polycarpi, 28, 379, 380, Romanum, 348.
Martyrologies, **378** ff
Martyrologium Hieronymianum, 379, Romanum, 322
Martyrs, Acts of lost, 379

INDEX 403

Mary of Cassobola, 30.
Matthew, apostle, 55, Gospel of, 21, 46, 48, 51, 56, 71, 73, 96, 192, 194, 214, 328, 348, 376
Matthiæ Traditiones, **55**, 71.
Maximian, 388, 389, 390.
Maximilianus, martyr, 388.
Maximilla, 94, 153.
Maximinus, 193, 201, 253.
Maximus, **224**, 237, 238; of Alexandria, 354, bishop (Numidia), 295, bishop, 353, confessor, 105, 116, 150, 151, 162, 172, 192, 222, martyr, 386, presbyter, 292 f., 294, Thrax, 176.
Mazdai, king, 93
Megethius, a Marcionite, 246.
Melchiades, 301.
Meletian schism, 219, 220.
Meletius, 221
Melito of Sardis, 92, **123** f., 144, 165, 170, 222, 259, 278, 330.
Mellitus (Melito?), 129.
Memian, 239.
Menander, 68, 70, 107
Mennas of Constantinople, **198**, 238.
Merozanes of Armenia, 210.
Messiahship of Christ, 288
Methodius of Olympus, 36, 132, 161, 200, **235** f, 246.
Metrodorus, Marcionite, 385, 386.
Micah, 192
Military profession, 274.
Milotho (Melito?), 129
Miltiades, **121** f, 128, 153.
Minor Prophets, 192.
Minucius Felix, 132, 133, **138** f., 259, 263, 289, 309, 319
Modestus, **144**
Modesty, 275, 298.
Modianus, bishop, 295
Monarchianism, 333, 346.
Monoimus, the Gnostic, 82
Monophysite controversies, 32
Monophysites, 220.

Montanism, 157, 26f.
Montanist, controversy, 124, writer, 384.
Montanists, 122, 147, **152** f, 155, 173, 257, 276, 381 See also Anti-Montanistic Writings.
Montanus, 153, martyr, 387.
Moses of Chorene, 75, 76, 243, 365.
Moyses, presbyter, 292 f
Muratorian Fragment, 16, 36, 41, 42, 44, 82, 92.
Musanus, **144**.
Musonius (Stoic), 164, 172.

Naassenes, 54, 55, 82, 83.
Nahum, 192
Nampulus, bishop, 295.
Narcissus of Jerusalem, 158, 247.
Nartzallis, martyr, 382
Natalis, M. Cæcilius, 141.
Nemesianus, bishop, 295, 297.
Neo, martyr, 387
Neoplatonism, 306.
Nepos, of Arsinoe, 207, **208**
Nero, 24, 127, 366, 368
Nerva, 20.
Nestorians, 116, 233.
Nestorius, 325.
New Testament, 11, 84, 98, 109, 118, 134, 140, 148, 149, 173, 179, 253, 300
Nexocharides, 95.
Nicæa, Second Council, 91.
Nicephorus Callisti, 123, 197, 325, 326, 327, 330, 332, 333, 336, 366
Nicephorus, Stichometry of, 20, 37, 55, 65, 89, 90, 91, 93, 171, 366, — (Antirrhet), 171, martyr, 387
Nicetas of Serra, 214.
Nicolaitans, 84.
Nicomedians, Epistle to, 156.
Nicostratus, confessor, 293, 294.
Noetus, 332.
Nonus Marcellus, **277**.

Novatian, 133, 207, 279, 298, 299, 302, **344** ff, 349, schism of, **210** f, 285, 294, 345   See also Anti-Novatianist Writings.
Novatianism, 296
Novatianist affairs, 351, 352.
Novatianists, 304.
Numbers, 184, 239
Numidicus, presbyter, 293.

Octavius, 139
Odes of Solomon, 85
Œcumenius, 61, 171, 254.
Œdipean nuptials, 131.
Old Testament, 21, 25, 84, **98**, 127, 149, 173, 179, 204, 300
Ophitic writings, **82** f
Optatus, bishop, 295, of Mileve, 65, 257, 350
Optimus, proconsul, 386
Opuscula Montani, Priscillae et Maximillae, 152.
Origen, 19, 23, 29, 31, 38, 41, 44, 50, 51, 54, 55, 56, 61, 66, 68, 70, 71, 73, 74, 104, 115, 124, 126, 160, 164, **173** ff, 205, 206, 208, 214, 221, 224, 227, 228, 229, 236, 239, 240, 241, 245, 246, 247, 249, 252, 254, 255, 330, 336, 348, 350, 352, 366, 376, 377.
Origenists, 88, 94.
Origin of evil, 246, 338.

Pachomius, bishop, **219**.
Pacianus, 89, 284
Palatina, 40
Palestinian martyrs (Eusebius), 379.
Palladius, 96, 173, 176, 343
Palmas of Amastris, 158.
Pamphilus, 161, 174, 177, 190, 192, 193, 194, 195, 197, 200, 218, **253** f
Pantænus, 160, **162**, 163, 247.
Paon, martyr, 381
Papias, 26, **46**, 48, 100, 149
Papylus of Thyatira, martyr, 381.

Papyrus, Brucianus, **85**, Rainer, **47**.
Παράφρασις Σήθ, 83
Parousia of the Lord, 223
Paschal, controversy, 123, 124, **155**, **158**, 170, 204, 213, 214, 216, 218, 220, Writings, 346
Passio Carpi, Papyli, etc **381**, Cassiani, 388, Genesii mimi, 388, Irenaei, Episc Sirm 389, Jacobi, Mariani, etc 387, Montani, Lucii, etc. 387, Perpetuae et Felicitatis, 278, **384**, Petri Balsami, 390, Philippi episc 390, Pionii, **385**, Pollionis, etc 389, Polycarpi, **380**, Procopii, 388, Quirini episc. et mart 390, Quiuionis, etc 391, Rogatiani et Donatiani, 388, Savini, 388, Sereni mart. 390.
Passion of Peter and Paul, 90
Passover, 125, observed by Christ, 339.
Pastoral Epistles, **16**, 27, 33, 79, 359, 369, 370
Patripassian Monarchianism, 154, 268.
Patrology, 1
Paul, 49, 72, 78, 103, 149, 174, 268, 366, 368, 369, Apocalypse of, 38, Epistles of, **15**, 21, 22, 25, 27, 33, 78, 79, 119, Theology of, 137, and Seneca, **17**, presbyter, 115, of Samosata, 206, 215, 228, **243**, 244, 353, 354, of Tella, 179.
Paulinus of Nola, 376
Paulli Praedicatio, 62, 300.
Penance, 270, 275, 353.
Pentadius, Brother, 313.
Peratæ, 82, 83
Perennis, judge, 383.
Peregrinatio ad loca sancta, 365, 370.
Περὶ παρθενίας, 66
Perpetua, Vibia, 272, 273, 278, **384**
Perpetua and Felicitas, 41, 278, **384**
Persecution, 243, 271, 273, 274, 295, 299, 308, 310, 315, (306 A D.),

221; (in Gaul), 382, by Diocletian, 348, 379, Maximinus, 201; Scapula, 264, 274, Severus (202), 163, 175, 328, 337.
Peter, 48, 52, 70, 90, 366, 368, 372 f., Apocalypse of, **36**, Epistles of, 18, 25, 27, 33, 38, 42; Gospel of, 37.
Petrus, Abselamus, ascetic, 391; of Alexandria, **219**, Balsamus, martyr, 390, Diaconus, 244
Philadelphians, Ignatius to, 30.
Philagrius, 232
Philastrius, 78, 88, 91, 94, 150, 277, 332.
Phileas, martyr, 390; of Thmuis, **219**
Philemon, Epistle to, **15**, 79, 195, Roman presbyter, 212.
Philip, the Arabian, 141, 192, 196, 204; of Gortyna, **144**; of Side (excerptor), 47, 130, 146, 218.
Philippi, Church at, 27
Philippians, Epistles to, **15**, 26, 30, 79, 194
Philippus of Heraclea, martyr, 390.
Philo, 195, 204.
Philocalia, **178**, 182, 184, 186, 187, 188, 190, 191, 192, 193, 194, 196, 198, 202, 245, 376.
Philogonius of Antioch, 222.
Philoromus, martyr, 390.
Philosophers, Writings against, 104, 267, 269, 334
Philosophy, Importance of, 168.
Philostorgius, 241, 345.
Philumene, 82.
Phœnix, Myth of, 316
Photius, **2**, 3, 23, 63, 89, 90, 91, 93, 94, 101, 106, 112, 114, 115, 116, 123, 130, 132, 146, 152, 168, 169, 171, 174, 200, 217, 218, 237, 238, 240, 251, 253, 254, 321, 322, 324, 330, 331, 332, 333, 334, 336, presbyter, 203
Pierius of Alexandria, 217, **217**, 253.
Pilate-Literature, 53.

Pinytus of Cnossus, 157
Pionius, martyr, 381, **385**.
Pistis-Sophia, 55, **84** f.
Pius of Rome, 42, 44, 72.
Placita, Pseudo-Plutarch (Aetius), 112, 138.
Plagiarisms, 169.
Plato, 140, 165, 236, 237, 306, 331.
Plotinus, 85.
Pneumatomachian controversy, 232
Poems of, Commodianus, 318 ff, Cyprian, 303, Hippolytus, 342, Lactantius, 316; Tertullian (?), 279. See also Hymns, and Psalms.
Polianus, 297.
Politianus, 259.
Pollio, lector, martyr, 389.
Polycarp, 19, 22, 30, 31, 147, 149, **380**, 381, 385; Epistle of, **25** ff., 33.
Polycrates of Ephesus, 124, 155, 158.
Pompeius, 296.
Pompeius, M, 110.
Pomponius, bishop, 290.
Pontianus, Bishop of Rome, 322, **350**.
Pontius, deacon (Vita Cypriani), **281** f, 288, 289, 299, 387, an " ecclesiastical man," 157.
Pontus, Epistle to church in, 156.
Porphyry, 85, 240.
Pothinus, 147.
Prædestinatus, 73, 153, 194, 276.
Praxeas, 268, 279.
Prayer used at Rome, 24.
Preaching of Peter, **60** f., 103, 374 f
Primus, bishop, 296.
Priscillianists, 91, 92, 94.
Privatianus, 295.
Probus, 314, philosopher, martyr, 390.
Prochoros, 92.
Proclus, of Miletus, 239, the Montanist, 267, 321; bishop, 295, 353.
Procopius, of Gaza, **2**, 111, 183, 184, 189, 191, 195, 208, 220, 238, martyr, 388.

Prophecy, 173.
Prophetical Writings, O.T., 109, 166, 264, 337.
Protevangel of James, 56.
Protoctetus, presbyter, 201.
Proverbs, 134, 186, 191, 234, 240.
Prudentius, 281, 323, 386, 387.
Psalms, 179, 185, 191, 205, 223, 240, 326, of Bardesanes, 76, Gnostics, 84, Hierax, 223, Marcion, 82, the Naassenes, 83, Valentinus, 72.
Psalterium Athelstani, 60.
Psellus, Michael, 251.
Pseudo-Abdias (Virtutes Andreae), 95.
Pseudo-Athanasius (Fides Nicaena), 66, (Περὶ παρθενίας), 66, (Praec. ad Antiochum), 39, (Σύνταγ. διδασκ), 67
Pseudo-Augustine (De poenitentia), 95.
Pseudo-Clement (Homilies, etc), 371 f, (Recognitions), 76, 371 f. (De Virginitate), 361 ff.
Pseudo-Clementine Writings, 62, 363, 367, 371
Pseudo-Cyprian (Ad Novatian.), 344, 349, (Adv Aleatores), 41, 66, 156, 300, (Adv. Judaeos), 332, (De bono pudicitiae), 347, (Celsus De Jud incredulit.), 302, (De Pascha computus), 339, 347, (De Rebaptism.), 62, De Spectaculis), 347.
Pseudo-Hegesippus (De bello Jud), 89.
Pseudo-Hippolytus (Dionys. Areop) Adv Beron., 343
Pseudo-Justin (Quaest. et Resp ad Orthod.), 63, 147, 204.
Pseudo-Melito (Apology), 122.
Pseudo-Mellitus (De Passione Joann), 92.
Pseudo-Origen (Exposit. lib. Job.), 245.

Pseudo-Plutarch (Placita), 112, 138.
Pseudo-Tertullian (Adv. Haeres), 72, 81, 150, 279, 332, 349, (Adv Judaeos), 105, 263; (Adv. Marcion.), 279, 349.
Ptolemæus, 73.
Puppianus, 296

Quadratus, apologist, 100 f, early Christian prophet, 101, Bishop of Athens, 101, L. Statius, proconsul, 390.
Quartodecimans, 150, 170.
Quintilla, 270.
Quintus, bishop, 296
Quirinus, 288, bishop, martyr, 390.

Recognitions, Pseudo-Clementine, 371 f.
Recta Fide, De See Dialogus, etc.
Resurrection, 111, 131, 133, 149, 173, 199, 214, 268, 317, 338, 369.
Reticius of Autun, 349 f.
Revelation, 169
Revocatus, martyr, 384.
Rhodo, 78, 81, 82, 119, 143 f, 153, 154.
Rhossus, Church at, 157.
Rogatianus, bishop, 290; confessor, 291; martyr, 388, presbyter, 293.
Roman baptismal symbol, 355; bishops, 155, 350, church, 23 f., 155, 335; symbol, 59.
Romans, Epistle to, 15, 79, 118, 192, 194, Dionysius of Corinth to, 156; Ignatius to, 30, 149.
Rufinus of Aquileia, 41, 60, 66, 125, 126, 153, 174, 178, 181, 182, 183, 184, 185, 186, 191, 193, 194, 197, 198, 199, 203, 205, 211, 230, 245, 246, 254, 314, 345, 360, 376, 377, 380; confessor, 293, grammarian, 314.

INDEX 407

Rule of faith, 151, 160, 232, 345.
Rusticus the prefect, 106

Sabellian controversy, **212** f
Sabellianism, 231
Sabellians, 54, 351
Sabellius, 209, 346.
Sabina, martyr, 385
Sabinus, 243
Sacra Parallela, **2**, 61, 109, 110, 112, 114, 116, 133, 151, 169, 207, 237, 239, 325
Samuel, Books of, 185.
Satornilians, 107.
Satornilus, 68, 70.
Saturninus, martyr, 384, presbyter, martyr, 389, P. Vigellius, proconsul, 382
Saturus, martyr, 384.
Savinus, martyr, 388.
Scapula, 264, 267, 274.
Scillitan martyrs, **382**
Scholia, 181
Secunda, martyr, 382
Sedatus, bishop, 290.
Semi-Arian controversy, 232.
Seneca and Paul, correspondence, **17**
Sententiae episcoporum, 353.
Septuagint, 179, 219, 244
Serapion, Epistles to, 200, of Antioch, **52**, 122, **157**.
Serenus, Epistle to Zenas and, 115.
Serenus, martyr, 390.
Sergius, confessor, 291, Paulus, **125**.
Servilius Paulus, proconsul, 125
Sethites, 82, 83, 84, 85
Severa, 204.
Severians, 82, 84, 85.
Severus, 314, Septimius, 96, 223, 224, 248, 266, 328, 337, 380.
Sextus, **224**, Empiricus, 334
Shepherd of Hermas, **38** ff
Sibylline Books, 37, 320, 357.

Sidonius, 294.
Simeon Metaphrastes, 253, 374, 379, 381.
Simon, a Gnostic, 68, **Magus**, 90, 107, 368, 374
Sistelius, 240
Sixtus of Rome, 212, 297, II. of Rome, 299, **351**, III of Rome, 379
Smyrnæans, Ignatius to, 30
Socrates, the Gnostic, 231, historian, 157, 190, 222, 235, 236, 241, 345, 352.
Solomon, Odes of, 85.
Song of Solomon, 151, 181, 182, 186, 190, 191, 241, 326, 348, 349.
Sophists, **97**, Christian, 138.
Sophronius, **3**
Soranus, 269
Soter of Rome, 123, 153, **155**, **156**.
Spanish martyrs, 387
Speculum Augustini, 16
Speratus, martyr, 382
Spiritual interpretation, 208.
Stephanus Gobarus, 112, 146, **152**, 215.
Stephen of Rome, 211, 296, **351**
Successus, bishop, 297.
Suidas, 203, 244, 248, 251.
Sulpicius Severus, 367
Συμφωνία, 83
Σύνταγμα διδασκαλίας, 67
Susanna, Story of, 199, 202, 252, 327.
Sylvester, 222
Symbol, African, 355; Alexandrian, 355, Cæsarean, 355, Gregory Thaumaturgus, **229** f, 232, 233, 356, Irenæus, 355, Lucian, **244**, 356, Roman, **59**, 356.
Symbols and creeds (see Confessions), 355.
Symmachus, **96**, 179, 309.
Syncellus, 247, 248, 249, 250, 251, 329, 333, 339
Synodal writings, **350** ff.

INDEX

Synods, African, 353; Alexandria (231–2 A.D), 352, Antioch, Third, 243, Antioch (268), 354, Arabia, 352, Bostra (244), 352, Carthage (251), 352, Carthage (255–6), 353, Rome (251–2), 352.
Synoptic gospels, 47, **48**, 49, 50.
Syrian martyrology, 379.

Tales, Gnostic, **69**, **88** ff.
Tarachus, martyr, 390.
Tarphon, Rabbi, 110.
Tarsians, Ignatius to, 30
Tatian, 98, 106, 113, **117** f, 121, 131, 132, 143, 144, 165, 233, 249, 259.
Tatiana, Sister, 201
Teaching of the Twelve Apostles, **63** f, 300 See Didache.
Telesphorus, 212.
Tertullian, 2, 41, 72, 73, **78**, 80, 81, 82, 92, 105, 106, 107, 110, 111, 117, 121, 122, 124, 133, 134, 141, 148, 149, 150, 152, 153, 155, 156, 165, 224, 247, 253, **256** ff, 280, 283, 284, 287, 289, 298, 303, 309, 319, 335, 345, 346, 350, 355, 370, 383, 384
Tertullus, bishop, 290.
Tetrapla, 180
Thaddeus, 95, 364 f.
Thascius, 295
Theatrical shows, 271, 297.
Thecla, 237, 369.
Thelymidres of Laodicea, 210.
Themison, Montanist, 153.
Theoctistus of Cæsarea, 161, 175, 248
Theodas, 71, 74
Theodora, martyr, 389
Theodoret of Cyrrhus, 51, 76, 120, 126, 143, 165, 197, 222, 241, 325, 326, 327, 329, 334, 336, 338.
Theodorus, Alexandrian advocate, 218, bishop, **219**, (Gregorius), 227; Studita, 92.
Theodotion, 179.

Theodotus, **74**, 169, excerpts of, **74**
Theognostus of Alexandria, **217**, 218
Theologumena Arithmeticae, 216
Theology, Christian, 217, 311
Theonas, bishop of Alexandria, 218, **225**
Theophilus, 249, 268, a certain, 337, of Antioch, **132** f, 140, 224, 247, 267, 309, bishop, 353, of Cæsarea, 158, chronographer, 134.
Theophilus of Patara, 239.
Theophylact, 51, 54
Theopompus, 231
Theotecnus of Cæsarea, 215, 216, 353.
Theseus, 323
Thessalonians, **15**, 79, 188, 194
Thnetopsychitae, 352
Thomas, 364.
Thyestian banquets, 131
Tichonius, 348
Timotheus, 207, of Alexandria, 94, 361–2.
Timothy, 16.
Titus, 16, 188, 195, 367.
Tobit, 65, 103
Toleration, Gallienus' edict of, 206
Tradition, Catholic conception of, 265.
Trajan, 29, 33, 44.
Trallians, Ignatius to, 30
Transmission of early literature, 1.
Tricentius, 220
Trinity, 345 f, economic, 268.
Tritemius of Sponheim, **3**, 307.
Trypho, 204, **205**, dialogue with, 110
Turibius of Asturica, 91, 92, 94.
Tuscus, consul, 388.
Two Ways, The (see Duae Viae), 21, 66

Urbanus, 294.
Ursinus, monk, 300.

Valarses, Armenian king, 76.

A D	Syria and Palestine	Asia Minor	Greece	Egypt	Rome (Italy)	North Africa	Occident	Unknown or Uncertain
Before 70	Ur-Matthew				(Paul)			
54–64 ±		Paul						Matthew
After 70					Mark?			Luke
75–100 ±		I Peter		Barnabas				Hebrews
Towards close of first century		Apocalypse of John						
About 100	Gospel and Epistles of John				I Clement			James Bapt Symbol
About 100?			Preaching of Peter		Hermas			
After 100 / Before 150	Didache Gospel of Peter			Apoc of Peter Gospel of Egyptians				Pastoral Epist II Clement
About 105–117? / About 140?		Ignatius Polycarp (d 155)						
First decade second century		Papas						
125–126			Quadratus Aristides (?138)					
About 130				Basilides				Agrippa Castor
About 150	Aristo of Pella				Valentinus Marcion Justin (d 163–7)			
After 150		Acts of Paul and Thecla		Jude II Peter	Heracleon Ptolemaeus			
Between 160 and 180	Tatian	Miltiades Apollinaris Melito	Dionysius of Corinth Philip of Gortyna		Tatian Rhodo Hegesippus (Minucius Felix)	Scillitan martyrs (180)	Lyons and Vienne Irenaeus (d 189+)	Athenagoras Musanus Modestus
After 180	Theophilus to Autolycus			Pantaenus				
About 200	Serapion (d 209) Bardesanes (d 222)	Apollonius		Clement (d – 215)	Caius	Tertullian (d 220+) Perpetua and Felicitas (203)		
About 220	Julius Africanus (d 240+)				Hippolytus (d 235+)			
About 230	Alexander of Jerusalem (d 250)			Origen (d 254)				
About 250		Gregory Thaumaturg (d 270±)		Dionysius (d 265)	Cornelius (d 253) Novatian	Cyprian (d 258)		Commodian
About 260	Paul of Samosata (d 268+)			Theognostus and Pierius	Dionysius (d 268)			
After 270	Lucian (d 312)						Victorinus of Pettau	
About 300		Methodius (d 311)		Petrus (d 312)		Arnobius		
After 300		Lactantius		Alexander (d 326)			Reticius Lactantius	

INDEX

Valens, a Valentinian, 238, 246
Valentinianism, 75, 86.
Valentinians, **73** f., 148, 149, 150, 169, 246, 267, 268. See Anti-Valentinian Writings.
Valentinus, 53, 69, **71** f., 73, 74, 78, 107, 169.
Valerian, 206, 213, 281, 288, 297, 345, 384, 386, 387
Valerian's persecution, 213, 215, 296
Valesius, 211
Varro, 259, M Terentius, 263.
Veiling of virgins, 274
Venantius Fortunatus, 317.
Vespasian, 20
Vestia, martyr, 382.
Vettius Gratus, 386
Vibius, 323
Victor, bishop, 290, 293, 295, 297, of Capua, 121, 147, 150, **155**, 158, 200, 203, 204, 301.
Victorinus (De metris, etc.), 314; Afer, 348; of Pettau, 279, **347** f.

Vincent of Lerins, 259
Vienne and Lyons, 382
Vigilius of Tapsus, 302
Virgil, 318
Virginitate, De, epistles, **361**.
Virgins, dress of, 274, 284.
Virtutes Andreae, 95.
Vitalius, 233.
Volusianus, 299
Vulgata, 39.
Vulgate, 121.

Water used in sacrament, 295.
"We-source" of Acts, 58
Witch of Endor, 185, 241, 325.

Xenocharides, 95.

Zechariah, 192, 328.
Zenas and Serenus, Epistle to, 115.
Zephaniah, 192.
Zephyrinus, 321, 322, 341, **350**

www.ingramcontent.com/pod-product-compliance
Lightning Source LLC
Chambersburg PA
CBHW052128010526
44113CB00034B/1023